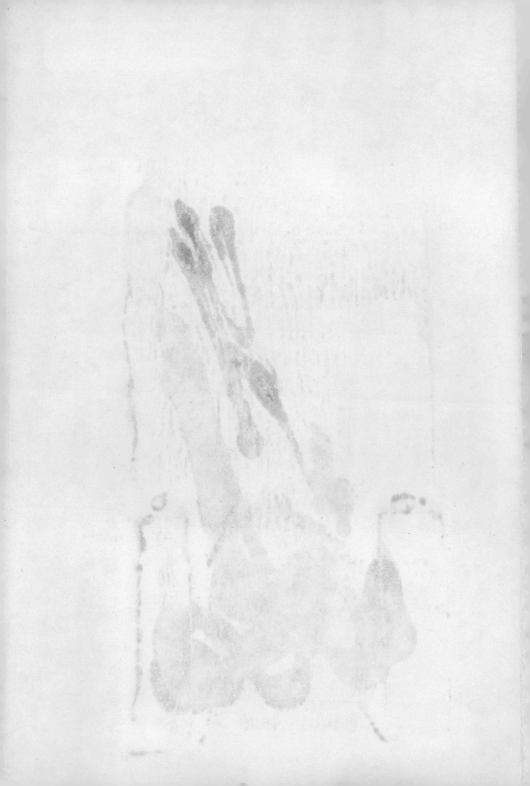

Social Behavior: Its Elementary Forms

Social Behavior | Its Elementary Forms

George Caspar Homans
Harvard University

Under the General Editorship of
ROBERT K. MERTON
Columbia University

Harcourt, Brace & World, Inc.
New York · Chicago · San Francisco · Atlanta

To the memory of

Bernard DeVoto
Charles Pelham Curtis

Friends and Teachers

Preface

In this book I am especially indebted to four men. First, to Paul E. Breer, who as a Harvard graduate student spent most of one year arguing with me about the right way to formulate the main argument. Sometimes he convinced me; sometimes I convinced him; sometimes both of us remained unconvinced; but the result in every case was increased clarity. Second, to Abe Zaleznik, C. R. Christensen, and Fritz J. Roethlisberger, of the Harvard Graduate School of Business Administration, who were my partners in carrying out research in which some of the ideas embodied in this book were tested.[1] The many hours spent in their company were always entertaining, intellectually and otherwise.

I am also indebted to the men who read and criticized the first draft, in whole or in part, or who straightened me out in other ways: Michael Argyle, Otomar J. Bartos, Peter M. Blau, Eugene Galanter, Douglas L. Oliver, B. F. Skinner, Ralph Turvey, and William F. Whyte; to Louis B. Barnes and James V. Clark for permission to use their unpublished theses for the degree of D.B.A. at the Harvard Graduate School of Business Administration; to Mrs. Martha Robinson, who typed the final manuscript, and to my wife, Nancy Parshall Homans, who drew the figures.

As for organizations, I am indebted to the Center for Advanced Study in the Behavioral Sciences for giving me, in ennobling sur-

---

[1] A. Zaleznik, C. R. Christensen, and F. J. Roethlisberger, *The Motivation, Productivity, and Satisfaction of Workers* (Boston, 1958).

vii

roundings, physical and intellectual, a whole year free from regular academic duties, in which I wrote the first draft; to the Ford Foundation, which gave me a small grant used, among other things, for the preparation of the manuscript; and to The University of Chicago Press for permission to reprint excerpts from Peter M. Blau's book, *The Dynamics of Bureaucracy.*

GEORGE CASPAR HOMANS

Contents

For o thyng, sires, saufly dar I seye,
That freendes everych oother moot obeye,
If they wol longe holden compaignye.
Love wol nat been constreyned by maistrye.
Whan maistrie comth, the God of Love anon
Beteth his wynges, and farewel, he is gon!

GEOFFREY CHAUCER
The Franklin's Tale

Introduction

My subject is a familiar chaos. Nothing is more familiar to men than their ordinary, everyday social behavior; and should a sociologist make any generalization about it, he runs the risk that his readers will find him wrong at the first word and cut him off without a hearing. They have been at home with the evidence since childhood and have every right to an opinion. A physicist runs no such risk that the particles, whose social behavior in the atom he describes, will talk back.

The sociologist's only justification is that the subject, however familiar, remains an intellectual chaos. Every man has thought about it, and mankind through the centuries has embodied the more satisfactory of the generalizations in proverbs and maxims about social behavior, what it is and what it ought to be. Every man has his price. You scratch my back, and I'll scratch yours. Do as you would be done by. You can't eat your cake and have it too. No cross, no crown. Fair exchange is no robbery. To each his own. *Noblesse oblige*. Whosoever hath, to him shall be given. . . . And so forth. What makes the subject of everyday social behavior a chaos is that each of these maxims and proverbs, while telling an important part of the truth, never tells it all, and nobody tries to put them together. Has *noblesse oblige*, for instance, anything to do with fair exchange? In the same way every man makes his own generalizations about his own social experience, but uses them *ad hoc* within the range of situations to which each applies,

1

dropping them as soon as their immediate relevance is at an end and never asking how they are related to one another. Everyone has, of course, every excuse for this shortcoming, if it be one: social experience is apt to come at us too fast to leave us time to grasp it as a whole. Nevertheless, the purpose of this book is to bring out of the familiar chaos some intellectual order.

The Subject Matter

What kind of social behavior will this book deal with? Although I have just spoken of "ordinary, everyday social behavior," much behavior that is perfectly ordinary and everyday is not part of its subject. This is a book that will try to explain behavior and not just describe it; and while it will talk incidentally about many things, its true subject matter is what it tries to explain. It will try to state and explain a number of findings about the behavior of men, but only so far as their behavior has the following characteristics. First, the behavior must be social, which means that when a person acts in a certain way he is at least rewarded or punished by the behavior of another *person,* though he may also be rewarded or punished by the non-human environment. We shall not, for instance, be interested in explaining that a farmer's son plants corn in a certain way because it will get him a crop, but we might well be interested in explaining why his behavior changed if his father praised or blamed him for planting as he did.

Second, when a person acts in a certain way toward another person, he must at least be rewarded or punished by *that* person and not just by some third party, whether an individual or an organization. A department store, for instance, may instruct a salesgirl to behave in a certain general way toward customers, and reward or punish her, by promotion or discharge, for obeying or disobeying the instructions. We shall not be interested in explaining why the store gave her those instructions and tried to enforce them, but we might well be interested in explaining why a particular customer's behavior toward her affected the salesgirl's behavior in a particular way. Here the immediate contact is between the salesgirl and the customer, and it is their behavior that we might be interested in explaining, and not the behavior of the store, which is, for the moment at least, a silent third party to the transaction.

Third, the behavior must be actual behavior and not a norm of be havior. I have just spoken of the instructions that the store gave the salesgirl. In connection with their larger and more permanent social groupings—families, associations, firms, communities, and whole societies—men have evolved a long list of expectations, roles, customs, norms, rules, and laws, all of which are verbal instructions addressed to a relatively large number of persons placed in similar circumstances and telling them how they *ought* to behave, and what rewards or punishments they ought to expect if they do or do not behave in that way. Thus I assume that the store's instructions were addressed to all the salesgirls in a department, and indeed there would be little economy in formulating rules were they not to apply to a relatively large number of persons. It takes time for rules to get formulated, and once formulated they tend to stay on the books for relatively, though not absolutely, long stretches of time. In the meantime the actual behavior of individuals goes on, changing with changing circumstances. Often it corresponds closely to the applicable rules, but often it does not, not only because men disobey the rules but also because no rule can spell out in enough detail how persons should behave in every contingency. Much social science is rightly devoted to explaining why the rules are what they are: why, for instance, the physician's role in our society is what it is, or why the custom of a certain primitive society calls for marriage between a man and his mother's brother's daughter. But this book will not undertake to explain the rules. Instead, taking the rules said to apply in a particular situation as given, it will try to explain the actual behavior. Its subject matter is, then, the actual social behavior of individuals in direct contact with one another.

Why "Elementary"?

I do not think we need a different kind of explanation for the development and enforcement of rules from what we need for the subject matter of this book, but we may need a more complicated explanation. It may well be a more complicated business to explain why the physician's role in our society is what it is than to explain why a particular physician, faced with the rules, behaves as he does. Because it is relatively easy to explain, and for no other reason, I have called the subject matter of this book *elementary* social behavior. I might have called it *informal* social behavior, as we do in industrial sociology. There we speak of the *informal organization* of a group of workingmen, meaning their social behavior so far as it is not called for, though it may not be specifically forbidden, by the rules of the factory. But I have never liked this word *informal,* which smells of old clothes and after-hours. Elementary social behavior occurs at all times and never lacks form.

When I say that this book will not undertake to explain why the more or less explicit rules of a society or some organization within it are what they are, let me be quite clear what I mean. To say that this book will not explain them does not mean that it will disregard them. On the contrary, I shall need to know what the rules are in any particular situation in order to explain what I have undertaken to explain —the elementary social behavior. I shall need to do so if only because, after all, the rules and the sanctions attached to them do often determine in large part the way persons actually behave. But this book will not undertake to explain the nature of the rules themselves and instead will simply take them as given.

But let me illustrate. I shall not, for instance, deal with the behavior of a man so far as he contributes his labor to a firm and gets paid at the end of a week or month, in accordance with the terms of a fairly explicit contract. It is not two individuals that are dealing with one another here, but an individual and a corporation. I shall not undertake to explain this transaction itself, but I shall nevertheless need to know its terms in order to explain the other things I am interested in. Thus I shall be much interested in the way two men, both employees of a firm and members of the same department, help one another at work, even when the formal rules of the firm do not require them to do so. Here the social behavior is elementary in the sense that the two men are in face-to-face contact, and each is rewarding the other directly and immediately: each is enabled to do his work better here and now. But their immediate reward may get some of its value from what it contributes to a more distant one: by doing his job better each man may improve his pay and his chances for advancement in the firm; and I shall need to take account of the more indirect, impersonal transaction between each man and the firm in order to explain fully the more direct, personal transaction between the men themselves.

In the same way, I shall not be concerned with the behavior of a man so far as he holds authority over others by reason of appointment by a public or private corporation. Thus I shall not be concerned with the behavior of a supervisor so long as he acts as the representative of a firm, employed to get his subordinates to carry out its rules. I shall, on the other hand, be much interested in the behavior of a man who, through his own exertions as an individual in his face-to-face dealings with other individuals, acquires influence over them not *de jure* but *de facto*. But it is not impossible, though it may be difficult, for a supervisor to exercise both sorts of authority, and then, if I am to explain his actual behavior, I shall certainly have to take account of the power he exercises by virtue of his official position. I shall have to take account of it, but I shall not have to explain why he was given that power. That question I shall leave to other social scientists.

It is not simply from strict obedience to the formal rules of an organization that elementary social behavior is to be distinguished. It is also to be distinguished from obedience to the norms that a society has inherited from its past, whether or not they are embodied in any formal organization. Our society, for instance, has inherited certain unwritten rules or norms about how a physician ought to behave toward his patients and toward other physicians. It has inherited what sociologists call the physician's *role*. If a student of elementary social behavior were interested in studying physicians—and in this book I shall not be interested in so doing —he would concern himself, among other things, with how particular doctors actually behave in direct contact with other doctors. Whereas the doctor's role lays down those ways in which doctors ought to be the same, he would in fact observe that doctors differ greatly in their behavior toward other doctors. Doctors do not live up to their role equally well, and the role itself leaves plenty of room for variations. But it is the variations, that is, the actual behavior, that our student would have to explain. To do so, he would of course have to know what the physician's role is in our society since, for instance, the respect in which a doctor is held by his fellows may vary with the degree to which he measures up to the physician's role. But my student of elementary social behavior would leave to other social scientists the task of explaining why the role got to be what it is, and take upon himself the job of explaining the variations in actual behavior once the role is given.

Since sociologists often call things like roles and their attendant sanctions *institutions,* and behavior so far as it conforms to roles *institutionalized* behavior, elementary social behavior might be called *subinstitutional.*[1] But remember always that the institutional framework of elementary social behavior is never rigid, and that some elementary social behavior, pursued long enough by enough people, breaks through the existing institutions and replaces them. Probably there is no institution that was not in its germ elementary social behavior.

This leads to my next point. Another reason for calling our subject elementary social behavior is that its characteristics, far more than those of institutionalized behavior, are shared by all mankind. Institutions, whether they are things like the physician's role or things like the bureaucracy, have a long history behind them of development within a particular society; and in institutions societies differ greatly. But within institutions, in the face-to-face relations between individuals that spring up every day and sometimes disappear as quickly, characteristics of behavior appear in which mankind gives away its lost unity. Would you see primitive social behavior in the United States, you need not go to the Navaho country. Any working group in a factory is as primitive. And the similarities reveal themselves the more clearly, the less fully the behavior in question is institutionalized—in our society a street gang is a good example. Naturally the rewards created and distributed in a street gang are not just like those in a hunting band; but given the difference in rewards, the propositions describing the behavior of individuals realizing rewards of some kind through face-to-face transactions are probably much the same for the two groups. At the level of elementary social behavior there is neither Jew nor Gentile, Greek nor barbarian, but only man.

Although I believe this to be true, I cannot demonstrate that it is so; for most of the field and experimental research that tells us about the characteristics of elementary social behavior has in fact been carried out in Western societies, particularly in the United States of America, and so the grounds for a sufficient comparison with other societies are lacking. There is no inherent reason why anthropologists studying primitive societies should not have studied their elementary social behavior, and some of them have studied it, but naturally they are more concerned with getting on record the institutions, the formal rules of

[1] See T. Parsons, *The Social System* (Glencoe, Ill., 1951), p. 552.

the societies they study—those things in which societies most differ—than with making the continuous, direct observations of a rather small number of persons on which our knowledge of elementary social behavior depends. Accordingly, though I believe that the general features of elementary social behavior are shared by all mankind, I believe it as a matter of faith only, and the evidence that I shall in fact adduce is almost wholly American.

Small Groups

If elementary social behavior is the face-to-face contact between individuals, in which the reward each gets from the behavior of the others is relatively direct and immediate, then the study of elementary social behavior depends on observations of such face-to-face contacts, and these cannot easily be made of any large number of persons at one time. Accordingly, my subject is often called the study of small groups; I have called it so myself, but I am now persuaded that the name is misleading. Small groups are not what we study but where we study it. Consider two sorts of social network. In one, Tom is in contact with Dick, and Dick with Harry, but Harry has no connection with Tom. This has been called an *open* network, and many of the chains of influence between men are of this sort. In another, Tom is still in contact with Dick, and Dick with Harry, but the chain is now closed by Harry's being in contact with Tom, and so networks of this sort have been called *closed*.[2] There is no reason to believe that the networks differ in the main propositions that describe elementary social behavior within them, but they obviously differ in the costs of observation. To study behavior in the open network an observer must be present on two different occasions, once for the Tom-Dick contact and once for the Dick-Harry one; for if Tom were ever, for instance, in the same room with Harry at the same time, the two would presumably come into contact with one another, and then the network would no longer be open. If, on the other hand, the network is closed, Tom, Dick, and Harry can all be in the same room within the same span of time, and an investigator can, within that time, get information on the contacts among all three of them. Accordingly, an investigator studying elementary social behavior can make his observations faster, and there-

[2] E. Bott, *Family and Social Network* (London, 1957), pp. 58-59.

fore at less cost, by concentrating on a closed network than he can by concentrating on an open one. But a closed network is what we ordinarily mean by a single small group. No more than any other activity is social research immune to considerations of cost, and accordingly most research on elementary social behavior has been carried out on small groups in which each member is in contact with every other in closed networks. But we must not confuse the particular sort of situation in which research is conveniently carried on with the subject of that research. Most, though not all, of the research examined in this book will be research on small groups, but its subject is still elementary social behavior.

Explanation

Now that I have told you what I shall study, I must tell you what I want to do with it; and perhaps a good way for me to begin will be to describe, as I see it, the relation of this present book to its predecessor *The Human Group*.[3] Though that book dealt with groups, some of them were not really very small, one being the whole population of a New England town. The groups that the present book deals with will be, on the whole, much smaller. But the difference between the two that I want to underline now goes deeper than the size of groups. It is a difference in intellectual aims: *The Human Group* did not try to explain much of anything, while *Social Behavior* will at least try to explain.

To say that *The Human Group* did not try to explain much of anything is not to say that what it did try to do was negligible. In it, I tried to do two things. I chose from the literature five detailed field studies of human groups, ranging all the way from a group of industrial workers to an entire town. And of these studies I first asked what classes the observations made by the investigators might reasonably be divided into. The question was not what classes of observation the investigators, according to somebody else's theoretical views, should have made, but what they really did make. And I tried to show that the observations made by the different investigators might be divided into the same four classes: sentiments, activities, interactions, and norms. I need not define these terms here, as they will come in later.

[3] G. C. Homans, *The Human Group* (New York, 1950).

The second question I asked of the five studies was what propositions about the relations between the four classes of variables the studies gave support to. I was not interested in any old propositions but in propositions about the relations between variables, propositions of the general form "x varies as y." The question again was not what propositions ought to have been tested against the data, or how they ought to have been tested, but what propositions did approximately and empirically hold good, whether or not they had any right to do so. And I tried to show that several such propositions did hold good in more than one of the studies; for example: "The higher the rank (or status) of a person within a group, the more nearly his activities conform to the norms of the group."[4] *Rank* was defined as favorable sentiments expressed toward a man by other members of his group.

Some sociologists, and particularly those who make what I shall call "anatomical theories," are apt to refer patronizingly to propositions like this as "mere empirical generalizations," but for me they are our most enduring possessions. Give me a man's actual findings, and I care not what theory he may have built them into. As Mr. Justice Holmes used to say, "Men's systems are forgotten, their *aperçus* are remembered."[5] Science has been built by some of the damnedest methods, but the strategy I follow starts with a scanning of the literature within a particular field in search of the sheer, approximate, empirical propositions, and with an effort to state them in some single set of concepts, that is, some single set of terms.

This was as far, practically, as *The Human Group* went, but it is no place to stop forever. The inevitable next step is to ask why the empirical propositions should take the form they do, and this is to ask for explanations. Once you have established that the height of the tides varies with the phases of the moon, your next step is to ask why this proposition should hold good. And once you have established that the higher a man's rank in a group, the more closely his activities conform to its norms, you will ask why it should be so. The only way to get an answer is to borrow from somebody else's work, if you can, or invent for yourself, if you must, a set of more general propositions, still of the same form as the empirical ones, from which you can

[4] G. C. Homans, *op. cit.,* p. 141.

[5] M. DeWolfe Howe, ed., *Holmes-Laski Letters,* Vol. I (Cambridge, Mass., 1953), p. 277.

logically deduce the latter under specified given conditions. To deduce them successfully *is* to explain them.

The new propositions are more general in the sense that empirical propositions other than the ones you started with can also be derived from them under other givens—and this is what prevents them from being mere inventions. Thus Newton's Laws, which explain the tides, also explain the orbits of the planets. The process of borrowing or inventing the more general propositions I call *induction,* whether or not it is the induction of the philosophers; the process of deriving the empirical propositions from the more general ones I call *explanation,* and this *is* the explanation of the philosophers.[6]

The first process, the process of building up from the empirical to the more general, is very different from the second, the process of building back down from the general to the empirical. The first is an act of creation, which has no rules of procedure that will ensure you success; the second has definite rules, the rules of logic. My strategy is that deductive explanations should be inductively arrived at. But this particular book is only concerned with the second process. It tries to explain, as explanation has just been defined, why empirical propositions about elementary social behavior, both those cited in *The Human Group* and others, should take the form they do. I shall not deny that the propositions themselves have become somewhat refined in the process. Thus the proposition about a man's rank and his activities in a group I now believe holds good in some circumstances but not all.

Much modern sociological theory seems to me to possess every virtue except that of explaining anything.[7] Part of the trouble is that much of it consists of systems of categories, or pigeonholes, into which the theorist fits different aspects of social behavior. No science can proceed without its system of categories, or conceptual scheme, but this in itself is not enough to give it explanatory power. A conceptual scheme is not a theory. The science also needs a set of general propositions about the relations between the categories, for without such propositions explanation is impossible. No explanation without propositions! But much modern sociological theory seems quite satisfied with

[6] See R. B. Braithwaite, *Scientific Explanation* (Cambridge, England, 1953).

[7] I am thinking particularly of the work of my colleague and friend Talcott Parsons. See especially T. Parsons and E. Shils, eds., *Toward a General Theory of Action* (Cambridge, Mass., 1951); T. Parsons, *The Social System* (Glencoe, Ill., 1951); T. Parsons and N. Smelser, *Economy and Society* (Glencoe, Ill., 1956).

itself when it has set up its conceptual scheme.[8] The theorist shoves different aspects of behavior into his pigeonholes, cries, "Ah-ha!" and stops. He has written the dictionary of a language that has no sentences. He would have done better to start with the sentences.

The other part of the trouble is that when the theory does contain sentences, they tend to take the form of qualitative, anatomical sentences about human behavior, such as "All organizations have communications systems"—not that a truly modern theory would use words as close to common sense as these.[9] Sometimes the descriptive statements in the new language help students see the phenomena in a new light; sometimes they seem to redescribe the phenomena without adding anything, translating into an unfamiliar language what is just as well said in a familiar one. No science can get along without making such statements, if only to say what its subject matter will be, and my effort to define elementary social behavior consists of a set of statements of this sort.

From the qualitative, anatomical descriptions, moreover, deductions can be made. If all organizations have communications systems, and the Standard Oil Co. of New Jersey is an organization, then it has a communications system. You might even say that its being an organization explains why it has a communications system—unless "having a communications system" was part of the definition of "organization" to begin with, in which case the reasoning gets circular. But the real difficulty lies deeper than this. What strikes us most forcibly about organizations is not that they *have* communications systems but that the systems vary greatly along several dimensions. Some, for instance, have many communications centers (offices); others have few. And the anatomical propositions help us little in explaining the variations. They can be made capable of explaining the variations only, I think, when they are turned into propositions of the general form "x varies as y," even if x and y can each take only two values, as when a particular feature of behavior is either present or absent.

If a conceptual scheme and anatomical propositions are enough to constitute a theory, this book is not a book of theory. Instead it is a book of explanation. It will state a number of general propositions of the general form "x varies as y" about elementary social behavior, and

[8] See H. L. Zetterberg, book review in *American Sociological Review*, Vol. 23 (1958), pp. 95-96.

[9] See J. G. March and H. A. Simon, *Organizations* (New York, 1958), pp. 7-8.

then try to show, perhaps not always successfully or rigorously, that a number of less general propositions, which investigators have found to hold good empirically, may be deduced from the general ones under specified given conditions. To deduce them is to explain them.

The General Propositions

I said earlier that the seeker after explanation would have either to invent for himself or borrow from others the set of more general propositions from which the empirical propositions may, under given conditions, be deduced. Newton had to invent his own; I have taken the easy way out and borrowed. Faced with empirical propositions from *The Human Group* and the large number of other experimental and field studies of elementary social behavior that have appeared since World War II, I have come to believe that the empirical propositions may most easily be explained by two bodies of general propositions already in existence: behavioral psychology and elementary economics.[10]

It is true that both sets of propositions will take a little extrapolating before they are ready to explain what is observed of elementary social behavior. Behavioral psychology is a set of propositions that come mostly from experimental studies of animals, usually in nonsocial situations. It must be extrapolated—and this is quite a distance—to men and to a social situation: one in which the behavior of one person affects, and is affected by, the behavior of another. As for elementary economics, it is a set of propositions describing the behavior of men exchanging material goods for money in a so-called perfect market: one in which the behaivor of any one buyer or seller has little effect in determining the market prices. Elementary economics does deal with men and with a social situation, for exchange is obviously social; and to serve as an explanation of elementary social behavior it needs a different kind of extrapolation from that which behavioral psychology needs. From apples and dollars, physical goods and money, it needs to be extrapolated so as to apply, for instance, to the exchange of intangible services for social esteem in a market that is far from perfect. As the two sets of propositions, behavioral psychology and elementary economics, are stretched in these respective directions, they seem to

[10] In saying this I necessarily reject Durkheim's view that sociology is *not* a corollary of psychology. See E. Durkheim, *Les règles de la méthode sociologique* (Paris, 1927), p. 125.

me to mesh with one another and form a single set; but rather than trying to prove that this is so, I shall later suggest what the set might be.

An introductory chapter is not the place for details. Briefly, both behavioral psychology and elementary economics envisage human behavior as a function of its pay-off: in amount and kind it depends on the amount and kind of reward and punishment it fetches. When what it fetches is the behavior, similarly determined, of another man, the behavior becomes social. Thus the set of general propositions I shall use in this book envisages social behavior as an exchange of activity, tangible or intangible, and more or less rewarding or costly, between at least two persons.[11]

I must confess that I shall be so anxious to emphasize the connection between a particular kind of behavior and its pay-off, so anxious to get motive into the system, that I shall have little to say about how the connection got established in the first place. Sketchy indeed will be the propositions in the field of psychology sometimes called perception, propositions about the processes connecting a man's environmental stimuli with his choice of courses of action—how likely they are to lead to reward and how valuable the reward is likely to be. In this field, which may include some of the most complicated processes of thought, I shall have to take many things for granted without explanation. This book pretends to be a complete psychology no more than it pretends to be a complete sociology.

My set of general propositions gets no high marks for originality. In its vulgar form it must be the oldest of all theories of social behavior, and it is one we still use every day when we say, "I found so-and-so rewarding," or "I got a great deal out of him," or even "Talking to him took a great deal out of me." Men have always explained their behavior by pointing to what it gets them and what it costs them. That mine is an explanation of the same sort I claim as one of its positive advantages. Modern social science has been so sensitive to the charge that its findings are old or obvious, so ready to go out of its way to show how common-sense explanations are wrong, that it has ended by painting a picture of man that men cannot recognize. Thus of all our many "approaches" to social behavior, the

[11] My own earliest statement of this view is G. C. Homans, "Human Behavior as Exchange," *American Journal of Sociology*, Vol. 63, No. 6 (May, 1958), pp. 597-606.

one that sees it as an economy is the most neglected, though it is the one we use every moment of our lives—except when we write sociology. But even then, in our unguarded moments, sociologists find words like *reward* and *cost* slipping into what we say. Human nature will break in upon our most elaborate theories, but we seldom let it have its way with us and follow up systematically what these words imply. If you will read any writing in sociology, you will find all sorts of theories and explanations, besides the one the sociologist says he is using, slipping in surreptitiously to plaster up cracks in the argument and dropping out again as soon as the need for them has passed. The economic explanation seems so far to have been kept under the table for use in this way. I intend to bring it out into the open. I am not out to destroy common sense but to make explicit and general the wisdom it embodies.

The Plan of the Book

Because this book aims at explanation, its form will be different from that of *The Human Group*. In its method of exposition tha: book was heavily inductive. A chapter describing in common-sense terms the behavior of the members of a particular group was always followed by another chapter pointing out the different classes of observations made by the man who first studied the group and the various propositions that seemed empirically to hold good of the data. Then came another chapter describing another group, and so on. What came first was always the data in detail.

In its method of exposition, this book will be much more nearly, though never perfectly, deductive. After a short chapter about the findings of behavioral psychology on the subject of animal behavior, I shall present in the two following chapters my set of general propositions. In the rest of the book I shall try to illustrate these propositions and show how they may be used to explain a number of familiar features of elementary social behavior—first those features that are least dependent on the presence of an organized group and last those that are most dependent. I dare not say that my explanations will be complete: no explanation ever is. All explanations must leave some things unexplained, and mine may leave rather more than most. I dare not say that mine will be rigorous: when one is using the English language instead of mathematics one can never be sure there is not some slippage in one's deductive logic. But explanation is what I shall aim at. I shall try to bring order out of the familiar chaos by showing that a variety of features of elementary social behavior may be explained by a single set of propositions, under different given conditions.

Only some of the features of elementary social behavior shall I try to explain. Let no one say I have disregarded his favorite one. Of course I have, and I could not help it. No one has ever gotten it all in, and no one ever will. Indeed I have disregarded some of the most famous of all. Mother love and sexual love are surely elementary social behavior, yet I have nothing to say about them whatever. Nor at the other extreme of importance have I much to say about embarrassment, though it is singularly interesting. All I can say is that the features I do talk about are all important and all familiar.

For each of the main empirical propositions that I shall try to explain I shall provide research evidence. In *The Human Group* I confined myself pretty much to field studies of real-life small groups— studies of groups not formed for experimental purposes, and studies made in more or less the same way as that in which an anthropologist maps out the organization of a primitive tribe. In this book the research evidence will come from such studies but also from studies made of groups artificially formed for experimental purposes in laboratories. It will come also from those studies of small groups that take advantage of a very special situation: because a number of groups are similar in some respect the investigator is able to test statistically an hypothesis whose truth may be masked in any one of the groups but which reveals itself as a central tendency when he takes all of them together. Such, for instance, is a study of the relation between the friendships and the geographical locations of people living in a number of apartment buildings all identical in layout.

Just as some experimentalists criticize field studies for their lack of rigor, so some field workers criticize experimental studies for their artificiality: they claim the experimental findings have no bearing on real life. I cannot agree. The laws of human behavior are not repealed when a man leaves the field and enters the laboratory. Naturally the same laws working in different circumstances lead to different results, but not, once the circumstances are taken into account, to inconsistent results. Experimental studies and field studies each can do some things the other cannot do. Each illuminates the other, and I propose to give due regard to both.

Because I shall take up in succession a number of different features of elementary social behavior, and because the more experimental and statistical researches usually aim at testing only a single hypothesis or a small number of them, this book will not offer in evidence what *The Human Group* did: fully rounded field studies of particular groups (or at least as far rounded as the original investigators made them), in which one can see how a number of different features of social behavior are related to one another in a particular situation. *The Human Group* is still the best place to find a few such researches presented in reasonably brief compass; for even when I do cite field studies in the present book, I shall tend to detach and isolate single findings from the many each presents. Yet in order to make good this deficiency in some degree I shall, at the end of the book and by way of summary of what has gone before, present a single field study, which was not yet made when *The Human Group* was written, and show how a number of the propositions that I shall have cited separately earlier in the book apply jointly in the behavior of the people concerned.

In evidence for each of the main empirical propositions, I shall try to cite the results of at least two pieces of research. Because of the variety of theoretical languages in which propositions have been stated, social scientists have failed to appreciate how many different times some of the same ones have been rediscovered. To cite two pieces of research that support a proposition will be enough to suggest that it does not hold good by accident. To cite more would be to overload the book with skimpy descriptions of many researches at the expense of adequate descriptions of a few. Every professional reader will find some of his favorite studies left out, and many excellent pieces of research will get no mention because for my purposes they do not illustrate a particular point as well as others do. As I shall not put forward every possible proposition about elementary social behavior, so I shall not cite every piece of research supporting the ones I do put forward. In no sense is this book a survey or review of the literature.

Now that I have made every claim for the book and disarmed in advance every conceivable objection, it is time to go to work. At this point I give up the competitive "I" and we, my readers and myself, assume the collaborative "we."

Animal Behavior

Chapter Two

We begin at what may seem a long distance from human social behavior—at the behavior of individual animals. And a long distance it is: not for one moment do we imply that the behavior of men and the behavior of animals is the same. But if they are not the same they may yet be similar, and similar in just those ways that will most interest us.

The reasons why we start from a distance are two. Some of the propositions that we shall want to use in describing and explaining the behavior of men are more firmly established for other animals, because investigators can more often experiment with animals under controlled conditions than with men. Second, anyone concerned with the unity of science ought to show, when he can, that the propositions holding good within his special field of interest illustrate those holding good within a wider one.

We shall not be dealing with all behavior, whether animal or human. In particular we shall have little or nothing to say about the conditioned or unconditioned reflexes: things like the knee jerk or the eyelids' closing when an object comes at them fast, but we shall deal instead with *operant behavior*. Should we wish to avoid using this unfamiliar term, we may call it *voluntary* behavior to distinguish from the "involuntary" reflexes, but we do so at the risk of thinking we know what the "will" is and getting into interminable arguments about its "freedom."

Operant behavior we shall illustrate with the behavior of the common pigeon, because it is the favorite experimental animal of my favorite experimental psychologist, B. F. Skinner, whose way of stating generalizations about behavior we shall use here.[1] His generalizations, at least those main ones that most interest us, do not differ in substance from those of other experimental psychologists but do differ in language.

Operant Conditioning

Suppose, then, that a fresh or naïve pigeon is in its cage in the laboratory. One of the items in its inborn repertory of behavior which it uses to explore its environment is the peck. As the pigeon wanders around the cage pecking away, it happens to hit a round red target, at which point the waiting psychologist or, it may be, an automatic machine feeds it grain. The evidence is that the probability of the pigeon's emitting the behavior again—the probability, that is, of its not just pecking but pecking the target—has increased. In Skinner's language, the pigeon's behavior in pecking the target is an *operant;* the operant has been *reinforced;* grain is the *reinforcer;* and the pigeon has undergone *operant conditioning.* Should we prefer our language to be ordinary English, we may say that the pigeon has learned to peck the target by being rewarded for doing so. However, if we use ordinary English we must take care to remember the actual events our words refer to.

In a normal man, a psychologist can at will elicit a knee jerk. He is rarely able to specify the conditions in which a fresh pigeon will peck the target the first time. He cannot, for that matter, do so for any operant in any animal: this circumstance, indeed, defines what he means by the word *operant.* Usually he can only wait until the pigeon pecks the target spontaneously and then reinforce the peck. Not until then does the psychologist, as representative of the physical and social environment, begin to get some control over the pigeon's behavior. That the same is true of fresh humans, every mother knows. You can put the baby on the pot but you can't make him perform—at least not

[1] B. F. Skinner, *The Behavior of Organisms* (New York, 1938), *Science and Human Behavior* (New York, 1953), *Verbal Behavior* (New York, 1957), *Cumulative Record* (New York, 1959).

then and there. You can only wait until the blessed event occurs and then reward him—with coos of approval or, better still, by taking him off the pot. Although people are well aware of such dramatic cases, they find it hard to believe that all human behavior, no matter how subtle, is shaped by the differential reinforcement of quite simple actions produced the first time as if by chance. But then people once had a hard time believing that all the myriad and complex forms of life could have been produced by the slow, shaping action of natural selection on the variations, produced as if by chance, in simpler forms.

We say that the pigeon has learned to peck the target, but we need not dwell on the learning. Once the behavior has been learned a psychologist like Skinner is no longer interested in how it was learned, and "learning theory," as it is sometimes called, is a misleading name for his field of research. Instead he is interested in what variables thereafter determine changes in the rate of emission of operant behavior. The same thing will be true of us in this book: we shall be less interested in how men learn what they do than in what they do after they have learned it, and this is a big limitation on what we have to say.

Deprivation and Satiation

For the sake of sticking pretty close to everyday language, we shall call any particular sort of learned behavior, like pecking the target, an *activity* and not, as Skinner does, an *operant;* and we turn now to the variables that determine the rate of emission of an activity. These variables are of two main kinds: the state of the animal, and the rate of reinforcement. The first is obvious. The hungrier the pigeon is— the longer, that is, it has gone without food—the more often it will emit an activity that, like our peck at the target, has been reinforced with food. And the same is of course true of activities reinforced by things other than food, like water or sex. By the same token, the more nearly satiated the pigeon is—the greater the amount of food it has gotten in the recent past—the less often it will emit an activity reinforced with food. This means, though it is often forgotten, that the pigeon is then more likely to emit some other activity, including doing nothing. Deprivation and satiation are not, of course, separate variables but low and high values, respectively, of the same variable, and we have not stated two different propositions but a single proposition.

The Rate of Reinforcement

The effects of the other class of variable, which have to do with the rate of reinforcement, are more complicated. Let us begin with the easiest. If an activity is established in some *strength* by reinforcement —if, that is to say, there is some probability greater than zero that the pigeon will emit it—and if thereafter the psychologist ceases to reinforce it at all, the pigeon will emit it less and less often; the behavior is getting *extinguished*. But how long it takes to get extinguished depends greatly on what the psychologist did before he stopped reinforcing. If he reinforced the activity often or, which is more interesting, reinforced it intermittently, a very long time without further reinforcement may have to go by before the pigeon never emits it at all; and a single reinforcement, coming perhaps years later, may serve to reinstate it at nearly its original strength. In pigeons as in men the effects of past experience take a long time to wear off.

If in the sufficiently long run an activity never reinforced is never emitted, it should follow that an activity often reinforced is often emitted, and in general this is true. But much depends on the form the frequent reinforcement takes. The highest rates of emission are not obtained by regular, but by intermittent, reinforcement, particularly reinforcement at a variable ratio. Instead of giving the pigeon grain at, say, every third peck, the psychologist now reinforces the third peck, now the seventh, and so on, varying the ratio between pecks and reinforcements at random. This feature of the pigeon's behavior must help it survive in its natural or wild habitat, where it is most unlikely to find food at every *n*th peck but must still keep hard at work pecking if it is to get enough to eat.

Variable-ratio reinforcement clearly has the same effect on some men that it has on all pigeons. All one has to do is consider the charm of gambling, which is nothing else than an activity reinforced both at a variable ratio and in variable amounts. Indeed someone contemplating the energy wasted on the slot machine or one-armed bandit may cynically wonder whether American industry, with its constant-ratio wage payments—payments for every hour or every piece of work —has chosen the schedule of reinforcement best calculated to get most output from its workers. Nor is gambling the only example of

variable-ratio reinforcement in human affairs. The rewards of many enterprises from fishing to the writing of poetry are apt to come after variable amounts of work. But once having recognized the variable of variability itself, we shall nevertheless pay little further heed to it. The reinforcement of the human activities we shall be most interested in comes, if it comes at all, at something much more like regular intervals. It is not altogether a gamble.

But this is not our main point. Unlike the observations that the psychologist makes of pigeons in a laboratory, the observations that we make of men in the everyday world are not often precise enough to let us determine at what ratios, variable or other, their activities are being rewarded. Since we are finally interested in men and not in animals, we need entertain no proposition about the behavior of animals that is more precise than one we can verify for men. We need instead a proposition about the relation between the frequency with which an activity is emitted and the frequency with which it is reinforced that holds good, roughly and approximately, regardless of the reinforcement ratio. Such a proposition is the following: if a low rate of reinforcement leads to a low rate of emission of an activity, then, roughly and approximately, the more frequent the reinforcement, the more frequent is the emission of the activity. And if a particular activity is often emitted, this means, again, that some other activity is less often emitted.

Clearly this proposition holds good only while "other things are equal"; and among the other things is the effect of the proposition we stated earlier: that satiation decreases the rate of emission of an activity. The two effects are often related and are particularly apt to be so in the pigeon's wild state, where there are no experimental controls to keep them segregated. For if a pigeon's activity is reinforced with grain, a high rate of reinforcement may lead to satiation with grain and so to a lowering of the strength of the activity. Frequency of emission may be low for two different reasons: too low a rate of reinforcement—if emission is roughly proportional to reinforcement—or too high a rate—if emission is decreased by satiation. This leads us to the belief that, apart from the effects of regular as opposed to intermittent reinforcement, there is some particular rate of reinforcement at which the new reinforcement will just allay the pigeon's increasing deprivation and keep him pecking at a maximum rate. The pigeon will

do most work looking for food if he is just a little hungry all the time. As our example of an activity reinforced in operant conditioning we have used "a peck at the target." If from a distant point of view these words specify a particular kind of behavior, from a nearer one they cover a multitude of pecks. The pigeon, for instance, may peck gently or with some strength. By reinforcing a particular strength of peck and failing to reinforce a stronger or weaker peck, the psychologist may train the pigeon to emit pecks of a particular strength far more often than it does others. But in the way it is established and in the frequency of emission once it has been established, the new *discriminated activity* illustrates the same propositions as did the former, more generalized activity. Perhaps this is obvious, but neither in pigeons nor in men should we forget the possibility of rewarding different degrees within the same over-all type of activity.

Stimuli

In our discussion of experimental psychology, we have not so far mentioned a word that in many such discussions comes in at the very beginning—the word *stimulus*. We have done so deliberately: the heart of the psychology used here is not a stimulus and a response but an operant and a reinforcer (an activity and a reward), and the latter pair are what we shall mostly be working with later in the book. But once we have made this point, the time for stimuli has come. Suppose that the psychologist precedes by the ringing of a bell every occasion on which he reinforces a peck at the target. Quite soon the probability increases that the pigeon will emit the activity upon the ringing of the bell alone, and in this way the behavior has come under the control of some discriminable feature of the environment—the stimulus—other than the reinforcer itself. Indeed, any feature of the environment that the pigeon's sense organs are equipped to pick up may, once it has appeared in some conjuncture with the emission of a reinforced activity, tend on its subsequent reappearances to elicit that activity. But if, of course, on the occasion of these later reappearances the activity is never reinforced, the stimulus tends with time to lose its power to elicit.

This characteristic of its behavior is clearly useful to the pigeon in its wild state. To take one example, grain is specially apt to be present

in the neighborhood of a particular pattern of colored leaves and stalks; and an increase in pecking in the face of such a pattern is particularly apt to get the pigeon grain. If, moreover, the grain is unlikely to be plentiful except in the neighborhood of such a pattern, the control by the stimulus over the behavior allows the pigeon to economize, so to speak, on pecks: it will peck less often in places where it is not apt to find grain.

We shall not dwell here on the ways in which stimulus-control may be generalized or discriminated under different conditions of reinforcement. In our example, the target that the pigeon pecks is red. Once the psychologist reinforces its pecking the red target, the probability of its pecking any target vaguely reddish or indeed any red object increases. On the other hand, should the psychologist reinforce only pecks at crimson targets, the pigeon's effective discrimination between shades of red may go far. And of course a finely discriminated stimulus may become linked with a finely discriminated activity: a crimson target may become the signal for a peck of particular strength. But we can do no more than refer the student who wants further information on these matters to the textbooks of behavioral psychology.

What we want to emphasize here is the triple contingency in the relation between stimulus, activity, and reinforcement—the triple contingency in which a stimulus (the ringing of a bell) occurs on an occasion in which an activity (the peck at the target) is followed by a reinforcement (grain). It is such contingencies that bring the behavior of the organism under a more and more precise control by the environment, physical and social. Because the pigeon in its past history has met a large number and great variety of these contingencies, and because an activity once established loses strength slowly even under infrequent later reinforcement, the psychologist may find it difficult to predict in detail the pigeon's behavior in the immediate future. If its past experience is determining its present behavior, much knowledge of its past is needed for prediction. Such knowledge is hard enough to come by with an animal that the psychologist has brought up under controlled conditions in his laboratory. It would be still harder to come by with a wild pigeon. With a man, the fact that he can talk about his experience by no means solves the problem, as he may well have forgotten just those past contingencies that were most important in determining his present behavior.

Punishment and Cost

So far we have spoken of the psychologist's presenting the pigeon with positive reinforcers, such as food. But in its natural habitat—and the psychologist can readily arrange the equivalent in the laboratory—the pigeon will also encounter *aversive conditions,* or punishments. The punishment may come from the outside environment, as when the psychologist dumps a bucket of cold water on the pigeon. Or it may come from that peculiarly intimate part of the environment, the pigeon's own body, as when the repeated use of a particular set of muscles leads to fatigue. Under aversive conditions, any activity that lets the pigeon escape from the punishment is by that fact reinforced. Just as food is a *positive reinforcer* for any behavior on the part of the pigeon that is followed by its eating, so getting out from under the water is a *negative reinforcer* for any behavior accomplishing that result. In the positive case, the reinforcer gets presented; in the negative case, the reinforcer gets eliminated.

The triple contingency of stimulus, activity, and reinforcement applies to punishment too. If the ringing of the bell, instead of preceding the presentation of food, has preceded the drenching—if it has become an *aversive* stimulus—then on a new occasion the ringing renders more probable any behavior that has in the past allowed the pigeon to get out from under the water or avoid the drenching altogether. But remember that the actual punishment must have occurred at least once in the presence of the aversive stimulus before the latter can successfully set off avoidance behavior.

In the example used so far—the bucket of water—we have assumed that the pigeon could escape from the punishment or avoid it altogether. But some activities get both reinforced and punished, and sometimes they cannot get the one without incurring the other. Particularly common under natural conditions, and particularly relevant to the argument later in this book, are those mild punishments that the pigeon encounters and can hardly escape if it is to emit activity leading to positive reinforcement. Thus the pigeon may find its food only in the midst of brambles and thickets, making movement painful and difficult. The psychologist can arrange the equivalent in the laboratory: he may, for instance, arrange that the pigeon gets food only when it pecks a target so high off the ground that it must stretch its neck unnaturally far; or, as we suggested earlier, he may reinforce only pecks made with great force. The evidence is that, under equal conditions of deprivation, the pigeon will peck less often in the new situation than it would have done if the target were within easy reach or it did not have to peck so hard. A highly discriminated activity may be, but need not be, a relatively aversive one.

These unavoidable punishments are often cumulative in effect: they take time to make themselves felt. Indeed, there may be no activity that kept up long enough does not become to some degree punishing. Even when the psychologist cannot prove that true muscle fatigue is present, a pigeon that has repeated an activity over and over again without interruption shows increasing signs of difficulty in carrying it out once more. We cannot ask the pigeon whether it is tired or bored, but we can observe that the frequency with which it emits the behavior falls off without any change in the conditions of positive reinforcement. As frequent activity, frequently reinforced, may by producing satiation come in time to decrease in frequency, so frequent activity, frequently punished but not so severely as to put a stop to it forthwith, may come to decrease through some analogous cumulative effect.

Punishment that the pigeon cannot avoid if it is to emit activities positively reinforced we may call the *cost* of these activities. Whether it takes effect suddenly or cumulatively, cost tends to depress the rate of emission of the activity below what it would have been with lower cost. And by depressing the frequency of any particular activity, cost makes more frequent the emission of some alternative activity. Indeed, we may argue that, since any activity allowing the animal to escape or avoid punishment is by that fact reinforced, an increase in the cost of any one activity increases the reward of an alternative one.

We have not yet reached the end of punishments. So far we have included in punishment only the actual presentation of aversive conditions. But if the presentation of aversive conditions acts as a punishment, so does the withdrawal of reinforcing ones. Just as we may punish a child either by slapping him or by taking cookies away from him, so we may punish the pigeon in two corresponding ways: by drenching it with water or by removing grain in plain sight. We call them both punishments because they have the same effect: any activity leading to the replacement of the grain becomes reinforced just as surely as does any activity that gets the pigeon out of the drenching. Since the emission of any reinforced activity prevents by that fact the simultaneous emission of an activity leading to an alternative reward, and thus amounts to the withdrawal of the alternative reward—that is, to a punishment—we might argue that the costs, or unavoidable punishment, of any one activity include the withdrawn or forgone rewards of an alternative activity. But we doubt that pigeons act as if they were aware of this.

Since in this book we shall be greatly concerned with alternative courses of behavior, we cannot too strongly emphasize that extinction, satiation, and punishment incurred in emitting an activity all render more probable, at least for the time being, the emission of some other activity. If the pigeon that has gotten grain by pecking the target never afterwards gets grain in this way, it is more likely to peck something else or not peck at all. If by pecking it gets a lot of grain fast, it is more likely to emit other activities—for instance, activity reinforced by a drink of water. And if pecking leads to a drenching, it is highly likely to do anything else but peck. But though all three—extinction, satiation, and punishment—render more probable activities other than those extinguished, satiated, or punished, they do so in different ways and for different spans of time. The extinction of, the failure ever to reinforce, a particular activity leads to a permanent fall in the strength of the activity. Satiation leads to a temporary fall in strength until, for instance, the pigeon is hungry again. And the punishment of an activity once found reinforcing leads also to an ephemeral fall in its strength: after the punishment has been removed, the activity soon returns to its original probability of emission. This is hardly surprising, as the pigeon could not survive in its natural habitat if occasional punishment permanently deterred it from pursuing otherwise rewarding activities.

It is this characteristic of punishment that makes it so unsatisfactory, because so costly, a way of controlling behavior. Suppose there is an activity that we find undesirable but that nevertheless gets some reinforcement. Unless we are in a position to punish the activity every time it appears, it will soon reinstate itself. If accordingly we disapprove of a certain activity, let us say in our children, and want to get rid of it, we had better use, if we can, some other method than punishment. We had better use extinction, and see that the activity goes without reward: if a child cries to get attention we should see that he does not get it, though we may run risks in doing so. Or we should reward an alternative activity, praising him for not crying rather than punishing him for crying. But let us face it: this is not always Pollyanna's world. Control may be necessary at times when the only means of control at our command is punishment, however unsatisfactory. These times may also come less often than we think.

Emotional Behavior

The punishment that consists in the withdrawal of a positive reinforcement will serve to lead us to one final issue. We have used the peck at the target as our model of behavior that may be reinforced in operant conditioning. But there are forms of behavior that may not quite fit the model. At least mankind has persisted in thinking of emotion as somehow different from other behavior, whether in men or pigeons. Suppose that the psychologist has regularly fed the pigeon when it pecked the target, and then abruptly stops feeding it. The final result may be the extinction of the activity, but the immediate one is something else: the pigeon turns away from the target, flapping its wings and cooing hurriedly. Recognizing similar behavior in man, we may say that the pigeon is frustrated and angry because it did not get the food it expected—though, since we cannot talk to the pigeon, all we can refer to when we use the word *expected* is the fact that regular reinforcement suddenly stopped. If, moreover, the withdrawal of an expected reinforcement releases aggression in the pigeon or other animals, we might guess that the presentation of an expected reinforcement would release emotion of an opposite kind: something equivalent to the cat's purr. However rudimentary the expression of positive emotion in pigeons, in man it does not lack eloquence.

How is emotional behavior to be distinguished from operant behavior like that in our example, the peck at the target? We may suggest that the emotion, unlike the peck, has no possible use for the pigeon: all that flapping gets it nothing. But the lack of use will not set all emotions apart from other behavior: the pigeon will peck back in anger at another pigeon that has attacked it; its behavior is emotional, yet may save its skin. A better distinction between operant and emotional behavior is this: the probability that the pigeon will peck the target can be increased by reinforcement with food, water, or any primary reinforcer, but it is doubtful that the probability, or strength, of emotion can be increased in this way: the emotional behavior can only be released by a particular stimulus-situation. Thus aggressive behavior is simply released or triggered by a frustration or an attack. It may be that a semblance of emotion can be reinforced: a pigeon may perhaps be trained to put on an emotional act, but the act remains just that: it does not contain all the features of true emotion. Man may be more liable to emotion and certainly has an infinitely greater capacity for expressing it; and it may be easier with men than it is with pigeons to strengthen emotional behavior—the reality or the semblance—by reinforcement.

Summary

In summary, we are dealing with two organisms: the pigeon and the psychologist, and with two classes of variable: the frequency with which activities are emitted, and the state of deprivation of the organism. As for the first class, we have to consider both the frequency with which the pigeon emits activities and the frequency with which the psychologist does so: how often he rewards the pigeon. These variables may be directly measured. As for the second class, we have to consider only the state of the pigeon: we are interested in whether the pigeon is hungry but not in whether the psychologist is. Some of the variables of the second class may also be easily measured. If we want to know how far the pigeon is deprived of a positive reinforcer like food, we can weigh the animal or count the hours since it was last fed. Much less easily measured is the degree to which it is deprived of negative reinforcers, like escape from fatigue or escape from repeated mild punishment; but to understand the behavior we may still have to make some estimate.

Stated approximately and under the condition of "other things equal," the chief propositions relating these variables to one another are the following. The more fully an animal has been deprived of a positive reinforcer, the more often it emits an activity so reinforced; the more fully it has been satiated, the less often it does so. The more often an activity is reinforced, the more often the animal emits it; the more often an activity is punished, the less often the animal emits it. The withdrawal of a positive reinforcer releases the emotional behavior we call aggression, and the presentation of a positive reinforcer may release, besides the reinforced activity, some degree of positive emotional behavior. Finally, any increase in the frequency of a particular activity entails by that very fact a decrease in the frequency of an alternative activity.

Although we say that these propositions hold good only if "other things are equal," we still treat each one by itself and so do violence to reality. No one of them really works alone; each holds good under the condition that the others hold good simultaneously. We come closer to reality if we look at their combinations. Take, for instance, the first two propositions together. If an activity is often reinforced, it is often emitted; but frequent reinforcement may also satiate the animal and so decrease the frequency of emission. Or take the first and third. If an activity is often reinforced, it is often emitted; but the very emission may entail the inescapable punishment we have called cost, and this may lead in time to a decrease in the frequency of emission.

As we conceded at the beginning of this chapter, the behavior of the pigeon differs greatly from that of the man. The sensory and motor equipments of the two are obviously different, and so are the kinds of activity each can perform: a man can talk and a pigeon cannot, and though in return a man cannot peck and a pigeon can, we do not give it much credit for that. More important, the sheer number of different activities the organism can learn and have available for emission under appropriate stimulation is far greater for a man than for a pigeon, and so is the number of links that the organism can learn in a chain of activities leading to some final reinforcement: this may be what we mean when we say a man can think. So great are these differences that they make, if we please to say so, a qualitative difference in behavior. Yet, given the differences in what is learned and in the capacity for learning, the behavior of the two organisms may still be similar in what happens after learning has taken place—similar especially in that both may illustrate just those propositions we have outlined in this chapter: propositions relating the frequency of activities and the state of the organism. At least the behavior of man may be not inconsistent with these propositions.

Human Exchange: Terms

Chapter Three

In the last chapter we might have thought of the psychologist as engaged with the pigeon in an exchange of grain for pecks. But it would have been a one-sided sort of exchange. While the grain reinforces what the pigeon does, the pecks reinforce the psychologist not as pecks but as science: as a pattern that tells him something about animal behavior. And while the pigeon's behavior depends on how often he gets grain, the psychologist's does not depend on how often he gets pecks unless he lets it do so. With the psychologist the pigeon carries on the same kind of exchange that he does with the physical environment, which is what we mean when we say the psychologist is studying individual behavior.

In this book we are less interested in individual than in social behavior, or true exchange, where the activity of each of at least two animals reinforces (or punishes) the activity of the other, and where accordingly each influences the other.[1] Yet we hold that we need no new propositions to describe and explain the social. With social behavior nothing unique emerges to be analyzed only in its own terms. Rather, from the laws of individual behavior, such as those sketched out in the last chapter, follow the laws of social behavior when the complications of mutual reinforcement are taken into account. At least we shall assume so as long as we dare. We welcome new situ-

[1] See T. Parsons and E. Shils, eds., *Toward a General Theory of Action* (Cambridge, Mass., 1951), pp. 14-16; B. F. Skinner, *Science and Human Behavior* (New York, 1953), pp. 297-312.

ations, but new propositions we shall not go out of our way to look for. They will thrust themselves upon us soon enough.

Nor, though the pigeon is thoroughly social, is his the social behavior we are interested in, and so we say a reluctant good-bye to the endearing creature that has given us our start. Not only shall we adapt the propositions of individual behavior to the social situation, but propositions about pigeons to the human situation; and the latter may be the harder job. We shall have to extrapolate or generalize the propositions of the last chapter beyond the limits to which experiments on the pigeon have so far confirmed them—but perhaps not far beyond: a family likeness will persist. Taking our departure, then, from what we know about animal behavior, we shall state a set of propositions that seem to us fundamental in describing and explaining human social behavior, or human exchange. In the present chapter we shall define and illustrate the chief technical terms that will enter our propositions; in the next we shall put on record the propositions themselves; and in later chapters we shall show what further propositions or corollaries seem to follow under various conditions from the main set.

An Example

To help us visualize the sort of thing we shall have to do with, let us consider a characteristic human exchange. Suppose that two men are doing paper-work jobs in an office.[2] According to the office rules, each should do his job by himself or, if he needs help, he should consult the supervisor. One of the men, whom we shall call Person, is not skillful at the work and would get it done better and faster if he got help from time to time. In spite of the rules he is reluctant to go to the supervisor, for to confess his incompetence might hurt his chances for promotion. Instead he seeks out the other man, whom we shall call Other for short, and asks him for help. Other is more experienced at the work than is Person; he can do his own work well and quickly and be left with time to spare, and he has reason to suppose that the supervisor will not go of his way to look for a breach of the rules. Other gives Person help and in return Person gives Other thanks and expressions of approval. The two men have exchanged help and ap-

---

[2] A good description of social behavior in an office situation is found in P. M. Blau, *The Dynamics of Bureaucracy* (Chicago, 1955), pp. 99-116.

proval. Besides Person and Other, there is at least one other worker in the room, whom we shall call the Third Man, but we need not introduce him yet.

Descriptive Terms

In propositions describing what is common to such an exchange and many others, what technical terms shall we use? In this chapter we can only define the principal terms and leave the secondary ones to be defined when they first come in. We shall use two classes of terms: *descriptive terms* and *variables*. The descriptive terms are names for the kinds of behavior we shall talk about, and the variables, as the word implies, are names for the properties of behavior that we think vary in quantity. Suppose that one of our propositions is: "The more valuable to Person a unit of the activity Other gives him, the more often he will emit activity rewarded by the activity of Other." In this proposition, "activity" is a descriptive term: it refers to the kind of behavior we are talking about. But the words "more valuable" and "more often" refer to variables: we hold that *value* and *frequency* are properties of activity that may vary in amount. It is not activity that varies—this is only a descriptive term—but the frequency and value *of* activity—these are the variables. Let us take up the descriptive terms first.

In the last chapter we spoke of the pigeon's peck at the target as an *activity* because this is a shorter expression than "kind of behavior," and in the same way in the exchange between Person and Other we shall refer to giving help and giving approval as two different activities.[3] The number of other activities men may carry out, the number of different things they may do, is of course infinite, so we shall not undertake to enumerate them but only point to particular ones as they come up. One difficulty in definition the pigeon's peck does not share with many human activities. Compared with them, it is pretty sharply discriminated both as a unit and as a type of activity. But even the peck is not an utterly standardized thing: the pigeon may peck hard or gently, and as for a human activity, men may not only change the amount of it they put out but also change the activity itself by insensible grada-

[3] G. C. Homans, *The Human Group* (New York, 1950), pp. 34-35.

tions into one of another kind, without our being able to draw anything but an arbitrary line to mark where one stops and the other begins. Thus Other's advice to Person may be very helpful or somewhat less helpful; it may even turn by degrees into positively bad advice. We take note of this difficulty here, but we shall have nothing more to say about it at the moment. How we cope with it, so far as we cope with it at all, will become clear only later when we talk about *value*.

One of the activities men engage in is transferring physical objects and materials from themselves to others. Or the work a man does on the environment may result in his getting physical objects from it. In talking about exchanges of this sort, people are inclined to play down the act of transfer and emphasize only the objects transferred. Economics is particularly, though by no means wholly, concerned with the exchange of physical objects, including money. In short, our everyday practice tends to make a distinction between *goods* and *services,* that is, nonphysical goods, like the time a lawyer gives to his client. But neither economics nor psychology believes that goods differ from services in their effects on behavior. Both are reinforcers or punishers, and both may be measured in value and quantity in essentially the same ways. The only advantage for a social scientist that goods have over services is not the fact that he can measure their properties but the precision with which he can sometimes do so.

Although all the observably different kinds of things people do are, in our language, activities, we shall—because we shall spend a great deal of time talking about them—set apart a special class of activities and call them by a special name. The activities that the members of a particular verbal or symbolic community say are signs of the attitudes and feelings a man takes toward another man or other men—these we call *sentiments*.[4] When a man eats his breakfast, the members of the American community believe that this activity need not—though in fact it may—imply anything about his feelings toward his wife. But when a man kisses his wife, we Americans hold it to be a sign that the man loves her, even though at the moment the love may be of the most conventional sort. Sentiments need not be verbal symbols—a kiss is not verbal—but all sentiments do resemble language in that their connection with what they refer to is shared by a particular community and

[4] G. C. Homans, *op. cit.,* pp. 40-43.

not by all mankind—not in all societies is a kiss a sign of affection—and someone not yet a member of the community, a baby or a stranger, must learn its sentiments as he does its language. In our example, the thanks and approval Person gives to Other are sentiments.

Sentiments are not internal states of an individual any more than words are. They are not inferred from overt behavior: they *are* overt behavior and so are directly observable. They are, accordingly, activities. Because people say that they are the outward and visible signs of internal states—of the attitudes and feelings men take toward other men—we find it convenient to call them by a special term. But in their effects on behavior they do not differ from other activities: we need no special propositions to describe their effects, and unless we have some special reason for emphasizing the distinction we shall use the term *activity* to include sentiments.

Above all, sentiments resemble other activities in that they may reinforce or punish behavior. Those who read this book are taken by that fact to be men of the world, who know that when Person thanks Other he may not really feel grateful. As social scientists we may also believe that skilled questioning of Person might bring out how sincere he was. But sincerity is not a problem for us. The real question is this: Whether or not Person is sincere, does his expressed sentiment reinforce Other's behavior? What Other doesn't know won't hurt him, and so far as he takes the thanks at face value and acts as if it were a sign of approval, we care not if it be sincere. It would of course be another problem if Other penetrated the disguise—but then the sentiment would be another sentiment too. The language of love would have taken a turn for the worse.

Among the many sentiments we shall be particularly concerned with social approval. We hold that all activities and sentiments emitted by one man in response to the behavior of another are more or less reinforcing or punishing to the behavior of the other or, as we shall say, more or less valuable to him. But between, for instance, help (an activity) and approval (a sentiment) lies a difference of the same kind as that between, say, mail and money. Mail reinforces the specific activities that lead up to getting the mail, but money is used to reinforce, to reward, a much wider variety of activities. For this reason B. F. Skinner speaks of money as a *generalized reinforcer*. Social approval is another: one can reinforce a wide variety of human activities by providing social approval and similar sentiments in return.[5] In fact social approval will play somewhat the same part in our social economics as money does in regular economics—but obviously not quite the same, if only because approval, unlike money, cannot be physically transferred: if one man receives approval from another he cannot use *that* approval to get something from somebody else.

The last of our main descriptive terms is *interaction*.[6] We use it when we are not interested for the moment in the particular sort of behavior emitted—whether it is an activity or a sentiment, or a particular kind of activity or sentiment—but simply in the fact that the behavior, whatever it may be otherwise, is at least social. Men perform many activities, like fishing, that are rewarded by the non-human environment; but when an activity (or sentiment) emitted by one man is rewarded (or punished) by an activity emitted by another *man*, regardless of the kinds of activity each emits, we say that the two have *interacted*. We are specially apt to use this word when we are interested in the number of social contacts a man has with a second person compared with the number he has with a third. Then we may say that Person interacts more often with Other than he does with the Third Man. But note here that "more often" refers to a variable—frequency—and the "interacts" remains a descriptive term.

In *The Human Group*, the forerunner of the present book, these three descriptive terms, *activity, sentiment,* and *interaction,* were explicitly defined in much the same way they are here, but the definition of the variables was left implicit. We cannot allow this to remain the case. Our variables will fall into two classes: those that have to do with the *quantity* of activity or sentiment emitted and correspond to the frequencies of the last chapter, and those that have to do with the *value* of activity or sentiment and correspond, as we shall try to show presently, to the state-of-the-organism variables of the last chapter. No doubt these are not the only properties of activities that may vary, but they are the ones we shall deal with. Let us take them up in order.

[5] B. F. Skinner, *op. cit.,* p. 78. See also J. L. Gewirtz and D. M. Baer, "Deprivation and Satiation of Social Reinforcers as Drive Conditions," *Journal of Abnormal and Social Psychology,* Vol. 57 (1958), pp. 165-72.

[6] G. C. Homans, *op. cit.,* pp. 35-37.

Quantity

One of the variables that entered the propositions about pigeon behavior was the frequency with which the pigeon emitted an activity. Frequency is a measure of the quantity of activity; it is the number of units of the activity that the organism in question emits within a given period of time: the frequency of pecking is the number of pecks per minute or per hour. Frequency is measured by some kind of counting and presupposes units of activity that can be counted. In the case of the pigeon, the measurement of frequency is rendered easy by a fact we have already considered: a unit of activity such as a peck is naturally well defined; it has a beginning and an end, and so can be counted. Some measures of the quantities entering into human exchange are of this sort. So far as economics studies the exchange of commodities, some of its units of quantity are natural in that they are single objects, like apples, or they have been accepted by so many people for so long that they have become practically natural, like bushels of wheat, tons of steel, or dollars. But in many kinds of human exchange, including those of most interest to us, the unit of quantity is given neither by nature nor by long-established convention. Moreover, the character of the unit that can be adopted in any particular study depends on the circumstances in which the study is carried out.

Since much of the activity that enters into human exchange is verbal, let us examine some of the ways in which investigators have measured the frequency of verbal activity. The most rigorous method is probably that of E. D. Chapple,[7] but we shall use as our first example the method of R. F. Bales[8] because we shall want to examine later some of his research results. Bales studies the behavior of groups of some half-dozen students, assembled in a special experimental room to discuss a problem. From behind a one-way mirror, unobserved by the students, a research assistant scores on a moving roll of paper what they say. For him, the unit of activity is any item of symbolic behavior that has a discriminable meaning, even if it is only a laugh or a shrug

[7] E. D. Chapple, "Measuring Human Relations: An Introduction to the Study of the Interaction of Individuals," *Genetic Psychology Monographs*, Vol. 22 (1940), pp. 3-147; and "The Standard Experimental (Stress) Interview as Used in Interaction Chronograph Investigations," *Human Organization*, Vol. 12 (1953), pp. 23-32.

[8] R. F. Bales, *Interaction Process Analysis* (Cambridge, Mass., 1950).

of the shoulders. Each such unit he scores as being emitted by a particular member of the group and as being directed to a particular other member or to the group as a whole. He further scores it as falling within a certain class of activities or sentiments, in a scheme of classification devised by Bales. "Gives suggestion," "gives approval," and "shows tension release" (e.g., jokes) are some of the classes of activity in the scheme. The score will, for example, yield counts of the number of such units of activity emitted by each member to every other member or to the group as a whole in the course of an experimental session. It will also yield counts of the number of such units falling within a particular class of activity in the course of a session or any part of it. The difficulty with the method lies in training different observers so that they will score the same way, especially so that they will treat as units the same items of behavior.

Moreover, the Bales method can only be used in special circumstances, not easily realized: the group must be small, and the observer must be able to hear what each of the members says. Should we want to study groups under natural conditions—what some of us are pleased to call "real-life" groups—we may have to put up with cruder methods than Bales'. Suppose a man is to study social behavior on an office floor where some fifty men and women are working.[9] The best he may be able to do is get himself a seat at the back and watch what is happening. There may be a good deal of moving about and several conversations going on at once. Unless they go on right in front of him, he will not be able to score their content. That is, he will not be able to score the particular kind of activity that has taken place. But he may, for instance, be able to count the number of times in the course of a day he sees one person talking to another even if he cannot tell who started the conversations or what was said in them. And he can do the same for other pairs of conversationalists. After a time he will have scores of the number of times each person in the office talked to every other, and from these he can make up various subsidiary scores, for instance: the total number of conversations a particular person took part in or the number of different persons he talked to.

Should all else fail, the investigator may be reduced to asking people whom they talked to, and how often they talked to each one. This

[9] G. C. Homans, "The Cash Posters: A Study of a Group of Working Girls," *American Sociological Review*, Vol. 19 (1954), pp. 724-33.

method is liable to all the distortions that can creep into a man's perception of his own behavior, but it is not utterly unreliable, and sometimes the investigator can turn the distortions themselves to account. Suppose Person says he had lunch with Other, but Other fails to mention it. They cannot both be accurate, yet the very discrepancy may tell us something about the relation between the two.[10]

We said earlier that there are no accepted or natural units, such as single physical objects, in which to measure the quantity of most activities that enter into human exchange, but this is not quite true: there is one such unit, so obvious that we are apt to overlook it. One man can give another several apples at a time, but he can emit units of the activities we shall be most interested in, like talking, only one at a time. That is, each unit takes time, which means that we can always, in principle and if we find it convenient, turn the units of quantity into units of time: minutes and seconds. We can reasonably ask questions like this: Within an eight-hour day at the office, how many minutes did Other spend giving help to Person, and how many minutes of approval did Person give Other in return? And we can reasonably expect answers to such questions to correlate with other measures we may make of the behavior of the two men.

In this book the one thing we shall never be is methodological snobs. We shall never assume that "crude" is a synonym for "unreliable." No piece of research that is interesting for other reasons shall we reject just because someone has said its methods are unsophisticated. The choice of methods is an economic problem like any other. The methods of social science are dear in time and money and getting dearer every day. Sometimes they cost more than the data they bring in are worth in enlightenment. The propositions about social behavior for which we shall provide evidence are themselves crude, and the data supporting them need be no less so. For some purposes it may be enough to know that Person spent more time with Other than he did with the Third Man, and superfluous to know just how much time he spent with each.

Whatever the unit used—minutes of time, an item of meaning, or a whole conversation—measures of the quantity of behavior emitted by one man to another are usually called measures of the frequency of *interaction,* that is, measures of the frequency of social behavior. But

[10] P. M. Blau, *op. cit.,* pp. 123-26.

in this book we emphasize alternative activities, and so we must emphasize the obvious fact that even in social situations not all activity is social. An example is the activity Person and Other devote to "doing their own work" instead of exchanging approval for help. It is true that even doing one's own work is social activity in the sense that Person and Other give their paper work to the company, and get from the company in return salaries and, it may be, promotions. It is nonsocial only so far as we choose not to include the company as a member of the social group we are studying, the group formed by Person, Other, and the Third Man.

Since easily recognizable behavior, like conversations, may not take place, the quantity of nonsocial activity may be more difficult to measure than the quantity of interaction. It is not always so: if the activity results in standard units, such as completed pieces of work in a factory, if the management keeps records of output, and if the investigator has access to the records, he may have very good measures indeed of the quantity of activity. Should these conditions not be met, he may be reduced to estimating the amount of time spent in nonsocial activity, the amount of time, for instance, Person spends in doing his own work relative to the amount of time he spends getting help from Other. But a warning is badly needed here: the observer should never take for granted that he knows what activity is social and what nonsocial, even in the terms we have set above. Industrial output is itself an example. If for any reason the workers of a factory department have come to find it rewarding that none of their number should produce more than a certain number of pieces of work in an hour, then the output of each member is a social activity as well as a nonsocial one. Many apparently nonsocial activities come to be social ones in this way.

Value

We come now to the second class of variables, which we call *value*. We have chosen this term, not because its meaning is unambiguous, but because it is in common use and we do not propose to strain our memories with new words. A man emits a unit of activity, however that unit be defined, and this unit is reinforced or punished by one or more units of activity he receives from another man or by something he receives from the non-human environment: he may give another man help and receive approval, or he may bait his hook and catch a fish. The *value* of the unit he receives may be positive or negative; it is the degree of reinforcement or punishment he gets from that unit.

We must define value as value per unit received because we shall want to assert that the value of the first unit received is not necessarily the same as that of the next unit, or that the value of a single unit varies with the number of units received over a period of time. But just what the unit is taken to be does not make much difference to the crude propositions we shall want to formulate. The proposition "The more help Person receives, the less valuable he finds any further help" probably holds good regardless of what is taken to be the unit of help: it remains true whether the help comes in large chunks or small. Only if we wanted to say just how much more valuable the first unit was than the next should we need to specify the unit, and this is why in discussing in the last few paragraphs the measures of the frequency of activity, we argued that any consistent method of defining the unit of activity was for our purposes convenient, and that we did not need to insist on the use of any particular one.

Having tried to be careful at least once, we can later get away with more elliptical language. Thus we may say that Person found such-and-such an activity valuable, meaning either that the activity was his and it was reinforced by a separate activity of Other's, or that the activity was Other's and Person received it—consumed it, so to speak —with pleasure. That is, we may speak of Person's activity as being valuable to him because it gets him a valuable reward, or of Other's activity as being valuable to Person because it rewards Person. Strictly it is only the second meaning that conforms to our definition of value: it is always something one receives from another man or the environment that varies in value. But as this book goes on we shall relapse more and more into the sloppy but comfortable old clothes of every-day language, confident that the reader, if he feels the need, will be able to translate it back into more rigorous statements.

But we are only at the beginning of our difficulties with *value*. However wide our choice of units, we can still directly observe and count frequencies of behavior—the number of units of activity or other goods a man receives from another man or the environment within a given period of time. But how shall we measure the "degree of reinforcement" he gets per unit?

One possible method of measuring value depends on the assumption that a man will put out more units of activity within a given time to get a more valuable reward than he will to get a less valuable one. On this assumption, the number of units put out that are reinforced by a particular unit-reward is the measure of the value of that reward. At one time elementary economics toyed with a distinction between *value in use* and *value in exchange,* and inclined to argue that only the latter could be objectively measured. Then the value of a pound of coffee would not be measured by the reward a man got from drinking it up (its value in use) but by the money he paid to get it (its value in exchange, or *price*). The price could be readily determined, but how the reward gotten from drinking coffee was to be measured was not so clear.

We must reject this method of measuring value. The assumption on which it is based is in fact a definition of the variable *value:* the value of a reward is the amount of activity put out to get it, and all definitions are tautologies. It is our own choice which of our propositions we shall allow to become tautologies, true by definition, in order that others shall escape this fate and remain real propositions, capable of being supported or not supported with evidence. We intend to state real propositions of the "x varies as y" form about the relations between the quantity and the value of activity. If we say: the more valuable a reward the more activity a man puts out that gets him that reward, and our only measure of value is in fact the quantity of activity put out, then our proposition turns into a tautology, for x and y have the same measure: indeed they are simply the same variable. For the proposition to become a real proposition and not a tautology, x and y—value and quantity—must be independently measured. This means that we must find some measure of value other than value in exchange.

Economics has found itself in the same position. Although for many purposes it can do very well without value in use, the evidence is that it dare not abandon the notion altogether. Accordingly it speaks of *utility,* which is the same as our *value,* and of *marginal utility,* which is the same as our *value per unit-activity.* In spite of this identity of meaning, we shall continue to use the term *value.* For *utility* inevitably suggests that some things which do in fact reinforce a man's behavior, which are in fact valuable to him, are also useful to him in the sense of being good for him. But this is not always so: many men find tobacco valuable, but we have less and less reason to think it good for them.

The Measurement of Value

Having rejected one possible method of measuring value, we must find another one. The measurement of value is practically a problem of comparison, which may take two forms: Does a man find a particular kind of reward more valuable on one occasion than on another? And, on the same occasion, does he find a reward of one kind more valuable than one of another? Now you can ask a man, as you cannot ask a pigeon, both of these questions. You can ask him how much he "wants" a particular reward. And psychologists have tests more subtle than this for discovering and measuring the values of individuals. Sometimes they yield consistent results, and although we may suspect that answers to such questions are liable to all the ambiguities to which we know other statements men make about their own behavior are liable, we shall assuredly not be such fools as not to use them in the absence of anything better. But many researches did not or could not measure value through questionnaires, and the question remains what measures of value they did use, explicitly or implicitly. If we cannot, or will not, ask men about their values, what measures can we adopt that are as objective as, though they may be even cruder than, the measures we make of the quantity of activity?

The fact is that in principle we measure the values of men in just the same way as we measure the values of pigeons: we study the past history of the animal and of the species in relation to the animal's present circumstances. If we say: the more valuable grain is to the pigeon the more often it will emit pecks that are reinforced with grain, how do we measure *value?* We cannot ask the pigeon how hungry it feels or how much it wants grain. What the experimenter actually does is this. First, he knows from his experience with other pigeons that grain will reinforce the animal's activity, that grain is a reinforcer. Second, he weighs the pigeon or counts the hours since it last fed. In either case he examines the pigeon's past history of reinforcement: the value of grain to the pigeon is greater, the thinner the poor thing is or the longer it has gone without food. Then value and quantity have been independently measured, and the proposition is no tautology but a real proposition, abundantly capable of support with evidence.

In the same way we may say of Person: the more valuable help is to him, the more often he will put out an activity that is reinforced with help, and what we mean is this. First, we have reason to believe, because we know that he is unskillful at his job, that help is a reinforcer, a reward, to Person. And second, we examine his past history of being helped: we try to find out how much help he has received in the recent past. If he needs help and has gotten little of it recently, we say that help has a relatively high value for him at present. Then we have avoided measuring value as value in exchange; we have measured value and quantity independently of one another, and our proposition is a real proposition. Incidentally, we have avoided asking Person how much he values help and so having to cope with the possible ambiguities of his answer.

Although we say we have "measured" the value of help to Person, it is clear that we have not measured it very precisely, not nearly as precisely as the psychologist measures the value of grain to the pigeon by weighing the animal. What we are able to do is make with some confidence statements of the "more or less" type: Person while he is at the office values getting help more than he does struggling with his problems all by himself, or Person values getting help relatively more at some times than he does at others. Our propositions will be couched in terms no more precise than this, and we need ask of our variables no more precise measurement than is required by the propositions into which they enter.

The Two Components of Value

It should also be clear that we face with *value* a problem that we did not have to face with *quantity:* the measurement of value has two components and not just one. When we say that at a particular time a pigeon values grain highly we refer to two sorts of fact. We mean, first, that grain reinforces the pigeon's behavior, that grain is a reinforcer or, as some sociologists say, *a value* to the pigeon, that our pigeon, if deprived of both grain and, say, thistledown for the same period of time, and now offered both, will eat the grain rather than the thistledown. And we mean, second, that the pigeon has recently gone without grain. The first component is so obvious that we often, with pigeons, take it for granted: mankind's whole experience with pigeons has consistently taught the lesson that they like grain. Some of the values of men are of the same sort and we take them for granted for the same reason, but many obviously are not. Note finally that the second component of value is determined by a variable that is part of our system: the *quantity* of grain the pigeon has received in the recent past. But the first component is not a variable of the same sort. Indeed with pigeons we take it to be substantially invariant among members of the species; that is, we take it as a constant or, as the mathematicians would say, a parameter.

In the same way, when we say that Person values help highly, we mean, first, that help is a reward, *a value,* to him, and second, that he has recently gone without help. In assessing the first component we need not necessarily ask him if he wants help. Often we need only look at his past history as it affects his present circumstances. If he is employed to do a job that requires a certain amount of skill and through lack of either training or experience he has not got the skill, we may confidently say that help is a value to him. We may even say that he will value help relatively more highly than will a man like Other, who has already acquired skill at the job. Or better still, when he has been deprived for some time of both help and, say, social approval, and now he has a choice between getting one and getting the other, he will set a relatively higher value on help and a relatively lower one on social approval than will Other under the same circumstances. Note that, unlike the pigeon's need for grain, Person's need for help is not substantially invariant among members of his species. It is not even invariant with himself: as he acquires, with time, experience on the job, he may come to value help less. But even for him this second component of value will change relatively slowly, and for any brief period of time it may be taken as a constant.

"We may confidently say that help is a value to Person"—alas! we cannot say so all that confidently. We cannot say so with nearly the confidence with which we assert that grain is a value to the pigeon. Of most persons who lack skill on a job we may predict successfully that they will find help valuable, but sooner or later one will come along who is too proud to ask for help, one for whom pride has a higher value than being helped; and our predictions and explanations of the behavior of such persons will go wrong if we rely on our common knowledge that unskilled people value help. Values like pride, altruism, aggression—values that are, as we sometimes say, their own reward—are just the ones that give us most trouble in predicting and explaining the behavior of men.

Some men find some of the damnedest things valuable—or so it seems to the rest of us. Yet in principle we go about accounting for such values in just the same way as we go about accounting for other ones: we search the past histories of the persons concerned as they affect their present circumstances. The man who is too proud to ask for help may be one whose family thought itself no small pumpkins and taught him to think so too. If there is one thing we have learned from Freud it is that a man's past history, sometimes so long past that he has trouble talking about it, is a powerful determinant of his present behavior. Not only may he go on emitting on present occasions certain kinds of activity that were rewarded on past ones, but he may find valuable at present the kinds of reward he learned to find valuable in the past. Sometimes the exact mechanisms by which his past history led him to pick up his present values are obscure; sometimes it may be hard indeed to explain why his present values are what they are. A taste for duck may look easy enough; a taste for duty does not even look easy. Nor, thank God, is it, as we shall see, the business of this book to explain. All we assert here is that a man's past is where we must look for enlightenment; the past offers in principle the information we need to assess values independently of the amount of activity a man puts out to get these values at present.

The past in question may be an ancient one. Men, like pigeons, inherit certain values from their genetic past: food, water, sex, shelter, and so on. Others they have acquired as part of the ancient social history of their race: perhaps, for example, a value put on an affection more general than sex. Since by the very fact of their humanity the social experience of most men has been to some extent the same, we assume that to some extent they hold similar values.

More nearly alike than that of all mankind is the social experience of members of a particular society; they are apt to have acquired the same special tastes for the rewards they received at the hands of their mothers, fathers, and other members of their community, and they in turn may hand the same tastes on from generation to generation. This is what we mean when we say that certain values are characteristic of American culture, or that certain rewards are more highly valued in American culture than in Chinese. Still more similar are the values held by members of a subculture. If certain people are not just Americans but also Yankees—white, Anglo-Saxon, Protestants living in New England—we may have reason to believe that, while sharing many American or human values, they also hold certain values peculiar to themselves: a taste, perhaps, for the fruits of conscience as dearly won as a taste for olives. The more we narrow down from mankind to culture and then to subculture, the less reason we have to assume that common knowledge will tell us what the values are. Special research must take its place.

When we get down to particular groups of people, a special kind of reward, the reward obtained by conformity to a norm, becomes important. A *norm* is a statement made by a number of members of a group, not necessarily by all of them, that the members ought to behave in a certain way in certain circumstances.[11] The members who make the statement find it rewarding that their own actual behavior and that of the others should conform to some degree to the ideal behavior described by the norm. Our example is an output norm in an industrial group: a statement that no member ought to turn out more than a certain number of pieces of work in an hour or a day. Whereas we call the value put on social approval or on money a generalized reward, a norm remains specific to a particular situation: a different industrial group might value conformity to a different norm. Why the group should find conformity valuable is a question whose answer, again, depends on the past history of the members in a particular factory or industrial community.

Finally, we reach the individual as such. Though he be a man, an American, a Yankee, and a Raytheon worker, his values, the things that reward him, are never wholly determined by circumstances like these, which he shares with others, but always partly by his unique experience. And so far as values are unique to individuals, the more costly it is to determine what these values are; for a skilled psychologist would have to go over with each man the details of his past history. We shall never be able to afford much of this kind of research; our knowledge of values will always be imperfect, and the predictions we

[11] G. C. Homans, *op. cit.,* p. 123.

make from it will be gross and statistical, based on a few obvious similarities and differences, bound to go wrong in detail.

Without undertaking to explain in detail how and why he came by them, it is difficult enough to assess what a man's values *are*. Yet the limited practical problems we shall have to face in analyzing the results of research make the difficulty somewhat less than it looks. No man can do something about all his values at once. Accordingly, we shall not need to put all the activities a man finds rewarding in rank-order of their value to him, but only those two or three alternatives that stay open to him during a particular period of time. Nor shall we need to compare the values of many men but only the values of two or three of them, nor to set up absolute measures of value but only to say of two possible rewards that one is more valuable than another. If, moreover, values are precipitates of the past histories of men, including the past histories of their species, their societies, and their groups, then the more similar the past histories of two men, the more similar their values are apt to be. If, therefore, we positively know of any group we are studying that the past histories, the backgrounds, of some of the members are to some extent different from those of the others, we shall at least be able to say with confidence that the values of the members of each subgroup will be to some extent alike, and different from those of the other subgroup. Even if we cannot say just what the values are, this similarity will, as we shall see, put a powerful weapon of analysis into our hands. Above all, what we have said about measures of quantity goes for measures of value too: we shall do the best we can with what we have on hand, and eschew no piece of research that is interesting for other reasons just because its methods are crude or unsophisticated.

We have said that it may be hard indeed to answer the questions how and why mankind, or the members of a particular society, or an individual acquired the values they did acquire. In what has gone before we have not even tried to answer them, but have only pointed out where the answers are to be sought—in the past histories of the persons concerned. We have left them unanswered not because they are unimportant—on the contrary—but because they are not the sort of questions that this book undertakes to answer. What it does undertake to answer are questions like this: Why does Person put out so much activity that is rewarded by help? For this purpose we certainly need to know that Person values help highly, and even that he does so because he is unskilled at his job, but we need not go into further details. We take the value he sets on help and on other rewards as *given,* and then go on to explain why he behaves as he does in realizing these values. But we do not undertake to explain in turn why his values should be what they are. To satisfy our minds and because the explanation is obvious, we may sometimes in this book offer reasons why, but we are not bound to do so in every case—the only rules we must obey are those we set for ourselves—and sometimes we may simply take the word of other social scientists or of common knowledge that groups or individuals do hold certain values, without ourselves offering any explanation at all why they should do so. Our problem is not why they hold these values, but given that they do hold them, what they do about them. Accordingly, we need to know *what* the values are but not *why* they are.

Let us put the matter in another way. This book is concerned with current, face-to-face social behavior and its changes within rather short spans of time. One of the variables that must enter into propositions about such behavior is *value,* but the measure of value has, as we have seen, two components. Person values help highly if, first, he is the kind of man that needs help, and if, second, he has gotten little help in the recent past. The second component may vary within a relatively short span of time, and since such changes are among the concerns of this book, we shall indeed try to explain why Person has received little help in the recent past and this will of course require that we account for the quantity of help Other gives him. But the first component is apt, for any given individual, to change much more slowly. It is because he is unskilled at his job that Person sets a high value on help compared with other rewards, and it will take him some time to acquire the skill that will let him do without help. For the spans of time considered in this book, we may therefore treat the first component as a constant as far as Person is concerned. And since variation, not constancy, is what we undertake to explain, we treat the first component of value as simply given for any individual and do not feel that we must always explain it. Within the limits we set for ourselves, whatever varies we explain and whatever stays constant we take as given.

Our last difficulty with value is created by a fact so obvious that we may be inclined to forget it: an activity received by Person and valued by him is an activity emitted by somebody else. Accordingly, though we take Person's scale of values, the things he finds more or less rewarding, as temporarily constant, this does not mean that the value of what he gets need be constant; for Other may change his behavior and give Person a kind of activity that stands higher or lower in Person's scale. A man may change either the quantity he emits of a particular activity or the kind of activity he emits. And in changing the kind, he may change by degrees within one general class of activity: Other, while still offering Person helpful advice, may make it less helpful than it was before; or he may shift drastically and put out activity of quite a different sort. In analyzing human behavior it is always a question how different activities, whether the differences be small or great, shall be measured by a standard common to them all. It should now be clear that differences in kind between activities emitted are to be measured by their differences in value. That is, they are to be measured by their values according to the first component: the temporarily constant scale of values of the person receiving them. Other, then, can change the value to Person of a unit-activity he gives him by working on either the first component or the second. He works on the second component by holding constant the kind of activity he gives Person and changing the amount of it he gives him within a period of time: the more he gives, the less valuable to Person is any further unit of it. He works on the first component by changing the kind of activity he gives: he may offer Person a kind of activity that stands lower on Person's scale of values.

Summary

Our two main variables are, then, value and quantity: the value of a unit of activity received, and the number of such units received within a period of time. (Remember that an activity someone receives is an activity someone else puts out.) Value itself has two components, one constant for the periods of time that will concern us, and one variable. If we disregard the amount of an activity that a man receives, we may say that he values that activity more or less than he does another, and that his preference is temporarily constant: this is the first component. If, on the other hand, we take into account the amount of activity received, we may say that he values that activity more at some times than he does at other times: he values it less the more of it he has gotten in the recent past; this is the second component.

We should really speak of *value* and *quantity* as classes of variable. For instance, in stating propositions about the behavior of Person and Other, we shall want to subdivide each of the classes according to which of the two individuals and which of at least two alternatives is concerned. Then, in our analysis of the example we began with, the actual operating variables would be the following: (1a) the quantity of help Other gives Person within a given time, (1b) the quantity of some alternative activity Other gives to the environment or to some Third Man, (1c) the quantity of approval Person gives to Other, (1d) the quantity of some alternative activity Person gives to the environment or to some Third Man; (2a) the value to Other of a unit of approval received from Person, (2b) the value to Other of a unit of alternative activity received from the environment or some Third Man, (2c) the value to Person of a unit of help received from Other, and (2d) the value to Person of a unit of alternative activity received from the environment or some Third Man.

It is now time we turned to our main propositions.

Human Exchange: Propositions

Chapter Four

In the last chapter we tried to define the chief terms that would come into our propositions about human exchange and, so far as these terms were variables, to suggest how they could, however crudely, be measured. In the present chapter we turn to the propositions themselves—to the main propositions for which we shall offer evidence later. They will state relationships between variables, and in so doing they will avoid each of two extremes. On the one hand, they will avoid the form "x is some function of y," which says that any change in the value of y produces *some* change in x but says nothing about the direction or amount of the change. Such statements tell us a little but not much, and they are all too common in the literature of social science. Nor, on the other hand, will our propositions take the form "x is a specific function of y," such as x = log y, which says that a given amount of change in y produces a specific amount of change in x and in a specific direction. In the study of social behavior our measures are seldom precise enough to justify our saying any such thing. Instead our propositions will usually take the middle form "x varies as y," which says that the value of x increases with any increase in the value of y but does not say just how much it increases. Our present degree of precision in measuring the variables warrants this much precision in our propositions but no more.

Before each of our propositions should stand the words "other things being equal." But we can avoid actually putting them there if we admit it here, once and for all. Of course "other things being equal" has nothing to do with equality. It only means that we cannot look on any proposition as being alone in the world. In the observed phenomena variables other than the two or more that come into a proposition may mask or belie its truth. Other things equal, all bodies, heavy or light, fall according to the inverse square law of gravitation; but in this case other things are rarely equal, and a feather and a bullet do not fall the same way outside a vacuum. Of the other things that a proposition must live with, the most intimate are its fellow members of a set of propositions simultaneously true; our propositions aspire to making such a set, and therefore when we understand before each of our propositions the words "other things equal," we mean that its truth may be masked in concrete circumstances by the truth of others in its set. We shall soon give an example.

Stimuli

Let us now return to Person and Other, whom we left in the last chapter exchanging approval for help. Much of the activity each emits is at once a reward for and a stimulus to the activity of the other: when Other gives Person help he not only rewards Person but stimulates his thanks. Some of the activity has little reward-value. Such may be Person's original request for help: it may have little value for Other unless perhaps he finds the request flattering in itself. But it may still be effective as a stimulus. If in Other's past experience a request for help (the stimulus) has been the occasion on which giving help (the activity) has been followed by his getting thanks (the reward), Other is the more likely to give the help now. That is what we mean when we say that Other "expects" thanks for his help, or that he "perceives" the situation as one in which thanks may be forthcoming. Most men have gotten thanks under these conditions, but the odd man may turn up whose past experience has been different and who accordingly responds differently to the stimulus.

The power of the stimulus to elicit the behavior is no doubt greater when it has occurred in the past in conjunction with an activity that has been often rewarded, or with one that has gotten a particularly valuable reward. But since we shall speak later of the variables *frequency* and *value,* we shall say no more about them here and emphasize instead the similarity of the present stimulus to a stimulus of the past. Other is likely to give help if the present stimulus bears some resemblance to one in conjunction with which his giving help has been rewarded in the past: he may give help not only when Person asks for it but merely when Person looks helpless. The greater the similarity, the more likely he is to do so, and, by the same token, the greater the difference between the present stimulus and the past, the less likely he is to do so.

Accordingly, we offer the following as our first general proposition: (1) IF IN THE PAST THE OCCURRENCE OF A PARTICULAR STIMULUS-SITUATION HAS BEEN THE OCCASION ON WHICH A MAN'S ACTIVITY HAS BEEN REWARDED, THEN THE MORE SIMILAR THE PRESENT STIMULUS-SITUATION IS TO THE PAST ONE, THE MORE LIKELY HE IS TO EMIT THE ACTIVITY, OR SOME SIMILAR ACTIVITY, NOW.

We must confess once more to a great inadequacy in this book. Whatever establishes the similarities and differences in question—whatever makes men discriminate between stimuli—may be exceedingly complicated. It is far more complicated for men than it is for pigeons, if only because the stimuli may be verbal. The use of language is incomparably the biggest difference between the behavior of men and that of other animals. With a man the discriminations may be the result not only of his everyday experience but also of his formal education, his reading, and the verbal arguments he may have listened to. They may be unconscious or the result of conscious reasoning. Obviously the problem of the relations between stimuli, past activities, and present ones is of the first importance, yet we shall state no further general propositions about it, and accordingly this book falls far short of being a complete psychology. Instead we shall take up particular instances of the discrimination of stimuli when it becomes necessary for us to do so. We shall be especially concerned with two cases: when the fact that a particular *person* makes a request is the decisive feature of the stimulus, and when certain patterns of stimuli —the ones men describe by saying they did not get what they deserved—release emotional behavior. We shall not otherwise be able to understand either authority or justice.

We have a reason for not going further into the discrimination of stimuli. If we are to explain why a man gives a particular activity to another the first time, we are bound to look carefully at the stimuli and at the man's past experience with the activity when other stimuli like them were present. After that, when the same kind of activity is repeated on similar occasions, we can practically take the stimuli for granted and explain changes in the activity, in quantity and value, by looking at the way it is reinforced. Most of the activities we shall consider are of this sort, as is our example, the interaction of Person and Other. We look on their behavior toward one another as a repeated exchange of help for approval, in which each activity emitted by one man is rewarded by an activity of the other, in a chain. And we turn now to propositions about the effect of reinforcement on their behavior.

Value and Quantity

We cannot say everything at once even if everything happens that way, and therefore to make our task easier let us begin by putting on the behavior of Person and Other a restriction we shall later remove. Let us assume that, by whatever process of trial and error you please, the two have struck a tacit bargain as to the *kind* of service each will provide, and that for the time being neither will provide another kind: Other will not offer a better grade of help nor Person a warmer brand of approval. If, under this condition, an activity emitted by Person, once rewarded by an activity of Other, is not thereafter so rewarded, Person will sooner or later stop emitting the activity: if Other stops giving Person help, Person will in time stop asking for it; and if Person stops giving Other approval, Other will in time stop giving help. But we had better put the matter the other way around, and emphasize the number of times an activity *is* rewarded instead of the number of times it is not: (2) THE MORE OFTEN WITHIN A GIVEN PERIOD OF TIME A MAN'S ACTIVITY REWARDS THE ACTIVITY OF AN-OTHER, THE MORE OFTEN THE OTHER WILL EMIT THE ACTIVITY. From this proposition it follows that the frequency with which Other emits activity to Person will tend to bear some proportionality to the frequency with which Person emits activity to Other; for if either allows his rate to fall off, the other, by this proposition, will eventually let his fall off too. Concretely, the more often Person thanks him, the more often Other will give him help. Just what the proportionality is we shall soon consider.

Proposition 2 refers only to the frequency of activity, but we must also consider our other variable, its value. (3) THE MORE VALUABLE TO A MAN A UNIT OF THE ACTIVITY ANOTHER GIVES HIM, THE MORE OFTEN HE WILL EMIT ACTIVITY REWARDED BY THE ACTIVITY OF THE OTHER. The more Person needs help, the more often he will ask for it and the more thanks he will give when he gets it; and the more Other needs approval the more often he will give help. From propositions 2 and 3 it follows that the frequency of *interaction* between Person and Other depends on the frequency with which each rewards the activity of the other and on the value to each of the activity he receives.

The present proposition should also answer the question of proportionality that we raised above. The number of units of activity Person emits within any limited period of time in return for a specific number of units emitted by Other we shall call the *rate of exchange* between the two activities. It is the equivalent in our nonmonetary economics of price in regular economics, for the price of a commodity in money specifies the number of units of the commodity that may be exchanged for a given number of units of another commodity. By the present proposition, the rate of exchange between approval and help should tend to equal the ratio between the value Person puts on help and the value Other puts on approval; for if Person values help relatively more than Other values approval, then he is likely to give relatively more approval than Other gives help.

But (4) THE MORE OFTEN A MAN HAS IN THE RECENT PAST RECEIVED A REWARDING ACTIVITY FROM ANOTHER, THE LESS VALUABLE ANY FURTHER UNIT OF THAT ACTIVITY BECOMES TO HIM; and therefore, by proposition 3, the less often he will emit the activity that gets him that reward: the more help Person has recently received from Other, the less, for the time being, he needs any further help and the less often he will ask for help or give thanks. Accordingly this proposition may mask the truth of proposition 2, which says that the more often Other rewards the activity of Person, the more often Person will emit the activity. For if Other rewards him often enough to begin to satiate him, his own activity will tend to fall off in frequency. This is the sort of effect we refer to when we say the propositions hold good only with "other things equal."

So far we have only considered exchange between two persons. Let us now complicate matters by having a Third Man enter the exchange.

We are reluctant to face all the possible intricacies of a triangular relationship, nor shall we need to do so in order to explain most of the research findings reported later in this book. Let us accordingly consider only one special case. Let us assume that the Third Man is just like Person: both are equally unskilled and both set an equal value on help which they can only get from Other. This is what we shall mean when we say that Other commands a rare or scarce activity. We also assume that, in return for help, both offer the same kind of approval, and that therefore Other treats them both the same way. Both now start giving Other approval in return for his help, but his help must now be divided between the two of them. This means that at any given time each of them is apt to have received less help in the recent past than Person would have received when he was alone with Other, and that therefore, by proposition 4, any unit of help will at the given time be more valuable to each of them. But by proposition 3, the more valuable a unit of help, the more activity that is rewarded by help each of them will put out, and therefore the rate of exchange of help for approval is apt to take a turn unfavorable to both of them: each will come to give more approval for a unit of help than Person did when he was alone with Other. We may say, if we like, that Other's bargaining position has improved over what it was when he had only Person to deal with, even though no conscious bargaining need take place. Note the part played by the scarcity of help in producing this result—scarcity in the sense that Other is the only man who can supply it, and that two men now want it where only one did before. If there were any source of help alternative to Other, if Person could get from somebody else enough help to make up for the help Other now denies him, the value to him of a unit of help at any given time would not go up. In the absence of any alternative source, Person faces the problem of increasing the amount of help Other gives him; for if he leaves things as they are, he will only get half as much help as he did before. He can accomplish this result if he changes the kind of approval he gives Other so as to make it warmer and more admiring; for then a unit of approval will be more valuable to Other, and therefore, by proposition 3, Other will put out more help to get it. To both of these questions we now turn: first, to the effects produced by the presence of alternatives, and second, to the effects produced by changing the kind of activity emitted.

Cost

So far we have considered the exchange of rewarding activities, but we should obviously be false to the facts of elementary social behavior if we disregarded the exchange of punishing activities, or negative values. Let no one say our view of human behavior leaves out conflict. Conflict lies at its very marrow if only because, even in the exchange of rewards, it admits the possibility that one party will get a better bargain than the other. But this is not what concerns us now. Just as the amount of reward that Person gives to Other tends to increase with the reward Other gives to Person, so the punishments they give to one another tend to vary together too: the more one hits, the more the other hits back, for it is rewarding to hurt someone that hurts you. But while the exchange of rewards tends toward stability and continued interaction, the exchange of punishments tends toward instability and the eventual failure of interaction in escape and avoidance: the pain experienced comes to outweigh the pleasure of revenge. Victory, to be sure, is a reinforcer, but then in the exchange of hostilities only one side can win; the other runs away, and it takes two to make social behavior. Only if for some reason neither of the two men can avoid hostilities, or if the other aspects of the exchange are rewarding in themselves and the chances of successive victories falling to one side or the other are about equal, does punishing exchange persist. Many games meet the latter conditions. And in one family I used to know a boy and his two sisters exchanged cutting remarks for years, first one side and then the other getting one-up in this preliminary bout in the war between the sexes. Under these circumstances one may come to admire an adversary worthy of one's steel. In spite of the massive importance of wars in human affairs, it is still true that the exchange of rewards takes a larger share in social behavior than the exchange of punishments, if only because the latter, when at all damaging, puts an end to social behavior.

Besides exchanging reward for reward or punishment for punishment, Person and Other may exchange reward for punishment or rather for a stimulus presenting the threat of punishment. Suppose that Person asks Other for help, and hits him or says he will hit him if he does not give it. Since escape from or avoidance of punishment is rewarding, Other, if he complies, has exchanged rewards with Person; Other gives Person help; Person gives Other the chance to avoid punishment, and a kind of wry balance has been struck. But though we can make this out technically to be an exchange, its consequences are obviously different from the exchange of true rewards. Whereas positive reinforcement renders more probable the emission of the specific activity so reinforced, the threat of punishment renders more probable *any* behavior that avoids the punishment; and unless Person is able to arrange that Other has no more rewarding alternative than to comply with his specific demand, the threat may simply lead Other to avoid Person and his threat as much as he can. Moreover, the emotional results are different. In the positive case where Person and Other are exchanging help for approval, we assume that, over and above the immediate exchange itself, the two men each emit sentiments indicating that they find the exchange rewarding. So in the negative case we assume that Other may emit sentiments, or symbolic emotion, of hate or fear toward Person.

We are far from arguing that punishment can be altogether avoided in any social situation. Take leadership, for example. Most leaders must give some orders, many of which at least imply a threat; and even without giving orders, they may not be able to avoid punishing some of their followers: their decisions may have the effect of depriving the followers of rewards, of preventing their doing what they would have liked to do; and the withdrawal of a positive reinforcement is as truly a punishment as the presentation of a negative one.

The problem of punishment leads us to the more general problem of costs. Our argument is a familiar one in economics: a cost may be conceived of as a value forgone. Let us return for a moment to the pigeon. In emitting activity the pigeon may incur fatigue; fatigue is aversive or punishing, and it is a principle of behavioral psychology that whatever gets the animal out of punishment—even if it is only doing nothing—becomes by that fact a reward. According to this analysis, the pigeon is not faced just with reward and punishment but with two alternative rewards: the one it gets from carrying out the original activity and the one it would have gotten from escaping the punishment incurred in carrying out the original activity. So far as it persists in the original activity, we may say, anthropomorphically no doubt, that it is forgoing the value of relief from fatigue, and that the cost of the original activity is the forgone value of the alternative one.

Remember now that the withdrawal of a positive reinforcer is as truly a punishment as the presentation of a negative one: we can punish the pigeon as well by taking food away from it as by drenching it with water. But so far as a man cannot do two things at once, the emission of any one rewarded activity amounts—by that fact alone—to withdrawing the reward he might otherwise have gotten from an alternative activity open to him. True, he has not been deprived by anyone else; he has withdrawn the reward from himself, but he is punished none the less. And so we may extend, for the man if not for the pigeon, the notion of cost to include not only positively painful conditions incurred in carrying out an activity but also positively rewarding ones forgone. Indeed, as we have just argued, to accept punishment is to forgo reward.

For an activity to incur cost, an alternative and rewarding activity must be there to be forgone. When we say that one activity is an alternative to another we mean that it is not a perfect substitute for the other in the sense that it fetches an identical reward—the sense in which two nickels are usually a perfect substitute for a dime. Unless a real alternative is open to a man, and so forgoable by him, his activity costs him nothing. Thus economists argue that the reason why in most circumstances the air a man breathes costs him nothing is that he cannot forgo it if he would. And great captains try to arrange that their soldiers have no alternative to fighting the enemy, as Cortez did by burning his ships behind him. So far as they are able to get rid of running away as an alternative, fighting has no cost to their soldiers—which need not mean at all that the soldiers fear death the less. By this token we shall consider as costs only those forgone rewards that remain available throughout the period in which a particular activity is being emitted, as the reward of escaping from fatigue is open to the pigeon throughout the time it is pecking. If I am offered two jobs, only one of which I can take, no doubt I shall find it painful to make up my mind; but as soon as I have taken one and turned down the other, which is then no longer open to me because someone else has gotten it, then the rewards of the job I let go are no longer a cost to me in doing the job I took—which need not prevent me from regretting my decision.

An activity whose reward is forgone is an activity not emitted and so not observable. Accordingly, some would say, cost is no proper concept for a science, for a science deals in observables. It is true that we infer costs and do not directly observe them, unless we call direct observation the answers we get from a man when we ask him what an activity costs him. Yet cost, though a value forgone, is still a value, and the things from which we infer costs are no less observable than those from which we infer values. From a man's past history or the histories of others like him, we often have valid reasons for knowing that he finds a particular reward valuable and that an activity which would get him the reward is part of his repertory. From our observations of the current situation we have valid reasons for knowing that the reward is there to be had from other men or from the environment, and for knowing how long he has gone without it. Of course we may go wrong in particular cases. Our man may not be as other men: he may not have learned an activity that other men, whose past histories in other respects resemble his, did learn. One of the great mistakes we can make in understanding and predicting a man's behavior is to assume he is able to put out a particular activity, when in fact he is not. Even then it is often open to us to go back with him into his past history and discover the facts that would have put us straight.

The *cost,* then, of a unit of a given activity is the value of the reward obtainable through a unit of an alternative activity, forgone in emitting the given one.

Cost, as a value forgone, is a negative value, and accordingly we assume by proposition 3 above that the more cost Person incurs in emitting an activity, the less often he will emit it. We need no new proposition to say this, which need not imply that Person will stop emitting the activity altogether, for the reward it gets him may well outweigh the cost. We also assume, as in proposition 4, that the more often Person has emitted a costly activity, the more costly he finds any further unit of that activity. Either the cost itself increases independently and cumulatively, as in some kinds of fatigue, or the value obtained by successive units of activity declines with the number of such units obtained in the recent past, and so makes the forgone reward of an alternative activity relatively more valuable. That is, satiation with a particular reward makes the forgone value of an alternative one relatively greater.

With these ideas in mind, let us return to our example and look now at the alternatives open to Person and Other. Upon any single request for help Other, the skillful man, has two activities open to him: to help Person, for which he gets approval, or to do his own work, for which he gets a reward that, in the present context, we consider nonsocial. If he does his own work, he forgoes the value of getting approval; if he helps Person, he forgoes the value of doing his own work. Whichever action he takes, its cost is the forgone value of the alternative. In the same way, Person can either do his own work or get help from and give approval to Other. If he does his own work he forgoes the value of getting help. But if he chooses to get help what value does he forgo? We believe that under these circumstances he, like many men, forgoes the value that we ordinarily call self-respect, the feeling that he is good enough to do his own work without help, as the rules of the office say he should.[1] Of course if he is new to the office and its procedures, so that no one should expect him to do his work very well, his loss in self-respect may not be great; but this kind of question we shall postpone for a time. Person's cost, the value he gives up in getting help from Other, is loss in self-respect, or to put the matter in another way, his cost is a confession of his inferiority to Other. The social approval he gives Other is at the same time an admission of his own inferiority.

Profit

Our next argument has long been foreshadowed. We define psychic *profit* as reward less cost, and we argue that no exchange continues unless both parties are making a profit. Even the pigeon, when it finds its rewards and costs nicely balanced, may try to get out of the situation or indulge in emotional behavior rather than continue its exchange with the psychologist. But our argument is more familiar in the field of human buying and selling, and we shall illustrate it from this field.

Suppose I go into a store to buy a can of coffee at the price of one dollar. From one point of view the value of what I get is a dollar, the cost of what I give is a dollar, reward and cost both equal price, and therefore in terms of accounting I have made no profit on the trans-

[1] P. M. Blau, *The Dynamics of Bureaucracy* (Chicago, 1955), p. 108.

action. The same is true of the storekeeper: he makes no profit on this single transaction considered by itself. It takes at least two transactions to make an accounting profit, as when the storekeeper sells me the coffee for more money than it cost him earlier when he bought it from the wholesaler. In short, this point of view eschews any consideration of the psychological value of the coffee and the money to the store-keeper and myself.

But we in this book may not avoid psychological value, both positive and negative, and so we must take another look at the transaction. From this point of view the value of what I get is the value to me of a can of coffee. And what is its cost? In our terms it is not the dollar but the forgone value of the alternative uses I might have made of the dollar. Moreover, the value of what I get is greater than the value of what I have given up, for if at the moment I saw any better use for my dollar I should presumably not have bought the coffee. In our present terms, I have a profit. It may not be a great profit: I may be pretty evenly balanced between buying the coffee and not buying it. But a psychic profit for the moment I have.

Nor am I the only party to the transaction. How about the store-keeper? When he sells the coffee he has my dollar. That is his reward, but what is his cost? What has he forgone? Just as I have forgone the alternative uses of the dollar, he has forgone the alternative uses of the coffee; but in his position he has little use for it unless he sells it to someone. At the moment my dollar is more valuable to him than the coffee, and he too is making a psychic profit, even though later, when he balances his books, he may find that he has lost money, that he has no accounting profit, on this batch of coffee. The open secret of human exchange is to give the other man behavior that is more valuable to him than it is costly to you and to get from him behavior that is more valuable to you than it is costly to him.[2]

One further question: Why is it that the coffee is more valuable to me than the dollar, and the dollar more valuable to the storekeeper than the coffee? The reason is that, at the moment of the transaction, I am relatively—never absolutely of course—long on dollars and short of coffee, and the storekeeper is relatively short of dollars and long on coffee and other groceries. Once dollars and coffee are established as

[2] C. I. Barnard, *The Functions of the Executive* (Cambridge, Mass., 1938), pp. 253-55; N. W. Chamberlain, *A General Theory of Economic Process* (New York, 1955), pp. 80-85.

reinforcers, it is the degree to which we are deprived of them that determines their value.

So far we have considered the profit on a single transaction, but what if the transactions continue? Let us go back again to Person and Other. At the time of their first exchange both make a profit. Person badly needs help, and he does not give up much in self-respect in asking for help only once. Other is skillful and can well afford to give up a little time from his own work if he gets for it the warm approval of Other. Both having found the exchange profitable they repeat it, and what happens? Our propositions tell us that the more approval Other has gotten from Person in past transactions, the less valuable to him any further approval becomes; and the more help he has given Person, the more costly any further helping becomes in time lost from his own work. In the same way, the more help Person has gotten from Other, the less, for the time being, he needs any further help and the more costly he finds any further confession of inferiority. A little inferiority may not cost much, but the cost of much conspicuous inferiority may rise disproportionately. The profits from exchange decrease with the number of exchanges, that is, with the time spent in exchange. And there probably will come a time in the course of a day in the office when Other begins to feel that the cost of helping Person any more is greater than its reward, and spends the rest of the day doing his own work. Something of the same sort is probably true of Person. In other words, the less a man's profit on a particular unit-activity, the more likely he is to change his next unit to the alternative.

Let us sum up what we have had to say so far about profit. Though we use the word because it suggests a difference between two values, our profit is not the profit of accounting. Accounting profit is measured by comparing two transactions, such as the money a merchant spent for a pound of coffee with the money he later sold it for. For us profit is a matter of a single transaction. Profit is the difference between the value of the reward a man gets by emitting a particular unit-activity and the value of the reward obtainable by another unit-activity, forgone in emitting the first. This we call the profit per unit. If it is true that the more valuable the reward of a particular activity, the more often a man will emit it, but the more costly, the less often he will do so, then the less his profit per unit, the less likely he is to make the next unit he emits another of the same kind. This further means that he is more likely to change his next unit to the alternative activity; and the point of zero profit comes where the probability of change between alternatives is greatest. If we are to explain a change from one activity to the next we badly need the notions of cost and profit.

Changes in Kind of Activity

We now propose to take off the restriction we have so far laid upon our example. We have allowed each of our two men to abandon the activity he gives the other and change to an alternative nonsocial one—we have allowed Other to do his own work instead of helping Person—but we have not allowed either to change his social activity in kind. We have assumed that Other had only one kind of activity to give Person: a certain kind of help; and the question was not whether he would change it in kind but whether he would do so in quantity: how much of it he would give. And we have assumed that Person had only one kind of activity (sentiment) to offer Other: a certain kind of approval; and the question was not whether he would change it in kind but whether he would do so in quantity—how much of it he would give. Under this restriction, and once the initial values of Person and Other were given—once it was given that Person valued help and Other approval—the value of a unit of help or approval varied thereafter only with the quantity received: the more units received in the recent past, the less valuable any further unit. And the only bargaining between Person and Other—if we can call bargaining what is really a process of settling down—could only be over the rate of exchange of fixed activities: how many units of one were to be traded for a given number of units of the other.

In assuming that the activities remained the same in kind we have followed the practical example of both behavioral psychology and elementary economics. As an experimental science psychology begins by simplifying the experimental situation as far as it dares, and one way of doing so is to put the animal whose behavior is being studied in a position where it emits only a pretty standardized activity like pecks at a target. And elementary economics takes things like tons of steel as its model of the goods that enter into exchange. So long as they are in the market tons of steel remain unchanged, whatever may happen to them later; indeed it takes time and energy to change them by manufacture into something else.

But human activities as goods entering into exchange are not generally like standardized pecks or tons of steel. Even a pigeon will readily learn to change the kind of peck it makes—for instance, by pecking more forcefully—if it is rewarded for doing so; and people certainly learn, though some more successfully than others, to change not only the quantity they emit of a given activity but the kind of activity itself. And both sorts of change have an effect on value. In the last chapter we saw that the value of an activity to the person receiving it varied for two different reasons: because more or less of it had been received in the recent past (the second component) and because it changed in kind (the first component). A change in the kind of activity is generally, then, a change in its value to the person receiving it. It is generally also a change in its cost to the person giving it.

Now that we have allowed our two men to change their activities in kind, let us simply assume that each changes so as to make his activity more valuable to the other without an equal increase in its cost. Let us assume, for instance, that both Person and Other are pretty tired of exchanging approval for help on the job, and that Person now asks Other to listen to his story about a personal problem that faces him and to advise him about how to cope with it. His problem makes more difference to Person than his work in the office, and in return for sympathetic listening and sensible advice he gives Other a warmer kind of approval than he did before. In this new kind of exchange we expect that the two men will spend more time together and less apart, that they will interact more often, than they did when they were exchanging less valuable activities; for by proposition 3 above, the more valuable to a man the activity the other gives him, the more often he will emit activity rewarded by the activity of the other. Or, to put the matter the other way around, if the interaction between Person and Other increases, each must have made the activity he gives the other more valuable.

In this example we have made both Person and Other change their activity in kind, and both change it so as to make it more valuable to the receiver. Much more interesting is the case in which one man keeps his activity the same as it was before, while the other changes his activity in kind so as to make a unit of it more valuable to the first; for in this case we cannot assume that costs remain unchanged, certainly not the relative costs of the two men. Let us suppose, then, that Other keeps on giving Person the same kind of help as before, but that Person now changes his activity to give Other a more lavish praise. For a given amount of help given, Other's cost per unit remains the same since he gives the same kind of help, but his reward increases in value since he gets more lavish praise, and so his profit per unit help—the difference between his reward and his cost—goes up. On the other hand, Person's reward in help remains the same in value, but his cost in getting it increases since he gives more lavish praise, and this may be, unit for unit, a greater confession of his inferiority than any he has made so far. His profit accordingly goes down. What happens then to the quantity of activity that each emits?

But first, how might this change have come about? For some time we have forgotten about the Third Man, but he is still in the office and others like him may be there too. We shall remember that we made him just the same as Person: both were equally unskilled and both set the same value on help which they could only get from Other. This means that the Third Man does not represent for Person an *alternative source* of help, and so does not, in himself, increase Person's costs in getting help from Other. We shall now add that the two unskillful people find giving Other approval in return for help equally costly as a confession of inferiority. Under the condition that the activities of all parties were fixed in kind, we have seen that bringing in the Third Man had the following effects. Other divided his help between the two unskillful men; the quantity of help each got was less than what Person got when he was alone with Other; and the rate of exchange, the number of units of approval each gave in return for a unit of help, went up.

The two unskillful men face, then, the problem of increasing the amount of help Other will supply. By our proposition 3, they can do it by changing the kind of activity they emit so as to make it more valuable to Other, for he will then emit more help that is rewarded by this activity. They can make each unit of approval they give to Other a warmer kind of approval, implying greater superiority on the part of Other. Not only can they do so but, other things equal, they will, for men are perfectly capable of learning how to behave in practice as if they understood in theory the truth of the propositions we put forward here. They give the warmer approval and get more help, which means that Other spends less time doing his own work. That is to say, under the new rate of exchange they each give fewer units of approval per unit of help.

We suppose that the process goes something like this. Person goes to Other for help, gets it, and gives him an off-hand thanks. If the Third Man is also asking for help, Person may find that the next time he goes to Other, Other is reluctant to help him. Though Other finally does help him, Person may deem it expedient to change his next unit of thanks to take the form: "Thanks a lot. That was a great help." And Person will settle down to giving a unit of praise whose value to Other is great enough to keep him giving some help, and whose cost to Person is not great enough to prevent his keeping on asking for help. How lavish the praise will be depends on the bargaining power of the two parties: Other's monopoly of help and Person's need for it. Of course things may not go this way and either party may break off the exchange, but the very form of the breakdown will reveal the rewards and costs that have entered into the bargaining process. If the thanks that Person gives Other is not valuable enough to the latter, he may stop giving help and say, "I won't help that guy any more. He doesn't show any appreciation of what I've done for him." Or if Person thinks Other exacts too high a price for help, he too may break off and say, "That guy won't help me unless I crawl. I've got too much self-respect to do that any more. It isn't worth it." As usual, the withdrawal of reinforcement leads to the emotional reaction of hostility.

To go back—when Person and the Third Man must divide between them the help that only Other can provide, and neither gets as much as he did when he was alone with Other, their problem is to induce Other to give more. They can do so by increasing the warmth of each unit of approval they give Other in return. Unfortunately matters are not quite as simple as this. Because Other is giving more help than he did before, each extra unit of help is rapidly increasing in cost to him in terms of time lost from doing his own work, and this of course is tending to cut down the amount of help he offers. Though he is likely to offer to the two men together more help than he offered to Person alone, he is unlikely to double his production and give each as much as he gave to only one before. That is, the amount of help Other gives is unlikely to increase proportionately to the new demand for it.

Moreover the new kind of approval they give will increase the costs of Person and the Third Man, for each unit of approval now implies a greater confession of inferiority, and so each will tend to give less approval than he did before. But again we may well doubt that each gives only half as much approval, for each is getting a more valuable unit of help—more valuable because so long as Other has not doubled his production of help, each of the unskillful men is apt at any moment to be relatively further from satiation with it. Just where the exchange will settle down we cannot tell. But from our verbal argument, which suffers from our having to describe one after the other repercussions that really take place pretty nearly simultaneously, it looks as though the rate of exchange of approval for help at any particular time should equal the proportion profit per unit-approval bears to profit per unit-help.

Relation to Economics

It should be clear by now that what we have been saying owes much to elementary economics. One of the purposes of the last two chapters has been, indeed, to show that the principles of elementary economics are perfectly reconcilable with those of elementary social behavior, once the special conditions in which each applies are taken into account. Both deal with the exchange of rewarding goods. But elementary economics, the economics of price, tends in fact to deal with physical goods, like apples, though it is not bound in principle to limit itself in this way. Quite a number of physical objects can be exchanged at one time—several dozen apples, say, for a dollar—whereas our goods are activities, only one unit of which a man can emit at a single time. Physical goods are not readily changed into something else, not, at least, into something salable and then not without effort: it takes effort to change apples into applesauce, whereas a man can readily change his activity in kind, from one grade of approval, for instance, to a warmer one. Economics also has, in money-price, a measure of a commodity's value in exchange that is independent of the particular other goods it is exchanged for, whereas we obviously have no such thing. Economics further simplifies its problem by considering the exchange of commodities for money in a perfect market, one in which the behavior of any single buyer or seller has a negligible effect on prices. Our market, if we may call it that, is far from perfect: the behavior of each party has a marked effect on the rate of exchange of activities between them. And though to be perfect a market must have many buyers and many sellers present in it, no one buyer need enter into more than one transaction with any one seller, while we assume that the same two people will enter into repeated transactions with one another. This means that economics chooses not to consider how the fact that one man drives a hard bargain with another affects their behavior in the next transaction, for there need be no next transaction; and the economic market is "impersonal" in a way ours can never be.

Yet the similarities in the propositions of the two subjects shine through the differences in conditions. Take the Law of Supply in economics: the higher the price of a commodity, the more of it a supplier will sell. This is equivalent to—we dare not say identical with—our proposition: the more valuable the reward gotten by an activity, the more often a man will emit it. For in the Law of Supply the price of the commodity is the reward obtained by selling it. In the same way the Law of Demand—the higher the price of a commodity, the less of it a consumer will buy—is equivalent to our proposition: the higher the cost incurred by an activity, the less often a man will emit it. For in the Law of Demand the price of the commodity is the alternative reward a buyer forgoes when he spends his money on the commodity, instead of spending it on something else or holding it for a fall in prices. It should be obvious that the two laws are really the same law seen from the point of view of different alternatives. If the rewards of one activity rise in value relative to those of another, the receiver of the reward will emit more of the first activity and less of the alternative. And if the costs of one activity rise they render the rewards of another relatively more valuable, and so the receiver of reward will emit less of the first activity and more of the alternative. In either case the proposition, the greater the profit (reward less cost) of a unit-activity, the more often it will be emitted, sums up the facts.

By assuming, moreover, that the price of a commodity is almost independent of the action of any single buyer or seller, economics can specify the point, in price and quantity sold, at which exchange will settle down: it will be the point at which the rising Supply Curve intersects the falling Demand Curve. We dare make no such assumption and therefore, as we have seen, the point at which our sort of exchange will settle down—if it settles at all—is subject to more complicated repercussions than economics usually takes into account.

Total Reward

So far we have been chiefly concerned with two questions: What makes Person or Other change from emitting one activity to emitting an alternative one? and, What determines changes in the rate of exchange of activities between them? Both changes are matters of the short run, even the rate of exchange. For the rate of exchange is the number of units of help exchanged for a given number of units of approval, and since it varies as the relation between profit per unit-help and profit per unit-approval, it must always be referred to some short period of time, for the profit per unit may vary with successive units. But Person and Other are not present together in the office for a short period of time; they are present for a whole working day and many days. We cannot neglect this problem of the longer run, for the degree to which a man is satiated with a reward depends on the number of units of the reward he has received in the past, if only the relatively recent past. We must consider how he distributes his time between alternative activities over some period like a day so as to achieve some degree of satiation with the rewards he gets from each. More accurately, we must consider not just his profit per unit-activity but his total profit over a period of time from the alternative activities open to him: the varying profit per unit times the number of units of each activity, which can if necessary be measured in time.

As we know, the more approval Other has gotten from Person in past transactions, the less valuable to him any further approval becomes; and the more help he has given Person, the more costly any further helping becomes in time lost from his own work. In the same way, the more help Person has gotten from Other, the less for the time being he needs any further help and the more costly he finds any further confession of inferiority. The profits from exchange decrease with the number of exchanges; and there will come a time in the course of a day in the office when Other begins to feel that the cost of helping

Person any more is greater than its reward, and spends the rest of the day doing his own work. Or he may alternate between helping Person and doing his own work. Something of the same sort is probably true of Person.

Under these circumstances, our propositions obviously imply that both Person and Other will spend something less than the whole day together and something less than the whole day apart. The more profitable, moreover, to the other the average value of what each gives, the more time they will spend together in interaction. But if Person gives Other an activity that the latter finds more valuable than what he got before—a warmer approval, for instance—but that at the same time costs Person more to give, the effect on the distribution of activity is not so clear. In any event, since each makes a profit, however small, from every unit-activity he emits, or he would not emit it, each distributes his time among alternative activities in such a way that he achieves a greater total profit than he would have achieved by some other distribution. The student of economics will recognize that we are talking about our equivalent of indifference curves.

How shall we measure this total profit? An admittedly crude illustration will suggest how we might, in principle, measure it. Suppose both men are in the office for eight hours a day. If Other in fact gives Person two hours of help (thus giving up two hours he might otherwise have devoted to his own work) and gets two hours of approval for it, and gives the remaining six hours to doing his own work (thus giving up six hours of approval he might have gotten from Person), we believe that he has achieved a greater total profit than he would have done if he reversed the distribution and gave six hours to Person and only two to his own work. And we can try to estimate his total profit by subtracting his forgone reward from what he did not do from the reward he actually got from what he did. But at this point the notion of total profit may not be very useful. We need not compare how he in fact distributed his activity with an unreal or ghost distribution, the whole point of which is that it never existed. We may for the present purpose give up the notion of cost and only estimate his total reward: the varying value per unit of alternative activities times the number of units he emitted of each.

Although we assume that as Person and Other go on exchanging approval for help day after day, they may learn so to distribute their time between alternative activities that each achieves a greater total reward on later days than he did on earlier ones, we dare not assume that either man ever maximizes his reward. Economics says that each would maximize his utility if he so divided his day that the last unit of activity he exchanged with the other got him a reward just equal in value to the last unit he spent on his own work. In the language of economics, to maximize his utility, he should make the marginal utilities of his two activities equal. But we shall never be able to measure value precisely enough to discover whether a man maximizes his utility in these terms. Still less dare we say that both men ever maximize their rewards. Both would do so if each was ready to break off their exchange at just the same moment, but this is unlikely to happen often. The reward each gets is to some extent at the mercy of the behavior of the other, and Person may, for instance, want more help at a time when Other is beginning to find giving help distinctly burdensome. All we can usefully say is this: the two men will spend an amount of time together that gives each some reward but not necessarily the greatest conceivable reward.

At this point, too, a new effect makes the question of maximization, at least in the terms so far considered, somewhat irrelevant. It should be clear by now that Person and Other have two sorts of bargain to strike—if we can call a bargain what need not be at all the result of conscious bargaining. They must strike a bargain over the momentary rate of exchange: the number of units of approval being given at a particular time for a unit of help, and they must strike a bargain over the total amount of activity each gives the other over a longer period of time such as a day. Into both bargains intrudes a problem we have not so far considered. It is the problem whether or not each party considers he is getting not just a profitable exchange but "fair exchange," and to this problem we now turn.

Distributive Justice

In Chapter 2 we saw that, when a pigeon pecks but gets no grain, although the stimulus-conditions resemble those under which it was previously rewarded for pecking, the pigeon displays what looks to a human observer for all the world like anger and frustration: it turns away from the target, flapping its wings and cooing hurriedly. Attributing human thoughts to the pigeon, the observer is irresistibly drawn into saying: "The pigeon got mad when it did not get what it expected." Or even: "The pigeon got mad when it did not get what it thought it deserved." What the observer really refers to when he talks of the pigeon's expectations or deserts is its past history of reinforcement under particular stimulus-conditions. When conditions in some way similar to those of the past recur in the present, the pigeon, by our proposition 1, will be apt to emit the activity rewarded in the past. When it does so and the reward is not forthcoming, it will be apt to display emotional behavior.

Although the evidence for it is much less clear, we have also assumed by symmetry that when the pigeon *is* getting grain under the conditions in which it received grain previously, it will emit emotional behavior of a different sort, rudimentary perhaps, but still, by human standards, expressive of contentment and well-being: its coos will be long and low.

In the same way, men express anger, mild or severe, when they do not get what their past history has taught them to expect. The more often in the past an activity emitted under particular stimulus-conditions has been rewarded, the more anger they will display at present when the same activity, emitted under similar conditions, goes without its reward: precedents are always turning into rights. Among these stimulus-conditions one set will be especially important for the purposes of our analysis: the characteristics of the man who provides a reward. When one man makes a request of another and is turned down, although the conditions surrounding the other resemble those of men who have provided similar rewards in the past, the man that made the request is apt to display some degree of anger. The other is "the sort of man" who "ought" to have granted the request. By refusing to enter into exchange at all when he might have been expected to do so he has violated the first principle of fair exchange.

Another such set of stimulus-conditions is that surrounding the other men who receive a reward. Even a pigeon will be vexed if it sees another pigeon making off with food it has had its own eye on, and so certainly will a man unless he is a saint. The past occasions in which a man's activities have been rewarded are apt to have been occasions in which other men, in some way like him, have been rewarded too. When others like him get their reward now, but he does not, he is apt to display emotional behavior. This is the condition called *relative deprivation*.[3]

The patterns of stimulus-conditions that are capable of releasing emotional behavior in men are undoubtedly more complicated than those that release them in pigeons. By what processes of past learning the patterns have come to have this effect it is not the business of this book to explain. Our job is to make clear what general characteristics these patterns possess and what effects besides emotional behavior they call forth. For this purpose we must now go into further refinements.

So far we have only asked whether a man received a reward or did not do so. But all the evidence is that he may receive a reward, even a valuable one, and still display emotional behavior. The question is quantitative not qualitative. Did he receive as *much* reward, in value or quantity, as he expected—either as much as he should have received from a particular other man, or as much as men like himself received? The stimulus-situation includes, moreover, the costs as well as the rewards of activity; and the question for our man is whether he received as much reward less cost—that is, as much profit—for his activity as he had the right to expect.

So far, too, we have treated the person giving a reward as distinct from the person receiving one; but when two men are in a social, or exchange, relation with each other, each is both giving reward to the other and receiving reward from him, and the question for each man then becomes: Did he get as much reward from the other, less the cost to himself in getting that reward, as he had the right to expect? And did the other get from him, at a certain cost to the other, no more reward than *he* had the right to expect? Did Other give Person as much help as Person had a right to expect, without exploiting his monopoly of help to exact from Person more approval than Person had the right to expect him to get? For the two may, in effect, strike a bargain without Person's considering the bargain fair. Instead, Other may have driven a hard bargain. This is the problem of *distributive justice:* justice in the distribution of rewards and costs between persons.

But what does our man think he has the right to expect for himself and for another man with whom he has entered into exchange? His expectations are determined by the many features of the past histories

[3] R. K. Merton and A. S. Kitt, "Contributions to the Theory of Reference Group Behavior," in R. K. Merton and P. F. Lazarsfeld, eds., *Continuities in Social Research* (Glencoe, Ill., 1950), pp. 42-51.

or backgrounds of himself and the other—features that we shall call in this connection the *investments* of the two men. In Chapter 12, on Justice, we shall consider a variety of investments and their mutual relations. At the risk of gross oversimplification we shall consider only one of them here, and then only for purposes of illustration. This investment, and it is the most characteristic of investments, is a man's age. We have seen that Person asks himself whether he has received as much reward as other men, in some respect like himself, received. But one of the ways in which two men may be "like" one another is in their investments. Accordingly the more nearly one man is like another in age, the more apt he is to expect their net rewards to be equal and to display anger when his own are less. But, by the same token, to the extent that their investments are different, he may expect the other's net reward, his profit, to be greater or less than his own. If the other is older than he is himself, if the other has invested more time in living, then he may be content that the other should get a greater profit than he does himself, and he may display no anger when the other does get it. Remember that we have considered age in utter isolation from other investments. In real life there are many background characteristics of men beside their age that count, with different persons and in different cultures, as investments.

Later we shall offer evidence for a general rule of distributive justice; here we shall only state it baldly. A man in an exchange relation with another will expect that the rewards of each man be proportional to his costs—the greater the rewards, the greater the costs—and that the net rewards, or profits, of each man be proportional to his investments— the greater the investments, the greater the profit. This means that unless the investments of the two men are greatly different, each man will further expect the following condition to hold good: the more valuable to the other (and costly to himself) an activity he gives the other, the more valuable to him (and costly to the other) an activity the other gives him. Finally, when each man is being rewarded by some third party, he will expect the third party to maintain this relation between the two of them in the distribution of rewards.

Our proposition 5 then becomes: THE MORE TO A MAN'S DISADVANTAGE THE RULE OF DISTRIBUTIVE JUSTICE FAILS OF REALIZATION, THE MORE LIKELY HE IS TO DISPLAY THE EMOTIONAL BEHAVIOR WE CALL ANGER. Distributive justice may, of course, fail in the other direction, to the man's advantage rather than to his disadvantage, and then he may feel guilty rather than angry: he has done better for himself than he ought to have done. But he is less apt to make a prominent display of his guilt than of his anger. Indeed a man in this happy situation is apt to find arguments convincing to himself that the exchange is not really to his advantage after all.

Until we reached distributive justice we had no need to assume that Person and Other compared the rewards each got from the exchange. But the problem is different when we consider, as we must, the stimulus-situations that elicit emotional behavior. For with men the heart of these situations is a comparison. Besides exchanging rewarding activities with each other, both Person and Other do in fact perceive and appraise their rewards, costs, and investments in relation to the rewards, costs, and investments of other men. In effect Person asks himself: "Am I getting as much as other men in some respect like me would get in circumstances in some respect like mine? And is Other giving me as much as other men, in some respect like Other, would give?" In the meantime Other is asking himself the same sorts of question. When it comes, moreover, to comparisons with other men, the most important other man is the particular one with whom exchange is now taking place. Accordingly Person asks himself: "Is Other maintaining distributive justice in the exchange between us?" He may even ask: "Am I myself doing so?" And if distributive justice fails, anger rises.

Though both men make the comparison, there is no guarantee that they make it the same way, that each appraises the rewards, costs, and investments—both his own and the other's—on something like a scale of values identical with that of the other. Person may feel that distributive justice has been done when Other does not. Other, for instance, may appraise his costs in time lost from doing his own work at a higher value than Person does, and so feel angry that Person is exploiting him, while Person remains unconscious of any guilt. All we can say for the moment on this point is that the more similar the past experiences of the two men—the more similar, that is, what they have learned—the more likely are their perceptions to coincide. They are also more apt to agree on what the rule of justice is than on what components should count in applying it. While agreeing that net reward should be proportional to investments, they may not agree that age should count as an investment. Finally, they need not consciously formulate the rule of justice, as we have formulated it here. What we observe is that they behave as if they were conscious of it.

The withdrawal of an expected reward is not just something that releases emotional behavior; it is also a punishment, and its avoidance is accordingly a reward. Not only, therefore, do men display anger or, less prominently, guilt when distributive justice fails in one way or the other, but they also learn to do something about it. They learn to avoid activities that get them into unjust exchanges; they learn to emit activities that are rewarded by the attainment of justice, and by the same token, to forgo these activities becomes a cost to them. In short, justice itself becomes one of the values being exchanged.

At the very least, a man who finds himself at an unjust disadvantage learns to complain. Someone who is angry at another is in no shape to approve the other's behavior; or to put the matter another way, a man like Other can get approval from Person both by supplying him with services valuable in themselves and by supplying them on terms that meet Person's condition of justice. Unless he is ready to forgo the extra approval and accept the likelihood that Person will be less ready to exchange approval for help on the next occasion, he is apt to go some way toward allaying Person's anger: he will give him more help than he would otherwise have done, thereby increasing his own costs. Both increasing Person's rewards and increasing his own costs are moves in the direction of meeting Person's condition of justice. Whether or not he estimates the justice of the situation in the same way that Person does, whether or not he feels guilty of taking an unfair advantage, he will still make the move so long as he sets a high enough value on keeping up his exchange with Person. Naturally it is a man like Other who commands a supply of a scarce good that is most in danger of violating Person's notion of distributive justice, or, as we say, of exploiting him. But the shoe may be on the other foot, and if it is Other who begins to feel angry because Person does not show a fair appreciation of the help he is getting, Person may, for reasons of the same sort, increase the approval he gives Other.

According to the argument we have used right along, either man will be the more ready to drive a hard bargain and to forgo the reward he would have gotten from meeting the other's condition of distributive justice, the less valuable he finds that forgone reward. So complete may be his monopoly of the power to reward or punish the other's behavior that the other has no alternative but to keep on with the exchange, and then the monopolist has little to lose by being unjust. The tyrant can sometimes afford to disregard the feelings of his slaves. Or a man may have no such monopoly but still set little store by continuing the exchange, which may mean that his alternative sources of reward are many. In theory the perfect market of the economist meets this condition. When buyers and sellers are many and none can have a big influence on the price of a commodity, no single buyer can fairly hold it against a seller who refuses to sell him the commodity below the market: the seller is clearly hurting himself if he does so. Or if the seller does drive a hard bargain and the buyer resents the price exacted from him, it may not make much odds to the seller, for there are always more buyers where that one came from. This is what we mean when we say that the classical market is impersonal, or rather that economics, for its particular purposes, chooses to consider it so and no longer concerns itself with the problem of the "just price." In reality, of course, it is a rare merchant who sets no value on the "good will" of his customers. Certainly the sort of market we are dealing with in this book is far from impersonal. Though it holds no absolute monopolists—for our people are always free not to enter into exchange at all—neither does it offer a man many alternative sources of reward; exchanges between two persons tend to continue, and distributive justice does make a difference.

A man in exchange with another who finds, through the other's rising anger, that he is not meeting the other's view of distributive justice must reckon with the costs of persisting in his present line of action. He must reckon with the rewards in approval and in continuing exchange that he thus forgoes. He may ultimately come to forgo them, to find it more rewarding to maintain his own standards of justice, but they are not negligible: they are there to be forgone. This makes it somewhat academic to ask where, in the absence of considerations of justice, our two men would strike a bargain over the rate of exchange or the total amount of reward exchanged. For if the exchange is to persist, some move to set the bargains by the standards of distributive justice will probably be made. We need no new proposition to explain this: all we need add is a new kind of reward. To the primary rewards exchanged we add the rewards of establishing fair exchange.

Rationality

In this chapter we have stated five main propositions, which we took from the findings of behavioral psychology but modified so that they should apply to human exchange—the situation in which each of at least two men emits activities reinforced by the activities of the other. We have also drawn a few corollaries from the main propositions: our statement of the determinants of the rate of exchange is such a corollary. Some of these propositions and corollaries, together with further corollaries to be brought in later, we shall hope to illustrate with research findings in the chapters that follow. But before we do so we may be allowed a comment or two.

Let not a reader reject our argument out of hand because he does not care for its horrid profit-seeking implications. Let him ask himself instead whether he and mankind have ever been able to advance any explanation why men change or fail to change their behavior other than that, in their circumstances, they would be better off doing something else, or that they are doing well enough already. On reflection he will find that neither he nor mankind has ever been able to offer another —the thing is a truism. It may ease his conscience to remember that if hedonists believe men take profits only in materialistic values, we are not hedonists here. So long as men's values are altruistic, they can take a profit in altruism too. Some of the greatest profiteers we know are altruists.

We have also tried to show how, given the special conditions of exchange that economics chooses to confine itself to, our propositions and corollaries are wholly compatible with those of elementary economics. Indeed we are out to rehabilitate the "economic man." The trouble with him was not that he was economic, that he used his resources to some advantage, but that he was antisocial and materialistic, interested only in money and material goods and ready to sacrifice even his old mother to get them. What was wrong with him were his values: he was only allowed a limited range of values; but the new economic man is not so limited. He may have any values whatever, from altruism to hedonism, but so long as he does not utterly squander his resources in achieving these values, his behavior is still economic. Indeed if he has learned to find reward in *not* husbanding his resources, if he values *not* taking any thought for the morrow, and acts accordingly, his behavior is still economic. In fact, the new economic man is plain man.

Some readers may feel that in making men profit-seekers we have made them more or less "rational" than they really are. If "rational" behavior means conscious rather than unconscious behavior, the question of rationality is irrelevant for us. In the fields of endeavor we shall be interested in, conscious and unconscious behavior come out at the same place. Person can offer Other more lavish praise in return for more valuable help, his behavior can be utterly economic, without his being any more conscious of what he is doing than the pigeon is.

But two other and somewhat more interesting meanings have been given to rationality. The first is this: behavior is irrational if an outside observer thinks that its reward is not good for a man in the long run. A man is irrational if he likes what he ought not to like. In this sense, a man who takes some drugs, including tobacco, is behaving irrationally. So is a masochist, a man who finds punishment rewarding, though the criterion of "goodness" or "health" is not as clear. But since for the purposes of this book we take a man's values as simply given, we care not here—though we surely do care elsewhere—if they be rational. What we are interested in is what he does with them once he has somehow picked them up. Suppose a man is a masochist—is it still true that if he has taken a lot of punishment lately, he will find further punishment less valuable? Will the first kick in the teeth give him more kick than the last? Although we have not experimented, we have no doubt it will.

The second meaning of rationality is a little different. Whatever a person's values may be, his behavior is irrational if it is not so calculated as to get him the largest supply of these values in the long run. Here the emphasis is not on the kind of value being pursued—it may be capital gains or eternal salvation—but on the way it is being pursued: the emphasis is on calculation and the long run—the longer the better. An irrational man is either unwilling to forgo some immediate reward in order to invest in some greater future, or unwilling to acquire the knowledge and make the calculations that would show him how to reach that future. A large part of many sciences, from divinity to the Theory of Games,[4] is devoted to providing him with this knowledge

[4] J. Von Neumann and O. Morgenstern, *Theory of Games and Economic Behavior* (Princeton, 1944).

and enabling him to make the calculations. The Theory of Games should, for instance, make him better able to choose a strategy among alternative courses of action, when the risks and returns of each are matters of probability, not certainty.

Even without the benefit of a science, there are of course people whose elementary social behavior is rational in this sense. The social climber is an example. Using his implicit knowledge of the propositions we try to make explicit here, and prepared to accept—this is his characteristic heroism—certain immediate costs in self-respect, he may well wind up in a far higher social position than he would have attained without his calculations and his peculiar asceticism. A developing science of elementary social behavior should enable a social climber who will study it to reach the top more surely—so long as it does not also help other people to see through his schemes. Indeed it should help anybody who has some long-term social goal in mind, selfish or unselfish. But let the reader be warned: though he himself may draw conclusions from this book that will enable him to act more rationally, we shall not draw them for him. This is not a book on applied sociology.

Although calculation for the long run plays its part in human affairs, we make no allowance for it in our propositions, which are to this extent incomplete. We do not rule it out; neither do we rule it in. Our first justification is that we shall not often need it to explain the research results considered in this book. And our second lies in plain sight: calculation for the long run is the exception and not the rule. The Theory of Games is good advice for human behavior but a poor description of it.

But we have a still better reason for our lack of concern with rationality. All the good advice, from ethics to economics, that wise men give their fellows is meant to change behavior and not to explain it; but our business is with explanation. The advice tries to answer the question: Given that you value the attainment of certain ends, how could you have acted so as to attain them more effectively? But what men or pigeons could have done is what they did do, and much social science has gone to show some of the surprising reasons why they cannot do in fact what some wiseacre says they could. This does not mean that all the advice goes for nothing. So far as men will take it, so far as they will learn from it, it may change the way they behave the next time. But behavior observed is behavior past, and for the purposes of explaining how men have indeed behaved, it is seldom enough to ask whether or not they were rational. The relevant question is what determined their behavior—though of course the advice they have listened to may be among the determinants.

The people who will appear in this book are, if you like, no less rational than pigeons. If it be rational of pigeons to learn and take the shortest of two paths to a reward, so it is of our men. They choose among a few alternatives immediately open to them; they choose with little regard for the really long-term results of their choice, which sometimes surprise them. But the short-term results they do know, and they know them less as matters of probability than of certainty. If Person will only praise Other enough, he is pretty sure of getting help: the question is not whether he can get the result but whether he finds it worth the price. Within these limits, our men do not choose foolishly— that is, at random—but only in the way our propositions say they do. All we impute to them in the way of rationality is that they know enough to come in out of the rain unless they enjoy getting wet. To be sure, such rationality as we have now left them may not amount to much, for rational behavior in the present sense is only behavior that is determined.

Let us make sure we are not snobs about the common pigeon or the common man. When the future is uncertain and science weak, the pursuit of immediate reward is by no means irrational even by the austere standards of the Theory of Games. "A bird in the hand is worth two in the bush" is by no means always an unintelligent policy. And so far as the pursuit of rationality entails study, forethought, and calculation, and such things hurt, as they often do, the pursuit of rationality is itself irrational unless their costs are reckoned in the balance. The costs of rationality may make rationality irrational.

Influence

Chapter Five

In the last two chapters we defined the terms that were to enter our main propositions and then stated the propositions themselves. But we have supplied evidence in support of the propositions only for pigeons and not for men. In the remaining chapters we shall try to make good this deficiency. We shall try to show how a number of field and experimental researches illustrate the propositions or the corollaries that may be drawn from them. In so doing we shall hope to suggest how the propositions may be used to explain a variety of features of elementary social behavior. True, the different propositions will not all get the same support. For reasons lying in the varied interests and opportunities of many investigators, interests that need not have coincided with our own, research has been unequally distributed over the propositions and corollaries in our set. Some have received a great deal of attention, others little or none; but we hope none will turn out to be positively not confirmed: even if there is little evidence for them, there will be even less against.

Research on Influence

The first body of research we shall examine consists of studies on the process of influence: how one man, including an experimenter, manages to change, or fails to change, the behavior of others.[1] Clearly

[1] For a useful general statement see H. L. Zetterberg, "Compliant Actions," *Acta Sociologica*, Vol. 2, No. 4 (Copenhagen, 1957), pp. 179-201.

our propositions should apply to this situation. Clearly, too, it is an appropriate place to start, for the situation corresponds more closely to what happens the first time Person asks Other for help than it does to what happens when the two men settle down to a regular exchange of help for approval. Men are always under influence, but the influence is often most conspicuous at the beginning of exchange.

Much research on influence has been experimental and carried out in the psychological laboratory; the subjects for the most part have been American undergraduates. The typical investigator has brought together in the laboratory groups of undergraduates who, so far as he could arrange it, were no more than barely acquainted with one another before the experiment began. He has subjected them to experimental conditions that were not identical with, though often similar to, the conditions they encountered in their daily lives; and the experiment has seldom lasted more than an hour at a time. For these reasons the research on influence has tended to play down the effects of long-established ties between men, and has told us most about how they respond to rather brief efforts to change their behavior.

Because of the expense and other difficulties of keeping human subjects together in a laboratory for days or weeks at a time, the patterns that social relations assume as they settle down—the patterns of "practical equilibrium," as we shall call it—are best studied not in the laboratory but in field and other observations of "real-life" groups, such as groups of undergraduates living together in their regular dormitories or employees working together in factories. But we shall not be numbered among those people who argue that laboratory studies of social behavior have nothing to say about real life. On the contrary, we hope to show that the laboratory studies of influence imply many of the features observed in real-life groups in practical equilibrium. Between behavior in the laboratory and behavior in the world there is no sharp break.

We have stated our propositions as if they applied to the behavior of a single pair of men, Person and Other, with the Third Man brought in from time to time. But the laboratory research is seldom designed to study the influence upon one another of individuals forming a single pair. If the investigators are to use statistical methods in order to reveal a central tendency in the data, they must study the behavior of a number of persons under the same conditions. And the question then comes up whether propositions about a single pair could possibly apply to the research. The only answer is to see if in fact they do. We have the more reason to expect they will, in that the circumstances of many of the experiments turn them, in effect, into studies of a number of separate pairs, each made up of the experimenter plus one of the subjects, and minimize the influence of the subjects on one another.

There are few things that men have more personal experience with than trying to influence people. And many social scientists have experimented with influence and gotten revealing results. But in this book we never claim to survey all the research; we choose only a few good examples. Within the literature on influence we shall limit ourselves to work done by a single group of men with a single, more or less consistent, point of view. Since each of the men—Stanley Schachter, Kurt Back, H. B. Gerard, and others—worked at one time or another with Leon Festinger, we shall speak of them collectively as the Festinger Group. We shall take up some of their chief investigations.

Approval and Productivity

The first study we shall take up was conducted by Schachter, Ellertson, McBride, and Gregory.[2] The investigators formed the women undergraduates who volunteered for the experiment into groups of three, and told the members of each group that they would work together at making cardboard checkerboards. One member was to cut the cardboard into squares, another to paste the squares onto heavier stock, and the third to paint the boards with the help of a stencil. In their instructions, the investigators implied that a high rate of production was desirable.

What really happened was a little different from what the members thought was going to happen. In order that they might compare the members' rates of production, the investigators put all the girls on the same job—cutting. They took each one into a separate room and put her to work on that job, but allowed her to believe that the other two members of her group were working on pasting and painting. They also encouraged her to write notes to the others. These a messenger collected as if for delivery, but instead he delivered to each girl a set

[2] S. Schachter, N. Ellertson, D. McBride, and D. Gregory, "An Experimental Study of Cohesiveness and Productivity," *Human Relations*, Vol. 4 (1951), pp. 229-38.

of standardized notes purporting to come from the others. For all groups the first few notes were neutral, designed neither to slow down nor to speed up production. But after this settling-down or preinduction period, the notes used in half the groups urged the girl to whom they were addressed to speed up her production, and the notes used in the rest of the groups urged her to slow down production. The investigators called these +Induction and −Induction groups respectively.

The investigators further subdivided each set of groups as follows. Before she was introduced to the other members of her group, the investigators had talked with each girl privately. They had told the members of half of the groups in each set that "there is every reason to expect that the other members of the group will like you and you will like them." And they had told the members of the other groups that it had been impossible to bring together a congenial group, and that "there is no particular reason to think that you will like them or that they will care for you." For reasons that will appear later, the investigators called these High-Cohesive and Low-Cohesive groups respectively.

In all experiments of this kind the investigators should adduce evidence that their experimental manipulations have in fact been successful. For instance, they should show that the girls in the high-cohesive groups found the other members of their groups more congenial than did the girls in the low-cohesive groups. And the investigators did indeed ask the girls to answer a questionnaire, the results of which showed just this. In discussing other experiments on influence we shall, to save time, say nothing about this aspect of the procedure but simply take for granted that it was carried out successfully.

The success of experiments like this one and others carried out by the Festinger Group requires that the investigators deceive the subjects. Thus in the present case they told the members of some groups that they would not find one another congenial, when there was nothing about the girls that would really make them so. For this reason, it is part of the morality of social experimentation for the investigator, at the end of the experiment, to explain to the subjects what tricks he played on them and why he thought them necessary. But for deceit to be successful, the subjects must be deceivable, that is, naïve. So far as we social scientists explain our tricks to our subjects and describe the experiments in large lecture courses, we may be depleting the supply of that article we most depend on for experimentation: the naïve American.

But to return: the investigators in this experiment created groups of four different kinds: congenial groups asked to speed up (HiCo +Ind), noncongenial groups asked to speed up (LoCo +Ind), congenial groups asked to slow down (HiCo −Ind), and noncongenial groups asked to slow down (LoCo −Ind). As for the results of the experiment, the investigators present them in two sets of figures: first, the average change, either positive (speed-up) or negative (slow-

Mean Deviation from Level of Production in the Preinduction Period

	16′-24′ induction period	24′-32′ induction period
HiCo +Ind	+2.92	+5.92
LoCo +Ind	+2.92	+5.09
HiCo −Ind	−1.00	−2.16
LoCo −Ind	− .58	− .42

down), in the rate of production of the members of the different groups, as compared with the rate in the settling-down period before any influence was exerted; and, second, the number of members of each class of group that changed, or failed to change, their behavior in accordance with the requests they thought they were receiving from the other girls. These figures are shown in Tables 1 and 2.

What do these figures show? If we compare the two kinds of groups that were asked to speed up, a greater change took place in the rate of production and a larger number of persons complied with the requests apparently made to them in the high-cohesive groups than in the low-cohesive ones. But the differences were not great and were far from being significant statistically. Among the groups that were asked to slow down, the corresponding differences were highly significant. Much more change in the direction requested and many more people changing in that direction appeared in the high-cohesive groups than in the low-cohesive ones.

The lack of significant differences between the groups asked to speed up may be the result of the investigators' suggesting to *all* groups that high production was desirable and the expectation in many parts of American society that people should work harder if they can. All of the +Induction groups were swimming with the stream, and it was accordingly more difficult for the differences in cohesiveness to produce differences in production between them.

TABLE TWO

Accepters and Nonaccepters* of Group Induction

	Number of accepters	Number of nonaccepters
HiCo +Ind	13	0
LoCo +Ind	11	1
HiCo −Ind	11	2
LoCo −Ind	4	8

* "A *nonaccepter* is defined as a subject who, during at least one of the last two periods, shifted her rate of production in a direction opposite to that of group induction."

How shall we put the findings about the −Induction groups into the more general framework of human exchange? Let us ask first what is being exchanged. The social scientists of the Festinger Group often speak, as they do in this experiment, of *cohesiveness,* which they define as follows: "This property of groups, the attraction it has for its members, or the forces which are exerted on the members to stay in the group, has been called cohesiveness."[3] A number of different things may attract a man to take part in a group: his interest in the activities the group carries out, the social approval he gets from other members, the absence of any other group he can belong to, and so on. In our terms cohesiveness refers to the *values* of the different kinds of rewards available to members of the group: the more valuable to a group's

[3] K. W. Back, "The Exertion of Influence through Social Communication," in L. Festinger, K. W. Back, S. Schachter, H. H. Kelley, and J. Thibaut, *Theory and Experiment in Social Communication* (Ann Arbor, 1950), pp. 21-36.

members are the activities (or sentiments) they receive from other members or from the environment, the more cohesive it is. Although the possible kinds of reward are many, the subjects in this experiment in fact received only one, a sentiment that the investigators called "liking" and that we call social approval. It is true that the subjects did not receive it directly from the other members of their groups. Instead the investigator told them they were receiving it, and they seem to have believed him. From our common knowledge of Americans and perhaps of mankind we assume that many of the girls in the experiment found "liking" valuable. According, moreover, to their membership in high- or low-cohesive groups, they received more or less valuable liking: in some groups, they were led to believe, the other members liked them much, in others not at all. At any rate, social approval of two different values was one of the things being exchanged: it was the one the girls received.

Social approval, we shall remember, is a generalized reinforcer: it can be used to reward a number of different kinds of behavior. In return for social approval, the girls in the experiment were asked to give something. The other two members of their groups, or so they thought, asked them to change their activity in the direction of producing more or of producing less. As with Person and Other, so here, activity was being exchanged for social approval, a sentiment. And in the groups that were asked to cut down production, the experiment showed that the more valuable was the social approval they received, the more of the requested behavior they produced. Of course a paradox was built into the very nature of the experiment: in one sense the girls that got much liking *decreased* their activity, since they produced less, but in another sense they *increased* the kind of behavior they were asked for.

The proposition, of course, describes the statistical results or central tendency; it does not describe the behavior of every individual. Two girls, for instance, refused to decrease their production though asked to do so by fellow members of a congenial group. Why they did so we cannot tell without knowing more about them as individuals —more about their personal histories—than the report of the experiment reveals, which is nothing. This is a problem of most experiments that use statistical methods, and now that we have mentioned it here, we shall say no more about it later.

In this experiment activity was being exchanged for "liking";

yet we dare not say that the liking reinforced the activity, since the girls got the liking before they were ever asked to change their behavior. Instead we must argue as follows: the investigator's statement that a girl would find her fellow members congenial constituted a stimulus similar to those under which, in the past, a girl had found that compliance with a request was rewarded with social approval. She might expect that if she complied approval would be forthcoming, and so she was likely to comply.

But this may not have been the whole story, and what we shall call the justice phenomenon may also have been at work. At its simplest, justice demands that a girl who has received much from another should also give much to the other, and that a girl who has received little should give little. By this rule girls who got much social approval should have given much of the requested behavior, and by and large they did just that. We have the stronger reason for believing justice to have been at work in the fact that some girls, for whom the perceived reward was low in value, not only did not change in the requested direction but actually changed in the opposite one: asked to decrease production, they increased it. Did they look on the other members of their groups as positively depriving them of social approval that, as nice American girls, they had every right to expect? And did they change in a direction opposite to that requested in order to "get back at" their fellow members? Revenge is a form of justice.

Approval and Interaction

The second study we examine is by Kurt Back and called "The Exertion of Influence through Social Communication."[4] When a number of undergraduates had volunteered for the experiment, the investigator divided them into pairs in such a way that the members of no pair had previously been acquainted. The investigator introduced the two members to each other and then took each to a separate room where he gave him a set of three photographs and asked him to write a story about them. When each had finished his story, the investigator brought the two men together again and asked them to talk over what they had written. He emphasized that the purpose of the discussion

[4] *Ibid.* See also K. W. Back, "Influence through Social Communication," *Journal of Abnormal and Social Psychology,* Vol. 46 (1951), pp. 9-23.

was to help them improve their stories, but that they need not come out with a single story on which they agreed. The investigator had shown slightly different sets of pictures to each of the partners, so that their stories would be different and they would accordingly have something to discuss; but in their discussion he did not let them look at the pictures again and allowed them to believe they were talking about the same set. The investigator let the partners talk together for as long as they felt like doing so, and then sent each back to his room with the instruction: "Write what you now think to be the best story."

This part of the procedure was the same for all pairs. But as in the previous experiment, the investigator formed pairs that differed in their cohesiveness, some being highly cohesive and some not. Cohesiveness, we have seen, refers to the value of the rewards available in a group. In the previous experiment the investigators manipulated only one kind of reward: the congeniality of the members of the group. In the present experiment the investigator manipulated several kinds; in fact he formed three sets of pairs. He informed half of the pairs in the first set that they would get five dollars for the best story produced (high-cohesive) and half that they would get no monetary reward (low-cohesive). He informed half of the pairs in the second set that they had high prestige (high-cohesive) and half that they had low prestige (low-cohesive). But for the sake of brevity we shall consider only the third set. The results were much the same for all three sets, and the third set has the advantage for us that the rewards manipulated were the same as those of the last experiment.

When the students signed up for the experiment, the investigator asked each one a number of questions tending to suggest that he was interested in the student's social preferences. Then in forming the third set of pairs he informed the members of half of them that they would find their partners congenial, and half that he had been unable to put together the kinds of person that would make a congenial pair. The former were the high-cohesive pairs and the latter the low-cohesive ones.

And now for the results. Two observers were present at each of the pair-discussions, and tried to classify each as showing an active or withdrawing pattern. An active discussion was one in which the problem was taken seriously, argument lively, and the effort to reach agreement or persuade the other partner vigorous. A withdrawing pattern was not of this sort. Active discussion was significantly more characteristic of the high-cohesive groups than of the low-cohesive ones. As might be expected, the members of the former were more nearly alike in the number of attempts each made to influence the other than were the members of the latter: in the high-cohesive groups both members tried hard.

After the experiment was over, the investigator interviewed each subject and asked him how much pressure to change his story he felt during the discussion. The members of high-cohesive pairs felt more pressure than did the members of low-cohesive ones. And these differences in felt pressure produced different results. Comparison of the two stories written by each subject, one before and one after the discussion, showed that members of high-cohesive pairs were more apt not only to change their stories than were members of low-cohesive ones, but to change them in a particular way: one member was likely to change radically—to go over wholly to the other's opinion—whereas in the low-cohesive pairs the partners were inclined to compromise.

Once again, how shall we interpret these results? As for the rewards available for exchange, they are much the same as those of the last experiment: first, social approval or liking, and second, a change in activity, specifically a change in opinion toward agreement with the opinion of another man; and we have good reason to believe that men often find agreement with their opinions rewarding. But this experiment left a wider choice open to the subject than did the last one. Whereas in the last experiment a subject could only comply or fail to comply with the influence brought to bear on him, in this one he could either try to persuade the other man or eventually allow himself to be persuaded. The stimulus presented—the investigator's statement that the other member of a pair was congenial or uncongenial—had a bearing on both options. In the past experience of many Americans a man who likes you is a man who is particularly apt to reward you for changing your activity in accordance with *his* request, but he is also a man who is particularly apt to comply with *your* request—though the whole explanation why this should be so we cannot give until we reach our chapter on Authority. Since the stimuli in the highly cohesive groups suggested that either agreement or efforts to get agreement would be well rewarded, both sorts of behavior were frequent in these groups and correspondingly infrequent in the less cohesive groups, where compromise—that is, something less than full agreement—was the rule. We do not know why a particular member of a highly cohesive group finally decided to give in to his partner rather than to keep on trying to persuade him. All we could have predicted of these groups was that both giving in and trying to get the other man to give in were especially likely to occur.

In the difference between the "active" and the "withdrawing" pattern of discussion, the present experiment provided a better measure of the *quantity* of activity exchanged, of the frequency of *interaction* between the two men, than did the last experiment. The more closely the stimulus presented by the experimenter resembled stimuli of the past under which efforts to persuade another man had been rewarded with success, the more likely was the subject on the present occasion to emit efforts at persuasion. Since this condition held for both members of highly cohesive pairs, each made many efforts to persuade the other even though one of them eventually gave in.

Cost and Profit

In the two studies considered so far, the subjects of the experiment were asked by other members of their groups, or thought they were asked, to change their activity so as to make it more valuable to the others. The experimental conditions made clear the rewards they might expect to get from the change, in the shape of more or less valuable social approval, but the costs of the change were not made clear. The cost of any change is the value received from alternative behavior that must be given up in making the change; and nothing in the experimental conditions suggested what the alternatives might be or what value they might have. In the first experiment, for instance, a member of a high-cohesive group who was asked to speed up might expect to get social approval if he did so, but what, if anything, he gave up by increasing production was not at all clear. We turn now to an experiment that begins to suggest how a change in behavior depends on cost as well as reward. This study was carried out by H. B. Gerard, a member of the Festinger Group.[5]

[5] H. B. Gerard, "The Anchorage of Opinions in Face-to-Face Groups," *Human Relations*, Vol. 7 (1954), pp. 313-25.

The investigator brought his subjects into the experiment in groups of six. He gave the members of each group a case history of a labor-management dispute to read and asked each member to indicate his opinion on the probable outcome of the case by checking a point on a seven-point scale, which ran from "the union will be adamant" at one end to "the union will give in immediately" at the other. The investigator then broke the original groups of six into groups of three members each, and he made these groups of three different kinds. Of course we do not mean that he broke each original group of six into three groups of three men each, which would be impossible. We need only remember that he began by having several six-man groups to work with. One kind of group he made up of subjects who were in close agreement as to the outcome of the case, another of subjects that were in mild disagreement with one another, and a third of subjects who strongly disagreed.

The investigator further divided the groups of each kind into two subclasses. He told the members of half the groups that they would find one another very congenial, and he told the members of the other half that they would not get on well together. In short, he created experimental groups of six different kinds: High Attraction-Agree, High Attraction-Mildly Disagree, High Attraction-Strongly Disagree; and Low Attraction-Agree, Low Attraction-Mildly Disagree, and Low Attraction-Strongly Disagree.

Each of the three-man groups then met for a face-to-face discussion of the case. The investigator observed the discussion, and at the end of it asked each man to indicate his current opinion on the outcome of the case. In this way he could determine how much change in opinion the discussion brought about.

Finally, about a week later, the investigator called in each man by himself, ostensibly to represent his group in a further discussion of the case with a member of another group. In fact this "member of another group" was, unknown to the subject, a paid participant, coached to behave as follows. In the new discussion he took a position on the outcome of the case that was, so far as possible, two steps removed on the scale from the last opinion expressed by the subject, and removed in a direction that would, if his persuasion was successful, pull the subject further away from the opinions expressed by at least one other member of his group. The subject was told that he would only find the paid participant fairly congenial. Once more the investigator observed the discussion and at the end asked the subject to indicate his final opinion on the outcome of the case. He could thus determine how many subjects changed their opinion toward that expressed by the paid participant, which represented a clear alternative to group opinion.

As for the results, members of high-attraction groups made more influence attempts in the first discussion than did members of low-attraction ones, and these attempts seem to have been more successful, for at the end of the discussion the opinions of members were more nearly alike in the former than in the latter. These findings are similar to those of the studies we have considered earlier and serve to confirm them. We shall be more interested in further findings, which seem to suggest something new. These findings are summed up in the following two tables.

TABLE THREE

Percentage of Subjects Changing Toward Someone in the Group

	Agree	Mildly-disagree	Strongly-disagree
High-attraction	0	12	44
Low-attraction	0	15	9

TABLE FOUR

Percentage of Subjects Changing Toward Paid Participant

	Agree	Mildly-disagree	Strongly-disagree
High-attraction	7	13	25
Low-attraction	20	38	8

One word to explain the meaning of these tables. The figure 44, for instance, means that of all members of high-attraction, strongly-disagree groups, 44 per cent changed their opinions in the direction of those held by some other member of their group. Comparing the sums of the rows in these two tables, we see that high-attraction people were more apt to change toward someone in the group than were low-attraction people, and that low-attraction people were more apt to change toward the paid participant than were high-attraction people. This is in accord with findings described earlier: if a group is giving you much, in this case liking, you are under pressure to give it much, in this case a change of opinion toward agreement with its views. By the same token, if a group is giving you little, you will be little apt to give it agreement. Indeed you may change your opinion so as to depart from agreement even further, that is, in the direction of the paid participant.

So far so good; but when I first scanned these tables I was less struck by the differences between them than by their similarities. In both tables members of the same type of group showed similar tendencies simply to change their opinions, whether the change was toward the group or toward the paid participant. Thus in both tables the persons who changed least were the members of high-attraction, agreement groups and low-attraction, strongly-disagree ones, while those who changed most were the members of high-attraction, strongly-disagree groups and low-attraction, mildly-disagree ones. And members of groups of the other two types displayed medium propensities to change.

The investigator is unable to account, or rather to account fully, for these different propensities. He says, for instance, "The 8 per cent figure for the low-attraction, strongly-disagree condition is perplexing. The figure is too low to be accounted for by chance. There seems to be no reasonable explanation for this inordinately low figure."

Since the experimenter is unable to provide one, let us see if we can provide an adequate explanation. Two kinds of question need to be answered: Why do different subjects change or fail to change their activity, that is, their opinion? and, If they do change, why do they change in one direction rather than another, toward the group or toward the paid participant? In the present experiment, the second question is secondary to the first.

Let us assume that there were available to the subjects at least three different kinds of reward for changing their opinions or failing to do so. The first was social approval by the group, which was purchased by agreement with it. The investigator takes for granted the existence of this reward; indeed his experimental design tried to give it a higher value in the high-attraction groups than in the low-attraction ones, and we too shall not find it hard to accept. The second reward was the value some men find in agreement for its own sake and apart from any social approval it may get them. As Festinger argues, disagreement with others is, at least on the face of it, not consonant with the truth of a man's own opinion: if his opinion is correct, it is absurd that others should disagree. Conditions like this, in which some of the facts before a man are incongruent with other facts, Festinger calls *cognitive dissonance,* and he claims that dissonance is often painful and its reduction rewarding.[6] This is not to deny that on some social occasions what we find entertaining is the very difference of opinions. In any event consonance may be purchased at too high a price, and accordingly the third reward available to a subject in this experiment was the maintenance of his personal integrity, achieved by sticking to his own independent and publicly expressed opinion on the issue of the case.[7] The investigator does not mention this reward, but we cannot make sense of the results without it, or something much like it.

In different degrees for different subjects, depending on their initial opinions and group membership, these rewards were in conflict or competition with one another: some subjects could not get one without giving up one of the others. Now according to our argument in the last chapter, when a course of action requires a man to give up one reward in order to get another, we speak of the cost of the action as the value of the forgone alternative. Cost is negative value, and the higher the cost of an activity, the less likely a man is to emit it. We also introduced the definition:

$$\text{Profit} = \text{Reward} - \text{Cost}.$$

And we argued that the less was a man's profit from a particular activity, the more likely he was to change and emit some other activity. But we were skittishly careful not to commit ourselves on whether a man acted so as to maximize his profit.

In the light of this argument, consider the members of the different groups in the present experiment. The high-attraction, agree people got cognitive consonance; they got much in the way of approval by the group and they had to give up for it little or nothing in the way of personal integrity, for their independent views happened to be in ac-

6 L. Festinger, *A Theory of Cognitive Dissonance* (Evanston, 1957), pp. 13, 18-19.

7 B. P. Cohen, "A Probability Model for Conformity," *Sociometry,* Vol. 21 (1958), pp. 69-81; see especially p. 75.

cordance with those of the group. Their profit was high, and they changed little. The low-attraction, strongly-disagree people were getting much in the way of integrity and they were not giving up for it much in the way of valuable approval, for they were members of low-attraction groups. Reward minus cost was high for them too, though not perhaps quite so high as it was for the high-attraction, agree people, for they were not getting consonance; and they too changed little. This is our explanation for the low figure of 8 per cent, which the investigator was at a loss to account for. But note that for these people profit was high for reasons the reverse of those that made the profit of the high-attraction, agree people. For the latter, approval was the reward, forgone integrity the cost—in their case little or nothing. For the former, integrity was the reward, forgone approval the cost, which in their case too was little or nothing.

The high-attraction, strongly-disagree people were in a very different position. They were certainly not getting consonance; they were perhaps getting much in the way of maintenance of their integrity but their costs in doing so were high too, for as members of high-attraction groups they were thus giving up much that was valuable in the way of social approval. Their net profit was low, and so they were very prone to change their opinions. We cannot say that their profit before change was zero, for our measures are not of the sort that yield absolute figures. But we may reasonably argue that their profits were less than those of most other groups. And the same was true of the low-attraction, mildly-disagree people. They did not get a great deal in the way of visible integrity, for their opinions were only in mild disagreement with those of others in their groups; but neither were they giving up much in the way of potential approval, for they were members of low-attraction groups. Unlike the high-attraction, strongly-disagree people, who had both high rewards and high costs, the low-attraction, mildly-disagree people had low rewards and low costs; but they resemble the former in that their net profit—the difference between the two—was low; and they too were prone to change. The members of groups of the remaining two kinds had medium profits and also medium propensities to change.

Once we have explained the different tendencies to change, the question comes up why people should have changed in one direction instead of another. No one that changed his opinion could have made it at once less like that of a member of the group and less like that of the paid participant; any change would have had to be toward agreement with someone, for the paid participant always took a position on the opposite side of the subject's own from that taken by other members of his group. He represented a source of consonance and social approval alternative to the one provided by other members of the group. He was not a particularly valuable source, but he was better than nothing, and some people must have felt that by moving toward agreement with him they were not abandoning all their integrity; at least they were not abjectly giving in to the group. If subjects changed, the evidence is that they changed so as to get the more valuable potential reward: members of high-attraction groups toward agreement with the group, members of low-attraction ones toward the "fairly congenial" paid participant. As we have said, this last finding is in accordance both with the two earlier experiments and with the propositions of the last chapter.

For the first time in the series of experiments we have been examining, we have evidence here for a person's alternatives to complying with influence exerted on him by his group. We have an alternative reward, in integrity, and an alternative person, the paid participant, from whom social approval may be gained. It is always the presence of alternatives that allows us to introduce the notion of profit. If profit is defined as the difference between the reward of a particular course of action and the forgone value of alternative courses, the evidence seems to be that the less their profit, the more likely people are to change their behavior, and to change it so as to increase their profit. And if whenever a man's behavior brought him a balance of reward and cost, he changed it away from that which got him the less profit, there might well come a time when, other circumstances remaining the same, his behavior did not change further because he had successively abandoned all the behavior that brought him less profit. That is, his behavior would be stabilized, at least for the time being. And so far as this were true for every member of a group, the group would have a social organization in equilibrium. Don't tell me that this is no problem. Many sociologists spend years describing and analyzing social structure without once asking themselves why it is that behavior persists long enough for them to describe and analyze it at all. Structure is not a given: it is itself the result of social process.

Alternative Sources of Reward

In the last experiment, we were forced to consider for the first time the effect of alternatives to a particular course of behavior. In our argument, and in ordinary human experience, alternatives are important because they raise the cost of any activity and so render more probable the emission of some other activity. The rule is: no alternative, no cost. In the last experiment the alternatives were of two different kinds: a reward other than social approval, and a person, other than the members of the group, from whom rewards of one kind or another might be obtained. We shall be particularly interested in the latter kind of alternative. Although our model so far is a two- or three-man group, we shall try to use its propositions to account for behavior in larger groups. One of the common features of such groups is the appearance of subgroups within them. In a four-man group members O and P may interact particularly often with one another, and Q and R particularly often. The reason may be, for instance, that O and P find in one another sources of reward alternative to those offered by Q and R. In the last experiment, the alternative person, the paid participant, was artificially introduced. We turn now to an experiment that suggests a more general condition producing alternative persons from whom a man may get reward.

This experiment was carried out by L. Festinger and J. Thibaut.[8] The investigators formed a number of groups of from six to fourteen members each. They gave the members of each group a problem to consider—half of the groups getting a problem in football strategy, and half getting a problem on what should be done about a delinquent boy. The members of each group read the case, and then each one made public to the others his opinion about it by putting up a card in front of his place at table indicating his position on a scale of possible opinions. Then the investigators gave each of the subjects a sheet purporting to contain new information on the problem—half of the members getting information that would tend to push their opinion toward one end of the scale, and half getting information tending to

[8] L. Festinger and J. Thibaut, "Interpersonal Communication in Small Groups," *Journal of Abnormal and Social Psychology*, Vol. 46 (1951), pp. 92-99.

push it toward the other end. The investigators did this in order to get a good dispersal of opinion and hence an active discussion.

The investigators asked each member after reading the new information to indicate his current opinion; and they drew attention to each opinion so that everyone should be aware of the differences. Then they told the members to discuss the case with one another not by word of mouth but by writing notes. The members handed their notes to the investigators who logged them in their record and then delivered them. In this way the investigators got a measure of the quantity of communication. After the experiment they asked each member to indicate, as before, his current opinion.

Besides giving them different problems to work on, the investigators differentiated the groups in two further ways. They told half the groups that the members "were selected in such a way that we believe you all will have about an equal interest in this problem and about equal knowledge about it." And they told the other half that members were chosen so as to be as different as possible in their interest and knowledge. They called these the homogeneity and heterogeneity conditions respectively.

The investigators further told one third of the homogeneous groups that they were interested in observing how a group reached a unanimous decision, one third that there was somewhat less need for uniformity, and one third that there was none at all. They created a similar division among the heterogeneous groups, except that for the first third they said that instead of unanimity, a plurality would be enough. In short, the investigators tried to create six different experimental conditions: Homogeneous, under High, Medium, and Low Pressures toward Uniformity, and Heterogeneous under similar differences in pressure.

And now for results. First, with increasing pressure toward uniformity, there was in fact greater change of opinion in the direction of uniformity. The investigators asked for different degrees of uniformity and by and large they got them. This result will hardly surprise us. Naïve Americans are nice people, and they will give investigators what they want so long as they themselves incur no great cost in doing so. As for the quantity of communication (interaction) measured by the number of notes written, more communication was directed at persons holding extreme opinions than at those closer to the mode. To get agreement with his opinions is valuable to a man, but once he has gotten it from some of his companions, the conversion of the others who still disagree becomes relatively more valuable to him: there is little advantage in preaching to the converted. Since the converted in this experiment were on the average those close to the mode, the unconverted were those that held out for extreme opinions; and in accordance with our argument in the last chapter, more interaction will be addressed to persons that can furnish the more valuable reward than to those that can furnish the less. But in the heterogeneity conditions, especially those of medium and low pressure, this tendency to communicate to the extremes became steadily less marked as the discussion went on. The reason was probably that, as we shall see, the efforts to get agreement were less successful in heterogeneous groups than in homogeneous ones, and a man will not go on indefinitely emitting behavior that is not rewarded.

More interesting, indeed, than the effects of differences in pressure were the effects of differences in homogeneity: the change toward uniformity of opinion was less in the heterogeneous groups than in the homogeneous ones. We interpret these results as follows. The investigators presented the members of the heterogeneous groups with a stimulus to the effect that they differed greatly among themselves. Now the experience of many men has been that, however queer their opinions may be, they are more apt to run into people with similar opinions in a group of varied than in one of uniform membership. Such people are sources of consonance and social approval alternative to the rewards to be gotten from agreeing with the mass of members. So long as members perceive these alternatives to exist, their costs in concurring in a uniform opinion increase and so they are less apt to concur. And so far as members fail to concur in a single opinion, the group may break up into subgroups, each made up of members holding similar opinions. This is what the investigators mean when they say that the reason why the heterogeneous groups were less likely to produce uniformity of opinion was that the members of these groups were more likely to see that the formation of subgroups was possible. The heterogeneity of the members is one of the conditions in which any one member of a group is apt to find that others are alternative sources of reward. In the present experiment heterogeneity played the same part implicitly that the paid participant played explicitly in the last one.

Similarity as a Source of Reward

In the next experiment we pursue the same issues that we did in the last. But in this one the investigators went still further toward artificially creating a particular distribution of opinion—or the belief that there was such a distribution—and they were able to observe still more precisely the reactions to it. The experiment was carried out by Festinger, Gerard, Hymovitch, Kelley, and Raven.[9]

The investigators formed groups of from six to nine members each, told the members of half the groups that they would find one another congenial (high-cohesive groups), and the members of the other half that they would not do so (low-cohesive). They made other experimental divisions among the groups, but we shall not go into them.

The members of all the groups read a case study of a labor-management dispute, no doubt the one we have heard of before. After reading the case, each member wrote down on a slip of paper a letter identifying himself and indicated on a seven-point scale his opinion on the probable outcome of the case. But these opinions were not made public as they were in the earlier experiment. Instead the investigators collected the slips in such a way that no member knew what were the opinions of the others.

This left the investigators free to create a fictitious impression of the distribution of opinion, which they did by handing to each member a slip of paper purporting to show the opinion of every other member in relation to his own. They led about two thirds of the members of each group to believe that they were "conformers." Each conformer received a slip showing one person in the group holding an opinion three steps removed from his own on the scale, two persons (one person if the group had only six or seven persons in it) holding an opinion only one step removed, and the rest agreeing exactly with his own opinion. Each "deviate," on the other hand, received a slip showing that he was alone in the opinion he held, that one or two persons held opinions two steps removed from his own, and that the rest of the group agreed on an opinion three steps removed.

Suppose that a man's identifying letter was "D," that he actually

[9] L. Festinger, H. B. Gerard, B. Hymovitch, H. H. Kelley, and B. Raven, "The Influence Process in the Presence of Extreme Deviates," *Human Relations,* Vol. 5 (1952), pp. 327-46.

held opinion "4" on the scale, and that he was a member of a seven-man group. Then Table 5 shows, first, the kind of slip he would get if he were treated as a conformer, and, second, the kind he would get if treated as a deviate.

Apparent Distribution of Opinion

Opinion	Given to conformer	Given to deviate
1		
2		
3		
4	D B C F G	D
5	A	
6		A
7	E	B C E F G

After the investigators had given out the slips and everyone knew the apparent distribution of opinion, each member again wrote down his current opinion and the degree of confidence he felt in it. This allowed the investigators to determine how much effect the perceived distribution of opinion had in changing either the members' actual opinions or their confidence in them. After this, the investigators told the members that they might write notes to others about anything they liked, including the case. These notes were collected but not delivered, and, in the number of words written, furnished the investigators with a measure of the quantity of communication (interaction) directed by each of the members to each of the others.

And now for the results. First, deviates showed greater readiness to change their opinions than did conformers, and less confidence in them. A person who sees that the majority of his group agrees on an opinion different from his own is in a state of "cognitive dissonance": the information he gets from the others is in conflict with his belief that his own opinion is correct. Many people find it valuable to escape from cognitive dissonance, and so deviates are apt to change their opinions. Second, somewhat more change occurred in high-cohesive groups than in low-cohesive ones. Besides the reduction is dissonance, a deviate might expect to get from the majority, in return for his agreement with them, a more valuable social approval in a high-cohesive group than in a low-cohesive one. Third, more communication occurred in the high-cohesive groups than in the others. But these general results we have encountered in earlier experiments; the nuances of communication are more interesting. Deviates that changed their opinion communicated less than either conformers or nonchanging deviates; for a man who has chosen to be changed has by that fact less need to change others. In the high-cohesive groups conformers and nonchanging deviates communicated, on the average, about equal amounts; but in the low-cohesive groups the nonchanging deviates communicated less than the conformers, as if they doubted not only the possibility of changing people that did not like them but also the value of doing so.

Still more interesting were the different persons to whom conformers and nonchanging deviates addressed their communications. In both high- and low-cohesive groups, conformers communicated more to the extreme deviates—that is, to members holding opinions three steps removed from their own—than they did either to members only one step removed or to those that already agreed with them. Besides seeing a good chance of changing the opinion of a man who was alone in it, they may have found it more valuable to preach to the unconverted.

But the behavior of the nonchanging deviates, at least in the high-cohesive groups, was quite different. Though the conformers communicated most to them, they did not communicate most to the conformers. Instead they communicated most to the few members that held opinions only two steps removed from their own—to those, that is, whose opinions most nearly resembled their own. A deviate may have seen that it was more difficult to change the opinion of a member of a conforming majority, especially when that opinion was quite different from his own, than it was to change the opinion of a man who had, at best, only one other man to support him in that opinion—especially when it more nearly resembled the deviate's own. At any rate, the experiment suggests that when members of a group emit different activities, any one member may find in others whose activities are similar to his own a source of reward alternative to others whose activities are different. The quantity of interaction between persons whose activities are similar in relation to the quantity of interaction between persons whose activities are different is something that will much occupy us later in this book.

Note that in explaining the behavior of the subjects in this experiment as in others, we have always referred, at least by implication, to their presumed past experience, particularly their social experience. We have, for instance, just assumed that in the past experience of many people, a stimulus to the effect that a majority holds a uniform opinion has been the occasion when efforts to change the opinion of a member of the majority are apt to have gone unrewarded; and we have used this assumption to explain why the deviates made few efforts to change the conformers. We social scientists are in the curious position of trying to demonstrate the truth of our propositions by experiments on people who already, for all practical purposes, know some of the propositions and adjust their behavior toward others accordingly. The fact that the behavior of men is always in part determined by their past experience means that the report of no experiment in social science can ever include all the information needed to explain its results. Indeed in the absence of information on the past histories of the particular subjects in an experiment, we are forced to fall back on common knowledge about the usual experiences of people in some way like them. We could avoid this necessity only by experimenting on truly naïve subjects, but by the time we are allowed to get at them, when they are undergraduates, our subjects are already so old that, at best, they are only relatively naïve.

Our only comfort is that we are not alone in this difficulty. Even in physics, scientists have found that the past histories of the materials they work with make a difference in their present behavior. Take iron—and the hull of a ship may be considered a single piece of iron. The present magnetic properties of a ship's hull are determined in part by its past history: where and on what heading it was built, what latitudes it has sailed through, and what buffetings it has taken from the sea. Since a scientist never has adequate information on these matters, he can never predict except very grossly what the present magnetic characteristics of the hull will be. In the last war this complicated the problem of making ships safe from magnetic mines.

When Influence Fails

The final experiment we shall consider comes properly at the end of the chapter, for it is concerned with the end of the process of influence. It deals less with the stimulus-conditions under which people comply with the demands others make of them than with the way others react when they fail to comply. It is concerned with what happens when influence fails. The experiment is the work of Stanley Schachter.[10]

The investigator formed a number of groups, each having from eight to ten members, and set them all to work reading and discussing the case of a juvenile delinquent, the question at issue being what should be done with him. On this question a number of opinions might be held, running all the way from "All he needs is a little more love" to "He ought to be sent to jail." The investigator also saw to it that the groups differed in cohesiveness, but because the details of how he did so would take more time to describe than they are worth, all we shall remember here—and it is only approximately correct—is that a cohesive group in this experiment was not one whose members were persuaded they liked one another but one in which they discussed something they were really interested in.

Into each group the investigator introduced three persons, treating them just as if they were ordinary members. In fact and unknown to the other members they were paid participants, coached by the investigator ahead of time to behave in certain ways in the course of the discussion. The so-called "mode" supported an opinion in agreement with the most commonly held opinion as it began to emerge in the group. The "slider" began by taking an extreme position, usually in favor of sending the delinquent to jail, and then slowly shifted toward the mode, as if the other members' arguments had persuaded him. And finally the "deviate" maintained an extreme position unchanged throughout the discussion.

The investigator observed the course of the discussion, recording the number of communications, including influence attempts, each person addressed to each of the others. Then at the end of the session he administered two tests to the members, designed to reveal the degree of social approval each one accorded to the others. First, he told the members that at a future meeting of the group it might be necessary to leave somebody out, and so he asked each member to list the others in rank-order beginning with the person he would most like to have

[10] S. Schachter, "Deviation, Rejection, and Communication," *Journal of Abnormal and Social Psychology*, Vol. 46 (1951), pp. 190-207.

remain with the group and ending with the person he would least like. This the investigator called the sociometric test. Second, he explained that for the purposes of a future meeting it might be necessary to form subcommittees of the group. These committees—Executive, Steering, and Correspondence—he so described that the first seemed the most attractive, the second next, and the third least. He then asked each member to write down the names of the other members that he would like to see serving on each committee.

And now for the results. As might be expected, the two measures of social approval showed the same tendency. At the end of the experiment, the deviates in the different groups received a lower degree of sociometric choice than did either the modes or the sliders: members were more apt to say that they ought to be left out at the next meeting, and this tendency was even stronger in the more cohesive groups than in the less. The deviates also got more nominations for the "worst" committee and fewer nominations for the "best" than did the others. As we have argued before, a man often finds it valuable that another should agree with his opinions. Should the other persist in not agreeing, he is not apt to give the other any activity that rewards the other's behavior, whether it is social approval or an opportunity to do an interesting job. But as usual this was not the whole story, and undoubtedly justice was at work also. If another is giving a man little agreement, crude justice demands that he give the other little approval. In failing to agree the other may, moreover, be withdrawing a reward that the man has come to expect, and he may accordingly meet the withdrawal not just with indifference but with positive hostility. Since a man is more apt to expect agreement from his fellow members of highly cohesive groups, he is also apt, in these groups, to be more hostile when he does not get it.

As for the quantity of communication (interaction), more communication was addressed to the deviate than to either the mode or the slider, and this was in accord with the results of experiments reported earlier. It took a little time for the general group opinion to jell out of the discussion, and accordingly a little time before the others recognized the deviate for what he was. As they began to do so, the number of communications addressed to him tended to increase, whereas the number addressed to the mode or to the slider remained more nearly steady. But the increase did not go on indefinitely. In the more cohesive groups, when it appeared that the deviate was not going to submit to the influence brought to bear on him, the number of communications addressed to him tended to fall off. In ordinary language, the majority gave him up as a bad job. In our language, a man will not continue forever to emit activity that has gone unrewarded. The situation toward which these groups tended at the end of the meeting was one in which the deviates received little interaction and little positive sentiment, and in which, by the same token, the conformers, holding the majority opinion, gave relatively more interaction and sentiment to other conformers—that is, to persons whose activities were similar to their own. We must emphasize this final situation, as we shall soon be turning to groups in practical equilibrium, and these are groups in which, for the moment, influence has brought about all the change it is capable of. Where it could succeed, it has succeeded, and where it could not, it has failed.

Summary

It is now time for a summary of these experiments on influence. Not every variable was a factor in every experiment, but the variables entering one or another of these experiments were of the same kinds as those we defined in earlier chapters. Indeed this is the reason why we chose to consider these experiments instead of others. These variables are: the amount of activity emitted by a person and received by another, and the value, including negative value or cost, of the activities exchanged. When the amount of activity was measured, it was usually the amount of verbal communication addressed by one man to another. Aside from influence attempts, the activities exchanged were of two main kinds: what we have called sentiments, or expressions of different degrees of liking or social approval, and what we have called activities proper, including such things as an expression of agreement with another's opinion or a change in physical production in accordance with another's request. Activities were in fact often exchanged *for* sentiments of social approval. Both sentiments and activities proper differed in value to the persons that received them: an expression of warm approval was presumed to be more valuable than one of indifference, and agreement with one's opinions more valuable than disagreement.

An independent variable is one whose values an investigator manipulates experimentally, and a dependent variable is one whose values he simply observes. In these experiments the investigators sometimes treated a particular variable as independent, sometimes as dependent. In the first experiment, for instance, they manipulated the value of sentiment and then observed the effect of the manipulation in changing production; whereas in the last they manipulated opinion, through the paid participants, and then observed its effect on sentiment. In the first, they treated sentiment as an independent variable; in the last, as a dependent one.

The variables the investigators manipulated might be either actual rewards or stimuli to potentially rewarding activity. To hear that another man likes you may be a reward in itself, but it is also a stimulus resembling those under which, in the past, your compliance with a request was apt to have fetched you much valuable approval. This past experience is what we refer to when we say a man expects certain behavior from others; and since the experiments tell us nothing about the past experience of the subjects except that they were American undergraduates, we have necessarily appealed to common knowledge in arguing what that experience must have been. In the order in which we have arranged them, the earlier experiments had more to do with the stimuli to compliant or noncompliant behavior, while the last one had more to do with actual compliance or noncompliance and the reactions to it—with what happens when influence has either succeeded or failed and in either case has done all it can.

Some of the main propositions to which these experiments seem to us to give support are the following. We state them under the usual condition of "other things equal," for when we say something is an experiment we mean that it was designed to keep at least some other things equal. The more valuable, then, to Person the activity (or sentiment) he gets or expects to get from Other, the more valuable to Other the activity (or sentiment) Person gives to him. And the more valuable to Person the activity he gets or expects to get from Other, the more often he emits activity that gets him, or he expects will get him, that reward. But as the expectation goes unrealized and his activity goes unrewarded by Other, Person emits the activity less and less often.

Since the cost of Person's activity is the value of the reward that he would have gotten by another activity, forgone in emitting the first, the presence of alternative activities open to Person tends to increase the cost to him of any one of them. The less his current profit from his behavior—the less, that is, the excess of value over cost—the more apt he is to change his behavior; and he changes it so as to increase his profit. The alternatives open to Person may be not only different activities but different Others who may reward them; and the more heterogeneous these Others, the more likely it is that some of them will do so. As between different Others, Person tends to emit more activity to—that is, interact more often with—that Other in exchange with whom he gets the greater profit. When the similarity of his own activity with that of another is valuable to him—a condition that does not always obtain, but does obtain for the similarity of opinions—and when some people have actually failed, or will probably fail, to change their activity so as to make it like his own, Person will interact more often with Other, the more similar Other's activity is to his own.

Remember always that these experiments have to do with influence, with attempts to change behavior. The stimulus-situation is such that Person expects more or less strongly to get more or less valuable reward, either in sentiment or in other activity, by changing his own behavior or by getting others to change theirs. As time goes on, these expectations are either realized or they are not. In either case, the social situation tends to become one in which no new change occurs. Person will cease trying to influence others who have not changed their activity so as to make it more valuable to him, which means that he will interact relatively more often with others whose activity does reward him. The propositions that describe the final situation are the following. Person interacts more often with Other, the more valuable Other's actual activity (or sentiment) is to him, and the more often Other emits that activity. And since he may give sentiment in return for Other's activity, the higher is the degree of social approval he gives to Other.

We believe these propositions either are the same as, or follow directly from, the propositions we put forward in the last chapter. But then we had no evidence, outside pigeon behavior, to support them; now we have some. We do not claim that they are at all out of line with everyday social experience; indeed we should be much surprised if they were. We do claim it is something to find them supported not just by experience but by experiment.

Conformity

Chapter Six

In the last chapter we studied experiments on influence, on the conditions under which men succeed or fail in changing the behavior of others, and on the results of their success or failure. In the present chapter and in several to follow, until we get to authority and social control, we shall shift our interest to the situation that arises when influence appears to have done its best, when it has accomplished all it can, and when therefore the behavior of a person or of the members of a group has settled down, at least for the time being, to something like stability. This situation we shall call *practical equilibrium,* and we shall state propositions that seem to hold good of individuals and groups in practical equilibrium.

Some of these propositions will look different from those that hold good of influence. For instance, when the members of a group are trying to change the behavior of others, they will direct most interaction to the member whose behavior most needs changing, that is, to the man who has so far failed to yield to the influence they have brought to bear on him. At practical equilibrium, on the other hand, when influence has done all it can and this man still holds out, he is just the one they will interact with least. Although the two propositions look like opposites, it should yet be clear from the last experiment reported in the last chapter that both follow from our set of general propositions. Men will put out much activity to get a valuable reward, but if the reward is not forthcoming, the amount of activity will fall off.

Practical Equilibrium

Practical equilibrium is not a condition in which no change of behavior occurs. A sociologist studying a working group in a factory often feels justified in treating it as if it were in practical equilibrium, yet changes are going on all the time as the workers finish old jobs and start new ones, as they go out to and come back from lunch and coffee breaks. But these changes are regular and recurrent: no new kind of change seems to occur. The behavior of the group is in practical equilibrium in the sense that one day's work is much like another's.

Changes other than recurrent ones may also be going on; indeed they must be, if only because the members of the group are growing older by the minute. But for our purposes their behavior is still in practical equilibrium so long as the investigator's methods of observation fail to detect the changes, or so long as he treats them as if they had no great cumulative effect during the time he is with the group. We must always remember how short a time even a fieldworker spends with a group—perhaps six months at most and often much less. If the observations he makes—and they may be crude—both toward the beginning and toward the end of this period—and it may be short—yield much the same results, then the behavior of the members of the group is in practical equilibrium. If, for instance, Person interacts with Other more often in the course of a day than he does with the Third Man both toward the beginning of the sociologist's stay and toward the end, then to this extent and by this measure Person's behavior is in practical equilibrium. Usually the sociologist does not report his making any such observations but simply allows us to believe that this is what they would have shown if he had made them.

We speak of *practical equilibrium* instead of plain *equilibrium* in order to avoid the almost mystical arguments that have encrusted the latter word in social science. We make no assumption here that the behavior of a man or a group tends toward equilibrium. The process in which a man seeks his social profit under the condition that others are seeking theirs at the same time may not lead to stability but to an endless jockeying for position—though that too may manifest stability of a sort. Nor do we assume that if a change from practical equilibrium does occur, behavior necessarily reacts so as to reduce or get rid of it. There is no homeostasis here: no belief that a group acts like an animal body shaking off an infection. Should some groups under some circumstances behave this way, there is no evidence that they do so always. Nor do we, like the so-called functional sociologists, simply assume that equilibrium exists and then use it to try to explain why the other features of a group or a society should be what they are. If a group is in equilibrium, they say, then its behavior *must* exhibit certain other features. For us, on the other hand, specific effects must follow from specific causes, but more than that we do not ask of the behavior of any group: there is no more *must* about it. Practical equilibrium, then, is not a state toward which all creation moves; it is rather a state that behavior, no doubt temporarily and precariously, sometimes achieves. It is not something we assume; it is something that within the limits of our methods we observe. It is not something we use to explain the other features of social behavior; it is rather something that, when it does occur, is itself to be explained by these other features. And what are these other features? The propositions that actually hold good of behavior in practical equilibrium; and these will be our first interest in the chapters that follow.

Because groups in practical equilibrium are ones in which the process of influence has had time to work itself out, they are more likely to be real-life groups than groups formed temporarily for experimental purposes, and therefore our evidence in what follows will come more from field studies and from certain kinds of statistical studies than from the kind of research we relied on in the last chapter.

Norms

It is really intolerable that we can say only one thing at a time; for social behavior displays many features at the same time, and so in taking them up one by one we necessarily do outrage to its rich, dark, organic unity. One feature of many groups in practical equilibrium is that a number of members, in one or more ways and in greater or lesser degree, are similar in their behavior. Neglecting the other features, we shall in this chapter concentrate on this similarity, its causes and results. We shall consider the question of conformity.

The first and most obvious thing to be said is that if members of a group are to resemble one another in their behavior, some of them must find this similarity valuable or rewarding. Similarity is not always rewarding. In some circumstances the members of a group may do better for themselves if they behave differently than if they behave alike. They may get more wood and water for themselves if one man remains a hewer of wood and another a drawer of water than if each does both. The division of labor means differences in labor, and it often pays off. But we are now dealing with the case in which similarities rather than differences are valuable.

One kind of valuable similarity took a prominent place in the experiments reported in the last chapter: similarity in expressed opinion. The investigators did not find it hard to assume, nor did we find it hard to accept, that many men are rewarded by others' agreement with them. Indeed this example is so obvious that we shall use another one here. In many groups at work in factories, the members resemble one another in the number of pieces of work each turns out within a given period of time, such as a day. Their behavior is often called restriction of output, not because the actual output need be at all unsatisfactory to management, but because similarity among workers in the amount they produce necessarily means that some are producing less than they might otherwise have done.

We are not bound to explain why a workingman finds it valuable that he and his fellows doing the same job should peg production at a particular figure. For us it is enough that he does find it so. We take his values as given by his past history, and often by a past more remote than that, and we seek only to account for what he does with them. But were we to ask him, he would have no trouble telling us why restriction is a good thing. If he or his fellows much increased the number of pieces each put out, management would cut the price paid per piece so that he would be doing more work for the same pay. He may well be mistaken: a modern management, watched by a modern union, might do no such thing; but that is no concern of ours: in this book we care not if men's values be rational or not. Or he might argue that in the absence of restriction the faster workers would show up the slower ones like himself, and bring down upon them the wrath of management. Even more important, if restriction has been practiced for any length of time, any conspicuous change in output might draw management's attention to what has been going on and lead to a drastic shake-up. And the workingman would never be at a loss to find other good reasons for restriction. Since it is more important that there be a peg than that the peg go in a particular place, the actual number of pieces that are to be produced tends to become an arbitrary figure, often some round number close to management's published standard for an average worker. Using this as an example of norms in general, we shall say that a *norm* is a statement made by some members of a group that a particular kind or quantity of behavior is one they find it valuable for the actual behavior of themselves, and others whom they specify, to conform to. The important thing is not that the behavior is conformity but that it is valued.

The Determinants of Conformity

The next question is what determines conformity to a norm. When we say that some people conform to a norm "for its own sake," we mean that they are rewarded by the result that the norm itself, if obeyed, will bring. In our example, some workingmen conform to an output norm because it brings them some kind of protection from management. So long as management does nothing, regardless of its reasons for doing so, their behavior is rewarded. We make no assumption that all members of a group find conformity to a norm valuable for its own sake but only that some of them do. Suppose that Person is a man who finds it valuable that his own behavior conform to a norm, and that Other's behavior do so too. If Other holds the same values as Person, so that the conformity of each is valuable to the other, then Person rewards Other and Other rewards Person in much the same degree. The exchange between the two is balanced, and we have argued that when the condition of distributive justice is realized, each party is apt to emit, over and above the immediate exchange itself, sentiments of liking or social approval rewarding to the other.

Even if Other does not hold quite the same values as Person, even if, to return to our example, he is not much worried about what management may do, he may still conform. For as we saw in the last chapter, people often reward conformity with social approval, as they reward other activities they find it valuable to receive; and Other, though himself indifferent to the norm, may still conform for the sake of the approval it gets him from people that are not indifferent. He conforms for the approval's sake and not for the norm's sake. Several experiments in the last chapter suggested that he is the more apt to conform, the warmer the approval he may expect to get for it.

Mind you, once Other has conformed, he is not likely to admit that he did so because he was bought by social approval. He will say that he really believes that conformity to the norm is valuable for its own sake. Indeed he may come to talk just like Person, a true believer from the beginning. So far we have talked as if men brought to their current groups the values precipitated by their past experience; but what is happening now will be past experience in just a moment, and besides bringing old values to new groups, men acquire new values within them. What they have once done for the sake of something else, they come to do, for all we can tell, for its own sake.

Mind you, too, Other in conforming may not get a particularly high grade of social approval from Person. If many members of the group are conforming so that conformity is not a scarce good or one at all hard to come by, Person may not give Other more than perfunctory approval. As we shall see in a future chapter, the highest approval goes to activities that are both valued and rare. But Person will certainly not dislike Other or ostracize him.

Only if Other values an activity incompatible with conformity strongly enough to forgo the approval that conformity would have brought him will he fail to conform. Whether or not he holds such values depends on his past history, on how he has behaved and how that behavior has been rewarded. In the case of output norms in American industry, we have reason to believe that people who have had a certain kind of past history, a rural, white-collar, or Protestant background or some combination of these—people, that is, who have picked up the values Max Weber called the Protestant Ethic—are more likely to be nonconformists and produce more than the output norm than are people with urban, blue-collar, or Catholic backgrounds.[1]

If Other fails to conform, then, as the last experiment in the last chapter and everyday experience both suggest, Person will direct much communication to him in an effort to get him to change his behavior. When the attempt fails, and his behavior remains unre-

[1] M. Weber, *The Protestant Ethic and the Spirit of Capitalism,* translated by T. Parsons (London, 1930); W. F. Whyte, *Money and Motivation* (New York, 1955), pp. 39-49.

warding to Person, the latter will not simply disapprove of him but positively dislike him. For if many people have conformed, so that conformity appears to be something a member could provide with little cost to himself, Person will expect Other to conform; his failure to do so becomes not just a failure to reward Person but an active withdrawal of reward from him, and the withdrawal of reward is met with hostility. Other has not lived up to the standards of fair exchange. At the extreme, Person will strike back at him or try to get the other members of the group to ostracize him, to send him to Coventry, so that he will have no chance whatever of getting any social reward.

Whether or not Other conforms does not depend simply on whether he finds sufficiently rewarding some activity—like hard work as a moral value—that is incompatible with his conforming to a norm—like the norm of pegged production. It also depends on whether he can find companions in his nonconformity. Should he fail to conform, he forgoes social approval from at least some of the members of his group, and this cost will be the greater the less open to him are alternative sources of social approval. If, for instance, there is no other group he can escape to, he is more apt to give in. Savages, who seldom have another tribe than their own that they can join, are great conformers. He is also more apt to give in if no other members of his own group share his values: the lot of the isolate is often hard. But if there are such persons—not just nonconformists but nonconformists of his own stripe—then he may not have to give up social approval altogether. Even a single such man seems to be a great comfort, and robs the group at one stroke of the greater part of its power. In this man the nonconformist has a source of support and social approval alternative to the approval offered by the rest of the group and now forgone by him. This is what the investigators meant in one of the experiments in the last chapter when they said that a member was less likely to conform if he saw the formation of subgroups was possible. If, indeed, there are enough members who share values opposed to those of other members, the group may split up into mutually hostile subgroups. We are far from knowing just what conditions are necessary in order that a norm should become accepted as a norm for a whole group, to which all members give lip service even if they do not all conform fully. We suspect that what is needed is a certain number of members that value conformity to the norm for its own sake, a certain number that are indifferent to the norm but value the social approval that conformity gets them, and an opposition that is divided against itself: its members fail to conform, but in different ways and for different reasons.

It should be clear that in this discussion the author and readers of this book are not Organization Men: we are not assigning a high moral value to conformity, to the man who goes along with the gang. We are only making the obvious point that nonconformity often has a price; and if we take any moral stand it is that the good nonconformist pays the price without feeling sorry for himself. Too many people complain when they can't have their nonconformity and eat it too. They want the best of both worlds, and if they got it they would be unfair to the rest of us.

Most studies of groups in practical equilibrium are not geared to testing all we have said about the relations between conformity and social approval. But they are geared to testing and have tested one corollary that seems to follow from our argument. Suppose a piece of research is pretty coarse-meshed: of a number of groups it tells us only that so many members of each conformed to a norm or failed to do so, and only that so many members of each expressed liking for other members or failed to do so. The research may lump together as conformists people who conformed for different reasons, some for the norm's sake and some for the approval's. It may lump together liking of different degrees, or confuse a low degree of approval with a high degree of positive disapproval. But so long as our argument is right in finding any link between conformity and social approval, we should expect such a study to show that the larger the number of members that conform to a group norm, the larger is the number that express social approval for other members. We cannot say that one variable in this corollary is the cause and the other the effect, for the liking may have produced the conformity as well as conformity the liking. But grossly and statistically we should expect the relationship to hold good, and we shall now see that it does.

Conformity and Liking

The first piece of research we shall consider formed part of a larger study reported by Festinger, Schachter, and Back.[2] Right after World War II the Massachusetts Institute of Technology built two temporary housing projects to meet the influx of married students and their wives. The elder project was called Westgate and the younger Westgate West, and Westgate is the one that will mostly concern us here. The couples lived in flats in one-story houses, and the houses were roughly grouped into nine courts, each given a name. The houses of a court faced one another across a grass plot.

Early in the life of the project, the students set up an organization to look after their interests as tenants, especially in dealing with the university administration. The investigators interviewed every couple and among other things found out how each felt about the tenants' organization: whether they were favorable toward it or not, and how much time they devoted to its activities: whether they were active in it or not. According to their attitude toward and activity in the organization, a couple would fall into one of four classes: favorable-inactive, favorable-active, unfavorable-inactive, and unfavorable-active. For obvious reasons there were no members of the last class, which left three.

The investigators next examined the distribution among the Westgate courts of the couples belonging to the different classes, and discovered that in nearly every court a majority of the couples belonged to a single one of the three classes. The position of the majority might differ from one court to another—in one it might be favorable-active, in another unfavorable-inactive—but there was a definite majority position in every court but one, and even in that court a single class held a strong plurality. So unlike was this distribution from anything chance might have brought about that the investigators felt justified in calling the majority or plurality class in each court the *court standard*. We should call it the group norm.

That a majority of couples living in a particular court followed the

[2] L. Festinger, S. Schachter, and K. W. Back, *Social Pressures in Informal Groups* (New York, 1950).

court standard in their opinion and behavior did not, of course, mean that all couples followed it. The investigators called the members of the majority in any particular court *conformers* and the members of all other classes *deviates*. Let us make sure we understand just what this meant. A couple that was unfavorable to and inactive in the tenants' organization, and lived in a court whose standard was unfavorable-inactive, counted as conformists; whereas if they had lived in a court whose standard was favorable-active or favorable-inactive they would have counted as deviates. The courts differed a good deal in the percentage of conformers in their whole membership, the figure ranging from 77 per cent in one court to 46 per cent in the single court where the standard was followed by only a plurality. The proportion of conformers (and hence of deviates) in the courts is one of the two variables that this study related to each other.

In their interviews the investigators also asked each couple the following question: "What three people in Westgate or Westgate West do you see most of socially?" Apparently in order to avoid having an extra variable to deal with, the investigators allowed each couple only a fixed number of choices. Without this restriction the couples no doubt would have varied greatly in the number of choices they made. The question as asked appears to refer to our interaction variable, to the sheer frequency of social contact between couples. In practice, the investigators always refer to the answers as friendship-choices, as if they had a sentimental component. We shall follow the same practice, and justify it later by showing why interaction is often linked to interpersonal liking.

From the raw data, the investigators readily calculated a score showing the number of friendship-choices made by couples living in any one court and given to other couples living in the same court, as a percentage of the total choices made by court-members, the scores ranging from 67 to 47 per cent. This constituted the second variable, which the investigators, as members of the Festinger Group, called *cohesiveness*.

There remained only to relate the variables to one another. The investigators put the courts in rank-order according to their percentages of conformers, put them also in rank-order of cohesiveness, and calculated the correlation between the two rank-orders. They found it very high: "The more cohesive the court (that is, the greater the proportion of 'in-court' choices), the smaller the proportion of people who deviated from the court standard."[3] We cannot fail to see that this is the same proposition we stated earlier in the chapter.

The investigators recognized that their measure of cohesiveness might be misleading. Suppose that half the couples in a court chose one another, that the other half also chose one another, but that no couple in one half chose any couple in the other. The index of cohesiveness would then show the court to be highly cohesive, whereas in any ordinary sense of the word it would hardly be cohesive at all but deeply divided into two, possibly antagonistic, subgroups. The investigators corrected their measure so as to allow for this possibility, and then recalculated the correlation. They found it to be higher than ever, and they concluded that a low percentage of deviates really was related to something that might be called general or widely diffused friendliness within a court.[4] In other studies of this sort no such correction was made, and in that case we cannot rule out the possibility that high in-group choice disguised deep division.

The finding for Westgate was rammed home by its contrast with the finding for Westgate West, the second housing project. The buildings of Westgate West were of two stories; they all faced one way in rows instead of clustering around courts, and they had been more recently built and occupied than those of Westgate. Westgate West, indeed, may have been so new at the time of the study that its residents had not had time to develop standards of behavior and attitude characteristic of each building, such as had certainly developed in the courts at Westgate. Of course it was possible to discover for each building in Westgate West what sort of opinion and behavior toward the tenants' organization had been adopted by the largest number of couples. But these "standards" did not seem to operate as true group standards like those of Westgate. The individual couples decided about the tenants' organization without much influence, whether successful or unsuccessful, from other residents of their building. The buildings differed greatly, and far more than did the courts of Westgate, in the number of their "deviates," which would hardly have been the case if much social pressure had been applied. And accordingly the investigators found in Westgate West no correlation between conformity and cohesiveness

[3] L. Festinger, S. Schachter, and K. W. Back, op. cit., p. 93.
[4] Ibid., pp. 94-95.

such as stood clearly revealed in Westgate. It was not that the correlation was different: statistically there was no correlation between the two variables at all. Let us take note of the fact that here, as often elsewhere, the relationship between two variables may itself be dependent on the value of a third variable, and that as this changes the relationship may disappear or even reverse itself.

But we have not done with the M.I.T. housing projects. A further question is this: What do we know about the deviates besides the sheer fact that they were deviates? Earlier in the chapter we argued, in effect, that the reason why the number of conformers in a group should vary with the number of members expressing liking for other members was that individual deviates would not be liked, so that the more there were of them, the less would be the general friendliness. The Festinger study showed that the conclusion held good, but did the premise also? We may have been right for the wrong reasons. To answer the question we must know about the choices given to individual deviates and not just the general level of friendliness in a group. Comfortably enough, the investigators and ourselves seem to have been right for the right reasons; for deviates received not only from members of their own court but from members of other courts fewer choices than they gave, whereas conformers received more than they gave. What is more, deviates in one court, when making choices in other courts, tended to choose conformers rather than fellow deviates. That is to say: deviates tended not to get together among themselves.

This information about deviates is no more than we had a right to expect. What we did not expect, though we shall later come to do so, are facts of another kind. Although most of the Westgate buildings faced one another around courts, a few corner buildings faced away from the courts, and the entrances to their flats opened on the street and not the grass plots. From these corner buildings deviates were especially likely to come. We cannot be sure why they did so, but we can make a guess or two. Because of their isolated location, couples in these buildings were less likely to come into easy interaction with fellow members of their court than were couples more centrally placed, and therefore other members were less likely to try to get them to conform to court standards. Moreover, these couples may have judged that even if they did conform, they were unlikely to reap the full reward in social acceptance. When one is giving a party, one has trouble remembering people that live in out-of-the-way places, and it costs one more to find and invite them.

In this connection, it is interesting that those few couples who deviated even though they lived in central flats on the inside of the courts received even fewer friendship-choices than did deviates on the corners. These couples must certainly have been subjected to influence. In failing to comply with it they were withdrawing from the others, much more conspicuously than the corner deviates who geographically were not members of the court at all, a reward the others had reason to expect. Hence the hostility toward them was greater. If all the signs show you to be a member of the group but you do not behave like one, the other members will be even more against you than against someone who behaves just the way you do but whom they have had no reason to consider a member. Whether or not our explanation is correct, let us at least remember that deviates tended to come from corner houses, for in a later chapter we shall take up geographical location as one of the environmental determinants of social behavior.

Besides friendship-choices and conformity to group norms, the investigators in the course of their interviews learned many other things about the students' social life. For some couples, social life centered in Westgate; for others, the parties they went to and the friends they visited lay mostly outside. Putting this information together with the other things they knew, the investigators found that deviates were much more apt than conformers to get their society outside the project. Once again we know the facts but not their reasons, which might be of two different kinds. Before they came under the influence of fellow members of their court, a couple might already have formed social ties outside. Commanding this alternative source of social reward, they would find the approval they might get from fellow members relatively less valuable, and so their inducement to conform would be weaker. In this case, their outside ties would be a cause of their deviance.

But there is another possibility. A couple might have had no outside social ties before coming into the project. If they nevertheless failed to conform, the other members of their court would have denied them social reward, and this in turn would have led them to look for it on the outside. In this case, their deviance would be a cause of their outside ties. No doubt both processes were at work at Westgate, but all we know for sure is the mere fact of the correlation between deviance and outside social ties. What is more, this confession may be a sign that we have milked the Westgate research dry.

Output and Liking

The second piece of research we shall examine was the work of Stanley Seashore.[5] We shall limit ourselves to that part of his research most nearly comparable to the M.I.T. study. The results of the two researches are much alike in spite of their differences in setting.

The research was carried out in a large factory in the Middle West making heavy machinery and employing between ten and twenty thousand workers. The smallest recognized unit of human organization in the plant was the "section" of from ten to thirty men assigned to a particular manufacturing job. Sometimes duplicate sections followed one another on successive shifts. For the investigator these sections were the groups to be studied, just as the courts were the groups studied by the investigators at Westgate. For various practical reasons, such as his failure to get reliable production records for some sections, the investigator was forced to leave some of them out. He wound up studying 228 sections with a total of 5871 members.

One of the two main variables in the study was the productivity of workers. For those jobs in which output could be measured as the number of pieces finished in a given time—and these were the jobs included in the research—management had set up standards of production by time-study, and informed the workers every day of their productivity expressed as a percentage of the standard. If a man produced four pieces of work a day on a job for which the standard called for five, his productivity was 80 per cent. This procedure allowed the investigators, as it did the management, to compare the productivity of workers doing wholly different jobs. One man might be welding, another machining, but their productivity was the same if each produced 80 per cent of the standard for his own job. The investigator got a record in this form of the average productivity for three months of every worker in the sections he studied.

[5] S. E. Seashore, *Group Cohesiveness in the Industrial Work Group* (Ann Arbor, 1954).

The second main variable was the cohesiveness of the group, just as it was in the M.I.T. study, but in the present one the investigator measured it in a more complicated way. He asked all the workers in his sections to answer a questionnaire that included, among others, the following three questions: Do you feel that you are really part of your work-group? If you had a chance to do the same kind of work for the same pay, in another work-group, how would you feel about moving? How does your work-group compare with other work-groups in the factory on each of the following points: the way the men get along together, the way they stick together, and the way they help each other on the job? From the answers to such questions the investigator calculated a score for each worker and a score for the average cohesiveness of the members of a section. The larger the number of men in a section that said that they felt part of the group, wanted to stay in it, and thought it was better than other comparable groups, the higher the section scored on cohesiveness. It seems quite fair that the investigator should call this an index of cohesiveness, as it evidently tried to measure the reward workers got from associating with others in their section.

Now that we have seen the way the underlying variables were measured, let us look at the relations between them. The more cohesive a section was, the more likely it was to show little variability in the productivity of its members. That is, the greater the liking members expressed for their association with other members of their section, the more similar they were in productivity. The investigator did not take time to make a firsthand field study of any section, but no one familiar with American industry would doubt that sections whose members were similar in productivity must have been sections whose members had adopted, and largely conformed to, an output norm such as we described earlier in this chapter. If this interpretation is correct, the first finding of the factory study is exactly the same as that of the M.I.T. study: the more cohesive the group, the larger is the number of its members that conform to a group norm.

Someone familiar with industry would also guess that in the more cohesive groups productivity as reported in the output records may not have been quite the same as actual productivity. Workers that adopt an output norm are often in a position to control their output records by reporting as produced more or less work than they have really produced; and their norm is not just that the actual output of the workers should be alike but that their reported output should be so. Should this have been the case, it would not invalidate the findings of the investigator, for a norm of reported output is just as truly a norm as a norm of actual output, and conformity with it is just as truly conformity.

When the investigator said that members of a cohesive section were apt to be similar in productivity, he implied nothing about the level at which they were similar. One section might have adopted for its norm a high level of production, say 120 per cent of standard; another might have adopted a much lower one, say 80 per cent of standard. Why a section adopted the particular level that it did the investigator could only have explained if he had made a detailed study of each section, especially the past history of its relations with management. But this formed no part of his design. So long as the members' output clustered close to 120 per cent in one section and close to 80 per cent in another, the two were alike in the aspect of behavior that interested the investigator, which was the degree of uniformity within the group. In this he resembled the investigators in the Westgate study, who cared little what the particular standard of a court might have been so long as they could count the number of members that conformed to it.

From the finding about within-group similarity in productivity, a finding about between-group similarity followed directly. The investigator divided the total number of sections into two parts, putting the high-cohesive sections in one and the low-cohesive sections in another. And he found that the between-group variability in productivity was greater in the high-cohesive groups than in the low-cohesive ones. But let us put this more clearly. The productivity score of a group was the average productivity of its members. Compared with one another, the productivity scores of the low-cohesive groups scattered themselves less widely over a range of possible scores than did those of the high-cohesive groups, again compared with one another. Part of the reason for this we have already seen. High-cohesive groups were those whose members tended to cleave to an output norm, but the absolute level at which they set the norm could be anywhere: high, middle, or low. Accordingly a comparison of the scores of such groups might show them widely dispersed over a range: their between-group variability was high.

Unlike those of a high-cohesive group, the individual members of any single low-cohesive group tended to be widely dispersed in their productivity. Instead of clustering near a norm, their individual production records might be low, middle, or high. For this very reason, the productivity score of the group as a whole—the average productivity of its members—would tend to fall near the middle of the possible range. And since the same thing tended to hold good of other low-cohesive groups, and their scores, too, fell near the middle of the range, the dispersal of their productivity scores was low—or at least lower than that of the high-cohesive groups. The high-cohesive groups were low in within-group, but high in between-group, variability; the low-cohesive groups were high in within-group, but low in between-group, variability. Of course these two findings are not independent of one another: they are the same finding looked at in different ways.

Just as in the M.I.T. study we learned more about the deviates than simply the fact that they were deviates, so in the present study we learn more about the members of high-cohesive groups than just the fact that they were high-cohesive. The investigator discovered that they were more apt than members of low-cohesive groups to have the following characteristics: to be similar to one another in age, to be of long-standing service in the company, and to feel that other people in the company thought they had good jobs. All of these things might have served to increase their cohesiveness. As we shall see in a later chapter, people that are similar in background—and age is one way of being similar—are apt to be people who have learned to emit and to enjoy the same kinds of activities, and so are well able to reward one another. People who have long service in a company are apt to have good jobs in a company, and indeed the high-cohesive members said that others thought their jobs were good ones. As we shall see in another later chapter, groups whose members are of high status are often highly cohesive, because interaction with others of high status is itself rewarding. But just as with the M.I.T. research we postponed further consideration of geographical location, so with this one we shall postpone further consideration of social background as an environmental determinant of social behavior.

Summary

Men give social approval, as a generalized reinforcer, to others that have given them activity they value, and so make it more likely that the others will go on giving the activity. One of the kinds of activity some men find valuable is that their own behavior and that of others they are associated with in a group should be similar in conforming to a norm, a norm being a statement of what their behavior ought to be in given circumstances. Why they should find the conformity valuable is beyond the province of this book to explain. Though some values are not difficult to explain, we take them simply as given. People that find conformity valuable reward conformers with social approval, but they withhold approval from those that will not conform, or even express positive dislike for nonconformists as having denied them a reward they had the right to expect.

Some members of a group conform for the norm's sake, that is, for the external reward, such as protection from management, that conformity gets them; and some for the approval's sake, but both will come to say that they do it for the norm's. The more a member values an activity incompatible with conformity—and again we do not undertake to explain why he should do so—and the more valuable are his sources of social approval other than the conformers in his group, the less likely he is to conform: a companion in misery is still a companion. As groups approach practical equilibrium, when all who can be induced to conform have done so, and all who cannot have not, at least one corollary to our set of general propositions seems to hold good: the larger the number of members that conform to a norm, the larger the number that express approval for other members.

Competition

So far in this book we have been largely concerned with the exchange of rewarding activities, particularly the giving of some kind of service, including conformity to a norm, in return for expressions of social approval. But if we confine ourselves to behavior of this sort, we are sure to call down upon our heads the wrath of the social scientists who make a profession of being tough-minded. "Never play down conflict," they would say. "Not only is conflict a fact of social life, but conflict has positive virtues and brings out some of the best in men." It turns out that these very scientists are no more willing than is the rest of mankind to encourage conflict within any body of men they themselves are responsible for. Conflict is good for other people's subordinates, not their own. But we must refrain. It is all too easy to ask men to practice what they preach. A trap that none can escape is no fun setting. On the general point the tough-minded are surely right: no one can deny, or ever has denied, that conflict is a fact of social life; and as students of elementary social behavior we had better devote a short chapter to the exchange of punishing activities, if only to show we are aware of it. We shall also need it to explain some of the phenomena that will turn up in later chapters.

Cooperation and Competition

In practice we shall confine ourselves to one sort of punishment. People can hurt one another directly, as by trading blows, but they can also do so by depriving one another of rewards. They can either present negative reinforcers or withdraw positive ones. The first case is so obvious that we shall not bother with it further, but consider only the second. So far we have been mostly concerned with cooperation between men. Cooperation occurs when, by emitting activities to one another, or by emitting activities in concert to the environment, at least two men achieve a greater total reward than either could have achieved by working alone. In the example we have used so often, Person and Other by working together get respectively more help and more approval than either could have gotten without cooperating. The situation usually contrasted with cooperation is competition. The contrast need not lie in the fact that the two men now work alone. It means rather that each emits activity that, so far as it is rewarded, tends by that fact to deny reward to the other. The activity, if reinforced, withdraws reinforcement from the other. In this chapter we shall be concerned with competition as a special form of conflict.

According to common sense and the elementary considerations we put forward in Chapters 2 through 4, a person who punishes another by denying him a reward is apt to arouse in him the emotional reaction of anger. Compared, therefore, with two men in cooperation with each other, we should expect two men in competition to express little liking for each other; and since they are not exchanging rewards, we should expect them to interact with each other no more than they can help, except to trade hostile actions.

Obviously matters are not as simple as this. The competition, as in many games, may be interesting enough in itself to provide rewards that outweigh the costs of losing. Since, moreover, competition is apt to result in one man's deprivation relative to another, it always raises the question of distributive justice. If both competitors accept the rules of the game and play fair according to the rules, then it is just and right that the man who has played better should win and the loser's natural hostility will be much diminished. Even so, there is plenty of evidence that it is hard work being a good loser: it goes against the old Adam. Even in games, the threat of hostilities is always present and may even add to the excitement. In short, the proposition that loss in competition tends to arouse anger remains true, though its truth is sometimes masked by stronger forces.

Naturally there is nothing in what we have said to prevent the competitors' learning how to divide the rewards of their activities between themselves instead of each man's trying to deny reward to the other. Under these conditions, they may interact often and express much mutual liking—but then they are cooperating and no longer competing.

Cooperation versus Competition Between Individuals

A good piece of research on the questions we have just raised, research that brings out clearly some results hardly surprising in themselves, was carried out by Morton Deutsch.[1] His subjects were about fifty students in a course in elementary psychology at the Massachusetts Institute of Technology. Before the experiment began, the investigator had every subject take certain personality tests. Using the results of the tests, he formed ten groups of five men each, each group matched with the rest in its members' range of ability and personality. He then had each group discuss a problem in human relations, gave it a score on the productivity of its discussion, and then formed two sets of five groups each, each set including the same proportion of high- and low-scoring groups. Having matched groups and sets of groups, he was ready for the experiment proper.

Each group in both sets met separately once a week for a number of weeks. At each session the investigator gave the members two problems: a logical puzzle and a problem in human relations. The members were to discuss each problem, reach a solution, write it up, and turn the report in to the investigator. Since the logical puzzle admitted of a single best solution, while the human-relations problem did not, he expected that each would bring out a different sort of discussion.

So far the investigator had treated the two sets of groups the same way. Where they differed was in the way the members were to be

---

[1] M. Deutsch, "The Effects of Cooperation and Competition upon Group Process," in D. Cartwright and A. Zander, eds., *Group Dynamics: Research and Theory* (Evanston, 1953), pp. 319-53.

rewarded. In every one of the five groups that got the *cooperative* treatment, he told the members that every week he would give them a score, as a group, on how well they worked together in solving the puzzle problem, and that every member of the group achieving the highest average score for the whole series of meetings would be excused from writing one term paper in the course but would nevertheless receive the highest grade he could have gotten for the paper. In the same way, the investigator would score, for quantity and quality, the discussions and solutions of the human-relations problem. Every member of the group that received the highest average score would receive the highest grade; every member of the group that received the next highest score would receive the next highest grade, and so on. In short, in the cooperative treatment every member of a group would receive the same reward for his participation, and the value of his reward would depend on how well his group did.

In the *competitive* treatment, the investigator told the members of each group that every week he would rank each member on the amount he personally contributed to the solution of the puzzle problem, and that the member who achieved the highest average score for the whole series of meetings would be excused from one term paper but get the highest grade. In the same way, he would rank each member on his personal contribution to the discussion of the human-relations problem, and would give the member that received the highest average score the highest grade, and so on. In short, in the competitive treatment the reward obtained by each member would depend only on his individual activity and not at all on how well his group did. Moreover, a high score received by one man necessarily meant a lower score received by others. Yet just like the members of a cooperative group, the members of a competitive one were required to turn in, as a group, written solutions to the problems set before them.

The investigator expected the different conditions to produce different kinds of behavior. To discover what the differences were, he had four observers watch each meeting of each group, recording certain specific kinds of behavior while the meeting was going on, and, after the meeting, making certain over-all ratings of the members' behavior. When a meeting had ended, the investigator also asked the members themselves to answer a questionnaire, and then again, one week after the last meeting, he asked them to answer another questionnaire about the experiment as a whole. We need not describe the observations and questionnaires in detail, but only look at some of the more interesting results.

One of our main propositions says that the more valuable the reward a man gets by emitting a particular activity, the more often he will emit it. In the cooperative groups, a member was to be rewarded for any activity that contributed to his group's doing well; in the competitive groups, each member was to be rewarded only for his own activity, regardless of the success of his group. True, he did not get the reward during the course of the experiment itself: it was to come later. But it is much to the credit of American teachers that the occasions in the past on which they have promised rewards have generally been occasions on which the appropriate behavior on the part of their students has in fact been rewarded—in short, they have kept their promises—and therefore their promises are apt to stimulate their students to appropriate activity on the next occasion. It is, then, hardly surprising that members of cooperative groups displayed much cooperative behavior, and members of competitive groups much competitive behavior.

Specifically, the two sets of groups did not differ in "involvement," as rated by the observers, or in interest in the task, as rated by their own answers to the questionnaires. But they did differ greatly in other ways. Members of cooperative groups were more likely to express interest in the ideas of their fellow members—and, after all, the others' ideas might contribute to rewarding *them*. The observers also rated the members of these groups as more "group-centered" and better at working together—and, after all, they were rewarded for working together. Members of competitive groups, on the other hand, expressed a greater desire to excel others—and, after all, they were to be rewarded if they excelled others. In short, the investigator got from each set of groups the kind of behavior he was prepared to reward, and it would have been startling if he had not.

Less directly obvious but still thoroughly in line with our propositions were the findings that members of cooperative groups expressed greater friendliness for one another than did members of competitive ones, gave others more encouragement, and expressed less aggression toward them. As we have seen over and over again, social approval is a generalized reinforcer that a man may use to reward, and so render more probable, the emission by another of any activity that rewards *him*. In the cooperative groups, almost any idea that a member put forward might contribute to the solution of the problems. Therefore it was apt to reward his fellow members and bring out their approval in return. In the competitive groups, on the contrary, the good ideas that a member expressed would help him but hurt his fellow members. His good ideas, by getting him a high score, would withdraw reward from the rest. Hostility is a common reaction to the withdrawal of a reward, and therefore in the competitive groups friendliness was at a low ebb and aggression high.

We must now consider findings that are still less obvious until we come to think about them—but something that takes thinking about before it seems obvious is not obvious at all. Two men reward each other, and thus cooperate with each other, when each provides the other with a service that he could not do for himself at all or could not do at such low cost. Sometimes the services the two men provide are similar, as when both put their weight into moving a rock neither could move alone. But often the services are different, which means that each man becomes a specialist as far as their cooperation is concerned. Thus in our example, Other became, in effect, a specialist in giving help and Person a specialist in giving approval. Competition, at least under the conditions we are interested in here, is much less likely to promote specialization and the division of labor. People who compete with one another are after the same reward, and when, as is often the case, the reward may only be obtained through one kind of activity, the activities of competitors are apt to become similar rather than different. Indeed some business firms make this a conscious rule of competition. If a competitor is selling two lines of goods, the firm must sell goods in the same two lines. To leave the other an unchallenged market in one line and compete with him only in the other is to hand him a better over-all competitive position, and thus the goods sold by the two firms tend to get more alike. In short, cooperators are more apt than competitors to differ from one another in the kinds of activity they put out.

How did this difference show itself in the experiment? The observers kept a record of the total amount of time every member contributed to the discussion of the problems. That is, they recorded how much he interacted with the other members of his group. They reported more "communications difficulties" in the competitive groups than in the cooperative ones—and, after all, the members of those groups could reap little reward from listening to their competitors' ideas. The observers also found that competitive groups did not differ from cooperative ones in the total amount of interaction, at least in the discussion of the human-relations problems; and this finding runs counter to our expectation that other things equal, competitors, since they are not rewarding one another, will interact with one another less than co-operators will. But in this case the other things were not equal. In the competitive groups, members were to be rewarded for their individual contributions, in quantity and quality. But what they were contributing to was supposed to be a discussion. That is, they had to speak up and announce their ideas to the others before they could get any advantage at all. Though they had no need to listen, they certainly needed to talk, and for this reason there was as much interaction in competitive groups as in cooperative ones. This was more true of the human-relations problems, for which there was no single best solution, than it was of the logical puzzles, in which a member of a competitive group could get a high score by thinking quietly and saying nothing until he was ready to come up with the one right answer.

Although the two sets of groups did not differ in their total amount of interaction, they did differ significantly in the way the interaction was distributed among the members. Members of competitive groups were more nearly alike in the amount they interacted than were the members of cooperative ones. In the competitive groups a man could hope to get a high grade only if he himself talked: he could not afford to let anyone else do all the talking. Accordingly, discussion in these groups tended to find all members participating more or less equally. In the cooperative groups, on the other hand, a member who had nothing useful to say could shut up, let better men talk, and still hope to get a good grade. His grade was the grade of his group, and anyone who could raise the level of the group's discussion could reward *him,* just as he could reward the others just by keeping still. He also served by only standing and waiting. For this reason, members of cooperative groups differed greatly among themselves in the amount they interacted.

A division of labor means differences in labor. A man who shuts up and lets others talk is differentiating his behavior from that of the others. He is none the less a specialist for the fact that his specialization is keeping still. This tendency of members of cooperative groups to show greater differences among themselves in the ways they behaved than did members of competitive groups showed itself also in the way they went about writing up the solutions to the problems. In these groups, particularly in the human-relations problems, two or more members would be writing up different parts of the solution at the same time. In the competitive groups it was more usual that each member in turn would take over the job of writing up the whole solution, while the others gathered around and told him what to write. Once again, the members of these groups tended to make their contributions similar and equal. Moreover the written solution made little difference to members of a competitive group. Though they were required to turn one in as a group, it could not reward them. Only their individual contributions, not their joint contributions, could reward them, and for this purpose it was better to talk than to write.

We turn finally to the difficult question of the differences between the two sets of groups in what the investigator calls their productivity. The cooperative groups solved the puzzle problems more rapidly than did the competitive ones, whose members had little to gain by helping one another out. For the human-relations problems, since they admitted of no single best solution, there could be no such clear-cut measure of productivity as the time taken to reach a solution; but at least the cooperative groups wrote more words in the reports they turned in to the investigator than did the competitive ones, to whom, as we have seen, the report in itself made little difference. Another and very different measure of productivity brought results that must have saddened the heart of the high-minded investigator. From the grades that the students received in the first term paper following the experiment, there was no evidence that the members of cooperative groups had learned any more psychology in the course of the experiment than had the members of competitive ones. However much the cooperators may have helped one another in other ways, they did not help one another to learn.

In any case we shall be in no hurry to draw from this experiment any general conclusion that cooperation is better than competition, or the group better than the individual, for accomplishing any task. All depends on what we mean by "better," including the long- and short-term costs of being "better." There are of course situations in which a group is clearly better than an individual in the sense that the group can do something that a single man could not do at all: two men may be able to move a rock that one man alone could hardly stir. But when the job could be done either by an individual or by a group, the problem gets more difficult. Take the case of the logical puzzles. Suppose the rest of us could not solve puzzles ourselves but needed to get them solved. Apparently a cooperative group can solve them faster than a bunch of competing individuals, and if we wanted the answers urgently enough, we might ask a group to give us them. But a group whose members can get together to solve puzzles may also be a group whose members can combine to establish a monopoly of puzzle solving and make the rest of us pay a high price for their work, while competing individuals may be much less well able to do so. If we needed the answers less urgently, we might prefer to give the job to the individuals and settle for slower solutions at a lower price per solution. This is the problem of what is better in the long run.

Then there is the problem of alternative uses of manpower. Suppose we were employing men to solve logical puzzles and to do other kinds of work. A group of five men working together can solve a logical puzzle faster than can five men working in competition with one another. But while the first five are working as a group they are all tied up, and none of them can be spared for other work; whereas the second five are essentially working as individuals, which means that we who have other things we could use these men for can leave one of them to work on the puzzle and set the rest to work elsewhere. Unless the individual we left were an outstanding logician, the advantage of the group might be even more pronounced. But except when we needed a solution in a hurry, it would not be enough for the group to solve the puzzle faster than the individual. Unless it solved it five times faster, putting the group to work on the problem would be an inefficient use of manpower. Most comparisons between groups and individuals in their effectiveness at accomplishing tasks put the individuals at an unfair disadvantage by failing to look at the alternative uses for their time. So let us not be carried away by the easy assumption made by many American social scientists that there is something inherently good about cooperation and bad about competition, everywhere and across the board. Let us examine each case on its merits.

Rivalry Between Groups

Let us now turn from competition between individuals to competition between groups, and look at the effects of competition on the structure of a group. The experiment we shall use to illustrate this point was carried out by John Thibaut.[2] The subjects were boys from ten to twelve years old attached to settlement houses and summer camps near Boston. The boys came to the experiment in groups of ten to twelve members each who had known one another, who had lived and played together, for some time. The investigator began by asking every boy to answer a questionnaire in which he was to put down in order of his preference the four other boys he would most like to have on his team if his group was divided into two teams to play games. With the benefit of this information, the investigator did in fact divide each group into two teams of from five to six boys each. As far as he possibly could, he arranged each team so that every member would find about an equal number of the boys he had chosen on his own team and on the other one. The investigator also arranged that an equal number of the more popular boys would be on each team. These popular boys—those in the top half of each team in the number of choices received—he called the *central* members; the rest he called the *peripheral* ones.

The investigator was now ready for the experiment proper. He had the two teams from each group play a series of four games, in each of which one of the teams had to serve or assist the other, to take the less interesting and inferior part. "In one game they served as 'human arches' for the other team to run under, in another they were a 'human chain' for the other team to buck against, and in the third game they held the target for, and retrieved, thrown beanbags"—beanbags thrown by members of the other team. The same teams took the inferior position in all the first three games. These the investigator called the *low-status* teams; the others, who regularly took the superior position, he called the *high-status* teams.

After the first three games, an observer encouraged the members of

[2] J. Thibaut, "An Experimental Study of the Cohesiveness of Underprivileged Groups," *Human Relations,* Vol. 3 (1950), pp. 251-78.

the low-status teams to protest unanimously to the investigator about the way they had been treated, and this they were not backward in doing. With half these teams the investigator accepted the protest and allowed them to take the superior position in the fourth and last game: he allowed them to throw the beanbags, which was the game the boys found most fun. But he rejected the protest of the other half and kept them in the inferior position for the last game. Thus there were, according to the treatment they received, four kinds of teams:

1. Consistently low-status.
2. Consistently high-status.
3. Successful low-status (who took the superior position for the last game).
4. Displaced high-status (who lost their superior position for the last game).

During the games observers kept records of the amount and kinds of behavior, verbal or other, produced by the members of each team; and after the last game the boys answered a questionnaire similar to the one they started with.

Some of the results were just what might have been expected. Before being divided into teams, the members of each pair of teams had all belonged to the same group, and the teams were equal in the number of popular boys each possessed. Nothing, therefore, in the backgrounds of the two teams justified the fact that one of them got preferential treatment. For one team to take the most interesting part in every game clearly violated the rules of distributive justice. Not only was the other team deprived of reward, but unjustly deprived, and its members displayed the characteristic emotional reaction. As it became increasingly clear over the first three games that they were getting unfair treatment, their hostile communications directed at the high-status team steadily increased in amount. After that, the communications of the successful low-status teams—those that had displaced the high-status teams for the favored position in the last game—fell off rapidly, while those of the unsuccessful teams mounted still further but became a little less aggressive, as if the members were beginning to give up hope of bettering their lot as far as the games were concerned and were trying instead to get in with their more favored opponents.

The high-status teams did little to return these attacks. Presumably they held the same standards of justice. Though willing enough to take advantage of their favored position, they felt guilty and embarrassed. There was no reply they could make when the low-status teams complained that they were unfairly treated, for it was an obvious fact. Their emotional reaction, if we may call it that, was to avoid their less favored opponents.

More interesting, because less obvious, were the results of the questionnaire that all the boys took after the last game. Compared with the way they had chosen before the games began, the members of all teams tended to shift their choices toward members of their own team and away from the other team. But within this over-all tendency, there were great differences in the amount by which within-team choice increased, both as between teams of different sorts and as between central and peripheral members. The least increase, and it was so small as not to be statistically significant, took place in the successful low-status teams and in the high-status ones they had displaced in the last game. For these teams something had been done to meet the conditions of justice and to make their status equal by exalting the humble and bringing down the proud—especially as the last game was beanbags and the most interesting of all. Neither team in these pairs was consistently superior over the whole series of games, neither remained very hostile toward the other, and accordingly boys on one team did not remain alienated from their old friends on the other.

We are left with the consistently high- and the consistently low-status teams and with their central and peripheral members. The order of the different categories of subjects in the amount by which they increased the number of their within-team choices was the following:

1. Peripheral members of high-status teams.
2. Central members of low-status teams.
3. Central members of high-status teams.
4. Peripheral members of low-status teams.

Between the first two of these categories the increase in within-team choice was statistically significant.

How shall we explain this rank-order? We believe that two sorts of effect, one positive and one negative, tended to increase choice within teams. Positive was the effect of the increased reward a boy got from being a member of a high-status team. Ultimately, of course, he got this reward from the experimenter, but he got it through his association with the other members of his own team and therefore we should expect his liking for them to increase. Negative was the effect of the hostility expressed toward him by members of the low-status team, which tended to cut him off from his old friends in that team and so increase his relative friendliness toward members of his own team. This effect is most eloquently described in the words of the old song: "I don't give a damn for any damn man who don't give a damn for me."

These tendencies had different strengths within different categories of boys. The first of the two effects—the reward effect—was apparently the more generally powerful. For the greatest change toward within-group choice occurred among the peripheral members of high-status groups, and they were just the boys that had gained most by their favored treatment. From ranking as second-class citizens in their original groups they had, in effect, risen into the privileged class. They responded by increasing greatly the liking they expressed for the other boys in whose company they had won these rewards. We do not argue that the hostility expressed toward them by members of the other team played no part in repelling them toward their own, but we can only explain the magnitude of their increased choice by pointing to their increased reward.

But the second, or hostility, effect was powerful too. For if the greatest change toward within-team choice occurred among the boys who had gained most, the second greatest occurred among those who had lost most. The experiment brought the central members of low-status teams down in the world. From ranking as first-class citizens in their original groups they had become members of the proletariat. And they had been brought down unjustly: there was nothing in their previous records as popular boys that justified any such treatment. Theirs was the greatest relative deprivation measured out to any set of boys in the experiment, and they repaid with hostility the others who had benefited at their expense. There is evidence from the records the observers kept of behavior during the games that, in return, they provoked many hostile reactions from members of the high-status teams. And thus repelled, they turned their expressions of liking inward, toward their companions in misery.

The third largest increase occurred among the central members of high-status teams. They had benefited from the favored treatment given their teams, but not as much as had the peripheral members, since they, unlike the peripheral members, were of high status to begin with. Accordingly they increased their choice for the boys in whose company they had made these gains, but not nearly as much as did the peripheral members. The increase in liking was proportional to the increase in reward.

Finally, the least increase occurred among peripheral members of low-status groups; it was not statistically significant, and it varied greatly from team to team. If the central members of high-status teams had least to gain from the experimental treatment, these boys had least to lose. They had less to lose than the central members of their own teams, for they were of low status to begin with. At worst they were only confirmed in their position of inferiority: the treatment they received was perfectly consistent with their previous position, so that, in effect, little injustice was done them. Though they expressed some hostility toward members of the high-status teams, and increased their liking for members of their own, they did not do so to any great extent. Indeed they tended to react less with hostility than with efforts to escape. Even before the games they were, as peripheral members of the original groups, getting few social rewards; now they were getting even fewer, and the observers noted that, of all the categories of boys, they were the ones who most often tried to get out of the situation altogether by paying no heed to the games or asking the investigator to let them do something else.

On this interpretation, the order of the different sets of boys in the amount by which they increased friendship-choice within their own teams was their order, first, in the *amount* by which their rewards changed, for better or for worse, in the course of the experiment: the greater the change in reward, the greater the increase in choice; and second, in the *direction* of the change: with the amount of change held constant, an increase in reward produced a greater increase in choice than did an increase in deprivation. The results can be summed up as follows:

1. High-status peripherals—most gain.
2. Low-status centrals—most loss.
3. High-status centrals—least gain.
4. Low-status peripherals—least loss.

Summary

The results of this chapter are elementary indeed. People who compete with one another are in a position to deprive one another of rewards, and the withdrawal of a reward stimulates the emotional reactions of hostility and aggression. The strength of the reaction depends not on the absolute amount of the deprivation but on its amount relative to some standard of distributive justice, and on this point we shall have much more to say in a later chapter. People who compete with one another are not rewarding one another, and, therefore, except for the expression of the hostility itself, their frequency of interaction will be low unless the form of competition requires interaction. People who compete with one another are emitting activities that are rewarded in the same way, and so far as this reward can only be attained by one kind of activity, people who compete are more likely to become similar in their activities than are people who cooperate.

As for competition between groups, it is, for the reasons already given, likely to increase the hostility members of one group express toward members of the other. So far as members of one group previously had friends in the other, the hostility is apt to get in the way of the friendship, and therefore members will be more apt to express social approval for fellow members of their own group. If one of the groups manages to compete successfully, to get rewards for itself and deny them to the other, the members of the group have rewarded one another and will therefore tend to increase their expressions of liking for one another: the greater the reward, the greater the liking. The members of the unsuccessful group have been deprived by the members of the other, and therefore will be hostile toward them: the greater the deprivation, the greater the hostility. And therefore, again, the greater will be the probability that they will express liking for fellow members of their own group. Accordingly, both reward and deprivation may increase within-group choice.

Esteem

Chapter Eight

The present chapter will return to a theme prominent in Chapters 5 and 6: the relation between the activities performed by the members of a group and the sentiments of liking or social approval accorded them by other members. In those chapters the activities in question were acts of compliance—compliance by members to the norms of the group or to requests made of them by other members. So far as they conformed at all, members were equal in their conformity, and they were, for all we knew, equal also in the social approval they received from others. In the present chapter we turn from equality to inequality. In real life the members of a group are apt to be much more elaborately differentiated in the kind of activities they give other members than we have allowed them to be so far, and they are, correspondingly, much more elaborately differentiated in the amount of approval they receive from others. We shall be particularly interested in members who can emit rare and highly rewarding services, and who command in return much approval from many others.

Value and Scarcity

When we say that the members of the groups in earlier chapters were equal in their activities, we speak, of course, too freely. Some of them were—those that conformed to a norm or complied with a request made of them—but not all were, not the deviates. We assumed, moreover, that members either conformed or did not do so, whereas in fact there may be different degrees of conformity. But for the purposes of the present argument let us assume that conformists, as such, are alike in their activity.

What, moreover, do we mean when we say that conformists were equal in the approval they received from others? We mean only that, while deviates certainly got less approval than conformists, the research reports give us no reason to believe that any one conformist received more approval than another. As conformists, they were social equals, though in other respects they may not have been so.

The next question is this: What are the characteristics of an activity for the performance of which men receive roughly equal amounts of social approval from others? To get any approval at all, a man must perform an activity valuable to others; and, as we have argued right along, others often find it valuable that the behavior of one of their companions should, like their own, conform to a norm. Yet from the present point of view what is important about conformity is not just that it is valuable but that it is in ample supply. Any old fool, so to speak, can conform, for many in fact do conform—including the very people that are giving approval in return.

More accurately, the capacity to provide the valuable activity is not just widespread in the group but perceived as being widespread. That is to say, the stimuli associated with the present members of the group are similar to those of men from whom in the past the members have had no trouble getting conformity. A workingman sees no reason why one of his fellows should not work to an output norm and produce just so many pieces of work a day. It looks easy, and so he expects the other to do it if asked. When the other does not do what he expects, he has in effect been deprived of a reward, and he repays deprivation with hostility. Of course the workingman may be wholly wrong in thinking the other "can" conform, for if the other sets a high value on activities incompatible with conformity it is practically very difficult for him to do so. At the same time it is hard to blame the workingman: the obvious stimuli connected with the other man and his job suggest that he could easily stay within the output norm if he only wanted to.

When we say that the capacity to perform an activity is in ample supply we obviously mean that there is a relatively large number of people able and willing to perform it more or less equally well. In that peculiar market in which the members of a group are at once suppliers and demanders of conformity and approval, no one participant can hold out for a higher price in approval in return for his conformity than can any of the others: there are too many suppliers of the same service. Each will get about the same price from the others, and perhaps no very high one at that: if conformity is to be elicited at all, it may not take much approval to bring it out. As we argued in Chapter 6, if there are plenty of potential conformers, no actual conformer receives from the others a very high degree of approval—at least not on that account alone—though he is certainly not rejected. In short, an activity for which men receive roughly equal amounts of social approval is one that a relatively large number of them can supply.

But—and here we strike close to the heart of the present chapter—by no means all the activities that the members of a group find it valuable to receive are in ample supply. Some are in short supply indeed. An example is the service we had Other supply to Person and the Third Man—his ability, founded on superior skill and experience, to advise his friends about their clerical work. Remember that short supply is a relative matter: it is a question of the relation between supply and demand. To be in short supply it is not enough that a service be rare; it must be both rare and valuable to others. Nor is it enough that it be valuable in itself; the number of members that demand it must be large in proportion to the number that can supply it. If only one man wants a particular service that another member can supply, that service is not in as short supply as one that many other members want and only a few are able to supply. And, obviously, for many members to find the same service valuable, many members must, for any number of possible reasons, share the same values. Such a service was Other's advice in our toy society of three men: both Person and the Third Man wanted it, but only Other could supply it. Activities like these are the activities that lead to differences between men in the amount of approval they receive from others.

But even this is not an adequate statement. What do we mean when we say a man "is able" to supply a service? Many men are able, in one sense of the word, to supply services that they do not in fact supply, presumably because the costs they incur in doing so are high relative to the value they put on the rewards they get in return. Only a man who is not only able but willing to supply a rare and valuable service commands high approval from his fellows. Indeed a man who "could" supply a service, in the sense that the signs associated with him resemble those of other men who have supplied the service, but who does not in fact supply it, will not reap approval but resentment. He has deprived his fellows of an expected reward.

In contrast, then, to someone who can only supply a common service, a man who can supply a rare one, valued by many members of his group, is able to command a high price for it in approval. In effect, though not consciously in the sense that they tell themselves they are doing so, several members are bidding against one another for his services, and they run the price up. Whereas a common service like conformity tends to make the members of a group equal in the amount of approval they received from one another, the capacity to supply a rare service gets the men who actually do supply it a larger amount of social approval than other members of their group get. They are superior to the others and no longer their social equals.

But let us speak a little more carefully. What do we mean by "running up the price" of an activity? If many members of a group find it highly rewarding to receive an activity that only a few of their number can supply, and if the few do actually supply the activity to the many, then we should expect—according to the argument put forward in Chapter 4—that each of the members would give either more units of approval or a warmer kind of approval for each unit of the activity they receive than they would have given for an activity less in demand or more in supply. We should also expect that, over a period of time, the men supplying the activity would receive a greater total reward, in terms of number of units of approval times the value per unit, than members providing an activity in ampler supply. Unfortunately our methods are seldom precise enough to measure the exact number of units or, especially, the value per unit. But what, for instance, we can easily do is ask the members to report on their behavior. We can ask them, after a period of time, to say how much approval they give to each of the others, specifically whether they approve of a particular man more than they approve of others. And then, if our argument is correct, we should expect that a man providing such an activity would get more approval from any member who received it than would a man providing an activity in ampler supply. We should further expect that since many members demand and get the service, many of them would give him that amount of approval.

The greater, then, the value of an activity to those receiving it, and the larger the number of members of a group who find it valuable to receive compared with the number who provide it—the more fully the activity possesses both these properties, the greater will be the social approval the man providing it is apt to get from every member he gives it to, and the larger the number of such members is apt to be. We have spoken as if our man put out only one kind of activity. In fact he may put out many kinds, and they may not all win him the same amount of social approval. But let us for the moment assume that they do all win him the same amount, and leave until later the problem of the relationship between his different activities.

Esteem and Status

We want a word for this dimension in which the members of a group differ from one another, and we shall use *esteem* rather than *status*. We define *esteem* as follows: the greater the total reward in expressed social approval a man receives from other members of his group, the higher is the esteem in which they hold him.[1] But this does not mean that we propose to abandon *status*. Social approval is an actual reward, but any activity (or sentiment) may be a stimulus as well as a reward, and we shall use *status* to refer to the stimuli a man presents to other men (and to himself). In other words, we shall use *status* to refer to what men perceive about one of their fellows.

The stimuli that make up a man's status include the kinds of reward he receives—among them his esteem itself—the kinds of activity he emits, and anything else about him, like the kind of clothes he wears or the kind of house he lives in, provided that these stimuli are recognized and discriminated by other men. To serve, moreover, as the sorts of stimuli that determine a man's status, people must be able to rank them, in comparison with the stimuli presented by other men, as relatively "better" or "worse," "higher" or "lower."

[1] See P. M. Blau, *The Dynamics of Bureaucracy* (Chicago, 1955), p. 107. In G. C. Homans, *The Human Group* (New York, 1950), p. 140, I called this dimension *rank,* but *rank* refers to a position in any rank-order, and this particular social ranking is only one of the ways in which men may be ranked.

Thus the fact that one man gets higher pay than another, if known to their companions, gives the first man a higher status than the second, at least as far as that kind of stimulus is concerned. Status is a matter of perception, and of perception that puts stimuli in rank-order.

It is easy to show that esteem is not the same thing as status. In the early stages of the development of a group, several members may give one of their companions much social approval so that he is in fact enjoying high esteem, and yet no single member may have come to recognize what the others are doing. Unless each member perceives not only that he is giving approval to the man in question but that many others are doing so too, esteem cannot be one of the stimuli that make up the man's status; and even then it is never the only one, for everything he does, or is done to him, presents some stimulus to his companions. When the members of a group have been together for some time, when they not only act in certain ways but perceive that they are doing so, a man of high esteem is generally one of recognized high status too, but even then there may be members who admit his high status without themselves according him much social approval. For the next few chapters we shall be much concerned with esteem, with the actual social approval the members of a group emit to one of their number, but in later chapters we shall change the emphasis and have more to say about status. In particular we shall see that men often find it rewarding to manipulate the stimuli they present to others—rewarding because the stimuli help determine what activities the others emit to *them*. The manipulation of status-stimuli becomes itself an activity that may receive social reinforcement.

Let us now make a few general comments on our argument up to the present. It will help us to understand that a man's esteem depends on the relative rarity of the services he provides if we take a larger look at the ways in which a man may help others. Obviously not every man that helps others gets high esteem from them. If he has capacities of heart, mind, skill, experience, or even strength that they do not have, and he uses these capacities to reward others, he will get esteem from them. But if his capacities are of a kind that they also possess, or if these capacities are widely available in the group, he will not get much esteem even if he uses them in such a way as to reward the others. Many workingmen, for instance, help other workingmen in minor ways to do their jobs, as by holding equipment in place while the others work on it. But this kind of help is quite different from the rare skill and experience that Other puts at the service of Person and the Third Man. No doubt it is a convenience; no doubt it is pleasant to get, and the man who gives it will not lack social approval. But a large number of people could have supplied it; above all, the man being helped could have done the same sort of thing himself. It is a valuable service but not a rare one, and because not rare not so very valuable; and it does not command a high price in esteem. Indeed the man providing such a service is a servant rather than a superior of the man being helped.

Roughly stated, the rule, as we all know, is this. If I ask you to do something I cannot do, I recognize you as my superior and my request is no more than a request: you are free to refuse, though if you do so without good reason you forfeit my esteem. If I ask you to do something that I can do too, I admit you to be at best my equal. But if I ask you to do something that I also can do, and there are other valuable things I can do but you cannot, you are my inferior and my request comes close to being a command. For this reason we have the proverb that a leader will not ask his men to do something he would not do himself. But we are getting ahead of our argument.

A more interesting and perhaps more difficult case than helping is joking. Suppose a member of a group is a real humorist, particularly good at cracking jokes. No one can say this is not a rare ability or one that other members will not find valuable, and yet the humorist is seldom held in the highest esteem. The reason may be that, though members enjoy jokes, the pleasure is one that they can forgo without a pang. In competition for esteem with a man who can provide services the members feel they must have, the humorist is apt to come out second best. If, of course, he commands other and more serious abilities besides joking, he may be in good shape, but he seldom seems to have them. Indeed it is his very incapacity in other areas and his willingness to laugh at himself about them that allows him to laugh at others with impunity. For joking is apt to be ambiguous: criticism may be buried in the laugh like a stone in a snowball, but the criticism is still there. One will fail to resent criticism only when it comes from a man who cannot be a serious rival. Hence court jesters must be people who otherwise are out of the market for esteem.

We must mention also one peculiar kind of rare capacity that can bring a man esteem in certain kinds of informal groups, such as boys' gangs. This is a high capacity to coerce with physical violence. It may not look like a rewarding capacity at all, but we must remember that the withdrawal of a threat reinforces behavior that leads to this result, and so, technically, a man who can beat up the other members commands a rare ability to reward them. But even in boys' gangs it is doubtful that physical prowess alone is enough to win a member high esteem. He must be able to provide positive rewards as well, for in boys' gangs it is often easy to escape physical violence by running away.

Let us not be in any hurry to generalize from what happens in the small group to what happens in society at large.[2] The status, pay, and other rewards that go to the more public positions in the larger society may not be determined by the supply of, and demand for, valuable services in quite the same way that esteem is determined in elementary social behavior. Or better, such forces may have determined the status of an occupation when it first appeared on the scene of history, but once the occupation got established as an institution, its status tended to perpetuate itself at a price higher or lower than it might later have fetched in the open social market. Thus the knight on horseback was once in high demand and low supply, and he commanded high status and other emoluments. Even before the use of gunpowder he became a drug on the market, but by that time his heirs had acquired enough land and political power to maintain their status for several centuries. In elementary social behavior, on the other hand, esteem is not to be had unless a man provides for the members of his group social values that they really enjoy and find it hard to come by. Of course an outsider may have trouble understanding why they want them; the values may look pretty queer, but it is enough for us that they do want them. In elementary social behavior there is no unearned income, and it is this contrast that makes us so often dissatisfied with the status and wealth accorded to some public figures.

We are now ready to look at a couple of pieces of research that bear on esteem. As usual the research reports will not be detailed

[2] See R. L. Simpson, "A Modification of the Functional Theory of Social Stratification," *Social Forces*, Vol. 35 (1956), pp. 132-37.

enough to support every point in our argument. They will, for instance, not tell us much about the supply of and demand for valuable services. But if our argument is correct, at least two generalizations should hold good. First, the higher a man's esteem, the more valuable the activities he gives to other members of his group. And second, the higher a man's esteem, the fewer are the members that are held in esteem equal to his; for so far as his esteem depends on his providing rare activities, the number of other members that offer such activities must be few.

The Distribution of Esteem

Our first piece of research is famous in social science and is reported in two books, one by J. L. Moreno and the other, giving more detail, by Helen Hall Jennings.[3] We shall rely on the latter. The investigator worked in the 1930's at the New York State Training School for Girls at Hudson, New York, whose inhabitants were more than 400 girls between twelve and sixteen years of age, committed by the Children's Courts for sexual delinquency. At the end of their stay, the school hoped to turn them out as useful citizens, able to support themselves; for this purpose it provided academic and vocational training, but relied above all on the way of life of the school itself. Although the girls were mostly children of poor parents, they were not otherwise unrepresentative of the population at large. No girl was committed that was known to be psychotic, below the normal range in intelligence, or in any other way unlikely to benefit from the training given.

The girls were used to psychologists and to taking psychological tests, and so it was with no overmastering anxiety that they met to take a test of a new kind. The investigator asked every girl to write down in order, without consulting the others, the names of the other girls she liked or disliked in each of four aspects of local life: living, working, studying, and spending leisure time. This test the investigator called the *sociometric test*. In no absolute sense of the words was it any more social or more metric than any other measure of social behavior that might be devised; but inventors may call their inventions

---

[3] J. L. Moreno, *Who Shall Survive?* (Washington, D.C., 1934); H. H. Jennings, *Leadership and Isolation,* 2nd ed. (New York, 1950).

what they will, and *sociometric test* has stuck as the name of questionnaires like those used by the investigator at Hudson.

To be more specific, let us take up the "living" criterion. The living quarters at the school consisted of a number of houses, in each of which roomed a group of from twenty to thirty girls, jointly responsible for its housekeeping and other matters of house concern, under the supervision of a housemother. In the sociometric test, each girl was asked to name the other girls she would like to live in the same house with, whether or not she was in fact living with any of them at the time. When one girl named another, the investigator spoke of her "choosing" another. The questionnaire at Hudson, unlike the one used in the M.I.T. housing project, did not limit a girl's choice: she could name as many others or as few as she wished. In the same way, each girl was asked to name the others she would not like to live in the same house with. This the investigator called "rejection."

The school gave vocational training in shops that also provided useful services to the community: a laundry, a beauty parlor, and the like. In each of these shops seven to fifteen girls worked together, not necessarily the same ones that lived together. And in the sociometric test, each girl was asked to name the others she would or would not like to work with in the shop (choice or rejection on the working criterion). The test did not require that a girl's choices on different criteria should overlap: she was free to choose a girl for working that she had rejected or simply failed to name as someone she would like to live with; but, as we should expect, there was in fact a certain amount of overlap. The same rules applied to choice and rejection on the two other criteria: spending leisure time with a girl and studying with her. On the studying criterion, the girls made rather few choices; and choices for living tended heavily to overlap choices for working. Therefore, in presenting her results, the investigator paid no further attention to choice for studying, combined in a single set of figures the choices for living and for working, and thus was left with two criteria: living-working, and leisure.

In our language, the sociometric test was a measure of sentiment, though a crude one. It showed how much liking or social approval each girl gave to every other: she liked (and chose) her, remained indifferent to (and failed to name) her, or disliked (and rejected) her. In the test, the girls expressed their sentiments to the investigator and not to the other girls. Although the research has nothing to say on the matter, we have no doubt that they expressed roughly the same sentiments to one another, and that the sentiments were recognized. There may well have been a girl or two who was not herself aware that all the other girls liked her who in fact chose her on the test. But studies that have gone into the perception of choice as well as choice itself have found that, while the correlation is seldom perfect, there is generally a significant correlation between the people that a man thinks will choose him and those that actually do.[4] At any rate we assume here that the sentiments expressed in the sociometric test were also real values exchanged at the Hudson School.

Besides the sociometric test, the investigator also questioned the girls about their *social contacts*. She asked each girl to list all the other girls she took the trouble to speak to on her own account and not just because the others spoke to her first, and to list them without regard for her feelings toward them, friendly, indifferent, or hostile. Since this *social-contact test* was a measure of *interaction*, we shall pay no further heed to it until we come back to that subject.

The findings of the Hudson research were many; we shall mention only a few of them, and we mention the first only to get it out of the way. The investigator administered the sociometric test on two occasions eight months apart. Because old inmates were getting discharged from the school and new inmates admitted all the time, the girls that took the first test were not all the same as those that took the second. Indeed most of the results that the investigator reports have to do only with the 133 girls who were on hand to take both tests and lived in the same house on both occasions. Of these girls the sociometric data showed that each occupied much the same relative, if not absolute, social position on the occasion of the second test as she had on the first. For instance, each received about as many choices and rejections on the first test as she did eight months later. This does not mean that no change took place but only that there was some measure of social continuity or practical equilibrium. Indeed the evidence is that when a girl first came to Hudson she formed her opinion of others, and others theirs of her, pretty soon, and neither changed much after that.

[4] See R. Tagiuri, "Relational Analysis: An Extension of Sociometric Method with Emphasis upon Social Perception," *Sociometry*, Vol. 15 (1952), pp. 91-104.

The number of others a girl chose depended only on herself, and so might not mean much socially, but the number of others that chose her depended on these others, and meant a great deal. In our terms, it was a measure of the *esteem* in which she was held. True, the investigator might have used a more elaborate measure of esteem, for she had asked each girl not only to name the others that she liked but to put them in rank-order of how much she liked them. The investigator might have taken these data into account by multiplying every choice by a figure indicating whether it was a first, or second, or third choice, and so on. This would have had the effect of increasing the differences in esteem, for girls that got many choices also got many first choices.[5] But perhaps because the rank-orders would have introduced statistical difficulties, the investigator paid rather little attention to them and in measuring esteem gave all choices an equal weight.

In looking at the results of the research at Hudson, we begin, therefore, with the distribution of the 133 girls present for both tests, according to the number of others by whom each was chosen on the living-working criterion. We shall consider later the distribution of choice for leisure time. We give the results of the first sociometric test; the second showed the same general kind of pattern. The distribution is plotted in Figure 1.[6]

Along the vertical axis are plotted the number of girls choosing a given girl and along the horizontal axis the number of girls chosen by a given number of others. Thus the highest point on the graph indicates that one and only one girl was chosen by 21 others; the point furthest to the right indicates that 14 girls were chosen by 6 others each, and the point at the bottom indicates that 9 girls each received no choices at all.

Now consider the shape of the whole distribution. It is not what the statisticians call a "normal" distribution, forming a symmetrical bell-shaped curve. Instead it tapers toward the top and bulges toward the bottom like a beet or radish. This means that choice tended to focus on a small number of very popular girls, but that indifference (or failure to choose) did not focus nearly so sharply: more girls

[5] H. H. Jennings, *op. cit.*, p. 88.
[6] From the figures given in H. H. Jennings, *op. cit.*, p. 46: "Choosing the Subject, Test 1."

were chosen little than were chosen much. In other words, the number of girls held in high esteem were, as we expected, relatively few. Since similar distributions have been found in other sociometric studies, we have reason to believe that some general tendency had made its presence felt.[7]

Distribution of Sociometric Choice

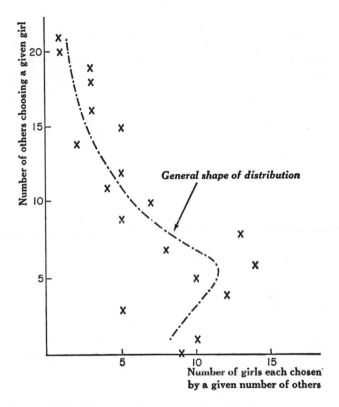

The distribution of rejections plotted in the same way does not produce the same kind of curve. True, a small number of girls were each rejected by a large number of others, but from then on the curves diverge. The rejection curve does not bulge in the lower middle

[7] See U. Bronfenbrenner, "A Constant Frame of Reference for Sociometric Research: Part II, Experiment and Inference," *Sociometry*, Vol. 7 (1944), pp. 40-75.

like that of choice. Instead the numbers increase fairly steadily and are greatest at the bottom, the greatest number of girls being those rejected by no one or by only one other each. That is, while rather few girls found no one to choose them, a very large number found no one to reject them.

What are the reasons for the differences between the two distributions? In the first place it is clear that rejection was not the same thing as low positive choice. If it had been many girls would have received many rejections, whereas in fact only a few did. To be positively rejected, a girl must have conspicuously violated whatever norms were current in the school, and in her peculiar way she must have been as rare a creature as a very popular girl. In the second place, a girl who was chosen just a little was not a girl who was also rejected just a little: she was more apt not to be rejected at all. For a girl that merely conformed, without being outstanding in any other way, would not have been rejected; and, while she might not have gotten much positive choice, she would assuredly have gotten some. There must have been many girls in this class of the inconspicuous and inoffensive, who had nothing much for them but certainly nothing against them. People who have nothing in their favor but common human goodness are the largest class in any society. And therefore we should indeed expect that, while few girls found no one to choose them, a very large number found no one to reject them.

Esteem and the Value of the Activities Provided

From now on we shall pay no further attention to rejections but confine ourselves to positive choices and look at the relation between differences in esteem and differences in the value of activities emitted. The investigator divided the distribution of positive choices into three parts, each containing about the same number of girls. She called the top third of the distribution, consisting of those girls each of whom was chosen by a large number of others, the class of the *over-chosen*. The membership of this class gave the investigator confidence that the residents at Hudson had answered the test sincerely, and that popularity as revealed by the test corresponded to popularity in the everyday life of the school, for eighteen out of the twenty elected members of the school council turned out also to be among the over-chosen. The investigator called the middle third of the distribution the class of the *average-chosen,* and the bottom third, which consisted, of course, of those girls each of whom was chosen by few others or by none at all, the class of the *under-chosen.*

The investigator then studied the kinds of activities performed by members of the three classes. Specifically, she interviewed every housemother, and in the course of the interview she talked over with her every girl living in her house. The investigator constructed a rough classification of the kinds of behavior housemothers complained about, such as quarrelsome, irritable, nagging, nervous, or rebellious behavior, and a similar classification of the kinds of behavior house-mothers were fond of praising, such as cooperative behavior, behavior that did not require supervision, evenness of disposition, willingness to do more than one's share of the work, and an ability to plan. Then in the course of the interviews the investigator noted down which girls the housemothers mentioned as displaying the approved or dis-approved kinds of behavior. When she tabulated the results, she discovered that the housemothers had, for every kind of approved behavior, mentioned far more members of the over-chosen as dis-playing it than they had members of any other class. They had men-tioned the average-chosen next most often and the under-chosen least. For most kinds of disapproved behavior the order of the classes was reversed: the housemothers mentioned the over-chosen least often, followed by the average-chosen and the under-chosen. But, signif-icantly, this was not true of all kinds of disapproved behavior. For rebellious, initiatory, retaliatory, and reticent behavior, the house-mothers mentioned more members of the over-chosen than of any other class. In short, with the exceptions noted, the housemothers found the behavior of the over-chosen more valuable than that of the average- and under-chosen.

But what do we care about the housemothers? It was the girls, not the housemothers, who answered the sociometric test, and we want to link the choices the girls themselves made with their own evaluation of the different kinds of behavior. We can make this con-nection if we argue that activities valued by the housemothers must often have been activities valued by the girls as well. The argument seems reasonable, and the investigator accepts it. Cooperative be-havior, evenness of disposition, willingness to do more than one's share of the work—all of which the housemothers praised, all of which they most often mentioned the over-chosen as possessing—must also have been activities that the girls themselves found rewarding in their companions. The very exceptions prove the rule. The few kinds of behavior that the housemothers disapproved of but mentioned the over-chosen most often as displaying—these were just the kinds of behavior that the girls themselves were apt to have looked on much more favorably. Thus rebellious behavior, described as "refusing to do what is requested by a person in authority," initiatory behavior ("behavior considered as too self-directive and too self-confident"), and reticent behavior ("does not bring personal problems to the housemother") were surely characteristic of independent girls, ready to lead and support their fellows in standing up to the housemothers on occasion. If, in short, the housemothers found rewarding most of the activities provided by the over-chosen, the girls themselves probably found all of their activities rewarding. And the more valuable to the other members of her group were the activities that a girl performed, the higher was the esteem in which they held her.

We shall notice that the behavior of an over-chosen girl tended to be valuable not just on one count but on a very large number of counts if not on all. We might conceivably have expected that a girl found to be cooperative would not also be found solicitous of the welfare of new girls, but in fact she was likely to be. Perhaps the rare capacity that she possessed was not some special ability but a rather general one that manifested itself in many ways. Perhaps what the psychologists call the "halo-effect" was also at work here: a tendency for a favorable, or unfavorable, judgment that a man makes of another on one count to spill over and color the judgments he makes of him on other counts. Perhaps the phenomenon resulted from what we shall call in a later chapter *status congruence*. Or some combination of these forces may have been operating. Let us take note of the facts, note also that we have not explained them, and pass on.

The Degree of Conformity to Norms

We have not done with the research at Hudson: we shall come back to it in later chapters; but for the moment we turn to another piece of research that got results similar to those we have considered so far. In the years just before World War II, T. M. Newcomb carried out an elaborate sociometric study of the whole student body, more than 600 girls in all, at Bennington College.[8] The investigator derived his measure of esteem from the answers the girls gave when each was asked which five other girls she would choose to represent the college at an intercollegiate gathering.

Bennington College, both faculty and students, was at that time dominated by a "liberal" climate of opinion and strongly supported the aims and ideals of the New Deal. The investigator asked every student to answer a questionnaire designed to measure the degree of her "political and economic progressivism," and then correlated the girl's score on this test with the number of sociometric choices she received. In every college class, from Freshman through Senior, he found that the girls most often chosen were the least conservative in opinion. Agreement with her opinions is rewarding to a girl, as to anyone else. In a college where "liberal" opinions rule, the girls who expressed liberal opinions most fully were presumably most rewarding to the others, and so most often chosen.

But it was not just in liberal opinions that highly chosen girls lived up most fully to the norms of the college. The investigator set up a panel of twenty-four students, each of whom was to name others whose reputation was most extreme for various kinds of behavior related to citizenship in the college community. From the judgments of the panel, the investigator calculated an index of the degree to which a girl was reputed to be "identified" with the community. If, for instance, she was named as "absorbed in college community affairs" or "influenced by community expectations regarding codes, standards, and so on," she was apt to get a high score for identification. Putting his earlier and his later measures together, the investigator found that girls high in "political and economic progressivism" were also high in identification with the community. Because they realized to a high degree in their own behavior the norms prevalent in their group these girls were highly chosen. But we must never forget the possible back effect or favorable spiral: by reason

[8] T. M. Newcomb, *Personality and Social Change* (New York, 1943), partially summarized in T. M. Newcomb, "Attitude Development as a Function of Reference Groups," in E. E. Maccoby, T. M. Newcomb, and E. L. Hartley, *Readings in Social Psychology,* 3rd ed. (New York, 1958), pp. 265-75.

of the esteem in which they were held, these girls were also in a position to maintain and support the very norms conformity to which gave them their popularity. By the same token, a girl held in low esteem is in no position to propagate the ideals, and they may be high ones, that she is prepared to live up to.

The girls held in high esteem were girls who measured up in high degree to the norms of their group. And this brings us back to a point mentioned at the beginning of this chapter. Earlier in this book we treated conformity as an all-or-nothing matter: we assumed that people either conformed or did not. But this is not fair to the evidence. Two men may both conform to the norms of a group well enough to earn no hostility from their fellow members, and yet differ in the degree to which they conform. In this case, the man who conforms the more closely often gets the higher esteem. In the Bank Wiring Observation Room, which was the last of the celebrated Western Electric researches, the workingmen firmly accepted an output norm: no one should produce more than 6000 "connections" a day. Almost all members of the group conformed fairly well, but Taylor (W3), who was the most consistent conformer, producing just the right number of connections almost every day, also enjoyed the highest esteem in the group.[9] But this was not the only reason for his popularity; and we shall see in a later chapter that persons of high esteem do not necessarily conform closely to all the norms of a group, though they certainly do conform to some of them.

Summary

At the beginning of this chapter we sketched an argument from which at least two conclusions could be drawn. The more valuable to the other members of a group are the activities a man emits to them, the higher is the esteem in which they hold him. And the higher the esteem in which a member is held, the fewer are the other members that get the same amount of esteem. The Hudson research provided some support for both propositions; the Bennington research provided support for the first but no evidence, one way or the other, that had a bearing on the second. On the grounds of research such as we have examined here, the author of the present book put forward in an

[9] G. C. Homans, *op. cit.*, p. 78.

earlier one the following proposition: "The higher the rank of a person within a group, the more nearly his activities conform to the norms of the group."[10] As a first approximate statement, and as a mere summary of the evidence without hint of explanation, this proposition served well enough, but we should now be able to recognize its inadequacy. It is not just conformity that gets a man high esteem (rank) in a group, so long as many members conform to more or less the same degree. He must also provide services for the others that are in short supply, services that they cannot easily get elsewhere, including not just conformity but a high degree of conformity. Nor in describing a man's activities as conformity or as the provision of services, such as helping others with their work, have we underlined their crucial feature. What is really important about conformity is not just that it is conformity; what is really important about help is not just that it is help. Instead the thing that is important about both is what they have in common: both are activities that, in different degrees, are valuable to other members who find them rewarding to receive. For high value received, men will return high esteem.

[10] G. C. Homans, op. cit., p. 141.

The Matrix of Sentiment

In this chapter we shall consider two different matters. First, we shall look at the distribution of favorable and unfavorable sentiments in greater detail than we have done so far; and, second, we shall take up some reasons for expressing favorable sentiments toward a man other than his ability to provide rare and valuable activities—though values of some sort will still be at stake. Both of these things can be well represented by the tables of figures that mathematicians call matrices.

Mutual Choice or Rejection

To say as we did in the last chapter that the more valuable to the other members of a group are the activities a man emits to them, the greater is the esteem in which they hold him, is not to say much in detail about the distribution of sentiment within the group. For instance, a man who is often chosen by others must himself do some choosing. How does he distribute his choice? Does he choose other highly esteemed members like himself, or does he choose people that few others choose?

In the attempt to answer questions like this let us set up another model group or toy society, somewhat larger than our old group made up of Person, Other, and the Third Man. The present group will have six members, called O, P, Q, R, S, and T. In the last chapter we showed that if a man is to enjoy high esteem in a group, he must provide services that many of the other members value, which means further that many of the members must share the same values. In our toy society, therefore, we shall assume that all six members value the same kinds of activities, that O provides these activities in their rarest and most valuable form—he may, for instance, be the most helpful member—and that the others provide less and less valuable activities in alphabetical order. Suppose further that, since this is a very small group and we can look at it closely, we allow each member to give a more detailed expression of his sentiments than the investigators allowed the girls at the Hudson State Training School. Instead of either choosing or failing to choose other members, he gives approval worth 5 to the member he likes most, 4 to the one he likes next most, and so on. (We shall not count the approval he gives to himself.) Finally, in accordance with our argument of the last chapter, let us assume that every member chooses other members in order of the value to him of the services they perform. Under these assumptions, the way each member distributes his choice to every other member, and the differences between the members in esteem, are represented in the accompanying matrix (Table 6).

TABLE SIX

A Model Sociometric Matrix

		Sentiment given to						Total given
		O	P	Q	R	S	T	
	O		5	4	3	2	1	15
Sentiment given by	P	5		4	3	2	1	15
	Q	5	4		3	2	1	15
	R	5	4	3		2	1	15
	S	5	4	3	2		1	15
	T	5	4	3	2	1		15
Total received		25	21	17	13	9	5	

Let us be sure we know what a matrix like this means. The figure 4, for instance, in the cell formed by the intersection of column P with row Q means that member Q gives to member P approval worth 4. The cells on the major diagonal are left empty because they can only represent the approval each member gives to himself. Since we have made the assumption—and it may turn out to be unrealistic— that the members are equal in the total value of the approval each *gives* to others, the figures in the "Total given" column are all 15. But we have made no such assumption about the total value each *receives*. The sums of the columns, marked "Total received," indicate the amount of approval received by each member from other members, and so correspond to the differences between members in what we have called *esteem*. Member O gets the most esteem, followed by the others in alphabetical order.

Simple and straightforward as this matrix is, simple and straightforward as were the assumptions on which it was constructed, it may nevertheless help to answer questions about the detailed distribution of sentiment in a group. At the beginning of this section, for instance, we asked how a member who was himself highly chosen would distribute his own choices. The matrix now tells us that, if the assumptions on which it was constructed are correct, he would tend to give his highest choices to other highly chosen members. Thus O, whose esteem is highest in the group, gives his first choice to P, who is in second place in esteem.

We have reason, moreover, to believe that the assumptions may in fact be correct, in the sense that they may correspond more or less well to conditions actually obtaining in some groups; for certain results that the matrix predicts or generates have been found to hold good in actual research. One of the things that the investigator at Hudson got interested in was mutual choice, which occurred when one girl chose another who chose her back. The investigator found that mutual choice occurred most often among the over-chosen girls and least often among the under-chosen.[1] Similar findings have been reached in other researches. To take one we are familiar with—the deviates in Westgate tended to receive little choice, and they were unlikely to choose other deviates as friends. That is, mutual choice

[1] H. H. Jennings, *Leadership and Isolation*, 2nd ed. (New York, 1950), p. 87.

was low among persons themselves under-chosen.[2] Both of these findings our matrix predicts or generates.

Let us see how it does so. Let us assume that the members of our toy society are girls like those at Hudson, and let us make the conditions under which they choose others similar to those allowed by the sociometric test at Hudson. We have had each of our toy girls put the others in rank-order of the approval she gives to each of them, whereas in taking the test the real girls either chose others or failed to do so. To make our toy fit the reality, let us say that any toy girl who took the test would have chosen another if she gave her approval worth 4 or 5. By this standard three of our girls made mutual choices: O-P, O-Q, and P-Q. All three of them include O and P, our equivalent of the over-chosen girls who made up the top third of the sociometric distribution at Hudson, and none of them includes the under-chosen girls S and T. In short, our toy does reproduce or generate the findings.

Why it should do so takes a little thinking. If, as our matrix assumes for our toy girls, each real girl at Hudson chose others in something like the rank-order of the value to her of the services these others rendered, and if many of the girls shared the same values—if, for instance, many of them valued friendliness and cooperativeness in their companions—many girls would choose the same other girls for much the same reasons, and this would be as much true of girls themselves highly chosen as it would be true of the rest. Accordingly a girl herself highly chosen would be apt to choose another highly chosen girl, and the other to choose her in return. The probable result would be much mutual choice among the highly chosen. By the same token a girl herself little chosen would be apt to give her choices to girls that many others had chosen and so *fail* to give her choice to another little chosen girl. The result could scarcely be other than little mutual choice among little chosen girls.

Some Unexplained Findings

Although our model matrix reproduces in gross some of the features of actual choice at Hudson and indeed in other groups, it

[2] L. Festinger, S. Schachter, and K. W. Back, *Social Pressures in Informal Groups* (New York, 1950), pp. 104-09.

falls far short of reproducing all of them. The reason may not be that the conditions assumed for our matrix often fail to obtain in real life. The reason may be rather that further conditions, which we have not allowed for in constructing our matrix, may obtain at the same time, and so complicate the real picture of the distribution of social approval. At any rate let us look at some of the discrepancies between our toy and the reality.

Our toy society has only six members forming a single, undivided group, whereas the real girls studied at Hudson numbered over a hundred and they were elaborately divided into subgroups, for instance, the cottages. Although the model predicts, and the data showed, that mutual choice was particularly apt to occur among the over-chosen, the investigator found that mutual rejection, while not as frequent as the other, was also more apt to occur among the over-chosen than among the under-chosen girls.[3]

This finding was almost certainly the result of competition and rivalry, which we did not allow for at all in our model. In Chapter 7 we saw that competition between people, since the result is apt to be that some of them withdraw reward from others, is also apt to lead to hostility between them. And of all forms of competition, competition for other people is the most savage. A girl that is another's rival for popularity, prominence, and power is apt not to like her much. In the nature of the case, only the over-chosen girls at Hudson could qualify for this kind of contest: an over-chosen girl and an under-chosen were much less apt to be rivals, and therefore mutual hostility was particularly rife among over-chosen girls. This obviously does not mean that all the over-chosen hated one another—the contrary was the case, as we have seen. It does mean that the place where mutual rejection was apt to occur, if it occurred at all, was among highly chosen girls. As for the under-chosen they were more likely to look on one another with mutual indifference than with either mutual approval or mutual hostility.

But even this finding about the mutual indifference of the under-chosen does not hold good to the last drop. In a few of the cottages at Hudson the investigator found tight little cliques. These were "closed" formations in the sense that each member of such a clique chose every other, and "overlapping" formations in the sense that

[3] H. H. Jennings, *op. cit.,* pp. 87-88.

they chose one another both on the criterion of living and working together and on the criterion of spending leisure time. What these cliques had in common was that the housemothers were particularly apt to complain of their members as showing "rebellious" behavior. But the cliques differed greatly in their positions in Hudson society. Some were made up of girls who were held in very high esteem indeed, but the rest of girls whom almost nobody chose except the other members of the clique. How cliques of under-chosen girls might form we shall consider in a later chapter under the heading of "companionship in misery."[4]

This overlapping of choices for living-working and for leisure brings us to the next discrepancy between our matrix and the data. In reviewing the research at Hudson we have so far considered only the pattern of choice on the first criterion. Choice on the criterion of spending leisure time with another girl displayed a rather different pattern, yet related in a curious way to choice for living and working. Fewer choices were made for leisure than for living-working; they were more apt to be mutual; and, finally, girls were apt to choose other girls for leisure who were more or less their equals in the number of choices they received on the living-working criterion—girls, that is to say, who were their equals in esteem.[5] Our matrix makes only a limited allowance for this tendency to choose equals. The girls at the top of our toy society tend to choose their near-equals, but not the girls at the bottom, whereas in the real society of Hudson the tendency was general from top to bottom, at least on the criterion of spending leisure time. This is the first appearance in these pages of the equality phenomenon, which will occupy us much in later chapters. All we need note now is that, if a tendency for people to choose their equals is to appear at all, they must first be made unequal in some respect. For to say that a girl chooses her equal in esteem is to imply that there are other girls who are her superiors or inferiors.

Finally, our matrix assumes that each member of the group has available for distribution to others a total supply of approval equal in value to the approval available to every other member. This is indicated by the figure 15, which appears in every cell of the "Total given" column. The assumption is unrealistic for two reasons. In

[4] *Ibid.*, pp. 248-50.
[5] *Ibid.*, p. 257.

the first place the investigator at Hudson found that besides receiving more choices than other girls, the over-chosen tended to give more too. They were also apt to report a larger *social-contact range,* that is, a larger number of other girls they took the trouble to speak to.[6] We shall have more to say about social contact when we come to Chapter 10 on Interaction.

In the second place, the value of the approval received by a member of a group depends in part on whom it comes from. As each girl not only expresses her approval of another girl, but begins to perceive that her companions are doing the same thing, this other girl comes both to possess esteem in fact and to be recognized as possessing it. At this point the approval that she in turn expresses becomes worth more, coming from her, to the girl that gets it than approval expressed by someone held in low esteem. Indeed to be praised by someone herself far from praiseworthy may be a dubious and embarrassing compliment. For this reason a more lifelike toy than ours, instead of making equal in value the approval given by each member, would weight it—that is, multiply it—by some figure representing the esteem in which she herself was held: the higher her own esteem, the greater the value of the approval she gave.

Change in Choice with Source of Reward

We have argued so far that a man gives social approval to another not just when he admires the other's activity in the abstract but when that activity actually rewards him. The data from Hudson were consistent with the truth of the argument but were not detailed enough to support it directly. We could see, for instance, that a "cooperative" girl was highly chosen, but the research did not supply us with enough information to affirm that many others chose her because her cooperative activities had rewarded them personally. We turn now to a study by Joachim Israel that does something to establish this link.[7]

We have two further reasons for taking up Israel's work. We like to examine research on both real-life groups and artificial ones formed

[6] *Ibid.,* pp. 50-51.

[7] J. Israel, *Self-evaluation and Rejection in Groups,* Stockholm Studies in Sociology, Vol. 1 (Stockholm, 1956), especially pp. 174-216.

for experimental purposes; and while the groups at Hudson were real, those in the present research were artificial. Israel's work also begins to tell us something about the reasons for one man's choosing another aside from sheer value received—reasons of equality and justice, which have already forced themselves upon us, and which will take much of our time in later chapters. It tells us about these things as a by-product of telling us about other ones: its incidental findings are in some ways more interesting than its main ones.

For once this is not an American study. From students at the University of Stockholm who volunteered for the research, the investigator formed a number of six-man groups which he then submitted to various experimental conditions, a different set of eight groups to each one, so that forty-eight men in all underwent each condition. In certain respects all the experimental treatments were alike. The members of every group sat around a table, each man identified by a letter. Then each man took, without help from the others, a pencil-and-paper test that purported to reveal how well he could draw logical inferences, but was so designed that he himself could not tell how high he scored. The investigator collected the papers, pretended to correct them, and then gave out what appeared to be the results. That is, he handed each member a sheet of paper which he said showed the member's own score and the scores of all the others, but, for reasons that will soon appear, the investigator did not let the members compare sheets. The subjects took tests of this kind several times, the same procedure being repeated every time. The investigator's object was to fix firmly in each member's mind the apparent logical ability of every other member as compared with his own. The score sheets given to each member showed him as getting, as his average over the series of tests, a score of middle rank (7), while one of the other members got, on the average, a score much higher (12) than his own, one somewhat higher (9), one the same as his own (7), one somewhat lower (5), and one much lower (2). In short, every member was led to believe that his own scores were middling, and that the scores of the other members were widely distributed over the range of abilities.

After having thus established these differences in apparent logical ability, the investigator told the members that the group was going to meet once again to solve logical problems, but that on this occasion two of the present members would have to be left out. Accordingly, each member was to write down the other members in order of his preference that they should remain with the group the next time. Note that while at Hudson the girls probably had a good idea which others chose them because they had lived with the others for a pretty long time, in the present experiment the groups were temporary and the investigator did not give out the results of the sociometric test. If esteem was given to others, it was certainly not received by them.

So far, the investigator treated all groups the same way. His different experimental conditions were designed to vary the degree to which a member found rewarding or valuable the apparent scores of the other members on the logical tests. He would then observe what effect these changes in the value of the others' activity would have on the choices a member gave to the others on the sociometric test.

We may perhaps think that choice in this experiment does not represent esteem at all. Certainly no bargaining, implicit or explicit, for the amount of approval to be rendered in return for a service, such as we believe takes place in effect in real-life groups, took place in these. A member was simply faced with information about the performances of others, and then asked which of them he would like to have stay around for the next meeting. Nevertheless we shall, though perhaps incidentally, discover forces at work in these artificial conditions that are also at work in real ones.

In the first experimental condition, called *cooperation-maximum,* the investigator told the members that at the next session each of them would be rewarded for the total score of the group on the logical tests: the higher the total score, the higher the individual member's reward, up to a maximum of fifteen Swedish crowns. The higher a member's score, the more likely he was to make a big contribution to the group's score at the next session, and thus to every individual member's reward. Accordingly it is not surprising that on the sociometric test members were very apt to give their first choices to the other member who scored 12, their second choices to the other who scored 9, and so forth: the higher the score the higher the choice.

In the second experimental condition, called *cooperation-close,* the investigator told the members that the most effective group was one in which all members attained the *same* score on the logical test, that a reasonable score would lie between 6 and 8, and that at the next session each member of the group would make more money the more nearly all the members got the same score. Since each member believed that his own average score was 7 and that this was a reasonable score, it is again hardly surprising that he was inclined to give first place on the sociometric test to the other member whose score was 7, second place to the members whose scores were 9 and 5, and so on. The actual figures are shown in Table 7.

Distribution of Choice: Cooperation-Close

Ability score	Sociometric ranking				
	1	2	3	4	5
12	5	1	4	33	5
9	10	35	3	0	0
7	32	10	6	0	0
5	1	2	35	10	0
2	0	0	0	5	43

We must not confuse a matrix like this with the sociometric matrix presented earlier in this chapter. The two are constructed on different principles, and their figures mean somewhat different things. For one thing, the earlier matrix showed the sociometric rank of the persons who gave sociometric choices; the present one only shows the number of first, second, etc., sociometric choices received by persons getting different scores on the logical tests. For instance, the figure 5 in the first column says that five men gave their first choices to the other member of their respective groups who obtained, so far as they knew, the score 12 on the logical tests; and the figure 5 in the fifth column says that five men gave their fifth choices to the other member who scored 12. Remember that every member had to put all the other members of his group in rank-order. Since there were eight groups of six men each, every column should add up to 48. They do not do so in all the tables that follow; mistakes must have been made, but they are minor in their effects.

It should be clear that the *cooperation-close* condition resembled experimentally the situation in real groups when members set a high value on the similarity of their behavior in conformity to a norm; and the more nearly a member conforms, the higher the approval he gets. In the present case, the norm was the score 7, and the nearer was a member's score to 7, the higher the sociometric choice he was apt to get. But the matrix reveals more than this. The next point to note is that score 9 got more second choices than did 5, and 5 more third choices than did 9, though if what paid off were scores close to 7, 9 was just as valuable as 5. In the same way, scores 12 and 2 were equally distant from 7 and equally "bad," but 12 got more fourth choices than did 2, and 2 more fifth choices than did 12. Thus the high scores in each column form a zigzag expanding from left to right: look at the series 32, 35, 35, 33, 43. In short, many subjects behaved as if they felt that when two scores were equally rewarding, the higher score deserved the higher choice. This is our first hint in this experiment of what we shall call the *justice-effect*.

In the third experimental condition, called *competition,* the investigator told the members that at the next session, to which, as usual, only four of them could come, each man would be given ten crowns before the tests started. After that, the member getting the highest score would receive five crowns from each of the other three; the member getting the next highest, four crowns from each of the remaining two; the member getting the third highest, one crown from the low man, who would thus be left with no money at all. Here the experimental situation put each of the members as individuals in potential competition with all the others. And the higher a man's score at the present session the greater the threat he represented at the next. Not surprisingly under the circumstances, the subjects tended to give their first choices for membership at the next session to the man with the lowest score, their second choice to the next lowest, and so on, as Table 8 reveals. The effect of competition was to concentrate the choices on the diagonal leading from column 1, row 2, to column 5, row 12. (We mean by rows 2 and 12 the rows in the matrix representing those scores on the logical test.)

But the concentration was by no means as marked as we might have expected. If all members had chosen others in accordance with their competitive interests, all scores off the minor diagonal would have

Distribution of Choice: Competition

Ability score	Sociometric ranking				
	1	2	3	4	5
12	7	2	5	7	*29*
9	1	10	8	*26*	3
7	14	5	*27*	0	2
5	6	*27*	6	8	1
2	*20*	4	4	7	13

been zero. Since this was not the case, some of the members must have made some of their choices on other grounds. Besides the effect of competition, two other forces were making themselves felt—forces weaker than competition but still discernible in the figures. First, there was a secondary concentration of relatively high figures on the other, or major, diagonal leading from column 1, row 12, to column 5, row 2. This distribution means that some members had some slight tendency to give high choices to persons that got high scores and low choices to persons that got low ones, notwithstanding that this ran counter to their own monetary interests. When the investigator asked them about these choices, they said they were influenced by a sense of fair play: a man who got a high score ought to get a high choice. Here the *justice-effect* is fully developed.

Finally, there was the tendency represented by the figure 14 in column 1, row 7. Since every member thought his own average score was 7, this relatively high figure means that some members gave first choices to others whose scores were the same as their own, even though, while not the most dangerous competitors, they were more dangerous than the low scorers. This we shall call the *similarity-* or *equality-effect.*

The fourth condition was called the *control* condition because, like the controls in other experiments, it was designed to determine whether the effects occurring under the experimental manipulations were really produced by them or would have occurred without them. In the *control* condition, the investigator told the members that the four who remained for the next session would each receive seven and a half crowns regardless of how well they scored. Accordingly a member had no financial interest, one way or another, in the scores of other members. They neither promised him any good nor threatened him with any ill, and he could afford to be disinterested. The results are shown in Table 9.

TABLE NINE

Distribution of Choice: Control

Ability score	Sociometric ranking				
	1	2	3	4	5
12	*24*	5	4	12	3
9	9	*26*	8	3	2
7	13	7	*19*	7	2
5	1	3	13	*24*	3
2	1	3	4	2	*38*

In this condition, since the members could afford to be disinterested, the justice-effect took over. The highest scores lay on the major diagonal from column 1, row 12, to column 5, row 2, just as they did in the *cooperation-maximum* condition. In that condition the members stood to gain personally by the high scores of others. Here they had nothing to gain, yet still distributed their choices in much the same way. They must have been carried away by admiration and a sense of fair play: a high score deserved a high choice. At any rate they tended to choose others according to the simplest principle of distributive justice: the "better" a man's behavior, the greater his reward in approval.

Though it was not so strongly marked as the justice-effect, the simultaneous presence of the similarity-effect may be detected in the secondary high figures in some of the columns. Consider, moving from left to right and from column to column, the series 13, 26, 13, 12, 38. These are the cells that got the highest figures in the *coopera-*

tion-close condition, when scores close to their own, that is, to 7, were valuable to members. The principle of choice then was that members chose other members more highly, the nearer the others' scores were to their own; and as between two members whose scores were equally close, they tended to choose the man with the higher score. In the present table we see some choice given to similars in the same way, though in the absence of any financial interest in similarity, the effect was less marked. Note that the justice-series (the major diagonal) and the similarity-series (the widening zigzag) coincide or overlap in certain cells: column 2, row 9, and column 5, row 2. The figures in these cells —26 and 38 respectively—are particularly high, as if they represented the sums of two effects.

The Effect of Subgroups

The two final experimental conditions introduced a new variable. All the experimental subjects were students at the University of Stockholm, but they came from a number of different schools within the university. Before the experiments began, the investigator had asked the students to rank the schools in order of prestige—or, as we should call it, status—and the results showed good agreement on a rank-order that put the Medical School at the top and the Teachers' College at the bottom. The final experimental conditions manipulated the school membership and hence the prestige of the subjects. With the subjects' knowledge, the investigator chose the members of each of these groups in such a way that it consisted of three students from the same low-prestige school and three from the same high-prestige school. As before, the investigator led each member to believe that his own average score was 7, and he so manipulated the other scores as to convince a member that the other two students from his own school received the high and low scores of 12 and 2 respectively, while the three students from the school not his own received scores closer to his own, that is: 9, 7, and 5. The investigator then put half the groups through the *control* condition as described above, and half through the *cooperation-close* condition. He called these new conditions *control-subgroup* and *cooperation-close-subgroup* respectively.

The results for the *control-subgroup* condition, shown in Table 10, should of course be compared with the results of the *control* condition without subgroups, shown in Table 9 above. The comparison shows that in the continued absence of any monetary incentive for choosing one member rather than another, the justice-effect was still powerful in the *control-subgroup* condition: the big figures still lie on the major diagonal. The similarity-effect, on the other hand, seems to have lost most of its force. The reason is obvious. The table shows that a member tended to favor members of his own subgroup, that is, people with scores 12 and 2, at the expense of members of the other sub-

TABLE TEN

Distribution of Choice: Control-Subgroup

Ability score	*Sociometric ranking*				
	1	2	3	4	5
12	*31*	5	5	6	1
9	5	*25*	6	7	5
7	7	12	*23*	4	2
5	0	1	11	*26*	10
2	5	5	3	5	*30*

group. Thus the subjects gave first choice to score 12 more often in this condition than they did in the *control* condition without subgroups: 31 to 24, and last choice to score 2 less often: 30 to 38. And since they favored the members of their own subgroup, whose scores were least like their own, they gave less choice to members with similar scores, thus making the similarity-effect much less prominent than it was in the earlier *control* condition. Yet we may, if we like, argue that the new condition got rid of one kind of similarity only to put another in its place: for a member's tendency to give high choice to others with scores similar to his own, it substituted his tendency to choose others whose prestige was similar to his own and who belonged to the same subgroup. We must be reminded of an earlier experiment in which choice increased within rival subgroups, and of the findings at Hudson showing that the girls tended to choose, for leisure, other girls whose esteem was similar to their own.

Let us look finally at the last experimental condition, *cooperation-close-subgroup,* and compare its results, shown in Table 11, with the results of *cooperation-close* without subgroups, shown in Table 7 above. In the present condition, as in the one we are comparing it with, subjects should have found the scores of others the more rewarding, the more similar they were to their own score, that is, to 7. Accordingly they should have chosen others in this order, and so by and large they did. As in the earlier condition, too, they showed signs,

Distribution of Choice: Cooperation-Close-Subgroup

Ability score	Sociometric ranking				
	1	2	3	4	5
12	12	4	7	*18*	7
9	9	*24*	10	4	1
7	*23*	10	12	2	1
5	0	7	*18*	17	6
2	4	3	1	7	*33*

when faced with two others holding scores equally close to their own, of giving the higher choice to the man with the higher score. The largest figures in every column appear, therefore, in the same cells as they did in the *cooperation-close* condition without subgroups: look at the series 23, 24, 18, 18, 33. The pure justice-effect was also at work, for the secondary high figures lie along the major diagonal.

But a comparison of the largest figures in the two tables shows that the tendency for subjects to choose others with scores similar to their own was weaker in the present condition than in the earlier one: the corresponding figures are always smaller. The reason is, of course, that subjects again displayed some little willingness to favor members of their own subgroups, and these were the men whose scores were least like their own. They gave, for instance, first choice to score 12 more often, and last choice to score 2 less often, than they did in the same condition without subgroups. What is more, this kind of behavior, if it was to show itself at all, had to overcome financial interests—though not very strong ones, as the pay was not at best enormous. Once again we see some men choosing others who were their equals in prestige and who were members of the same groups outside the experiment. We shall not lose sight of the phenomenon.

Summary

In the last chapter we were concerned with the determinants of the over-all ranking in esteem of the members of a group. In the present one we have taken a closer look at the detailed distribution, or matrix, of sentiment. To some extent the same general proposition to which the last chapter gave support—that a member gives more approval to another, the more valuable the other's activity is to him—accounted for the features of the more detailed matrix. Under the condition that many members shared the same values, it accounted for the large amount of mutual choice among members themselves highly chosen and the low amount of it among members chosen little. We have seen further evidence that a member's choice goes to others that actually reward him personally: as different members rewarded him in different circumstances, his choice followed them. But we have also encountered evidence not so easily summed up by this simple proposition. We have seen members choosing others, sometimes in the teeth of their personal interests, on straightforward grounds of distributive justice: the "better" the others' activity, not to the members personally, but in the abstract, the more apt they were to choose these others. Finally, we have seen members choosing others who were similar in some respect to themselves—similar in the kind of activity they emitted, similar in prestige, similar in their membership in larger groups. We do not pretend for one minute that these findings are surprising or at all out of line with everyday experience. We are not here to quarrel with common sense but to support it with more systematic evidence than common sense itself provides. Above all, we are here to explain it. From this point of view, the present chapter raises more questions than it answers, and it is clear we shall sooner or later have to pay much more attention to justice and to similarity, another word for which is equality.

Interaction

In recent chapters we have been mostly concerned with value, particularly with the value to Person of an activity Other gives him and the value to Other of the sentiment Person gives him in return. In the present chapter we shall turn to the second of our two main variables: the quantity of activity or sentiment Person emits to Other and Other to Person. We shall remember that, for us, quantity is a frequency: the number of unit-acts—however the unit be defined—emitted within a given period of time—whatever the period specified by the investigator. If we choose for the time being to forget about the kinds of activity or sentiment Person and Other exchange, and to concentrate instead on the sheer amount of contact between the two, we speak of the frequency of their interaction.

Interaction and Liking

Within the field of interaction, we shall begin by studying the relation between interaction and the sentiment of social approval or, as we call it for short, liking. In Chapter 4 one of our main propositions about elementary social behavior was the following: The more valuable to Person a unit of activity Other gives him, the more often he will emit activity, including sentiment, rewarded by Other's activity. Let us call it, for present purposes only, the first proposition. Remember that when we say "more often" we mean that the quantity of activity Person addresses to Other increases, and that the proposition holds good of Other as well as of Person himself. Now one of the activities Person may give to Other is the generalized reinforcer called social approval; and we have seen in recent chapters that the more valuable to Person is the activity Other gives him, the more valuable is the approval or liking Person gives Other. Let us call this for present purposes the second proposition. One of the possible consequences of the first two propositions taken together is the following third proposition: the more valuable to Person the activity Other gives him, the more valuable the approval he gives Other *and* the more often he emits activity, including sentiment, to Other. To put the argument more crudely, if Other does Person a service, Person is apt both to like him and to interact with him often. That is, Person's liking for Other varies directly as the frequency of his interaction with him. This third proposition, which should of course hold good *mutatis mutandis* for Other too, will provide us with most of our business in this chapter.

We already have some evidence that the proposition holds good, at least at practical equilibrium. Think back to the last experiment reported in Chapter 5 on Influence—Schachter's experiment called "Deviation, Rejection, and Communication." When the other members of the group came to recognize the deviate for what he was, they interacted often with him in an effort to get him to change his expressed opinion; but when he would not change—when, that is to say, he would not give them an activity valuable to them—they interacted with him less and less often and gave him little sociometric choice. As the group tended toward practical equilibrium, the conformists gave the deviate both little liking and little interaction compared with what they gave to other conformists: the less the liking the less the interaction.

Much other research shows an empirical relation between liking and interaction. In practice the two are often associated, though perhaps not always for the reasons we have just given. Let us consider briefly a number of examples rather than concentrating at length on one or two, as we have been doing in recent chapters. In an experiment reported by Potashin, the investigator used as his subjects the children in three grades of a primary school.[1] He gave them a simple sociometric test, and then put them together in pairs of two different kinds. The two members of every pair in one set were children that had chosen one another sociometrically; the two members of every pair in the other set were children that had not chosen one another. The investigator then gave each pair a standardized subject for discussion, and observed the interaction that followed. He found that the amount of uninterrupted discussion was greater in pairs of friends than in pairs of nonfriends. He also found, which may interest us later, that the differences between the two members in the amount each talked, and in the frequency with which each originated discussion, that is, began talking after a pause, was less for friends than it was for nonfriends.

The main finding, that friends interacted more often than nonfriends, can hardly surprise us. Friends are certainly people that have rewarded one another in the past: to meet a friend as the other member of one's pair in the new situation is to expect that his behavior will be rewarding, and so one is apt to interact with him often, which gives him an opportunity to be rewarding in fact. A person who is not a friend presents no such stimulus; indeed one may not even allow him an opening to show how rewarding, for once, he might be.

In the Potashin study of the relation between interaction and sentiment, the independent variable, the one manipulated by the investigator, was favorable sentiment. He put together pairs of children known to be friendly and pairs known not to be friendly, and then watched the differences in interaction that resulted. We shall soon see that the frequency of interaction may also be treated as the independent variable, an increased frequency leading to more favorable sentiment. On what grounds might we expect this to be true?

Suppose that two persons are, as we say, thrown together, that interaction between them is made easy and likely because they live near one another or work on the same job. If they interact at all, they emit activities to one another; and if no special factor is present that might bias systematically their values or their activities, the chances are that each one will find some of the other's activities valuable, if only be-

[1] R. Potashin, "A Sociometric Study of Children's Friendships," *Sociometry*, Vol. 9 (1946), pp. 48-70.

cause they may be obtained at less cost from him than from a third party at a greater distance: the distance of a source of reward adds something to the cost of getting it. And to the extent that each finds the other's activity valuable, each is apt to express favorable sentiment toward the other. For this reason, an independent increase in interaction between persons is apt to be associated with an increase in liking between them.

Let us look now at a couple of experiments that treated the frequency of interaction as the independent variable. In a study by Bovard,[2] the investigator began by forming four groups of college students, every group to discuss the same problems under the chairmanship of a man appointed by the investigator. He trained the chairman of two of the groups, which he called "leader-centered," to monopolize the discussion, so that all comments and questions would be addressed to him and answered by him and little communication would pass between the members themselves. He trained the chairman of the other two groups, which he called "group-centered," to behave quite differently. The chairman was to ask few questions, make few comments, and, if comments and questions were addressed to him, to turn them back to the members for discussion among themselves.

At the end of the meetings the investigator administered a sociometric test and found that the number of choices given by members to other members of the same group was less in the "leader-centered" discussions than in the "group-centered" ones. In our terms, he had experimentally discouraged interaction between members in the first kind of group and encouraged it in the second. And as we should expect from our argument, the liking of members for other members was less in the first than in the second. Naturally we do not claim that the interaction produced the liking directly. Instead, when the chairman of the "group-centered" discussion encouraged interaction among the members, he gave them an opportunity to reward one another, and the reward produced the liking. The word *affect* in the title of the study is the investigator's name for favorable sentiment. He showed that, practically speaking, one of the ways of getting people to like one another is to make them interact with one another. It is a method that works—other things equal. It is also one that Americans

[2] E. W. Bovard, Jr., "The Experimental Production of Interpersonal Affect," *Journal of Abnormal and Social Psychology*, Vol. 46 (1951), pp. 521-28.

believe in without benefit of psychology: if they can only get Tom and Bill together, the boys are sure to like one another.

A somewhat more complicated study was one made by the Sherifs at a summer camp for preadolescent boys.[3] For a time at the beginning of the season, the investigators allowed all the boys to go around together in a single group. At the end of this period, they got them to answer a sociometric test, and then divided them into two groups, equal in size and, so far as possible, equal sociometrically. That is to say, the investigators chose the members of the groups in such a way that any one boy would now find in his own group and in the other group about the same number of the boys he had chosen. The investigators then separated the groups for a time, each one playing and camping by itself. When they again administered the sociometric test, choice had shifted, and now the choices made by any one boy tended overwhelmingly to go to other members of his own group. Once again, increased interaction between some people had increased liking between them, and decreased interaction between others had decreased their liking.

But this was not all that happened. A further factor encouraged and complicated the shift in choices. Not only did the two groups camp and play apart for a time, but they also came to be rivals over which was to be considered the "better" group. As we saw in Chapter 7 on Competition, a rival is someone who threatens to deprive you of a reward; accordingly you are apt to meet him with some hostility; and if your rivals are members of another group, your hostility toward them is apt to increase your friendliness toward members of your own group. In the summer camp the boys' liking for members of their own group was fostered by their hatred for members of the other. Hatred is not too strong a word: the hostility waxed so great that the investigators decided the experiment had gotten out of hand and broke up the groups. It is interesting that the rank-and-file members of each group, those that received few sociometric choices, were more eager than the leaders to express hostility toward the other group. Vying for full acceptance, they behaved as if exaggerated hostility toward the others would win them approval from their own gang. At any rate, the increased hostility between groups and increased friendliness within

[3] M. Sherif and C. W. Sherif, *Groups in Harmony and Tension* (New York, 1953), pp. 229-95.

each of them was the effect not only of their isolation but of their rivalry. The investigators had produced experimentally a situation that occurs all too often in real life.

As a practical matter, the association between interaction and social approval is often observed. If, for instance, you watch the behavior of three people in the same room and discover that two of them interact more often with each other than either of them does with the third, you can bet that the two will express more liking for each other than they do for the third, and you will be right far more often than not. As Newcomb says: "So widespread and so compelling is the evidence for the relationship between frequency of interaction and positive attraction that Homans has ventured to hypothesize that 'If the frequency of interaction between two or more persons increases, the degree of their liking for one another will increase.' Actuarially speaking, the evidence is altogether overwhelming that, *ignoring other variables,* the proposition is correct in a wide range of circumstances."[4]

Limits to the Relation Between Interaction and Liking

But when I put forward this proposition in my earlier book, *The Human Group,*[5] none was more often attacked. Every reader, it appeared, could think of people, including himself, who interacted often with others and yet did not like them. Though the proposition holds good often, it obviously does not hold good always, and we must now look at the "other variables" that sometimes make it fail.

If two men interact and the activity of each rewards that of the other, each is apt to like the other and go on with the interaction—our proposition has no trouble handling that situation. If two men interact and at least one of them finds the activity of the other not rewarding or even positively punishing, he will sooner or later, if he is free to do so, look for some alternative source of reward. If he finds it, he will decrease interaction with the other man and give him little approval. Our proposition has no trouble with this situation either, for an association of little liking with little interaction is as much implied by the proposition as is an association of much liking with much interaction.

[4] T. M. Newcomb, "The Prediction of Interpersonal Attraction," *American Psychologist,* Vol. 11 (1956), pp. 575-86.

[5] G. C. Homans, *The Human Group* (New York, 1950), p. 112.

If, on the other hand, two men interact and at least one of them finds the other's activity punishing, but he is not free, as he was in the first two situations, to break off interaction with the other, then, as we know, frequent interaction between the two will not only not be associated with mutual liking but may even lead to increasing hostility. They are shut up together like two rats in a trap. Though our present proposition will not handle this situation, other propositions certainly will.

What makes the difference is whether or not a man is free to break off interaction with another whose behavior he finds punishing. If he is not free, our proposition about the relation between interaction and liking no longer holds good. What do we mean by "free" here? Let us consider a familiar example. Suppose that their mutual boss has ordered two members of a firm to work together on a problem, and as a result they interact often, perhaps more often than any other two members. Suppose that each finds some of the other's behavior punishing, if only because the two are rivals for promotion; each is trying to show the other up, and each thus threatens to withdraw reward from the other. When we say that neither is free to break off the interaction, we mean of course that if either did, and thus disobeyed his orders, he would have to forgo the rewards he might otherwise have received from his boss and the firm. Accordingly the two go on interacting frequently, but they will probably not like, and may even come to despise, each other. We believe that other exceptions to our proposition will fall into the same class as this one. When the costs of avoiding interaction are great enough, a man will go on interacting with another even though he finds the other's activity punishing; and far from liking the other more, he will like him less. Thus the members of some families and the neighbors in some villages keep on interacting, though they fight like leopards whenever they meet. Note that we have used an "economic" argument to explain exceptions to a proposition itself derived from an "economic" argument. "When me they fly, I am the wings."

Interaction and Esteem

We began this chapter with the proposition that the more Person likes Other, the more he interacts with him. As usual we began with a proposition stated in terms of the relation between only two men. We shall next, and again as usual, show what the proposition implies about a larger number of persons forming a group. On the assumption that a group consists of a number of pairs, we may go on to argue that the larger is the number of members that like other members, the more frequent is the over-all interaction between them; and we have already seen, for instance in the Bovard experiment above, that this is so. This subsidiary proposition, or corollary, is the analogue, in the relation between interaction and sentiment, to the corollary in Chapter 6: the larger the number of members that like other members, the more similar are the activities of the members in conformity to a norm. And just as we then went on from similarities to differences between members, so shall we now. If the main proposition of this chapter is correct, it should follow as a further corollary that the larger the amount of social approval received by a single member from other members (that is, the higher his esteem), the more frequent the interaction he receives from other members.

A great deal of evidence supports this corollary. Two famous field studies of real-life small groups: the Bank Wiring Observation Room, an industrial group, and the Norton Street Gang, a group of corner boys, both showed in an impressionistic way that the more popular members tended to receive most interactions.[6] But let me cite an investigation I made myself—a field study using techniques a little more quantitative than those used in the earlier ones.[7]

The investigator was studying a clerical department in a large public utility, which he called the Eastern Utilities Co. Of the members of the department ten, all girls, were each doing the same job, called cash posting. For present purposes all we need know about the job is that a cash poster went from one filing cabinet to another and pulled certain cards out of each one. The posting job required no collaboration between the girls and, unlike many jobs, allowed great freedom of movement. As the girls moved around the room from file to file, they had plenty of chance to meet and talk to one another. These

---

[6] G. C. Homans, *op. cit.*, pp. 145, 182, analyzing data from F. J. Roethlisberger and W. J. Dickson, *Management and the Worker* (Cambridge, Mass., 1939), pp. 379-548 (Bank Wiring Observation Room); and W. F. Whyte, *Street Corner Society* (Chicago, 1943) (Norton Street Gang).

[7] G. C. Homans, "The Cash Posters," *American Sociological Review*, Vol. 19 (1954), pp. 724-33.

features of the job are worth emphasizing, for if a girl's freedom to interact with others had been curtailed by the need to collaborate or to stay in one place, the results would not have been the same.

The investigator wanted to get a record of interactions in the department for a period of at least two working weeks; but since fifty people were present all told, he found it physically impossible to record every contact and took a sample instead. Every fifteen minutes during the working day he allowed his eyes to sweep the room, and he checked off what girls were talking to what other girls at that time. He could not by this method determine which of the girls had started a conversation nor which had contributed most to it. But he could readily make a count of the sheer number of times each girl had been seen talking to every other girl and thus of the total number of times a girl had taken part in conversations with others.

Analysis of the results showed a strong tendency for girls to talk to other girls in their own job-group within the department more often than they talked to members of other job-groups. Thus cash posters were particularly apt to interact with other cash posters. Where there were exceptions they were likely to be girls who talked to others formerly in their own job-group and only recently promoted out of it. But for the moment we shall pay no further attention to this finding, and concentrate instead on differences between cash posters in the number of interactions each received.

In the course of a long interview, the investigator asked each girl the sociometric question: "Who are your close friends in here?" She might name as few or as many friends as she pleased. In the investigator's experience a general question like this was just as apt to yield reliable results, to correlate with other ways of measuring liking, as were more specific sociometric tests, such as those used at Hudson, which named definite criteria for choice. He then put the cash posters in rank-order according to the number of others that named each girl as a friend; that is, he put them in rank-order of esteem. He put them also in rank-order according to the number of conversations each took part in; that is, he put them in rank-order of the interactions each received. And he found a high correlation between the two rank-orders. This finding is in accordance with our corollary.

Yet a critic may fail to be impressed. He may say to the investigator, "When a girl named another as her friend, all she meant was that she associated with her often, and so it is hardly surprising that there should be a correlation between choices and interaction received." There is this much merit in his criticism, that when the investigator asked a girl what she meant when she called another her friend, she might indeed refer to the fact that "she saw a lot of her." But this was not all she would say. She would also say that "she liked her a lot," that is, she would refer to what we call sentiment, and then go on to explain what it was about the other girl's behavior that she found rewarding. In short, in their discussions of friendship, the girls, like the rest of us when we are not being social scientists, would recognize implicitly the relations between interaction, activity, and sentiment that we are trying to make explicit here.

The Matrix of Interaction

Now that some evidence has supported our corollary about the relation between esteem and interactions received, let us see what else the main proposition of this chapter implies about the detailed distribution of interaction in a group. Let us set up, as we did in the last chapter, an artificial group, or toy society, made up of six members: O, P, Q, R, S, and T. And let us assume—it is a large assumption—that the members are agreed on the way each ranks the others on the amount of approval he gives them. Thus every member likes O best and gives him approval worth 5, likes P next best, and so on. (As usual we pay no attention to the amount of approval that a member gives to himself.) Accordingly the alphabetical order of the members is their rank-order in esteem. Our main proposition states that the frequency of interaction given by one person to another varies directly as the approval he gives the other, so let us say that if any member gives O approval worth 5, he will give him 5 interactions within some arbitrary period of time, and so on. The resulting matrix is shown in Table 12. The figure 1 in column T, row O, means that O gives T one interaction within the arbitrary period of time. It is not, of course, the absolute size of the figures but their size relative to one another that is important here.

Now let us consider the properties of this rather obvious matrix. First, its pattern of interaction is the same as the pattern of sentiment our six-member toy group displayed in the last chapter, which is scarcely surprising, as our present proposition holds that in general interaction and sentiment vary together. Second, it conforms to our corollary in showing that the higher a member's esteem, the larger the total number of interactions he receives from other members; for the total interactions received by each member are shown by the sums of the columns, and their rank-order is also the rank-order of the

A Model Interaction Matrix

		Interactions received						Total given
		O	*P*	*Q*	*R*	*S*	*T*	
	O		5	4	3	2	1	15
Interactions given	*P*	5		4	3	2	1	15
	Q	5	4		3	2	1	15
	R	5	4	3		2	1	15
	S	5	4	3	2		1	15
	T	5	4	3	2	1		15
Total received		25	21	17	13	9	5	

members in esteem. Third, the mutual interaction between two people is higher, the higher the average esteem of the two. Compare the figures 5 and 5 for the interactions between O and P, with the figures 1 and 1 for the interactions between S and T.

Plausible as it may appear at first glance, our matrix does not correspond to any real state of affairs, and that for a very obvious reason. It shows, for instance, member T addressing interaction to member O five times, but O addressing interaction to T only once. But is this a realistic result? If we assume, as we are free to do—for the matrix is after all only a toy—that T's five interactions were mostly attempts to get some valuable service out of O, then O's single interaction back shows that the attempts were not very successful. In real life we should expect, as the group moved toward practical equilibrium, either that O would increase the returns he made to T (or he would forfeit the high approval T had given him), or that T would decrease the number of attempts he made on O (for if an activity goes unrewarded, a man will in time cease to emit it). In either case the two members would become more nearly equal in the interactions each addressed to the other. Put it even more simply: most interactions between men take the form of talking. If I talk to you, you will find it hard not to talk back, and so the interactions each of us gives to the other will tend toward something like equality. For reasons that will appear later, we do not insist on absolute equality.

If what must happen in any one pair happens also in other pairs in the group, we should expect that members who receive much interaction will also give much. And since members who receive much are ones that stand high in esteem, we should expect members high in esteem to be high givers of interaction too. So obvious is this conclusion that we shall not bother to review the evidence supporting it, which is plentiful.[8] Yet the conclusion is not embodied in our matrix at all: whereas the members of our toy society are definitely unequal in the number of interactions they receive, they are equal in the number they give.

Let us, therefore, make an assumption that will bring the matrix closer to real life. Let us assume that the more interactions a member receives, the more he also gives, and correct the matrix accordingly. We do this by multiplying the figures in each row, which represent the interactions given by each member, by a figure representing his rank in interactions received. Thus each of the figures representing interactions given by member O should be multiplied by 6, since O holds top rank in interactions received. The corrected matrix is shown in Table 13.

In the new and corrected matrix, the rank-order of the members in esteem is their rank-order not only in the number of interactions received but also in the number of interactions given. Moreover the two members of many pairs are much more nearly equal in the number of interactions each gives to the other than they were in the original matrix. For instance, T still gives 5 interactions to O, but he gets 6 back instead of only one. But absolute equality we have not achieved. In fact

[8] For instance, B. Norfleet, "Interpersonal Relations and Group Productivity," *Journal of Social Issues*, Vol. 4 (1948), pp. 66-69.

a close inspection of the matrix shows that in every pair the member higher in esteem gives more interaction to the other than the other gives to him. On all these counts, except perhaps the last, the new matrix is more realistic than the old one.

In their research on small groups investigators have obtained matrices of interaction that have many points in common with our toy. Let us look at one of them, but without asking for the moment whether

Corrected Interaction Matrix

			Interactions received				Total given
		O	P	Q	R	S	T	
	O		30	24	18	12	6	90
Interactions given	P	25		20	15	10	5	75
	Q	20	16		12	8	4	60
	R	15	12	9		6	3	45
	S	10	8	6	4		2	30
	T	5	4	3	2	1		15
Total received		75	70	62	51	37	20	

it resembles ours because the people concerned behaved according to our propositions—without asking, that is, whether we were right for the right reasons. The matrix is shown in Table 14.

This matrix is a product of research by R. F. Bales and his associates.[9] They formed six-man groups that met for about an hour at a time and tried to reach by discussion some solution to problems set by the investigators. Note that the members of each group had a task to accomplish in common—a condition that certainly does not hold for all human groups. Aside from giving them the problem and re-

[9] R. F. Bales, "The Equilibrium Problem in Small Groups," in T. Parsons, R. F. Bales, and E. A. Shils, *Working Papers in the Theory of Action* (Glencoe, Ill., 1953), p. 129.

Aggregate Matrix for Eighteen Sessions of Six-Man Groups

		To individuals						Total to individuals	To group as whole	Total initiated
		1	2	3	4	5	6			
From individuals	1		1238	961	545	445	317	3506	5661	9167
	2	1748		443	310	175	102	2778	1211	3989
	3	1371	415		305	125	69	2285	742	3027
	4	952	310	282		83	49	1676	676	2352
	5	662	224	144	83		28	1141	443	1584
	6	470	126	114	65	44		819	373	1192
Total received		5203	2313	1944	1306	872	565	12205	9106	21311

quiring that they meet in a special observation room, the investigators did not restrict the members' behavior in any way. From a special observation booth, which let them see and hear the members without the members' seeing and hearing them, the investigators, among other things, recorded every act in the discussion as being made (initiated) by a particular member and directed at (received by) another member or the group as a whole. A unit-act consisted for the investigators of any word, set of words, or gesture, no matter how short, that made sense by itself in the circumstances of the discussion. In some circumstances the word "Oh?" alone might express doubt about what had just been said and so count as a unit-act.

From these records the investigators could make a count of the number of interactions (unit-acts) given by each member to every other one and to the group as a whole. The present matrix represents the aggregate of such figures for eighteen separate sessions of six-man groups. First, the investigators constructed a matrix for each separate session as follows. They arranged the members in rank-order of the number of interactions they initiated, the No. 1 man being the most frequent initiator, the No. 2 man the next most frequent, and so on. Then they filled in the matrix by indicating how many acts No. 1 directed to No. 2, how many to No. 3, and so on for him and then for the other members. Having thus constructed a matrix for each of the eighteen sessions, they arrived at the aggregate matrix by simply adding together the figures in the corresponding cells of the original matrices. Thus the figure 1238 is the total number of times that the eighteen No. 1 men initiated acts directed at their respective No. 2 men.

Remembering that only relative magnitudes and not absolute ones are of interest to us, let us compare this matrix with our own. In both, the more often a member receives interaction, the more often he gives it too. But the members that initiate often do so proportionately a great deal more often in the Bales matrix than in our own: the frequent talkers do much more to monopolize the conversation. The reason lies in part in the simple 6, 5, 4, . . . series that we used to construct our matrix. Though it is a natural series to use, it need not correspond closely to the way interaction is distributed in real life. The tendency of the high initiators to monopolize the discussion is even more marked when acts addressed to the group as a whole are included. In constructing our matrix we made no allowance at all for this kind of act.

Both in the Bales matrix and in ours the interactions given by each member of any pair to the other member tend toward equality without reaching it. But there the resemblance ends. In any pair in our matrix the member higher in total interaction gives more interaction to the other member than the other gives to him. The reverse is true of the Bales matrix: close inspection shows that in almost every pair, the member lower in total interaction gives more interaction to the other member than the other gives to him. Thus the No. 6 man in initiations gives 470 interactions to No. 1, while No. 1 gives 317 interactions to No. 6. There are a few exceptions to this rule, for instance, the pair made up of Nos. 3 and 4, but the general tendency is pronounced. The reason for this difference lies, of course, in the interactions to the group as a whole, which were possible in the Bales groups but which we did not allow for at all in our toy society. In the Bales groups, some of the remarks addressed by low interactors to high ones the latter did not answer directly but only indirectly—by talking to the group as a whole. Interaction tended to go upward—from low interactors to high—in pair relations, and thence from high interactors to the group as a whole. No chairman of any kind was appointed or elected in the Bales groups. In many real discussion groups, such as committees, the institution of a chairman formalizes the tendencies informally present here: members conventionally address the chairman, and the chairman addresses the group as a whole.

Remember that the Bales matrix was an aggregate matrix. Not every one of the eighteen single sessions would have shown the pattern so clearly: it came out only when the figures for all the sessions were summed up; yet we may guess that it represents a strong central tendency in groups of this kind. These were discussion groups: each had a single problem to consider as a group, and each member could easily talk to every other. If these conditions had not been realized, if, for instance, there had been no single group-task and the physical layout of the room made some members easier to talk to than others, we should not have expected so neat a pattern nor so heavy a concentration of interaction on a few talkative members.

In the same way we do not argue that every real group matches our model matrix, which is no more than the pattern of interaction our proposition predicts under a very special condition: that in giving social approval every member ranks the others in the same way. There is no reason to believe that this condition always obtains in real groups. Under different conditions the same proposition will predict different patterns. We shall use our matrix only as a kind of benchmark for comparison.

The Bales matrix bears a strong family resemblance to ours, and yet the resemblance may be spurious. The former was constructed by arranging the members of a group in rank-order of their initiation of interaction; it made no assumption that this rank-order was also the rank-order of members in esteem. But in constructing our matrix we did make just this assumption. Unless we can show that it also holds good in fact of the Bales groups, we have no right to cite his matrix in support of our proposition. The horrid fact is that we may not be altogether able to do so. As we shall see later, the high interactors in the Bales groups did get much social approval of a certain kind, but they were not particularly well "liked." We may have to distinguish between different kinds of social approval instead of lumping them all together as we have done so far. In particular we may have to distinguish between a principal ingredient of esteem that most Americans might call "respect" and another kind of social approval that most Americans might indeed call "liking." We only raise the question here; in later chapters we shall have much more to say about it.

Interaction with Equals

Just as in the last chapter we examined matrices of choice displaying some features—an equality-effect and a justice-effect—that our propositions have not explained so far, so in the present chapter we must look at an interaction matrix that has something in common with our toy matrix and with Bales' and yet differs from both. The matrix resulted from research by Riley, Cohn, Toby, and Riley.[10]

The investigators studied the girl students, some 1500 in all, in the 9th and 10th grades of eight New Jersey high schools. No doubt each grade in each school formed a true social group, but all the grades together obviously did not form one, and the results the investigators report represent, like those of Bales, an aggregate. Nor probably did any single grade have the sharp focus for interaction that the discussion of a set problem provided for Bales' groups. The opportunities for interaction were much more diffuse.

The investigators asked every girl to answer a questionnaire in which she was to name, out of the other girls in her grade, a certain number, say three, that she considered the most "popular." Then she was to name the three she thought were most "liked," and the three she thought were most "admired." Out of the results of the questionnaire the investigators put the girls in each grade in rank-order of "status." Note that "status" here is not the same thing as esteem, for each girl was not asked to name the others she personally liked most but rather the others she perceived as being generally best-liked. No doubt real esteem would have correlated with perceived esteem, but the research report tells us only about the latter. The investigators next

[10] M. W. Riley, R. Cohn, J. Toby, and J. W. Riley, Jr., "Interpersonal Relations in Small Groups," *American Sociological Review,* Vol. 19 (1954), pp. 715-24.

divided, by arbitrary cutting-points, the whole distribution of status-scores into six different status-classes, the highest being status 6 and the lowest status 1.

The investigators then asked every girl to answer a new questionnaire, designed to discover how much she was likely to talk to every other girl in her grade. They gave her a series of seven topics of conversation ranging all the way from relations with the opposite sex to problems of right and wrong—a long distance, we shall agree—and asked her to name the other girls she would be apt to talk to about

TABLE FIFTEEN

Status and Disposition to Communicate

	Status	Communication-choice received						Average given
		6	5	4	3	2	1	
Communication-choice given	6	*1.36*	.66	.39	.25	.16	.04	.47
	5	.88	*.81*	.52	.33	.19	.05	.46
	4	.81	.76	*.62*	.36	.18	.07	.47
	3	.69	.54	.42	*.38*	.20	.07	.38
	2	.60	.47	.34	.26	*.26*	*.11*	.34
	1	.49	.41	.26	.22	.26	.07	.29
Average received		.81	.61	.43	.30	.21	.07	

each topic. The larger the number of topics a girl said she would be disposed to talk about with another, the higher her score on communication with the other. From these individual scores, it was easy to calculate the average disposition to communicate between girls in any one status-class and those in another. Note that the investigators studied verbal expressions of a disposition to interact and not interaction itself. How much the girls' answers represented reality and how much wish we cannot tell; but even if they represented nothing but wish, the way that wished-for interaction was distributed would still be interesting. At any rate the matrix is shown in Table 15.

As usual, in studying this matrix we should not pay attention to the absolute scores but only to the relative ones. For instance, the important thing about the figure 1.36 is not that it is a particular quantity but that it is the highest figure in the matrix. It means that girls of the highest status-class (6) felt more disposed to talk to other girls of the same status than they did to talk to girls of any other status, indeed that there was more talking between girls of this status-class than there was within any other status or between any pair of statuses. In the Bales matrix and in ours the cells on the major diagonal were left empty because scores in them could only represent a member's talking to himself. In the present matrix they could be filled, because there were many girls in each status and they could perfectly well talk to one another.

The matrix displays many of the features of the Bales matrix and ours. The higher the average status of any two statuses, the higher their disposition to interact with one another. The more often the members of a status receive interaction, the more often they give it too, though the difference between statuses in interaction given is very small—proportionately much less than the equivalent differences in the Bales groups. Moreover the tendency toward equality between any two statuses in the exchange of interaction with each other is much less marked than it is in the Bales matrix. Even more marked, on the other hand, is the tendency for the lower status to give more inter action to the higher than it receives from the higher. The reason is, of course, that the present matrix shows perceived and not actual interaction: girls of high status were under no such pressure to respond to remarks addressed to them by girls of low status as they would have been under in real life.

For our immediate purposes the present matrix has one great advantage over Bales'. In the latter the rank-order of members in the receiving of interaction was simply taken as given and not related, as yet, to any measures other than those of interaction. In the present matrix, on the other hand, we can see that the rank-order on receipt correlates with the independently measured status of the girls. Thus the present matrix, unlike Bales', provides some support for our corollary that the higher the esteem in which a member is held, the larger is the number of interactions he will receive. True, the present research measures "status," that is, esteem as perceived and recognized in public, but we have argued that esteem always does become so recognized, and not inaccurately.

But there is one feature of the present matrix that appears neither in Bales' nor in ours. Look down the columns. In every column but one the highest figure lies on the major diagonal, making the series 1.36, .81, .62, .38, .26. The only exception to the rule is the figure .11 in the last column, column 1, and that is only one step off the main diagonal. If, moreover, we scan the other figures in each column, we see that they drop off steadily on either side of the highest figure, unless as in column 6 the high figure is at one end.

What does this well-marked pattern mean? The rows indicate whither each status-class gave its interaction; the columns, whence each class received it. The rows show that the higher the status of a class, the more interaction, or rather the more expressed dispositions to interact, another class gave to it. But the columns show something different. They show that so far as interactions received, not interactions given, were concerned, the members of each status-class received more interaction from other members of the same class than from any other. More than this, the nearer in status any two classes were to one another, the more interaction the members of one received from the members of the other. Thus, the members of class 4 received most interaction from other members of that class, next most from classes 5 and 3, and so on.

The differences between the present matrix and Bales' are probably made possible not only by the different method used in the research—questionnaire instead of observation—but also by the different nature of the groups. These were not discussion groups, their members meeting for a short time and focusing their communication on a single problem, but school grades, their members sharing many activities for months and years together. More interesting than the question why the matrices differ at all is why they differ in the way they do. Just as in the last chapter we observed a tendency for members to give approval not only to their superiors in activity but also to their similars, who were by that fact their equals, so now we observe a tendency for members to give their interactions, likewise, to their equals in status as well as to their superiors. Let us take due note once more of an equality-effect that remains to be explained.

The Origination of Interaction

When in one of the Bales groups we say that a member *initiated* interaction, we mean only that he emitted a unit-act addressed to another member or to the group as a whole. We have specified nothing about the position of that act in a series of interactions. It may have been the first of a series: the man may have asked the other to do something for him; but it may also have been the last: the man may have complied with the other's request and brought the series of interactions between them to a close. The unit-act that starts off a series of exchanges between two men after a period, long or short, in which no interaction between them has taken place, we shall speak of as the *origination*,[11] rather than the initiation, of interaction. To originate interaction with another, a man may have to move from where he is now into the presence of the other, as when Person leaves his own desk in the office and goes over to Other's to ask him for help. It may be worthwhile asking what determines which of a pair of men is the more likely to originate interaction with the other. What, for instance, determines that it is Person rather than Other who originates interaction between them?

One of our main propositions in Chapter 4 says that "the more valuable to a man a unit of activity another gives him, the more often he will emit activity rewarded by the activity of the other." Accordingly, after some break in their interaction, the man who is the more likely to emit the first activity in a new series is the one who finds the other's activity the more valuable. In the language of common sense, the man who needs the other's services the more is the man more likely to make the first move, and if necessary to go over to the other's place and ask him for his services, as Person asks Other for help.

But the man who values the other's activity the more is apt to be lower than the other in esteem. Consider our old group consisting of Person, Other, and the Third Man. Other is able to provide rare and valuable services for the other two: only from him can they get help in doing their work; but if one of them fails to provide Other with

[11] See E. D. Chapple and C. M. Arensberg, "Measuring Human Relations," *Genetic Psychology Monographs*, Vol. 22 (1940), pp. 3-147; and G. C. Homans, *op. cit.*, pp. 36, 247; but in both these books *origination* is used in a somewhat different sense from the present one.

approval in return, Other has an alternative source of approval in the third party, whoever he may be. In these circumstances, Other is in a superior bargaining position: Person and the Third Man both need his help more than he needs the approval of either one of them. Accordingly, both Person and the Third Man are more likely to go to him and ask for help than he is to go to them and volunteer it. They are more likely to originate interaction with him than he is to originate interaction with them. When he complies with their requests, they give him approval, which means that he has the highest esteem in the group. Therefore, in any series of interactions between two men, the lower in esteem is apt to be the more frequent originator. This also means that persons equal in esteem are apt to originate interaction for one another about equally.

We have been careful to limit this proposition to interaction between two men forming a pair. It may not apply to the situation in which one man originates interaction with a number of others at the same time, as when in the Bales groups one member addresses himself to the group as a whole. Then we have already reason to believe that the higher a man's esteem, the more apt he is to originate interaction; but we shall postpone to our chapter on Authority any further consideration of this problem.

As we have already had occasion to observe, men not only behave in ways described by our propositions, but come to perceive that they are doing so; and their perceptions make possible new activities rewarded by old values. The elementary mechanisms of social behavior would make a sufficiently complicated pattern if they were merely let alone to work their own way. But they are not let alone; one mechanism climbs on the back of another, and complication gets compounded. Suppose men come to recognize, if not in our words, then in their own, that the lower of two men in esteem is the one more apt to originate interaction with the other. Then if you can maneuver another man into coming to you before you go to him, you have established for all to see the outward and visible sign of your social superiority to him; you have presented a stimulus indicating that your status is the higher. This kind of maneuvering is a favorite sport in some bureaucracies: if you can get another man, hitherto considered your equal, to come to your office rather than your going to his, to discuss some problem, you are to that extent one-up on him. But you had better be careful: there is always a counter-ploy. If he is smart enough to show no reluctance about coming to your office, as if this kind of social climbing were wholly beneath him, and he makes this plain to any observer who may be present, including yourself, he has turned the tables on you; for the man who shows no anxiety about status is apt to have the highest status of all.

There are plenty of other examples of the secondary behavior created by men's recognition of primary social mechanisms. Suppose, for instance, that a man provides his fellows with valuable services, and so receives their esteem and interaction. Once his status gets recognized, this fact alone gives the others a new reason for interacting with him. For, as we have noticed in our matrices, a person who interacts often with a man of high esteem is apt to be held in high esteem himself; accordingly for a man to interact often with another held in high esteem becomes rewarding to him in its own right, and apart from whatever other rewards the interaction may bring him. It gets to be a good thing just to be seen in the company of such a person: by this sign our man can suggest to his fellows that his own status is high. By once acquiring esteem, therefore, a man automatically commands this further scarce good, permission to interact with him, which he may then exploit to acquire still further esteem. Social behavior is full of such favorable—or vicious—spirals.

Summary

In the present chapter we have considered the sheer quantity of activity one man gives to another, regardless of the kind of activity it may be. We began with an argument showing why, other things equal, the more a man interacts with another, the more he likes him. We then looked into the other things that, when they are not equal, prevent the proposition from holding good. When a man interacts with another and the other's activity punishes him, but he is not free to break the interaction off—under this condition frequent interaction is not associated with much liking. Returning to the original proposition, we then asked what corollaries followed from it; and we found, for instance, that the higher the esteem in which a man is held, the more interaction he receives from other members of his group. We then saw that the corollary fell short of fully representing the facts, and we asked why. This led us into the reasons for believing that the interaction each of two men gives to the other will tend toward equality; and we found this to imply further that, besides receiving much interaction from others, a man of high esteem is likely to give them much too. Finally, we saw why, in any pair, the man lower in esteem is apt to originate more interaction than the man higher. But as usual we also encountered findings for which our propositions so far provide no explanation, notably a tendency for men to receive much interaction from their social equals; and, again as usual, we postponed the consideration of these findings to a later chapter.

The Nature of the Givens

> **Chapter Eleven**

Now that we have stated a few straightforward propositions about the value of activity and sentiment and the frequency of interaction, and have also run into some findings about equality and justice that our propositions so far neither describe nor explain, we must take time out, before going on to these more complicated phenomena, for a topic of a new kind. This book undertakes to explain elementary social behavior, and the explanation of a phenomenon is a process of showing that a proposition or propostions describing it may be deduced from a set of more general propositions under specified given conditions. When we say that the propositions from which the deduction is made are more general, we mean that other phenomena besides the one in question may also be deduced from them under different given conditions. When we say that the conditions are given, we mean, first, that whoever is doing the explaining is not bound to explain *them,* though he may in fact be able to do so, and second, that the conditions are taken to be constant during the period of time under consideration.

In earlier chapters, in explaining various social phenomena, we did in fact take various social conditions as given. Thus in explaining why a rather small number of members got the highest esteem in a group, we assumed that many members set the same value on the same services, and that they could get these services from only a few of their fellows. But these particular conditions may not obtain in all groups;

and there may be other sorts of conditions, wholly different from any we have considered so far, that must from time to time be taken into account in explaining actual behavior. Accordingly this chapter will have two jobs to do: first, to illustrate a few out of the many different sorts of given conditions that may have to be taken into consideration, and second, to suggest how, under conditions different from those we have so far assumed to be given, our same propositions predict different actual behavior.

To understand the relation between descriptive propositions, general propositions, and givens, let us consider an illustration from physical and not social science. In most parts of the sea there are two high tides and two low tides in about every twenty-four hours. About twice a month these tides have an especially great range between high and low—the spring tides—and about twice a month an especially small range—the neap tides. Not only is this true of the sea; it is true also of lakes, though it takes careful measurement to detect the tides there. These are statements describing the phenomena. How does the natural scientist explain them?

He first takes as given the existence of the sun, of a certain mass; the existence of the earth, of a certain mass, rotating on its own axis once a day, revolving in orbit around the sun once a year, and largely covered with water; and finally the existence of the moon, of a certain mass, moving in orbit around the earth about once a month. For the purpose of explaining the tides the astronomer simply takes these things as given. This does not mean that the givens could not themselves be explained: no doubt the science of cosmology might explain them. But the scientist is not called upon to explain all things in the course of explaining one.

He next takes a general proposition, Newton's inverse-square law of gravitation—general because with somewhat different givens it can be used to explain phenomena other than the tides, for instance, the shape of the planetary orbits. And he proceeds to show that from this law it may be deduced that the water on the earth will bulge slightly in two directions, one bulge on the side nearest the moon and one on the side farthest away, and that correspondingly the water will be lower on the two sides of the earth at right angles to the direction of the moon. He shows further that as the earth rotates on its axis once a day, this double-ended bulge will tend, subject to friction, to maintain its alignment in the direction of the moon, producing at any one point on the earth's surface two high and two low tides.

Since the moon, although of much less mass than the sun, is also much nearer to the earth, the chief tidal effect is produced by the gravitational attraction of the moon. But the effect of the sun is not negligible. When sun, moon, and earth are in line, as they are when the moon is either full or new, the two forces combine to produce a particularly big bulge of water and hence the spring tides; but when the attraction of the sun is at right angles to that of the moon, the former cancels the latter to some degree and produces the neap tides. We shall not demonstrate here the logic of the deduction, but be well assured that the deduction does follow from Newton's law under the given conditions.[1]

The deductions do not account for all the tidal phenomena. They do not, for instance, explain why in some places like the Bay of Fundy the range of tides should be spectacularly great, nor why at different places high tide should occur at different times after the moon's passage over the meridian. Worse still, there are places where there is only one high tide a day instead of two. The explanation of these things would have to take account of new kinds of givens—the contour of ocean bottoms and shores, for instance—and use new propositions—those of fluid mechanics, for instance. But Newton's law, taken together with the given conditions we have mentioned, does explain the gross descriptive propositions about the tides that we started with. It explains no more than it was meant to explain.

Note, finally, that we may look on the givens as the environment of the tidal phenomena: earth, moon, and sun. In explaining anything we draw, in effect, an arbitrary line around it—arbitrary in the sense that we have freely undertaken to explain what lies inside the line, and that, if we had undertaken to explain more, we should have drawn the line differently. What lies outside the line we simply take as given. This does not mean that we are not interested in the effect of the environment on the phenomenon, for obviously we are. What lies outside the line we also take as constant, nor need this mean we lack interest in the effect of the phenomenon on the environment; and the tides do have an effect on their environment: for instance, they tend to

---

[1] See E. Mach, *The Science of Mechanics*, T. J. McCormack, trans. (La Salle, Ill., 1942) pp. 255-64.

retard the earth's rotation. But the effect is a very slow one, and at any particular time we take the environment as both given and constant.

Geographical Location

With this example in mind we are ready to consider the relations between descriptive propositions, general propositions, and givens in the explanation of elementary social behavior. And what we shall do first is illustrate a number of different features of the environment of behavior that must be taken as givens in explaining it. We insist that we can do no more than illustrate. No more than a textbook of physics can possibly survey all the circumstances in which the laws of mechanics may be applied, can we possibly cover systematically all of the sorts of givens that may from time to time play their part in determining the phenomena we are interested in.

Yet we shall not illustrate utterly at random. We shall concentrate on three classes of givens that turn up again and again in field studies of social behavior. First, features of the physical or functional proximity of men to one another that make them likely to enter into exchange. Second, features of the past histories, or backgrounds, of men that make them likely to hold similar values. And third, features of the positions men hold outside the group in question that make them particularly well able to reward their fellow members within the group. But we insist again that these classes, though often encountered, are not the only ones and do not exhaust the possible givens. In particular, the conditions established in any experiment, both those the investigator intended to establish and those he did not, must always be taken as givens in explaining its results.

Prominent among the givens are those establishing the geographical location of people in relation to one another. For illustration here we go back to the study by Festinger, Schachter, and Back of the M.I.T. housing development.[2] We do not go back to Westgate, considered in Chapter 6 on Conformity, but to Westgate West, the newer part of the development. All of the buildings of Westgate West were exactly

---

[2] L. Festinger, S. Schachter, and K. W. Back, *Social Pressures in Informal Groups* (New York, 1950), pp. 33-59. See also J. T. Gullahorn, "Distance and Friendship as Factors in the Gross Interaction Matrix," *Sociometry*, Vol. 15 (1952), pp. 123-34.

the same in their layout, which was quite different from that of West-gate. Each had two floors with five flats on each floor. On each floor the doors of the flats opened on a porch or gallery running the length of the building, the top-floor porch lying directly above the ground-floor one. From the ends of the ground-floor porch stairways ran up to the ends of the top-floor one. Figure 2 shows the layout and numbers the flats for ready reference.

FIGURE TWO

Schematic Diagram of Westgate West Building

Each flat was occupied by a young married couple, the husband a student at M.I.T. We shall recall that the investigators asked each couple to name its three closest friends in the project, and that in our terms these choices were expressions of sentiment. In Westgate West, the investigators were interested in discovering the relation between geographical position and the distribution of friendship-choices.

The first finding we all might have predicted. When the investigators plotted the choices made by couples in Westgate West against the positions occupied by these couples in the buildings, they discovered that, statistically speaking, a couple was most likely to choose another whose flat was an immediate neighbor to its own, one unit of distance away, next most likely to choose a nearest neighbor but one, and so on. The nearer a couple lived to another couple the more apt it was to become friendly with the other.

The next finding was a little less obvious. The investigators exam-ined the way in which couples on a particular floor distributed their choices to other couples on the same floor, and discovered that couples in the central flats—Nos. 3 and 8—were chosen as friends more often than other couples. When we say that these flats were central, we mean that the average distance from them to all other flats on their floors was less than it was for any of the others. Again, physical distance was governing sociometric choice.

The last finding we present was not obvious at all. It is shown in Table 16. Row 1 simply indicates the apartment positions on the ground floor, as given in Figure 2. Row 2 takes the total number of choices given by lower-floor people to upper-floor people and shows which flats on the lower floor these choices came from. Specifically, the high figures, 13 and 11, show that couples occupying end flats on the ground floor were more likely to choose people on the upper floor than were couples occupying other flats. Since the end flats lay at the

TABLE SIXTEEN

Geographical Location and Sociometric Choice

		1	2	3	4	5
1.	Apartment position	1	2	3	4	5
2.	Choices given to upper floor	13	5	8	6	11
3.	Choices received from upper floor	14	3	12	4	15

feet of the stairs leading down from the top floor, people living in them had an especially good chance to come into contact with upper-floor people. Yet people in the central flats (3) were more likely to choose upper-floor couples than were the people in flats 2 and 4, even though they were further from the stairs.

Row 3 tells the same sort of story. It shows how choices given by members of the upper floor were distributed among flats on the ground floor. End apartments were most likely to get choices from above, just as they had been to give them. The central flat came close behind but flats 2 and 4 got few choices. The reader will of course have observed that the number of flats on each floor was only five, and yet the choices given and received were far more than five. The reason is that Westgate West consisted of a number of identical apartment buildings, and the figures in the different cells in the table represent the sums of all the choices given or received by couples occupying the corresponding positions in the different buildings. Thus the figure 15 indicates that the several couples occupying No. 5 flats received a total of 15 choices from all the couples in top-floor flats. And the table represents an aggregate. A single building taken by itself might not, for one reason or another, have displayed the pattern that revealed itself when the figures for all the buildings were taken together.

These results constitute the descriptive propositions we have to explain. And what are the givens? Givens are data that are taken to be constant for the time being, and that are used in explanation but remain themselves unexplained; and so one set of givens is the physical layout of the buildings. As social scientists we are not called upon to explain the layout, though as amateur architects we might make a start at doing so. But this is not the only significant given. Just as important is the fact that the project was new, and that the couples were new to M.I.T., the project, and one another. Few of them had previous ties with other couples in the housing development or indeed elsewhere in the city. Moreover we may guess that they were a rather homogeneous set of people—all married, all of about the same age, and all students of engineering. If sharp differences in background had divided them, or if the investigators had studied the project when it was older— when couples had come and gone, when some old ties had been broken while others were still in force—the geography of the place would not have made its influence so clearly felt. One kind of given set the other free to do its work.

With these things given, our propositions must do the explaining. We put geography forward as something that affects, in the first instance, the quantity of activity given by one person to another. The nearer together people live, the more apt they are to meet and exchange some amount of activity, however little and however trivial, such as comments on the weather. The nearness need not lie in sheer physical proximity. It may also lie in the likelihood that paths will cross: someone coming downstairs is apt to run into people living at the foot. Once thrown together in this way, once they have exchanged some activity not positively punishing, they are apt to repeat the exchange and find it rewarding—provided that they lack alternative and richer sources of reward. In Westgate West the second set of givens— the homogeneity of the couples and their newness to the project— made it unlikely that they had access to better sources of reward than those near at hand. Accordingly exchange with near neighbors was likely to continue, and, as we have seen, frequent interaction is associated with favorable sentiment. Therefore, under the given conditions, the nearer two couples lived to each other, the more likely they were to become friends. And the more central the position of a couple on a floor—that is, the nearer they were, on the average, to other couples on that floor—the more likely these couples were to choose them as friends.

More difficult is the explanation of the pattern of choice between floors. People living at the foot of staircases are particularly apt to run into the people on the floor above that use those staircases. They are close to the others functionally if not in sheer physical distance, and hence are particularly apt to become friendly with upper-floor people. We need no new argument to account for this. But how about the large number of choices given to, and received from, the upper floor by the central couple on the lower floor? Physically and functionally it was, on the average, the couple on the lower floor that was farthest from the upper. We cannot explain this finding without making an assumption about indirect relations between people: if O is a friend of P's, and P is a friend of Q's, then O is apt to become a friend of Q's. The central couple on the lower floor was apt to have more friends on that floor than any other couple there. So far as these friends of theirs had any friends at all on the top floor, they were likely to become friends of the central couple's too. And so, in spite of physical and functional distance, the central couple on the first floor were apt to have many friends on the second.

We have spent some time on the case of Westgate West because it is an especially neat one. In an earlier chapter we cited findings of the same sort from Westgate: couples that lived in flats that did not face the court tended to have few friends in the court and to deviate from court standards. There are many other examples, but one may be enough. We shall remember the cash posters. Although they spent most of the time on their feet, moving from file to file, management had also assigned a small table to each girl, where she could take file trays that she was going to work on at some length. Management believed in our propositions, and changed the table assignments every year in order to prevent the girls with adjoining tables from becoming too friendly. Friendliness would lead to talking, and talking would interfere with work. But the damage—if damage it was—had already been done. When he arrived on the floor, the investigator found no tendency for girls with adjoining tables to interact with one another particularly often or to choose one another as friends. On the other hand, the social history of the department showed that girls who had sat next to one another during their first year on the job were indeed likely to become friends, and their friendship was likely to survive their later physical separation.[3] Proximity at the beginning was what counted.

Functional proximity between two persons is naturally not limited to staircases. People who work on the same piece of equipment or on different stages of the same job, so that one passes work on to the other, are particularly likely to interact and hence, other things equal, to become friends. And people that many others must interact with in the course of their work are apt to have many friends for much the same reasons that made the couples in the central flats at Westgate popular. Let us return for a moment to the Hudson State School for Girls. Each girl received vocational training, in the course of which she learned to provide services for other girls and the community; and certain sorts of jobs, notably telephone-operating and working in the store, were especially likely to bring her into contact with large numbers of others. Girls on these jobs were apt to report a large *social-contact range:* they took the trouble to speak to a large number of others, and they were also more likely than other girls to be highly chosen.[4] In cases like these, what throws people together is not a building with its doors and passageways but the management of some enterprise; yet the effect is the same. By breaking down an over-all task into parts and assigning each part to a person, the management has made it inevitable that this person will interact with some people more often than he will with others, and that some people will interact with him more often than they will with others. No more than he undertakes to explain why a building is laid out the way it is does a student of elementary social behavior undertake to explain why the management breaks down the task in a particular way—though he could doubtless lecture on the division of labor in general. All he says is this: "I shall take as given the way in which the environment, physical or social, sets different probabilities that persons will interact. These things given, I deduce from my general propositions that certain descriptive propo-

[3] G. C. Homans, "The Cash Posters," *American Sociological Review,* Vol. 19 (1954), p. 729.

[4] H. H. Jennings, *Leadership and Isolation,* 2nd ed. (New York, 1950), pp. 138-41.

sitions hold good of the observations. If they do, the general propositions are confirmed and the descriptive ones explained."

Perhaps by this time we need not insist that proximity, physical or functional, does not always have the effect that we have said it does, but has it only when other things are "equal," and they are not always so. People who are thrown together do not like one another unless they reward one another. Often they do reward one another, if only because near rewards are purchased at less cost than distant ones, but they need not do so always; and this leads us to the second of the three classes of givens we shall consider in this chapter.

Similarity of Values

In Chapter 3 we argued that the most important of all givens in explaining or predicting the behavior of men are their values, and particularly the relation of these values to one another. Of two kinds of activity, which does a man find the more valuable to receive? If we know things like this, if we can take his scale of values as given, we have taken the most important first step in explaining his behavior. By the same token, in explaining the behavior of two men toward one another, we need to know the relation between the values of the one and those of the other.

Sometimes it is the difference between their values that makes exchange between them probable, and in much that has gone before we have been concerned with the differences between people in the values they hold. Thus we assumed that, in the given circumstances, Person valued help more than he did approval, and Other approval more than he did help, and that this difference made exchange between them probable. In this case, the values of the two men were complementary.

But sometimes it is the similarity between the values of the two men that cements their relationship. A man's values are precipitates of his past history, or background, as we call it for short; and therefore the more similar the past histories of two men, the more similar their values are apt to be. Not only this: the more similar their backgrounds, the more apt they are to have learned to emit the same activities to get these values. When they fall into contact with each other, they are, accordingly, apt to reward and come to like each other. It is true that if they want the same thing and are competing with one another to get it, no love may be lost between them, but competition is not the only estate of man. Should both be interested in fishing, each will talk fishing when he is with the other and give him a good time. Certainly most people believe that common interests cement many relationships from marriage to ordinary friendship.

We are not called upon to decide which is more important in establishing human exchange, similarity of values or complementary differences between them. Which is more important in making a good marriage, the complementary needs or the common interests of husband and wife? Probably both are important. All we argue here is that if two or more men are similar in the values they hold—if this fact is given—then we are in a position to predict that they will probably reward each other and come to like each other. Even if the similarity in values is not given us directly, but we do at least know that the men have similar backgrounds, we can make the same prediction with a high probability of being correct.

Research on this point is not lacking. We cite one example, reported in a paper by Precker.[5] The investigator had been asked to find out what criteria the students and faculty of Bard College considered most important in assessing what a student had achieved in his education. He asked the whole population, students and faculty (some 300 in all), to suggest criteria, and they gave him some 1300. These criteria were, in effect, the names of values. He gave the list to three judges who condensed it into 39 main criteria, and these new criteria he submitted once more to the students, asking each one to put them in their rank-order in importance. At the same time he asked each student to name the three other students "he would most like to keep in touch with after graduation," and "the member of the faculty whom he would most like to have as faculty advisor."

The investigator then compared the way each student ranked the criteria with the way the persons he chose, both students and faculty, ranked them. And he found that the values of students tended to resemble the values of others whom they chose more than they did the values of others whom they had left unchosen. The similarity in rankings was greatest between persons whose choice was mutual, who had

[5] J. A. Precker, "Similarity in Valuings as a Factor in the Selection of Peers and Near-Authority Figures," *Journal of Abnormal and Social Psychology*, Vol. 47 (1952), pp. 406-14, cited in E. Katz and P. F. Lazarsfeld, *Personal Influence* (Glencoe, Ill., 1955), p. 60.

chosen one another. Of course we cannot tell from this study which variable to take as independent. Did similarity in values determine choices, as our argument would have it, or did choices determine similarity in values? It may at least be possible that two men brought together because they share a single interest should learn in the course of their association to share others. At any rate, the sheer correlation between friendship and similarity in values, or *value-homophily,* as it has been called,[6] is clear.

Suppose, now, the following to be a general proposition: the more similar the values of two persons, the more apt they are to like one another. Suppose also that the following descriptive proposition is true to the facts: Person likes Other more than he does the Third Man. Suppose, finally, that we have no present explanation why this should be so, such as that Person lives nearer to Other than he does to the Third Man. If we have independent reason to believe—independent of the descriptive proposition itself—that the values of Person resemble those of Other more than they do those of the Third Man, then the descriptive proposition is explained, for it can be deduced from the general proposition under the condition that the similarity of values is taken as given.

Similarity of Background

Sometimes we have direct information about the similarity of values, but even when we do not, we have argued that we can infer the similarity of men's values from the similarity of their backgrounds. If, for instance, Person and Other are both college students and the Third Man is a high school boy not planning to go to college, we can infer that the values of Person and Other resemble each other more than they do the values of the Third Man. And the larger the number of background characteristics two men have in common, the more similar we may expect their values to be. We may well be wrong in some instances, especially if we stop at the more visible aspects of background and so miss the hidden but perhaps more compelling events. At the hidden level, Person's background may resemble the Third Man's more than it does Other's. Yet if we are satisfied to explain the

[6] By R. K. Merton in a forthcoming study, see E. Katz and P. F. Lazarsfeld, *op. cit.,* p. 59.

general tendencies of behavior in a group of men, without accounting in detail for the behavior of every one of them, the costs of probing for hidden similarities may be greater than the additional information is worth. For many practical purposes all we need know are the obvious aspects of a man's background.

At any rate, the effects of similarities and differences in the backgrounds of men—similarities and differences that we do not undertake to explain but accept as given—are often very marked. Let us look at an example. Some years ago I was associated with members of the Harvard Graduate School of Business Administration in an intensive study of about fifty machinists and assemblers, both men and women, who formed a department in a company that we called the Industrial Controls Corporation.[7] The investigation did not begin with direct observation of the group but with an examination of the backgrounds of the workers as they were revealed by, or could be inferred from, the company's personnel records. The factory was in a city where a particular kind of background carries great weight, and this background was well represented in the department. The family names of the workers showed that about half of them were of Irish origin. Of course this did not mean that they had been born in Ireland. Far from it: the families of some of them had lived in this country for a century or more. Nor did it mean that they felt they were not Americans. It meant only that, when it came to distinguishing themselves from other Americans, they did so by saying they were "Irish."

When the investigators moved from the personnel records to the department itself, their sociometric tests and other observations showed that persons in the Irish majority were much more likely to be approved and accepted as members of the dominant cliques than were the persons of different ethnic background—German, Italian, French-Canadian, and so on—that made up the rest of the department. Nor did the Irish differ from the others in this way alone. The jobs in the department were of great variety and paid by the number of pieces of work completed. Many of the workers had adopted an output norm to the effect that whenever the management had set a standard for the output an average worker might expect to produce in a day on a particular job, no worker on the job should produce either much more

---

[7] A. Zaleznik, C. R. Christensen, and F. J. Roethlisberger, *The Motivation, Productivity, and Satisfaction of Workers* (Boston, 1958).

than the standard or much less: output should be kept right on the line. When the investigators studied the output records, they found that the Irish were more likely to be on-the-line producers, conforming to the output norm, than were the others, who tended to be either high or low in production.[8] Finally, the investigators asked the workers in the department to express, in answer to some rather straightforward questions, how satisfied they felt with the department and their jobs. From the answers the investigators simply divided the workers into two parts: the satisfied and the unsatisfied. They had devised various subtle formulas, based largely on such things as pay, seniority, and skill, which they had hoped would predict ahead of time how the members would be divided in satisfaction. But none of these measures correlated as highly with satisfaction as did the simple division into Irish and non-Irish.[9] Anyone familiar at first hand with industrial groups has had experiences of this kind, where differences in the backgrounds of workers have correlated with differences in their behavior.

Because people with similar backgrounds tend to hold similar values, they are apt to behave in ways that each will find rewarding, especially when they first meet—and what gets done then seldom gets undone later. They may not hold values greatly unlike those held by people of different backgrounds, but the values may be enough unlike to tilt the balance of behavior—if only in allowing the former to feel more at home with each other, because their style of life is more familiar, than they do with people of a different sort. At any rate, we believe that the Irish in the department were apt to find the behavior of other Irish particularly rewarding.

When people behave in ways that they find mutually rewarding, they are apt, as we know, to like one another and continue the interaction. Hence the Irish were apt to like other Irish and welcome them into their cliques, which in itself was no small reward. What was given in this group was not just that a few of the workers had an Irish background but that a majority of them did, so that their cliques were the leading ones. Had the ethnic groups been more nearly equal in numbers, being Irish might have made much less difference.

If the members of a group like one another, they are apt, as we saw in an earlier chapter, to conform to a norm that any part of the group

[8] *Ibid.*, p. 235.
[9] *Ibid.*, p. 273.

has accepted: they have much to lose, much to forgo in the way of social approval, if they fail to conform; so the Irish in the department were particularly good conformers to the output norms; and once they conformed, the approval they received from the rest of the gang was established. And this too made more difference than it might have elsewhere. For the condition of the company and the department within it was such that a worker might expect little advancement in pay or rank in return for high output on the job. In effect, social rewards were the chief rewards obtainable; and as the Irish got more than their share of them, they were on the average better satisfied than the other workers. What we have done is take as given not only the similarity in ethnic background but also certain other features of the situation—the Irish majority and the low value of rewards obtainable through the work itself—and with these things given, we have used our propositions to explain the clique-memberships, the on-the-line production, and the satisfaction of the Irish.

If persons with similar backgrounds are apt to reward and like one another and to conform to one another's norms, persons with different backgrounds are not apt to reward one another nor do any of these other things. In Chapter 6 on Conformity we suggested that people whose background was urban, Catholic, or lower-class were more likely to adopt rules restricting output than were people whose background was rural, Protestant, or middle-class, and who found a moral value in hard work. Something of the sort was true in the department. We have seen that the Catholic Irish were strictly on-the-line producers. So few people really went out for high production that we may not be justified in drawing any conclusion from them, but it is at least interesting that their backgrounds were different from those of the regular Irish. Very few of them were Irish in ethnic origin; and they had either themselves been, or their fathers had once been, white-collar workers, who had later come down in the world. They were not accepted by the regular Irish, whose norms they resented, and they tended to form a clique among themselves.[10] Indeed their high output may have been partly a result of their rejection. They may have kept it high in order to get back at the Irish who they knew disliked it. "He only does it to annoy, because he knows it teases."

[10] *Ibid.*, p. 337.

Status as a Given

A man's own background determines what he will find rewarding; the backgrounds of others determine which of them he will seek to get it from. In earlier chapters we have argued that the members of a group give most esteem to the man who is most able and willing to reward them. But why should one man be better able to do so than another? It turns out that the esteem a member gets within a group is often proportional to his status in a larger society, whatever that may be. It may be the local community. In the Eastern Utilities Co. I found a tendency for the popular girls and informal leaders to come from the suburbs as opposed to the center of the city, a tendency that the girls themselves noticed and found surprising because it upset what they took to be the order of nature: they had always supposed that "country" girls were less sophisticated than "city" girls and not more.[11] In fact, the distinction between suburbs and city was also a distinction, roughly, between middle and lower class: the higher the outside social status of a girl, the higher her esteem within the group.

The "larger society" may also be an organization of which the group is a part; and if the members of a group differ in their formal status in a company—some are better paid and have higher rank than others—the men that have the higher formal rank often, though certainly not always, have the higher informal esteem.

The reasons why this is likely to happen are pretty obvious. "Outside" status is apt to be associated with experiences that make people especially able to reward others, and rewarding others gets them esteem. Thus the middle-class girls from the suburbs were "sophisticated": as part of their style of life they had acquired a knowledge of interesting things to do, which the city girls might never have thought of. Or, in a factory, a man of high pay and rank will naturally have much knowledge and experience of the different jobs to be done, and so be well able to help others less skilled than himself. But we must also remember the secondary elaboration we mentioned at the end of the last chapter. If a man's external status, in the community or in the factory, is both high and well known, and if frequent interaction with

[11] G. C. Homans, op. cit., p. 729.

another is a sign of nearness in status with him, then being seen with him is rewarding in itself, and he has a new benefit to confer.

As students of elementary social behavior, of what is happening here and now before our eyes, we take such things as a girl's middle-class position or a man's pay and rank as given. We do not undertake to explain—though we could make a good try at it if we wanted to—why she belongs to the middle class or why there are classes at all, nor why the company has decided to give the man a particular rank or why it should have any ranks at all. But we use these givens, in conjunction with general propositions, to explain the descriptive propositions that hold good of elementary behavior, to explain, for instance, not just why some person should hold high esteem in a group but why a particular person does so in a particular group.

But let us look in more detail at another example. Let us go back to the factory department we talked of earlier, focusing now on its status-system rather than its ethnic divisions.[12] The group, including myself, that planned the research in the department wanted to see how good we were at prediction—a special kind of prediction. We, the investigators, were not trying to predict changes in the department over time. Instead we tried to predict data whose nature, at the time of prediction, was hidden from us. We should get for the department as many of the external givens as we could, and using them in conjunction with what we believed to be true propositions, we should predict certain things about everyday social behavior within the department. Only after we had written the predictions down should we go to the department, actually observe social behavior, and see if our predictions were correct. Descriptive propositions about actual behavior formed the "hidden data" we were to predict.

Because we did not want our predictions to be contaminated by any awareness of actual behavior, we took as our givens such information about the department and its members as we could get without going there at all. In fact we went to the company's personnel records. With their help we made a large number of predictions, but those that had to do with status will be enough to consider here. If, from the personnel data on the workers in the department, we could put them in order of official status in the company and unofficial status in the world of

---

[12] A. Zaleznik, C. R. Christensen, and F. J. Roethlisberger, *op. cit.,* pp. 169-98.

American labor, then certain things should follow. Since the ability to reward other members tends to be associated with outside status, and people who actually do reward others tend to get their esteem, then it should be a good bet that the order of members in outside status would also be their order in a number of measures of esteem or of things like interaction that are associated with esteem. And we made predictions to this effect.

There is at least one obvious weakness in this argument. People that are able to reward others do not always do so in fact, and industry is full of high-paid, senior workers that do not use their acquired skill and experience to help out younger men. Nor do the younger men always need help. In answer to this objection we can only repeat that people of high external status often possess the ability to reward others; at least a few will actually reward them. We should not expect perfect prediction, but the bet remains a good one.

It should be clear that the process of prediction runs parallel to the process of explanation. In both cases what is needed is a set of givens and one or more general propositions. The givens provide, for instance, the values of an independent variable in one of the propositions. The values of some dependent variable then follow from the propositions, and themselves constitute a descriptive proposition—in the present example the rank-order of members in measures of esteem. So far as the observations of actual behavior correspond to the descriptive proposition, prediction has been successful and the descriptive proposition has been explained. Of course if they do not correspond, neither prediction nor explanation has occurred. And even if they do, the problem remains of explaining why the general propositions should be what they are. They become in their turn descriptive propositions to be deduced from, and thus explained by, general propositions of a higher order. But at any one time in the history of science there must obviously be a few propositions that are used in explanation while remaining unexplained themselves. Thus for two centuries Newton's inverse-square law of gravitation remained without explanation. We are told that it can now be shown to follow as a special case from Einstein's theory of relativity.

But to return to the department. In the effort to describe briefly what the investigators did, we shall greatly simplify, while remaining true to its spirit. The methods of measuring external status were more complicated than we indicate here, and they were used to assess the average status of subgroups rather than that of individuals. From the personnel records, the investigators discovered that the department was divided into four subdepartments. Not every single worker, but the largest body of workers in each subdepartment fell into a particular category by pay and type of work. In the different subdepartments, the different categories were, respectively, relatively high-paid assemblers, high-paid machinists, low-paid assemblers, and low-paid machinists.

The next job of the investigators was to rank the subdepartments in order of external status. In the official ranking of the company and indeed in the wider world of American industry, pay is the most important measure of status, so the two high-paid subgroups should rank higher than the two low-paid ones. But as between the two groups roughly equal in pay, how determine the relative status of assemblers and machinists? From their general familiarity with American industry and the criteria by which it ranks jobs, both officially and unofficially, as "better" or "worse" than others, the investigators decided that machining would have higher status than assembly work because it requires more training, and that therefore the rank-order of the subdepartments in external status would be:

1. High-paid machinists.
2. High-paid assemblers.
3. Low-paid machinists.
4. Low-paid assemblers.

There appeared, moveover, to be no other conditions that might mask the effects of status. As far as the formal organization was concerned, in the location of work-places and in the flow of parts and completed units, there seemed to be no reason why one subdepartment should receive more esteem or interaction than another. The geographical and organizational givens were unlikely to bias the results. Accordingly the investigators predicted, by arguments like the one we gave above, that the order of subdepartments in external status would also be their order in various measures of esteem.

Once the predictions were on record, the investigators could go to the department and observe actual behavior. Analysis of the data thus collected showed that their predictions had turned out to be partly right. They were most nearly right at the top: in six out of eight measures of esteem and associated variables, the high-paid machinists ranked first, as they had predicted. They were most nearly wrong at the bottom: in all measures of esteem the low-paid machinists ranked fourth instead of third. Their specially low position was associated with a high degree of *status incongruence*, a variable which the investigators had failed to take sufficiently into account, and which we shall not discuss until we reach a later chapter in this book. The other two subdepartments were tied for middle position in the measures of esteem, so the actual ranking was:

1. High-paid machinists.
2. {High-paid assemblers.
    {Low-paid assemblers.
3. Low-paid machinists.

We have spoken of several "measures of esteem and associated variables." Two of them may serve as representatives of the rest: first, the number of friendship-choices given by members of a subdepartment to other members compared with the number given outside; and, second, the number of times members of the subdepartment interacted with other members compared with the number of times they interacted with outsiders. In Chapter 9 on The Matrix of Sentiment, we argued that persons high in esteem were particularly likely to choose one another, and in Chapter 10 suggested that the same was true of interaction. Using essentially the same arguments, the investigators had predicted that the members of subdepartments high in esteem would have a high ratio of choices and interactions within the group to choices and interactions outside. The actual rank-order on both ratios was: high-paid machinists, high-paid assemblers, low-paid assemblers, and low-paid machinists. The order was again as predicted, except for the unduly low position of the low-paid machinists.

Because this last study of the effects of external status on the behavior of men within a group may not be convincing when taken by itself, let us briefly consider another study, made by Hurwitz, Zander, and Hymovitch.[13] The investigators called a small conference in a Midwestern city to discuss problems in the field of mental health.

[13] J. I. Hurwitz, A. F. Zander, and B. Hymovitch, "Some Effects of Power on the Relations among Group Members," in D. Cartwright and A. Zander, eds., *Group Dynamics* (Evanston, Ill., 1953), pp. 483-92.

The conferees were forty-two in number; they included social workers, guidance workers, psychiatrists, psychologists, teachers, and nurses, chosen in such a way that half were high in status and half low. We may guess that the psychiatrists and psychologists were apt to be high, and the nurses and teachers low.

Each conferee then met at different times with four different six-man discussion groups, so arranged that each group contained both high- and low-status members, and that no two individuals were both members of more than one of the groups. Thus every conferee met in his four different groups a total of twenty other conferees. Before the conference began, each subject was asked to rate, with the help of a directory describing them, how much each of the persons he would meet was likely to influence his opinions and judgments. The average rating that each conferee received on his power to influence others correlated very highly with his external status. In every case but three, conferees high in status were also high in power to influence; and this is the first finding of the research. We shall say no more about it here, as power will be the subject of a later chapter of this book.

At the end of each discussion, the investigators asked each member to rate every other member on how much he would like to lunch with the other. This was the measure of liking. They also observed the course of the discussion, and kept a record showing how often each member talked to every other member. This was the measure of interaction.

The results, for both sentiment and interaction, will not surprise us. Members high in influence, whom we shall call the highs, received more liking than did the lows. That is, people high in external status and high also in the influence others felt they could exert, were also held in high esteem. The highs also expressed more liking for other highs than they did for the lows, but the lows more liking for the highs than for their fellow lows. This is equivalent to the finding at Hudson that mutual choice was greatest among persons themselves highly chosen, and lowest among persons themselves little chosen.

As for interaction, highs both received and gave more of it than did the lows, and lows were more apt to interact with highs than they were with other lows. These matrices of liking and interaction are thoroughly familiar to us. What this study does is connect them up with external status. A person who has relatively high status commands, because of the very experiences that earned him his status—he has, for instance, become a trained psychiatrist—a high capacity to emit activities rewarding to others, especially when, as in this case, their interests are similar to his own. His capacity to reward others is in turn apt to earn him high esteem. It will also mean that others direct much interaction to him, and that therefore he will direct much interaction to others. Once the differences in external status are given, our propositions predict the observed results.

But let us note one new point. Our argument explains the few interactions given by the lows as being the result of their having little to offer others, so that others address little interaction to *them*. The investigators suggest that something more than this was at stake: that the lows felt positively inhibited from communicating with people of higher status than their own. They raise the question of the costs of interaction, and sooner or later we shall have to pay much more attention to costs than we have paid here.

Variation in the Givens

We turn now to the second of the two tasks we set for this chapter: to suggest how, under conditions different from those we have so far assumed to be given, our same propositions predict and explain different actual behavior. Take our toy matrices of sentiment and interaction in Chapters 9 and 10. We derived them from our propositions under very special assumptions (assumptions in toys are the equivalent of givens in real life): that many of the members shared the same values, that the members could be put in a single rank-order in their ability to provide activities satisfying these values, and that no geographical barriers made it likely that anyone would interact more with one member than with another. Something much like these matrices is often observed in real groups, especially when the data from a number of different groups are summed up into an aggregate, so that the special givens of particular groups tend to cancel themselves out.

But there is no reason whatever to think that the conditions we have so far assumed for our toy group hold good of every real group. Let us play with our toy a bit. Let us assume that it still has six members, but that the six no longer share the same values, no longer find the same sorts of things rewarding. Let us assume instead that O, P, and Q share the same set of values, R, S, and T another set, and that within each subgroup of three persons, one member is best able to reward the other two, while the others are about equal. Let us say that O and R are able to provide the most valuable services within their respective subgroups. Under these assumptions our propositions predict the rather obvious distribution of approval shown in Table 17.

A Model Sentiment Matrix: Subgroups

		Sentiment to					
		O	P	Q	R	S	T
	O		1	1	0	0	0
	P	2		1	0	0	0
Sentiment from	Q	2	1		0	0	0
	R	0	0	0		1	1
	S	0	0	0	2		1
	T	0	0	0	2	1	
	Total received	4	2	2	4	2	2

If the two subgroups are competing for any scarce good, or if in any other way the members of one are seen as withholding from the other a reward the other has come to expect, then the mutual indifference between them—which we have indicated in this matrix by zeroes—will turn to hostility. A pattern something like this emerges in many groups. We lay no great weight on the matrix except as making a point that, though obvious, is often forgotten. Too many people confuse concrete patterns of behavior with general propositions about behavior. They assume that one pattern should go with one set of propositions. Nothing could be more wrong. With different givens a single set of propositions explains any number of patterns.

Instead of assuming a set of given conditions, deriving the resultant matrix from the propositions, and then asking whether it matches anything in real life, let us now reverse the process, look at an actual sociometric matrix that deviates from our toy one, and then ask under what given conditions it might be derived from our propositions. The matrix below (Table 18) attempts very roughly to reproduce at the level of a six-member toy the results Lemann and

TABLE EIGHTEEN

Sentiment Matrix: Solidarity of the Lower Class

		Sentiment to						Total given
		O	P	Q	R	S	T	
	O		5	4	3	2	1	15
	P	5		4	3	2	1	15
Sentiment from	Q	5	4		3	2	1	15
	R	4	4	3		2	2	15
	S	3	2	2	3		5	15
	T	1	2	3	4	5		15
Total received		18	17	16	16	13	10	

Solomon got from a sociometric study of three residential houses in a women's college.[14] The investigators gave each girl the same number of choices to make, a feature we have reproduced in our toy society by allowing each member to give the same total amount of social approval. And they divided the population into three status-classes: high, middle, and low, corresponding in our toy society to members O and P, Q and R, S and T, respectively.

Comparison of this matrix with our model on p. 165 shows that

[14] T. B. Lemann and R. L. Solomon, "Group Characteristics as Revealed in Sociometric Patterns and Personality Ratings," *Sociometry*, Vol. 15 (1952), pp. 7-90.

the differences are greatest in the lower ranks. Upper- and middle-class members behave much as they did in our matrix, except that the middle class gets a little more choice from, and gives a little more choice to, the lower class. But the lower class—S and T—behaves quite differently. Whereas in our toy society persons themselves of low esteem tended to give high approval to persons of high esteem and little approval, little mutual choice, to one another, in the present matrix they give little approval to persons of high esteem—and thereby reduce the esteem-scores of these people—but much mutual choice to one another. We are forcibly reminded of Jennings' finding at Hudson that, though the general trend of her data ran in accordance with our model, she found a few "overlapping and closed formations" of mutual choice at the very bottom of society.

With one exception, the investigators provide no reasons for the pattern of choice they found, and so we are free to ask ourselves what possible sets of givens—different from those we assumed for our model matrix—might, together with the same general propositions, have produced the present pattern. One possibility is that the members of the lower class roomed near one another in the dormitories, and so found in one another, at low cost, sources of reward to take the place of the liking denied them by the rest of the group. Another is that the members of the lower class, while sharing some values characteristic of the group as a whole, resembled one another in their values more than they did the members of other classes. If this were the case, we should argue that they would be particularly apt to reward and like one another. A third possibility brings in the problem of justice. If the members of the lower class saw that the upper class not only deprived them of approval but unjustly deprived them—if they felt they did not deserve the low esteem in which they were held—then, according to our argument in Chapter 7 on Competition, their sentiment toward the upper class would turn to hostility, and this would increase their liking for one another. There is this much reason for believing the last explanation may be the correct one in that the investigators studied rejections as well as positive choices, and they found that the upper and lower classes not only chose one another little but rejected one another much. But in the absence of further data we shall never be sure which explanation is correct; and all we want to suggest here is that, with different givens, the phenomena may be explained in a number of different ways and yet not require a change in our propositions. Certainly the phenomena are common and ask for explanation, for they add up to "companionship in misery" or "the solidarity of the lower class."

Because a great variety of descriptive propositions may be derived from a single set of general ones, depending on what is taken as given, a social scientist should hesitate before he claims that any of his findings contradict any of his colleagues'. Nature plays rough but not dirty, and Claude Bernard argued that there were no such things as contradictory findings:

> Starting from the principle that there are immutable laws, the experimenter will be convinced that the phenomena can never contradict themselves if they are observed under the same conditions; and he will know that, if they show variations, this must be the result of the intervention or interference of other conditions, which mask or modify these phenomena.[15]

Let the social scientist look well to the conditions of his experiment, both those he planned to establish and those he did not plan but established none the less. It may be that something about the experiment, hidden because it lies in plain sight, makes it quite unlike the one it seems to contradict. Let him do so not just because he is rightly reluctant to give a colleague the lie, but because apparent contradictions point to the unsuspected presence of new phenomena— phenomena that may have made the difference between the experiments. Contradictions should not destroy old findings but lead to new ones. We shall run into this problem in a later chapter, where we shall have to consider two apparently contradictory findings: people who interact often with others are much liked; they are also, it seems, much disliked.

Let me finally add a personal word. The kinds of things we have called *givens* in this chapter are the same as what I called in my earlier book the *external system*.[16] I now think this is too pretentious a term and suggests what is not true. If "system" means that a set of parts are related to one another, the givens sometimes do constitute a system: the geographical layout, the specializations, and the flow

[15] C. Bernard, *Introduction à l'étude de la médecine expérimentale* (Paris, 1865), 2e Partie, Chap. 1.

[16] G. C. Homans, *The Human Group* (New York, 1950), pp. 90-94.

of work in a factory department are givens for the social organization of the department, and they are related to one another. But givens do not always constitute a system. Geographical givens and the givens we have called *background* need not be related at all. If the word *givens,* on the other hand, is not pretentious enough to suit the reader's taste, let him try some other phrase like *parameters* or *boundary conditions,* the boundary being the arbitrary and imaginary line dividing elementary social behavior from what, for the purposes in hand, we choose to consider its physical and social environment in time and space.

Justice

We must now begin to tuck in some loose ends that in earlier chapters we deliberately left dangling; and first of all we must return to the problem of distributive justice: justice in the distribution between men of the rewards and costs of their activities. In Chapter 4 we made the following summary statement of the rules of justice implicit in much social behavior: "A man in an exchange relation with another will expect that the rewards of each man be proportional to his costs—the greater the rewards, the greater the costs—and that the net rewards, or profits, of each man be proportional to his investments—the greater the investments, the greater the profits. . . . Finally, when each man is being rewarded by some third party, he will expect the third party, in the distribution of rewards, to maintain this relation between the two of them."

We went on to state the following general proposition: "The more to a man's disadvantage the rule of distributive justice fails of realization, the more likely he is to display the emotional behavior we call anger." And finally we argued that men are rewarded by the attainment of justice, especially when just conditions are rewarding in other ways. For instance, I am more likely to demand justice when justice would bring me more money than when it would bring me less. Our statement was: "Not only do men display anger or, less prominently, guilt when distributive justice fails in one way or the other, but they also learn to do something about it. They learn to avoid activities that get them into unjust exchanges; they learn to emit activities that are rewarded by the attainment of justice, and by the same token, to forgo these activities becomes a cost to them. In short, justice itself becomes one of the values being exchanged."

In the preceding chapters we have encountered evidence that bore out these statements. For instance, we saw in Chapter 7 how the boys in Thibaut's experiment got angry at the others who were given an unjust advantage over them in playing games, and in Chapter 9 how some of the Swedish students gave high sociometric choice to others in their group who had apparently scored high on the logical tests: they said it was only fair to do so, even when such choice ran counter to their own interests. But the evidence has remained fragmentary and scattered, and we have not tried to fit it into any general scheme.

In the present chapter we shall try to make good this deficiency. We shall bring forward much more evidence on the rules of distributive justice implicit in the behavior of men and much more evidence on the way men behave in their endeavors to attain justice and avoid injustice. In fact these are two birds to be killed with one stone. Because the rules usually remain implicit, because we infer them from what men do rather than learn of them directly from what men say, a study of men seeking the condition of distributive justice will also tell us what that condition is. Our evidence will come from field studies of real-life groups: no laboratory experiments on justice have yet been carried out.

The Proportionality of Rewards

Let us begin by simplifying the problem: let us forget for the moment about what we have called costs and investments (we shall have plenty to say about them later) and consider only the rewards exchanged between two men. Under this simplification, the rule of justice says that the more valuable to Other the activity Person gives him, the more valuable to Person should be the activity Other gives him. But we shall take our first illustration not from the exchange between two persons but from the more general exchange between a man and the members of the group he belongs to.

The Norton Street Gang, described first in W. F. Whyte's *Street*

Corner Society[1] and again in my own book, *The Human Group,*[2] consisted of thirteen young men who in the year 1937 used to hang around together in the Cornerville district of Eastern City. Among other things they used to go bowling several nights a week. One of the members who often bowled was Alec. By reason of his performance in other activities he was held in rather low esteem in the group, but he fancied himself as a bowler and from time to time beat other members of the group in individual matches, including Long John, a highly esteemed member and a friend of Doc's, who was the leader of the gang. But when Doc instituted for the first time a regular bowling tournament between all the members, Alec did not do well. Good bowling takes confidence, and Doc and the other members saw to it that Alec's confidence was undermined by friendly heckling. In so doing, they maintained a state of justice. For as I said of Alec in *The Human Group*:

> In individual matches and when the leaders of the group did not gang up on him, he could do very well in bowling, but in other activities he did not conform very closely to group standards. He was boastful; he was aggressive in trying to improve his social ranking. He spent more time chasing girls than the other Nortons did, and, what was worse, showed that he was capable of leaving friends in the lurch when on the prowl. If his behavior had improved in these respects, his social rank might then have risen, and his scores in intraclique bowling competition might have been allowed to go up. As it was, his rank remained low.[3]

The first rule of distributive justice, as it emerges from this case, might be put as follows: the value of what a member receives by way of reward from the members of the group in one field of activity should be proportional to the value to them of the activities he contributes in another field. If the condition is not realized, the members will act in the endeavor to realize it, particularly, we should note, the leader. Alec's activities in one field were not of much value, indeed he violated important group norms; and so in another field, where the members were in a position to control the reward he got—and a good bowling score was a valuable reward—they kept it down. They kept the value of what he got "in line" with what he gave.

[1] Chicago, 1943.

[2] G. C. Homans (New York, 1950), pp. 156-89.

[3] *Ibid.*, p. 180.

The Proportionality of Rewards and Investments

We shall now complicate matters a little by bringing in what we have called investments. The rule of justice says that a man's rewards in exchange with others should be proportional to his investments. To understand what this means, let us turn to the Bank Wiring Observation Room, last of the celebrated researches carried out by Elton Mayo and his colleagues in the Hawthorne plant of the Western Electric Co.[4] The two principal jobs carried out in the room, wiring and soldering, need not be described here. It is enough to say that the wiremen got more pay than the soldermen, were presumed to be more skilled, and held more seniority. Of the nine wiremen six worked on so-called connector equipment and three on selector equipment. The differences between the two jobs were slight, but the connector wiremen were a little senior and got a little more pay than the selectors. There were three soldermen in all, one for each set of three wiremen, and they soldered in position the wires that the others had connected to terminals on the equipment.

In social activities two cliques had arisen—one centering in the connector wiremen and one in the selectors—and in these activities, as in skill, pay, and seniority, the first clique held itself to be somewhat superior to the second. To the first, or connector, clique but in a subordinate position as befitted his inferior job-status, belonged Steinhardt, the solderman for the first three connector wiremen. To the second, or selector, clique in the same sort of position belonged Cermak, who had replaced another man as solderman for the three selector wiremen. Matchek, the solderman for the middle group of wiremen, suffered from a speech defect and was hardly a member of Observation Room society.

All the men ate lunch in the room, sending out one of their number to pick up their food and drink from the plant restaurant. The question was who should be the "lunch boy"—note the word "boy." It was not a very valuable service; anyone could have performed it for himself, and it was menial: the lunch boy was a servant for the others. At the time the men were first assigned to the room Steinhardt had

[4] F. J. Roethlisberger and W. J. Dickson, *Management and the Worker* (Cambridge, Mass., 1939), pp. 379-584; also G. C. Homans, *op. cit.,* pp. 48-155.

reluctantly agreed to do the job. But as soon as Cermak came in as a solderman for the selector wiremen and was accepted as a member of their clique, Steinhardt was relieved and Cermak took over as lunch boy.

Why was it appropriate that he should do so? He was a member of the "worse" clique; he was a solderman, and soldermen held the lowest job-status in the room; of the soldermen he was the least senior and the last to come into the group. Accordingly the group assigned him the least rewarding activity at its disposal: his menial job was in line with the other features of his status. We say "accordingly," but note the difference between this case and the last one. In the Norton Street Gang, the behavior that earned Alec his low esteem in the group, and hence a bowling score in line with his esteem, was his own action, his own fault. But in the Bank Wiring Observation Room it was hardly Cermak's fault in any immediate sense of the word that he was a solderman of low seniority, the last man to enter the group, and assigned to the selector wiremen. These were what we have called elsewhere his background characteristics determined by the events of his past history. But they had the same effect as if they had been his own fault. Inasmuch as the other members of the group had more pay, seniority, skill, etc., than he, they were "better" than he was, they held higher status in the larger society, and so they did not, but he did, deserve the menial job. No doubt when he should have served his time as lunch boy and acquired, again with time, higher pay, seniority, and skill, and when someone should have come into the room with less of these background characteristics than he, then he would be able to shove the lunch-boy job off on the newcomer.

Because some of a man's background characteristics increase in value with the time and ability he has "put in" in various groups and jobs, we speak of them for the purposes of distributive justice as *investments*. Not all investments change: to be a Negro or a woman, as compared with being white or a man, are investments that in some groups never change in value yet are always weighed in the scales of distributive justice, and so some of us might say it was absurd to speak of justice here at all; but we must remember that we are talking about justice as seen by the members of a particular group and not about our own sense of justice, which is of course Olympian.

No doubt, too, there are societies in which fewer investments increase in value with time and ability than do in our own, many societies in which more investments are ascribed and fewer achieved. Ascribed or achieved, the second rule of justice is this: the value of what a member of a group receives from other members should be proportional to his investments.

Proportionality of Rewards, Costs, and Investments

Our next case introduces all three of the variables that come into the problem of distributive justice, and it differs from our previous cases in other respects as well. The parties at issue were not a group and an individual but two groups. The division of rewards between the two groups was unjust, at least in the eyes of one of them, but neither of the groups had done the injustice. Instead, the culprit was a third party, the management of the firm to which both groups belonged. Finally, this case, unlike the previous ones, does not show us how a group endeavoring to establish distributive justice decreased the rewards of others, but how it tried to increase its own. Both are possible strategies for establishing just conditions.

The firm in question was the Eastern Utilities Co., to whose Customers Accounting Division, home of the cash posters, we must now return.[5] The posters were only one of several groups of people that carried on special tasks in the division and in the same big room. This time we shall be concerned with the relations between the cash posters and the members of the largest group in the division, the so-called ledger clerks.

We shall not go into details about the cash posters' and ledger clerks' jobs. Like the other jobs in the division, they had to do with keeping the company's accounts with the customers who bought electric current and other services. Though no longer carried out by the methods of old-fashioned bookkeeping, cash posting resulted practically in recording on the customers' accounts the amounts of money they paid on their bills. The job had little variety; it allowed a great deal of movement from file to file, and the company felt it was the one job in the division that should be kept caught up with: all pay-

[5] G. C. Homans, "Status among Clerical Workers," *Human Organization,* Vol. 12 (1953), pp. 5-10.

ments were to be recorded on the customers' accounts on the day they were received.

Of the ledger clerks' job it is enough to say that they did everything other than cash posting necessary to keep the accounts up to date. They had, for instance, to record changes of customers' addresses and breakdowns of over- and under-payments. Each ledger clerk had a "station," which consisted of a block of files containing the accounts of people living in a particular section of the city, and at the station was a telephone with which the clerk was to answer calls made either by the customers themselves or by employees of the company, about the state of the accounts. As the investigator put it: "Whereas the cash posters had, in the main, to do one single, repetitive job on a production basis, requiring little thought but plenty of physical mobility, the ledger clerks had to do a number of nonrepetitive clerical jobs on a nonproduction basis, requiring some thought but little physical mobility."

All the cash posters and ledger clerks were women. Because the regular line of promotion in the division was from cash poster to ledger clerk, and many of the clerks had formerly served as posters, they tended to be older than the posters and to have more seniority in the company. But there was some doubt that the promotion was really a promotion, for ledger clerks received the same weekly pay as posters. Management considered posting to be so monotonous and under so much pressure for production that women would not be attracted to take it unless it fetched relatively high pay. In point of fact, when they got used to it the girls did not find posting as bad as all that; some of them, indeed, had refused the ambiguous promotion to ledger clerk, giving the reason that the extra responsibility was not balanced by higher pay. Finally we shall remember that cash posting was the one job in the division management felt it had to remain caught up with every day. To make sure of doing so, the supervisor every afternoon took some of the clerks off the stations and set them to work helping to clean up the posting. He did not mind if the ledger work fell temporarily into arrears.

With each of the girls the investigator carried out a long interview in which she was free to talk about her own job and those of others in any way she chose. They tended to compare jobs as more or less rewarding or costly along a number of different dimensions, which we have called values. Not all the values were shared by everybody in the division: thus the older women did not value the chance to move about in a job nearly so highly as did the younger girls. But most of the values were shared, in the sense that by these values everybody ranked jobs in the same way. Thus all agreed, as would most of us, that a job with higher pay was "better," on that count at least, than one with lower. Because they were shared and so could be used as the premises of an argument, these values were the ones most often cited in the discussion of distributive justice. The more important ones were pay, chance for advancement, variety, responsibility, and autonomy. Only the last was a word the women did not use themselves, and it represents the investigator's shorthand for the value implied when a girl said in praise of a job that "they [the supervisors] let you alone to do your own work." Some of the values were positive, such as pay, variety, and autonomy, and to the degree that jobs stood high on these values they were clearly rewarding. But some were negative, and jobs that stood high on these values were to that degree costly. Such, in one of its aspects, was "responsibility." When the girls said that one job was more responsible than another, they implied that more harm would be done if it was not done right. A responsible job might be exciting and stimulating, but it was also costly: it meant worry and risk or peace of mind forgone; and some girls found its uncompensated responsibility good enough reason for not taking the job when it was offered them.

In speaking of their job the ledger clerks said that in general they liked it: it had variety and interest. They did not see much chance for advancement, but then neither did anyone else in the division: as far as promotion was concerned all jobs were about equally bad. And they were satisfied with the absolute amount of their pay, in the sense that they recognized they could not get better pay in comparable jobs elsewhere in the city.

Relative pay was something else again. When the ledger clerks compared their job with the cash posters' they complained about the two jobs getting the same pay when theirs was the more "responsible." They also complained about being "taken off their own jobs and put down to work on posting." Notice the "down": their temporary afternoon assignment to cash posting was a loss in status as well as in autonomy. Finally they complained that their immediate supervisor did not "stick up for them." This meant that he did little to get these injustices set to rights. A typical statement was the following:

> I like the work. There's only one thing I don't like about it. Everybody talks around here as if cash posting was the only job that counted. They take us off stations to work on cash, and they think that the stations can just take care of themselves. The work piles up and you get behind. Of course we've got to get the cash out, but I think the station work is just as important. And it's much more responsible. Cash posting, most of it, is just mechanical, but station work is a responsible job. You have to deal with customers and with the stores, and if you don't do something right, someone is going to suffer. Of course that's true of cash posting, too, but there are a lot more things that a station clerk has to do. It's a more responsible job, and yet the station clerks get just the same pay as the cash posters. It seems that they ought to get just a few dollars more to show that the job is more important.

The complaints of the ledger clerks sound like another one of those problems, so frequent and troublesome in American industry, of wage differentials—problems not of the absolute amount of wages but of differences between groups in their wage rates. And so it is, for problems of wage differentials are problems of distributive justice.

The investments of the ledger clerks were greater than those of the cash posters: they had put in more time in the company; they had learned to do a more responsible job, one that the cash posters could not do. Distributive justice accordingly demanded that their rewards should be greater than the posters', and some of them were: their work was more varied and interesting. But not all were: they got the same pay as the cash posters, and they were allowed even less autonomy—whereas the bosses left the posters alone, they took the ledger clerks off their "own" job and put them "down" on posting. Apparently distributive justice demands not just that higher investment should receive higher reward in one respect but that it should do so in all. As the ledger clerks had accumulated larger investments than the posters, they should have gotten larger rewards, not only in variety and interest but in pay and autonomy too. The two respects in which the ledger clerks' rewards were out of line with their investments were just the two that they complained of and wanted to get changed. Only when investments and rewards were all in line would distributive justice reign.

So far we have only talked of rewards being in line with investments; now we must complicate things a little more by bringing in costs. When the ledger clerks spoke of the responsibility of their job they were apt to refer to its costs, which in this respect were higher than those of cash posting. When their day's work was over they would go home still worrying whether they had handled their accounts correctly, while the posters did not need give another thought to what they had done. The ledger clerks were content that their costs in responsibility should be higher. Had their costs consisted in mere drudgery, which any menial job may entail, they would have been much less ready to accept them, for such costs would have implied no superiority in their contribution to the work of the office. But costs in responsibility do imply superiority: a responsible job is one that many people cannot or will not undertake. To use a word we shall have much more to say about shortly, the responsibility of a job is *congruent* with its superiority in other respects. Costs of this kind a ledger clerk was ready to accept—so long as they were balanced by superior rewards. When they were not, the clerks felt there had been a failure of distributive justice. When they said, "We ought to get just a few dollars more to show our job is more important," they implied their acceptance of a third rule of justice, which we shall now add to our two earlier ones. What a member of a group gets in the way of reward should be directly proportional to what he gives up, his costs, provided that the costs are of a kind that others, his inferiors, are in no position to incur—costs of the kind we call congruent.[6] For there are costs and costs: there are the costs that imply superiority, such as the cost of facing danger, and there are costs that imply nothing of the sort, such as the cost of doing work that is dull and dirty but safe.

Now since we have defined profit as reward less cost, this rule implies that distributive justice would be realized if the profits of two persons or the members of two different job-groups were equal. Let us put the argument in terms of a simplified toy and arbitrary figures. Suppose Person, or anyone doing the same job, is getting

[6] See also L. F. Sayles, *Behavior of Industrial Work Groups* (New York, 1958), pp. 97-98.

pay to value 4, and Other, or anyone doing the same job as Other, is getting pay to value 3. And suppose that Person, in return for the pay and other considerations, is incurring responsibility to cost 2, while Other's cost is only 1. The features of Person's job are above Other's and in line on both counts of reward and cost: 4 is greater than 3 and 2 is greater than 1. But the profits of the two are equal, for $4-2=2$ and $3-1=2$. We must not argue for a minute that people can measure the rewards and costs of what they do in cardinal figures, but they surely do assess them in ordinal ones: they put the activities of different persons and subgroups in rank-order of rewards and costs. In these terms distributive justice among men is achieved when the profits of each are equal, in the sense that their rank-order on rewards is also their rank-order on costs. The ledger clerks failed to get justice because, while their costs were greater than the posters', their rewards, in pay at least, were equal.

Proportionality of Profits and Investments

But our statement is still inadequate, and to improve it we must tie it back into what we learned earlier. It does not take much knowledge of the world to realize that equality of profits does not sufficiently describe the reign of distributive justice among men. Some men do much less well than others but are still held to be getting no more than they deserve. Certainly one of the things that make the difference is the nature of costs. Some costs, while no doubt painful to incur, have the curse taken off them by being "good" costs, in the sense that they are the kind of costs incurred by someone who makes a superior contribution. Such, as we have seen, are the costs of a "responsible" job. Other costs imply no such superiority, and men will heap these costs on their fellows, who sometimes will not raise the question of justice even though their profits have suffered much damage. We are now considering the over-all or net profits men get from what they do; we are considering, for instance, how "good" a particular job is, taken as a whole. Here are two men, so closely associated that they cannot help comparing their profits; the over-all profit of one man is obviously less than that of another, and yet the former makes no complaint. When this sort of thing happens—and it does happen—what conditions make it possible?

Let us return for enlightenment to the Customers Accounting Division. So far we have considered only the ledger clerks' and cash posters' jobs, but there were a number of others, among them the so-called Address File. This job consisted in keeping up to date a separate file of customers' addresses by putting new cards in the file whenever information came in about a change of address or a new occupant of a house. It was recognized as the worst job on the floor: it got little pay, it was hopelessly monotonous, it was done in a place cut off from the rest of the floor by high walls of files so that the address girls could not easily talk to the others. It was indeed the local salt mine.

The girls on the Address File certainly did not like the job, and they were forever grumbling about its dreariness. Yet their complaints were quite different from the ledger clerks'. The ledger clerks complained about the rewards of their job relative to those of the cash posters'. The address girls made no such complaints about the relative position of their job against cash posting, the next job above it on the ladder of advancement. Though in absolute terms they were certainly badly off, they only complained about the job itself. They did not complain of being deprived in comparison with others, and it is always relative deprivation that raises the question of distributive justice. What made the difference? Whereas the ledger clerks' job was more desirable than the cash posters' on most counts but not on all, the address girls' job was worse than the posters' on all counts: it got less pay, less autonomy, less chance for social life, and vastly more monotony. Its costs, moreover, were not of the kind that implied any superiority. In effect any fool could do the work on the Address File, and its costs in monotony were also such as any fool could undertake to bear without special training. On any simple-minded assessment, then, the over-all profits of the Address File were less than those of cash posting, and so our statement that distributive justice consists in the equality of profits does not fit this case, for the file girls did not act as if they felt unjustly treated. However little they liked their job, they did not doubt the justice of their having it. Why did they feel so? Because they were the youngest girls and had least seniority in the department. That is, their investments were less than those of the cash posters; profits should be proportional to investments, and so it was right that they should have less profit. We are back to investments again. Just as it was right in the Bank Wiring Observation Room that the newest solderman should serve as lunch boy, so it was right in the Customers Accounting Division that the newest girls should be assigned to the Address File. As for the ledger clerks, their investments in age, seniority, and acquired skill were greater than those of the cash posters, and so in justice they should have gotten greater profits but did not: they got the same pay and less autonomy. Therefore they did, and the address girls did not, complain of relative deprivation.

Let us return to our simplified toy and arbitrary figures, and make them a little less simple, if still amounting to no more than a possibly illuminating metaphor. Let us still suppose that profit is some net figure, the result of subtracting cost from reward. Then, on the evidence before us, it looks as if distributive justice demanded not absolute equality of profits but equality of profits as a rate of return on investment. Suppose one man has invested $1000 and gets an income of $50 and another has invested $100 and gets $5. In investments and returns the two men are "in line" with one another: one has made a larger investment and also gets a bigger return. In one sense the two are, if "in line," also unequal: one certainly gets more. But in another sense the two are equals: each makes an income of 5 per cent on his investment. Justice is a curious mixture of equality within inequality. And since our toy, though only a toy, has its serious side, we suggest the following rule of distributive justice, which comprehends the others we stated earlier: a man in an exchange relation with another will expect the profits of each to be directly proportional to his investments, and when each is being rewarded by some third party, he will expect the third party to maintain this relation between the two of them. If the investments of two men, or two groups, are equal, their profits should be equal, and if their investments are unequal, the one with the greater investment should get the greater profit. But this statement is the one we started the chapter with: all we have done is examine the sort of evidence that bears it out.

Though we are far from feeling that this statement bears no relation whatever to what actually happens, it is practically not a very useful one. It sounds as if people made quantitative measurements of their investments and profits, and they do not. When they compare their activities with those of others, they can assess ordinal differences much more readily than cardinal ones: they can put jobs in rank-order of "goodness" more readily than they can say how much "better" one job is than another. As a practical matter, what made the address girls' job realize distributive justice in relation to the cash posters' was that on every count—pay, skill, variety, autonomy, and the investments of the girls that did it—it was "worse" than that of the posters. But they would have been at a loss to say how much worse. The important point was that all the features of each job were in line with one another. Accordingly we shall state the following as a rule of distributive justice that people practically seem to respond to: if one man is "better" than another in his investments, he should also be "better" than the other in the value of the contribution he makes and in the reward he gets for it; his cost in making it should be higher too, so long as it is the sort of cost that a superior contribution necessarily incurs.

The notion of distributive justice that we have put forward here, the notion that if one man ranks higher than another in one respect, he should rank higher in others too, the notion that investments, rewards, and costs should be "in line" with one another—this idea of justice is an ancient one. It was the one Aristotle was thinking of when he wrote about the debate between the parties of oligarchy and democracy: "For the one party, if they are unequal in one respect, for example wealth, consider themselves to be unequal in all; and the other party, if they are equal in one respect, for example free birth, consider themselves to be equal in all."[7] A more modern formulation is Jouvenel's: "What men find just is to preserve between themselves, as regards whatever is in question, the same relations that exist between them as regards something else."[8]

In applying this rule to the relations between the ledger clerks and the cash posters, we may seem to suggest that the two groups were in exchange with each other instead of each in exchange with the company so far as concerned the characteristics of their jobs. The fact is that they did behave a little as if they were exchanging with each other. Though it was not the cash posters' fault that the ledger

[7] Aristotle, *Politics,* Book III, Chapter 9. The reader should also consult the first great statement on distributive justice: Aristotle, *Nicomachean Ethics,* Book V, Chapters 3 and 4.

[8] B. de Jouvenel, *De la souveraineté* (Paris, 1955), p. 195.

clerks' pay was no higher, the latter showed some resentment of the posters as beneficiaries of injustice. In dealing with the ledger clerks the management of the Eastern Utilities Co. worked of course on a principle of fair exchange, but it was a principle that lacked, so to speak, detail. It might have been put, it was tacitly put, as: "We pay you good wages, and in return we expect you to do anything lawful that we ask you to do." Accordingly when the clerks complained that they were taken off their own jobs and put on posting, the supervisor said, in effect: "What do you care what work you do? You get paid just the same. When we take you off stations and put you on cash, we don't bawl you out if your station work gets behind"; and this was perfectly true: by its lights the management was fair. But the ledger clerks' definition of justice was more complicated. They were saying: "In return for hard work we expect you to pay good wages and, more than that, we expect you, in establishing the conditions of our work—wages included—to maintain distributive justice in our relations with the cash posters and other groups we associate with." Management had to maintain justice not only between itself and the different job-groups but between the job-groups themselves. No doubt it was a tall order, but it was one more easily filled if recognized.

We believe that men are alike in holding the notion of proportionality between investment and profit that lies at the heart of distributive justice. The trouble is that they differ in their ideas of what legitimately constitutes investment, reward, and cost, and how these things are to be ranked. They differ from society to society, from group to group, and from time to time in any one society or group. In the Customers Accounting Division, management talked as if only hard work and good wages ought to enter the balance, while the ledger clerks thought that other things about their job, like its autonomy, ought to count as well. Once upon a time high birth counted as a legitimate investment, but in our modern American society it counts officially not at all, though one can sometimes see it playing its part unofficially. Once upon a time, too, the fact of being a man rather than a woman counted as more of an investment than it does today in America. A man doing the same job as a woman might demand, in justice, more pay. Today he is much less likely to make his claim good. And all the arguments about surplus value from John Ball to Karl Marx are one long attempt to prove that what employers count as investments ought not be so counted, and that therefore they get more than their fair share of the returns of economic enterprise and exploit the workers. Of course none of the arguments prove it; such things are not capable of proof: they are matters of taste. Only perhaps for rather brief times and for rather small groups are men fully agreed not only on what the rule of distributive justice is but also on what particular investments, rewards, and costs should fairly be placed in the scales and at what weights. Men certainly assess their own investments and income, but to make a rule of justice work they must assess those of others on the same scale. The others, moreover, must agree at every point, which does not make consensus any easier to achieve. The evidence, as we might expect, is that consensus is easier to achieve among people who in similar backgrounds have acquired similar values; but even there it is always breaking down. This means there is no just society, though there may be societies and groups that are more or less just, to the extent that the rules of evaluation are agreed on and a rough proportionality between investment and profit is maintained. By these standards the Customers Accounting Division was a pretty just place. Except for the ledger clerks everyone was getting something like her fair share, and as for what happened to the ledger clerks, almost everyone agreed at least that it *was* an injustice — which is more than can be said for many places.

We are now in a position to clarify some of the things we said in Chapter 8 on Esteem. Consider, for instance, the way a man of high esteem evaluates a man of low. For the man of high esteem the other's activities are not particularly valuable, and so he does not give the other any high degree of social approval. But if these activities are in line with the man's investments, if they are no more than what might have been expected of him, then the man of high esteem, though not giving him much approval, will not despise him either. Poor soul, he is doing the best he can. The man of low esteem is not giving the man of high esteem a very good deal, but he is giving him a fair deal. The latter will like him for doing so, and the liking will take some of the curse off the former's lowly station. Low approval is not the same thing as disapproval, and only when a man behaves even worse than he is entitled to will he arouse the hostility of others.

Status Congruence and Social Certitude

A man's assessment of the justice or injustice that has been done him always depends on his comparing his investments, rewards, and costs with those of other men. That is, it depends on his comparing the stimuli presented by his own behavior, by the behavior of others toward him, and by the other things about him, like his background, with the corresponding stimuli presented by other men. We have been much more interested in *what* he compares than in *whom* he compares himself with. But these are the stimuli that determine his perceived status, as we defined status in Chapter 8. And just as we have seen that men put their characteristics, so far as relevant to the assessment of justice, into rank-order in comparison with the corresponding characteristics of other men, so in Chapter 8 we saw that they put the different kinds of status-stimuli they present into rank-order as "better" or "worse," "higher" or "lower," than those of others: status is always a matter of the perception of stimuli as falling into a rank-order. Finally, we have seen that justice is realized in the relationship between two men when the investments, rewards, and costs of one are all better than those of the other—or when, if the investments of the two are equal, their rewards and costs are equal too. Thinking now of status rather than of justice, we shall say that a condition of *status congruence* is realized when all of the stimuli a man presents rank better or higher than the corresponding stimuli presented by another man—or when, of course, all of the stimuli presented by the two men rank as equal.[9] The less fully this condition is realized, the greater the *status incongruence*. In the present connection, let us call the different kinds of stimuli by the name of *status factors,* and by way of illustration let us say that among the status factors of two women are their pay, their seniority, the responsibility of their jobs, and the worry they incur in doing these jobs. Then the relative status of the two women is congruent if the perceived pay, seniority, responsibil-

[9] This variable has been called by a number of names. See E. Benoit-Smullyan, "Status, Status Types and Status Interrelations," *American Sociological Review,* Vol. 9 (1944), pp. 151-61; G. Lenski, "Status Crystallization," *American Sociological Review,* Vol. 19 (1954), pp. 405-13; S. N. Adams, "Status Congruency as a Variable in Small Group Performance," *Social Forces,* Vol. 32 (1953-54), pp. 16-22.

ity, and worry of one of them are all greater than the corresponding status factors of the other.

If justice and congruence are both matters of perceived stimuli and both assessed the same way, why go to all this trouble to define this second term, *congruence?* Why would not *justice* alone be enough? The answer, as we shall now try to understand, is that congruence and incongruence determine new forms of behavior that are not easily subsumed under the pursuit of justice. When we say something is congruent, we mean that it is somehow in keeping with, in line with, something else. The current notions of men about the congruence of status factors depend on their past perceptions of social behavior. If, for instance, in their past experience it has been generally true that persons who took on much responsibility also got much pay, then their present perception that a man takes on much responsibility is congruent with the further perception that he gets much pay. But if a man who takes on more responsibility than another is seen to get the same pay as the other, the two facts are incongruent, out of keeping, out of line with one another. Sometimes the present assessment of congruence depends on men's having recognized just those relationships that we have been at pains to put forward in this book. Thus if it is generally true, as it is, that someone who gets high esteem is also someone who provides valuable services to others, then a man perceived as getting higher esteem than another but providing just the same services would be incongruent on the two status factors, esteem and services rendered. Or again, if it is generally recognized that persons high in authority are persons to whom many others come to ask questions, then a man who on some present occasion is supposed to have higher authority than another but is seen to go over to the other's desk and ask a question has tended to render his status incongruent in the eyes of his companions. He stands higher than the other on the status factor, authority, but lower on the status factor, direction of movement. Note this well: anything that can be perceived about a man may become a status factor.

Our next point is that status incongruence may be a cost to a man and its reduction accordingly a reward, even apart from considerations of justice. Why should this be so? Because a man's status factors are stimuli, and according to proposition 1 in Chapter 4, the stimuli presented to men are among the determinants of their behavior. The stimuli in question naturally include the stimuli presented by other men, and the behavior in question includes their behavior toward other men. If a person presents two incongruent stimuli to his companions, one of the stimuli suggests that he will reward (or punish) a different kind of behavior from what the other one does, and accordingly the companions may be in doubt over which kind to emit: they are getting two conflicting signals. Thus if one woman holds more responsibility than another but gets the same pay, a third party seeing them both may be tempted by the equality in pay to treat them as social equals and not to accord to the first woman the higher respect that her responsibility would otherwise deserve. The incongruence throws her status in doubt in the eyes of her companions. Or again, if one man is supposed to have higher authority than another, but nevertheless allows himself to be seen going over to the other's desk, he may lead his associates to wonder whether he really has the authority after all. Still worse, since behavior and not mere thinking is always the payoff, he may tempt them to treat him as if he no longer held higher authority. If, on the other hand, a person's status factors are congruent with one another, the fact suggests that a single main kind of behavior toward him will be rewarded: the stimuli to behavior are no longer conflicting. His status is established and certain rather than fluid and ambiguous. Status congruence is a condition of social certitude.[10]

But the woman in question will find it costly to be treated as the equal of someone she considers her inferior; and the man in question will find it costly to be treated as if he had lost authority. In general people will find incongruence costly because of the effects it may have on the future behavior of others toward them, and therefore any activity that helps them avoid or eliminate the incongruence may be rewarding. Distributive justice is a matter of the relation between what a man gets in the way of reward and what he incurs in the way of cost, here and now; status congruence is a matter of the impression he makes on, the stimuli he presents to, other men, which may affect their future behavior toward him and therefore the future reward he gets from them. There is a difference between the two phenomena

[10] A. Zaleznik, C. R. Christensen, and F. J. Roethlisberger, *The Motivation, Productivity, and Satisfaction of Workers* (Boston, 1958), pp. 56-66.

and so we have called them by different names, but of course the two may overlap. Thus the ledger clerks tried to get their pay increased, not only because it was just and equitable, in the light of the kind of work they did, that they should get more pay than the cash posters, but also because the fact that they were getting the same pay cast doubt on their status relative to the cash posters: theirs was a problem in which both justice and social certitude were at stake. But note that, though they complained much about pay, they complained little about the worry they incurred in doing their responsible job. No doubt the worry was costly to them; but responsible jobs are generally worrisome, and so worry is congruent with responsibility. Therefore their worry, unlike their pay, only confirmed their superiority in status. Their worry was a cost, but so far as social certitude was concerned, a "good" cost.

The Manipulation of Social Stimuli

In short, one of the activities of men that may receive social reinforcement is the manipulation of the stimuli they present to other men. But let us look at some examples. A man who is established as equal in status with another will hesitate before behaving in such a way as to cast doubt on his equality. In earlier chapters we saw that a person who went to another to ask for help was apt to be held in less esteem than the other. If people in general come to recognize this relationship between esteem and helping, then a man who goes to another and asks for help will suggest to his fellows that he is inferior in status to the other. His status has become incongruent, and so his asking for help will cost him something. Thus we argued that the cost Person incurred in the office by going to Other and asking for help was the confession he thus made of his inferiority to Other. Although the reward he got in the form of help might well outweigh its cost in inferiority, the latter still remained a cost. Our present argument suggests that the amount of cost varies with the other status factors of the person who asks for help. If he is already established by his other status factors as inferior to the other, his asking for help will cost him little, for it is congruent with his inferiority in other respects. But if he is already established as the other's equal, then his going to the other for help will be incongruent with his equality and so cost him much. He will be demeaning himself and putting his over-all status in jeopardy in the eyes of his fellows. We should therefore expect that men's equals would ask them for help less often than their inferiors would. By the same token, thrusting help upon a man who thinks he is your peer is an act of hostility to him, and your generosity is apt to earn you resentment and not gratitude.[11]

Let us look at an example. In a certain machine-shop, described by Zaleznik,[12] there were two classes of workers, called by different job-titles: machinists and operators. As the titles suggest, the machinists ranked higher than the operators in seniority, pay, and reputed skill. Operators often borrowed tools from machinists and went to them for help in dealing with mechanical difficulties: their asking for help was congruent with their inferiority in other respects. But machinists hardly ever borrowed tools or asked help from other machinists, and when they did so tried to disguise their behavior. They pretended it was not help they wanted but only a chance to compare notes, to discuss with a fellow expert technical problems of interest to both. Note that if it is costly for a man's equal to behave toward him in ways that imply inequality, it is all the more rewarding to behave in ways that imply no such thing. We shall have more to say on this matter in Chapter 15 on Equality.

In our last example we considered the case in which a man established as another's equal in recognized status tried to avoid behavior that would put the equality in question. We now turn to the case in which a man who is established as another's superior in most of his status factors, but who is in danger of losing his superiority in one of them, tries to establish his superiority in that one too. Let us consider a homely example. In certain supermarkets, a study of which we shall consider in greater detail shortly, the full-time workers got higher pay and generally held higher seniority than the part-timers. But sometimes the two were assigned to work together on the same job. In this situation, as one of the full-timers pointed out:

> A full-timer has got to show the part-timers that he can work faster than they can. It's better to work with them than against them, but he's got to show he's a better man.

[11] See Ralph Waldo Emerson, *Essays:* "Gifts."

[12] A. Zaleznik, *Worker Satisfaction and Development* (Boston, 1956), p. 75.

We might call this a case of *noblesse oblige*. No doubt it is just that a man who gets greater rewards than another should also incur higher costs in hard work, but it is also congruent that he should do so. To act otherwise is to cast conspicuous doubt on his status as a member of the "nobility." A worker's superiority in pay and seniority is congruent with his superior ability to do a job; the full-timers were superior to the part-timers in these other respects, and so they had to do the job better than the part-timers too, even if it meant working harder than usual.

Just as it is not always possible to establish justice, so it is not always possible to establish congruence; and in this case various kinds of accommodation may be worked out. A man who is superior to a second in other features of status is apt also to be superior to him in authority: higher status and higher authority are congruent. In many American restaurants the cooks are older men, with greater skill, seniority, and pay than the waitresses, who are women to boot. That is, the cooks are superior to the waitresses in what we have called investments. Yet the waitresses must pass the customers' orders on to the cooks; therefore they control what the cooks do, and control is the very guts of authority. At this moment cook and waitress are in a notably incongruent relation with one another.[13] Perhaps as a result of a process of unconscious adaptation, waitresses often give their orders to the cooks through a small window or over a high barrier, where the two can see one another with difficulty if at all, and the consequent impersonality seems to take some of the curse off the incongruence: one cannot, so to speak, feel incongruent with a mere voice. A man whose status factors are congruent is by that fact a man whose social position is established and unambiguous: one knows where one stands with him. Such, in a New England factory, is a skilled male worker, with high seniority and pay, a high school graduate and a Yankee. His high pay, for instance, is in line with the other things about him. Even his ethnicity (to use a dreadful word) is in line; for in the unavowed ranking of New England ethnic groups, the Yankees—white Protestants of colonial ancestry—still stand high.

[13] See W. F. Whyte, *Human Relations in the Restaurant Industry* (New York, 1948), pp. 47-63; the whole book is full of examples of status congruence and incongruence. See also C. I. Barnard, *Organization and Management* (Cambridge, Mass., 1948), pp. 221-23.

This does not mean that all Yankees have high status—far from it. But Yankeeness as such still scores; and a man who is a Yankee and has a good job would be on these counts congruent, whereas a woman of Syrian origin, holding a highly skilled job with much pay and seniority, would be incongruent indeed. Both her sex and her ethnicity would be out of line with the other factors that made her status.

What do we mean when we say that one knows where one stands with a person whose status is congruent? When we have in the past encountered other people who presented stimuli like his, we have found that a single main kind of behavior on our part, a single band or range, has been rewarded. But the stimuli presented by an incongruent person suggest that two or more different, and even incompatible, kinds of behavior may be rewarded. A woman attracts one kind of behavior to herself, a highly skilled machinist another; when faced with the combination of personages we are hard put to combine the behaviors, and so we feel uncomfortable. There is some evidence that people tend to avoid an incongruent person, to interact with him seldom on social occasions, or if he cannot be avoided, to pass off the embarrassment with a joke. It is as if the joke resolved the ambiguity. A familiar example is the behavior of men at some kinds of reunions. They are supposed to be old pals together, yet they may not have seen one another for years or indeed ever have been very friendly at Yale. On such occasions, exaggerated back-slapping and shouts of the "You out of prison, you old hoss-thief?" order can be—amazing as it may seem—appropriate. Certainly in the Industrial Controls Corporation, which we discussed at some length in the last chapter, some of the persons most incongruent in status—in the sense in which our female machinist was incongruent—were most apt to joke with the others and be joked at by them, the jokes being of a pretty pointed kind.[14] We shall not enter further into what the anthropologists call the "joking relationship," except to say this: a man's status incongruence may mean he is suffering from injustice; it may also mean he is suffering from ambiguity. The former makes him hostile, the latter makes others embarrassed, and both make trouble.

We have described some of the ways in which people manipulate social stimuli, in accordance with the principle of status congruence,

[14] A. Zaleznik, C. R. Christensen, and F. J. Roethlisberger, *op. cit.*, p. 377.

so as to avoid losing status; and we have described some of the accommodations, like joking, that may appear when congruence cannot be established. But before taking leave for the moment of the manipulation of social stimuli, we should give one example of the way men can use, or try to use, status congruence in order to raise their apparent status in the eyes of others. The example in question is one we have mentioned in Chapter 10. If it is true, as it generally is, that persons of high status are in frequent social interaction with other persons of high status, if high status and frequent social interaction are congruent, then a man who can often manage to be seen in the company of a person of high status on social occasions has, at least as far as that fact goes, established the presumption in the eyes of his fellows that his own status is high too. This method is a favorite with social climbers. Of course he may not get away with it: his fellows may simply resent his trying to get above himself, for he has probably increased his own incongruence. His status is perhaps high as far as social interaction is concerned, but it may still be low in terms of the value of the services he performs for others. The evidence is that men are afraid of incongruence when it may lower their status as perceived by their fellows but much less afraid of it when it may raise their status. This is hardly surprising, for an increase in recognized status is rewarding.

Congruence and Productivity

People find that there is something right, just, and appropriate about congruence. Accordingly when they are working together as a team, we expect that the degree to which they are congruent will make a difference to their effectiveness. If they are highly congruent, at least one factor that might otherwise have disturbed their collaboration has been removed. We turn now to a study showing how failure or success in establishing status congruence made a difference to the relations between workers and to the success of the firm of which they were part. When we examine the productivity of workers in a company, we are getting pretty far away from elementary social behavior, and we do so only for the sake of relating status congruence to one more variable. The study was made by J. V. Clark under the auspices of the Harvard Graduate School of Business Administration, and it was concerned with eight supermarkets belonging to a larger chain of stores.[15]

The investigator devoted most of his time to two of the eight supermarkets and, in them, to the "front end" of the store where the check-out counters stood side by side in a long line. In a fashion familiar to most Americans, a customer wheeled up to one of these counters a cart filled with the goods he had chosen from the shelves. There an employee took the goods from the cart, added up on a cash register the sum due for them, and packed them into a bag or bundle for the customer to take away after he had paid for them.

The number of customers that come into a supermarket, like any other food store, varies greatly from day to day and from hour to hour; therefore the supermarket's need for employees varies greatly, and it hires a great many part-time employees. In the markets studied in the research, about two thirds of the nonsupervisory personnel were part-timers, each working from ten to thirty hours a week.

When customers were few, few check-out counters were manned, and each was manned by a single full-time cashier who carried out all the operations of the counter, both "ringing" (adding up on the register the sum due from the customer, taking his payment, and making change) and "bundling" (taking the goods out of the carts and putting them into bundles to be taken away). When the customer-load got heavy more counters were manned and, to speed up the through-put, each was manned by two workers, one to "ring" and one to "bundle." The extra cashiers and bundlers were drawn partly from full-time workers usually busy in the "back end" where the merchandise was laid out on display, and partly from part-time workers, some of whom spent all their working hours at the "front end." The question that came to interest the investigator most was what made a good team—ringer and bundler—at a check-out counter. When in the Eastern Utilities Co. the ledger clerks were taken off their regular jobs and put on cash posting they did not have to work with the other posters: the jobs required no collaboration. But in the supermarkets a ringer and a bundler had to work together, if only in the timing of what they did, to put a customer through the counter.

Besides observing what went on, the investigator carried out pre-

[15] J. V. Clark, *A Preliminary Investigation of Some Unconscious Assumptions Affecting Labor Efficiency in Eight Supermarkets* (D.B.A. thesis, Harvard Graduate School of Business Administration, 1958), unpublished.

liminary interviews with eighteen workers in the two supermarkets, chosen so as to represent the different categories of workers. These first interviews were fairly "nondirective," designed to give the investigator a quick general impression of workers' attitudes toward their jobs. Later he interviewed the same workers at greater length, and this time tried to test out more systematically the ideas he had picked up earlier. Among the other questions he asked was this: "If you were suddenly called upon to go to the front end and bundle, arrange these people in the order in which you would *like* to bundle for them." Note the use of the word *for* here. In the workers' parlance, if you bundled *for* someone, that someone was a ringer: you were working *for* him (or her) as a subordinate.

The interviewer then showed the worker a series of cards, each card describing a particular class of person. For instance, one such series was the following: full-time male, part-time male, full-time female, and part-time female employee. The worker was to put the cards in the order in which he would prefer to bundle for the types of person described on them. Some of the dimensions of preference that were examined in other such series were age, marital status, education (whether in high school or college), and educational intentions (whether planning to go to college or not). These last two were brought in because most of the part-time help was of high school or college age. Indeed all the dimensions were ones that the investigator had come, through his first interviews, to believe were particularly significant to the workers. When the worker had put the cards in any series in order, the investigator asked him to explain why he had put them in that order. Besides the information from the interviews, the investigator secured from the personnel office the usual background data about each worker: pay, seniority, job-title, and regular job assignment.

We are now ready for the congruence problem. Bundling was the job that, as a regular assignment, got the lowest pay. It was probably also the most monotonous and least responsible. Yet at times of heavy customer-load, men from better jobs were moved into it, as the ledger clerks were moved into posting, and this created one kind of ambiguity: people working on jobs that were "beneath" them. But it was not the only kind or the most important one. If one went onto bundling, it made a difference whom one bundled *for*. This expression, regularly used, of bundling *for* someone showed that the employees felt the cashier was superior in responsibility and authority to the bundler, and indeed as a regular job cashiering got more pay. But at times of peak load people from other jobs were moved onto ringing as they were onto bundling, and then the question was bound to come up what combinations of different kinds of workers made pleasant or appropriate ringer-bundler teams.

From his interviews the investigator came to the conclusion that the following, not always consciously expressed, rules described the conditions the workers felt should obtain when two of them collaborated:

1. A person should be able to talk comfortably with whomever he works beside.
2. The status factors of a person's job should all be in line.
3. A person's job status (which is determined by the amount of pay, responsibility, variety, and autonomy) should be in line with his general social status (which is determined by his sex, age, education, and seniority).
4. A person should work *with* someone else of his own social status (sex, age, education, seniority, and religion).
5. A person should not bundle *for* a cashier of lower social status than his own.

Actually there are only two main questions that these rules answer. First, whom is it legitimate that I should bundle for, as a subordinate? And second, whom do I enjoy bundling with, as a companion? For cashier and bundler are at once companions and superior and subordinate. The answer to the first question is that I should bundle for someone the characteristics of whose regular job and social background are congruent, and superior to mine in other respects besides the superiority of ringing to bundling. And the answer to the second question is that I enjoy bundling with someone who, because his background is like my own, has many things in common with me, so that we can talk comfortably. We have earlier encountered each of these rules apart from the other. In the supermarket the two combined to make the preferred cashier one who was legitimately superior to the bundler but not so much superior as to be utterly unlike him.

Let us now tie down these points in detail, quoting from the interviews. First, cashiering (ringing or checking) was socially superior to bundling. As one male cashier said:

> You know I feel sort of silly saying it, but in the scheme of things in this store, when you are checking you feel superior to the people who are bundling and to the stock boys, and this superiority is because of the responsibility of the job.

In the supermarkets as elsewhere, one job was more responsible than another if more damage could result if it were done wrong. But if as a job cashiering was superior to bundling, then status congruence required that the cashiers be superior to the bundlers on some other count besides the job itself. Accordingly we hear that:

> It would be a very bad situation to have even a 20-29-year-old bundling for a 16-19-year-old ringer. That's a *must* for good personal relations. Another way of saying that, is that high school guys should bundle for college guys. The college guy would naturally feel superior, and it would induce friction if he bundled for a high school guy. You see, he would *feel* superior as a person but *be* in an inferior position on the job.

That is, ringing had higher job-status than bundling, and so the ringer should have higher social investments than the bundler—in this case more age and more education. Of course this does not mean that the condition of legitimacy was always realized in practice. Girls were thought of as having lower status than boys, at least boys of about the same age, and yet girls often rang the cash register and boys bundled "for" them—an ambiguous situation never wholly legitimate. Even in that most modern of American institutions, the supermarket, congruence still requires that the man have a better job than the woman.

As two employees worked at a check-out counter, a little talking helped along an essentially dull job, especially in the intervals between passing customers through the slot. And though the condition of congruence was satisfied if a high school boy who was also a part-time worker bundled for a cashier who was an older man and a full-time worker, the bundler might not find him particularly easy to talk to because his background was too much unlike the bundler's own. Congruence, then, was a necessary but not a sufficient condition for a good ringer-bundler team: the two should also be similar in background. Accordingly we hear statements like this:

> I'd like to bundle for the regular high school kids, though. [The speaker was one himself.] You could talk to them, you know? . . . The college kids would be too smart for *me*. You always like to bundle for someone your own age and class.

The resultant of the two demands for legitimacy and similarity was that a bundler most liked to work for a cashier whose investments were higher than his own, but not so much higher as to put comfortable talking out of the question. Especially suitable was someone whose investments the bundler himself expected to attain in time. Such a team might match a cashier who was in college with a bundler who was like the cashier in all respects except that he was not yet in college but aspired to go there: he was taking the college-preparatory course in high school. Such a pairing of bundler and cashier met the specifications for both congruence and congeniality.

Perhaps the combined effect of the two requirements was best described by a part-time employee who was also a high school boy planning to go to college:

> I always prefer to bundle for the male if he's a friend. Not all of them are your friends, though, and I'd want to bundle for those that are. In general, I'd bundle for the younger person first because you're more apt to be friendly with younger fellows than older people. But between a high school cashier and a college cashier, I'd bundle for the college person first. If a person is older, you look up to and respect him more. I'd bundle for the high school girl before I'd bundle for the college girl, though. I'd have more in common with a younger girl than with an older one.

Note that, though he would bundle for a college boy, he would prefer not to do so for a college *girl,* on the grounds that she would have too little in common with himself.

We turn now to the investigator's last finding about the supermarkets. The cashier and the bundler worked together in putting customers through the check-out counter, and we might expect any failure in the congruence and congeniality of the relation between them to have some effect on their joint efficiency. Indeed one girl said that when she was forced to bundle for a cashier of lower status than her own, she purposely slowed down the speed at which she worked.

The investigator succeeded in getting systematic evidence on this point.

The costs of manning the check-out counters formed a very large part of the total labor costs in the supermarkets. The investigator began by studying intensively two stores in the chain, Nos. 6 and 58. The former was much less efficient in its use of manpower than the latter: grocery department man-hours per $100 of sales were 3.85 hours in the former but only 3.04 in the latter; and operating gain as a percentage of sales was 3.89 per cent in the former but 5.67 in the latter. The investigator also had the impression that of all possible bundler-ringer pairs, fewer in No. 6 store could meet the conditions of congruence and congeniality than could do so in No. 58. That is, the evidence suggested that labor efficiency and number of suitable bundler-ringer pairs might be correlated. He decided to test this hypothesis, not just for the two stores but for a larger sample of stores in the chain.

The investigator knew that the part-timers did most of the check-out work: about 80 per cent of all customers were checked out by them, so that it was largely for them that matching the members of the check-out team in congruence and congeniality was a problem. Although he could not study the other stores at first hand, he knew that their jobs were the same as those of Nos. 6 and 58, and he had access to their personnel records. From these records he gave each part-time worker in the other stores a score on each of a number of different dimensions: for instance, a boy scored higher than a girl on the sex dimension, a college boy higher than a high school boy on the education dimension, and so on for the other relevant dimensions of an employee's job and background, such as pay.

Since each part-time worker might be assigned, at one time or another, to work with every other one at a check-out counter, the investigator calculated for eight different stores—by a method too complicated to be described here—the percentage of all possible pairs of part-time workers that could realize the conditions necessary for a good team: similarity of background and job characteristics, on the one hand, and legitimacy in the form of status congruence, on the other. And he discovered that the rank-order of the eight stores on this measure, which he called a measure of *social ease,* correlated almost perfectly with their rank-order on labor efficiency (man-hours of labor used per $100 of sales): the greater the social ease, the greater the efficiency. If the rank-order of the stores in efficiency was 1, 2, 3, 4 . . . , their rank-order in social ease was 1, 2, 3, 5, 4, 6, 7, 8. The two stores that were fourth and fifth in efficiency reversed that order in social ease, and this was the only departure from a perfect correlation.

The investigator was also able to show that none of a number of possible other explanations accounted for the differences in efficiency nearly as well as did differences in social ease. He then added a fascinating final twist. Of the two supermarkets he studied at first hand No. 6 had, when he first studied it, a lower score in labor efficiency than had No. 58. Later No. 6 went through a spell of heavy labor turnover, which may itself have been a sign that employees were dissatisfied with the social conditions they encountered. The investigator was able to show that the employees who came in as replacements possessed characteristics more apt to make them members of congruent and congenial pairs than did those who had left. And as the replacements came in, the labor efficiency of supermarket No. 6 rose. Congruence and congeniality in the relation between two men working together as a team do make a difference to their productivity.

Congruence, Liking, and Effectiveness

At least one other study reaches conclusions similar though not identical to those of the supermarket research. Stuart Adams, to whom we owe the term *status congruence,* studied the effectiveness of Air Force bombers in relation to the congruence of their crews.[16] He gave each member of each crew a score on a number of different dimensions of his background, his job in the bomber, and his social position—the dimensions being age, education, length of service, flying time, combat time, rank, the importance of his position in the crew, his reputed ability, and his popularity—the last two being determined by a simple sociometric test. Thus, to be obvious, an older man got a higher score on age than a younger one. From these scores on particular dimensions the investigator was able to develop a status-congruence score for each member. Thus an older man with long service would be highly congruent as far at least as his scores on these two

[16] S. N. Adams, "Status Congruency as a Variable in Small Group Performance." *Social Forces,* Vol. 32 (1953-54), pp. 16-22. I changed *congruency* to *congruence* because the latter has one less syllable.

dimensions were concerned. And from these scores for individual members it was an easy matter to construct a measure of the average congruence of each bomber crew.

The investigator then correlated the crews' congruence scores with their effectiveness as measured by the number of hits they got in practice bombing, and also with the results of two questionnaires—one on the degree of confidence members of a crew felt in one another and another on the degree of friendship they felt for one another. Congruence correlated highly with both confidence and friendship: the greater the congruence of a crew, the greater the average friendship of its members for one another—which is just what we should expect from the supermarket study if social ease encourages friendship. On the other hand, effectiveness as measured by scores in practice bombing correlated negatively, though not highly so, with congruence—which is not what we should have expected from the supermarket study if effectiveness is equivalent to labor efficiency.

A closer look showed the investigator that the relationship between congruence and effectiveness was curvilinear. That is to say, a bomber whose crew had very low congruence was apt to be a rather ineffective one. From then on an increase in congruence was associated with an increase in effectiveness until *medium* congruence was reached: the most effective bombers were those of medium congruence; but after that any further increase in congruence meant a sharp falling-off in effectiveness, until at the other end of the distribution a very congruent bomber was apt to be a very ineffective one. It was as if the members of such a crew were, by reason of their congruence, so much at their social ease that they spent their time enjoying one another's company instead of tending to business. It was as if, in the supermarkets, bundler and ringer spent so much time talking to one another that they neglected to put the customer through the slot. Although the pressure from the customers was enough to prevent anything like that from happening in the supermarkets, there are plenty of other situations in which the adjustment of workers to one another may become so good that it gets in the way of work. Unfortunately the man who investigated the bombers does not give us enough information to make sure this explanation is the correct one.

Summary

Besides actually exchanging rewards (and punishments) with one another, men act as if they find it valuable to realize fair exchange. At least they display emotional behavior when, by the standards of fair exchange, they perceive that they are deprived in comparison with others. Fair exchange, or distributive justice in the relations among men, is realized when the profit, or reward less cost, of each man is directly proportional to his investments: such things as age, sex, seniority, or acquired skill. As a practical matter, distributive justice is realized when each of the various features of his investments and his activities, put into rank-order in comparison with those of other men, fall in the same place in all the different rank-orders. This condition, which we call status congruence, is not only the condition of distributive justice but also that of social certitude: the status of a man in this condition is secure, established, unambiguous in the eyes of his fellows. To attain status congruence is a reward to men, and to forgo it, a cost; and they have learned various means by which they may attain the reward or avoid the cost. Congruence facilitates social ease in the interaction among men, and so when they are working together as a team, a congruent relationship between them, by removing one possible source of friction, should encourage their joint efficiency. Up at least to middle levels of congruence, the evidence shows that it does do so.

Satisfaction

Chapter Thirteen

Besides behaving in certain ways and getting various rewards, men also talk about how satisfied they are with the rewards they get. In a book on elementary social behavior, a chapter on satisfaction necessarily follows one on justice. In the last chapter we were concerned with showing how men define the condition of distributive justice when they think they are getting what they deserve. In the present chapter we shall be concerned with showing how their satisfaction varies when they fall short of getting what they deserve, for, as we shall see, distributive justice is a principal ingredient of satisfaction. But satisfaction is a tricky thing. It is a form of verbal behavior. We learn about human satisfaction from what men have to say about their "states of mind," and the study of satisfaction suffers from all the difficulties in interpretation that statements of this sort are heirs to.

The question that the study of satisfaction raises above all others is what relation it bears to other forms of behavior. Clearly, satisfaction is directly related to emotional behavior. The ledger clerks expressed dissatisfaction with their pay, and they were also angry. Indeed it may be superfluous to say that they were "also" angry: their dissatisfaction and their anger were the same thing. But the relation between satisfaction and nonemotional behavior is nothing like so clear. It is not at all clear that the more satisfied a man is with the reward he gets from a particular activity, the more often he will emit that activity. It is not at all clear, for instance, that the more satisfaction he expresses with his job, the harder he will work on that job. On the contrary, the job may pay him so well that after a time he would rather do something else than work for more pay. On the other hand, men will often work hard at a job without expressing any great satisfaction with its rewards. The ledger clerks kept on doing their job to the complete satisfaction of the management of the Eastern Utilities Co., even though they themselves were not at all satisfied with its pay. Let us put the matter as crudely as we can: men will often do things they do not like, and like things they do not do.

For this reason there is one statement we cannot make too strongly: satisfaction is not identical with profit, as we defined profit in Chapter 4: the two are not the same variable.[1] The profit of a unit-activity is the difference in value between its reward and its cost, cost being defined as the reward of some alternative activity forgone in emitting the first. If our argument is correct, the profit of an activity is directly related to the frequency with which a man will emit it: the greater the profit from doing it, the more often he will do it. But this is not necessarily so of satisfaction. Consider the dramatic situation we cited in Chapter 4. The soldiers of Cortez have landed on the shores of Mexico, and Cortez has burned his ships behind him. The natives are hostile, and the soldiers now have no alternative to fighting them. Under these circumstances, their profit from fighting is high and they will fight hard, but it would be silly to argue that they enjoy the situation they have been put in, though if they do fight and win, their satisfaction will be so great that it might better be called elation.

A student of social behavior must always be more interested in what men do than in what they say about what they do. He is a little like a general who cares not if his soldiers grumble so long as they will fight. Accordingly he will be more interested in profit than in satisfaction. Yet there are good reasons for devoting a chapter to satisfaction, provided its length is not out of proportion to the importance of the subject. With all its ambiguities men will talk about it, and social scientists will try to discover why men are satisfied or dissatisfied. Moreover, the

---

[1] See N. Morse, *Satisfactions in the White-Collar Job* (Ann Arbor, Mich., 1953), pp. 11-12, where she points out that satisfaction is not the same thing as motivation; see also J. Thibaut and H. H. Kelley, *The Social Psychology of Groups* (New York, 1959), pp. 21-23: their distinction between "comparison level" and "comparison level for alternatives" is related to the distinction between satisfaction and profit.

study of satisfaction brings in again, in a new and perhaps interesting way, some of the variables we have already encountered in other connections. In the present chapter we shall try to do two things. First, we shall try to discover what the main determinants of satisfaction are, and second, we shall try to answer the question we have already raised: What is the relation between a man's satisfaction with a reward and the amount of behavior he will put out to get that reward?

The Determinants of Satisfaction

We must repeat: the interpretation of verbal expressions of satisfaction or dissatisfaction is a tricky business. No doubt there are satisfactions and satisfactions: the elation attending the completion of a hard task may be different from the pleasure gotten from an ongoing activity. We shall confine ourselves to the latter. Our question is this: Suppose a man is performing more or less regularly a particular kind of activity; what circumstances make it more or less likely that he will say he is satisfied with the reward he gets from that activity? The best recent discussion of the determinants of satisfaction is Nancy Morse's book *Satisfactions in the White-Collar Job,* which we shall make much use of in the present chapter. Our general answer to the question is the one she makes: "The greater the amount the individual gets, the greater his satisfaction and, at the same time, the more the individual still desires, the less his satisfaction."[2]

Let us be sure we understand this statement. It says first that the larger the amount of reward a man gets within a given time by performing an activity, the more satisfaction he will express with that reward. So loose is men's talk, that he may speak as if it were the activity and not the reward that satisfied him: he may say he is satisfied with his job when it is its pay he means, and this makes one of the difficulties in interpreting statements about satisfaction. Satisfaction is a matter of reward. We must, if we can, identify the rewards and not just the activities, and discover which activities get which rewards: a man may say he is satisfied with his job when it is not its pay but the opportunity it affords for interaction with his fellow workers that satisfies him.

The statement says, second, that "the more the individual still de-

[2] N. Morse, *op. cit.,* p. 28.

sires, the less his satisfaction." As it stands, this is only intuitively adequate. For what do we mean by "the more the individual still desires"? Let us begin with a very crude formulation, reserving the right to modify it in the light of later evidence. Let us assume that there is a certain quantity of reward that, received over a given period of time, would satiate a man with that reward, so that for the time being he would perform no further activity so rewarded. Then the amount the individual still desires is the amount by which what he has already gotten falls short of satiating him. The more nearly he is satiated, the more nearly he is satisfied—which does not say much, for the two words *satiation* and *satisfaction* mean much the same thing and include the same Latin word: *satis,* "enough."

For any single person the amount that would satiate him with any particular reward is, we assume, constant for the time being. If this is the case, Morse's two determinants of satisfaction are necessarily related to one another; for the more reward a person has received, the less he has still to desire. But as between two persons, it may well take more to satiate the one than it does the other, and so the two may get the same amount of reward and yet one may be left with more to desire. Let us accordingly rephrase Morse's statement in the form of two propositions. (1) When two men would be satiated with the same amount of reward and one has gotten a larger amount than the other, the one that has gotten more is the more satisfied. (2) When two men would be satiated with different amounts of reward and one has gotten the same amount as the other, the one who is nearer satiation is the more satisfied. Note that the further a man is from satiation with a reward, the more valuable any unit of that reward is to him, and therefore we may say that of two men receiving equal amounts of a reward, the one who finds that reward the more valuable is apt to be the less satisfied.

It is sometimes possible to show how the two determinants—the amount of reward received and the amount still desired—work together. For instance, Morse reports a study of the satisfaction of white-collar workers with their chances for promotion in a company.[3] The study easily showed that employees were more satisfied with promotions the more confidence they felt in their chances of being pro-

[3] *Ibid.,* pp. 28-31.

moted. True, they had not actually received their promotions, yet it is not hard to see how this finding fits the first part of Morse's statement: the more the individual gets, the greater is his satisfaction. The investigator also asked the employees how "important" promotion was to them, and she found that among employees who felt the same degree of confidence in their chances for promotion, those who said that promotions were more important to them were less satisfied. It is not hard to see how this finding fits the second part of Morse's statement: the more the individual still desires, the less his satisfaction. In our terms, the more valuable is a reward to a man, the less likely he is to be satisfied with the amount of that reward he has gotten so far.

The Amount a Man Gets

Usually we must content ourselves with considering the two elements of satisfaction separately. As for the first, the amount a man gets, it is not hard to show that between two persons more or less similar in other respects, the one who is getting more of any particular reward is the more satisfied of the two. Indeed it is the assumption most men have always made, and they are surprised indeed when they run into an exception. We need not linger over the evidence. The workers of Irish origin in the Industrial Controls Corporation were on the average more satisfied with their life in the department than were other workers, and they had good reason to be. As we saw, they were particularly likely to get what social rewards were going in the way of being one of the boys, and other rewards in the department were few: there was little chance for promotion or for big raises in pay.[4]

But there are studies that seem to contradict the common-sense view that the more reward a man gets, the more satisfied he is with it. In World War II, the Research Branch, Information and Education Division, of the United States Army carried out a long series of studies on the attitudes and behavior of American soldiers. Among other things, the investigators studied attitudes toward promotion, and they found, for instance, that soldiers in the Air Force were much less satisfied with promotions than were soldiers in the Military Police, in spite of the fact

[4] A. Zaleznik, C. R. Christensen, and F. J. Roethlisberger, *The Motivation, Productivity, and Satisfaction of Workers* (Boston, 1958), p. 273.

that the actual chances for promotion were far greater in the former than in the latter.[5]

How shall we explain this apparently paradoxical finding? Note first that the finding gives us the average satisfaction of the soldiers in the two different branches of the service. No doubt the soldiers who had actually been promoted recently would have expressed satisfaction with promotions, but the questionnaire was not given to them alone; it was also given to people who had not been promoted. Now if there is much promotion in a particular branch of the service, some men will see many of their fellows promoted while they themselves are passed over, and this will lead them to ask whether the promotions are just and whether sufficient attention has been paid to their own abilities. It will raise the question of distributive justice—justice in the distribution of rewards among men—and justice, as we shall see more and more as we go along, is a principal ingredient of satisfaction. In a branch like the Military Police, on the other hand, where there has been very little promotion, the soldiers are much less apt to compare their fate with that of others and so to raise the question of justice. Promote everybody or promote nobody and soldiers will be satisfied with promotions, this study seems to say.[6] Unfortunately neither of these policies is satisfactory for other reasons.

This is the sort of problem that creates the demand for promoting people by seniority instead of by alleged ability. All parties concerned are more apt to agree that justice has been done if they are agreed on the sorts of things that should enter the balance and what weights are to be assigned them. If seniority is to count, it is easy for the parties to agree that one man has a higher investment in seniority than another and so, in justice, should be the first promoted. But if ability is to count, it is much less easy for the parties to agree that one man has a greater investment in developed ability than another. The former judgment can be "impersonal," the latter less obviously so. It reflects on the ability of the man who is not promoted, and he will be only human if he asks himself whether justice has been done him. Because of the dissatisfaction promotions by alleged ability are apt to arouse, most organizations make a compromise. At the lower levels, where high

[5] S. A. Stouffer, E. A. Suchman, L. C. DeVinney, S. A. Star, and R. M. Williams, Jr., *The American Soldier*, Vol. I (Princeton, 1949), pp. 250-53.

[6] See J. A. Davis, "A Formal Interpretation of the Theory of Relative Deprivation," *Sociometry*, Vol. 22 (1959), pp. 280-96.

ability does not matter so much, they are apt to allow more promotions by seniority than they do at the upper levels.

Let us now look at a somewhat more complicated, but still common, situation. So far we have considered the case in which two men want essentially the same kind of reward, even though one may want it more than the other does. But sometimes they want entirely different kinds. Suppose two men are doing the same job, and objectively they are getting about the same reward for doing it. One of them values this kind of reward highly, while the other does not do so. No doubt the latter would be satisfied with the amount of reward he does get, if only he wanted that kind. Instead he sets a high value on a different kind of reward, which the job is not giving him much of. Under these circumstances, the former is getting more of the kind of reward he wants than the latter is getting of the kind he, the latter, wants. Accordingly we should expect the former to be the more satisfied of the two. Let us look at an example.

In a study of a research laboratory attached to a manufacturing company, L. B. Barnes found he could divide the engineers in the laboratory into two different categories, which he called *professionals* and *organizationals,* according to differences in their backgrounds.[7] In their past experience, including lengthy technical training at universities, the professionals had acquired the values of academic, research scientists. The past experience of the organizationals was apt to have been somewhat different, and they tended to identify themselves with business and look forward to a career in the company. In point of fact the laboratory was asked to do little true research, and spent much of its time running routine tests and providing other services for the ongoing manufacturing operations of the company. Not surprisingly, the organizationals were much better satisfied than the professionals. By the acquired values of the latter, the rewards they got from the job itself were small. They were not doing what they were trained to do and liked to do.

We can look on the dissatisfaction of the professionals as a problem of social certitude. Whereas the kinds of work the organizationals did and the kinds of rewards they got for doing it were thoroughly congruent, thoroughly in line, with their investments, this was not true

[7] L. B. Barnes, *An Industrial Laboratory* (M.B.A. thesis, Harvard Graduate School of Business Administration, 1958), unpublished.

of the professionals. The kind of work they did in running routine tests was apt to cast doubt on their status as research scientists: it was beneath them. In the same way the ledger clerks resented their relatively low pay because it was incongruent with their doing a responsible job. If distributive justice is an important ingredient in satisfaction, so is its close relative social certitude. And there is plenty of evidence that research scientists in American industry are often dissatisfied.

The Amount a Man Still Desires

Much more interesting is the second main element in satisfaction— the amount the individual still desires. The more there is left for a man to desire of any particular reward, the more valuable any unit of that reward is to him. In Morse's study of promotion we have already seen that when two men are getting equal amounts of a kind of reward they both want, but one of them sets a higher value on the reward than the other does, the former will be less satisfied than the latter. And one of the reasons why a man sets a relatively high value on a particular reward is that his circumstances outside the place where he is getting the reward make his need for it high.

To look into this matter further let us return to Nancy Morse's *Satisfactions in the White-Collar Job.*[8] In her analysis of the attitudes of clerical workers in a large American company, she divided the different jobs into four classes and put them into the following rank-order: high-level technical, semisupervisory, varied clerical, and repetitious clerical. This was the order of the jobs in pay, responsibility, and variety, and their order in status within the company. It also turned out to be the rank-order of the jobs in the degree of satisfaction the people who held them expressed for the intrinsic rewards of the job itself, such as the sheer interest of the work. Here it is clear that satisfaction varies with "the amount the individual gets": the better the job, the greater the satisfaction.

But when the investigator asked the employees on the same jobs how satisfied they were with pay and promotions, the order of jobs almost reversed itself. In spite of the fact that they drew the highest pay, the high-level technical people were now least satisfied, the varied clerical somewhat more so, and the repetitious clerical still more. The semi-

[8] *Op. cit.,* pp. 55-75.

supervisory people, as the most satisfied, represented the only exception to a complete reversal of the rank-order. We shall have more to say about them later.

Leaving them aside, let us look at the others. The repetitious-clerical workers got less pay than the others and certainly had received little promotion, but they were most satisfied with both. Here it is evident that a person's satisfaction does not vary simply with the amount he gets. What is the explanation? When employees first came into the company, most of them began on the dullest and lowest jobs. But most of them were also youngsters, new to the labor market. Though they were far down the ladder of promotion, at least it looked open ahead. Though their pay was low, it was more than they had gotten before, and as persons of few outside responsibilities, they had few outside demands for pay put upon them. That is, the amount of pay they still desired was relatively low. If you wish, we shall agree at once that our desires for money are infinite; but once that point of doctrine is out of the way, we shall also agree, perhaps, that most of us would get by very well with something less than that.

As employees spent more time in the company, moved up to more interesting and responsible jobs, and got more satisfaction out of the job itself and its informal status, they also acquired wives and children —so many more demands on them for money. The pay increases that they got as they moved up in the company did not keep pace with their increasing need for pay; with every promotion they received, their chances for further promotion in the organization pyramid narrowed, and promotion of course meant more pay. Accordingly their satisfaction with pay and promotion declined. Indeed in some companies over-all satisfaction is highest in the least senior and in the most senior jobs, and is lowest in the middle. The least senior people are most satisfied with things like pay, and the most senior most satisfied with informal status and the intrinsic interest of their work, while the people in the middle are not much satisfied on either count.[9]

Another factor may have worked in the same direction. The higher a worker's status in the company, the more often management must have considered whether to promote him. And if management had ever passed him over for promotion, the question of the justice of promo-

[9] T. V. Purcell, *The Worker Speaks His Mind on Company and Union* (Cambridge, Mass., 1953), p. 79: the statement holds good of white but not of Negro workers.

tions must have risen in his mind, as it did among the soldiers of the Air Force. After all, a worker who is new to a company has had little chance of being considered for promotion, and the sight of others' being advanced over his head has not yet soured him. The older workers, moreover, may have felt that in taking on the responsibility of wives and children, they had also increased their investments and so, in justice, might expect more pay: not only did they need pay more than others did, but they had more right to it.

Now let us return to the semisupervisory workers who, we shall remember, ranked second on intrinsic job-satisfaction and tops on satisfaction with pay and advancement, and so constituted an exception to the rule that the order of jobs on the latter kind of satisfaction reversed their order on the former: the semisupervisory workers were more satisfied with pay and promotion than they ought to have been. It happened that most of them were women, and it is conceivable that women, simply as women, are more easily satisfied than men. Many of them were also single women, without heavy outside responsibilities and so without heavy demands made on them for pay; and of course even married women are seldom the chief supports of their families. But we must never lose sight of the part played by justice in determining satisfaction. By the standards current in American industry, the female sex is considered to have made a lower investment than the male, and so by distributive justice, to deserve a less good job than the male. This kind of discrimination may well vex a woman, but it has its compensations. It means that she expects less than a man does, and so is more satisfied if she gets anything like as much, for then less remains for her to desire. There is much evidence that on the average the women in American industry are more satisfied than the men. In short, the high investments of the married men tended to make them less satisfied, and the low investments of the unmarried women tended to make them more satisfied with pay and promotion than was justified by the sheer quantity of pay and promotion either group received.

Justice and the Level of Aspiration

It should be obvious that we have been drifting toward a definition of "what the individual still desires" that is somewhat different from the one we started with. We started by assuming there was a quantity of reward that, received over a given time, would satiate a man with that reward, and that the amount the individual still desired was the difference between that quantity and the quantity he had actually received. When we are talking about eating steak or some other physical reward, it may be more or less meaningful to speak of the quantity of steak that, eaten at a sitting, would glut a man; but when we are talking about pay, or variety, or autonomy, or promotion, it is by no means so clear what we might mean by satiation. What we have practically done is substitute for "quantity of reward that would satiate a man" "quantity of reward that is in line with his investments according to the rule of distributive justice." Then the amount the individual still desires of any particular reward is the amount by which the reward he has gotten falls short of this quantity, which we shall call the *satisfaction quantity*. This definition satisfies the proposition, for the more, in these terms, the individual still desires, the less indeed is his satisfaction.

Though it will fit a good deal, the new definition will not fit every case of dissatisfaction. In spite of the fact that, inside his company, a man's pay is utterly in line with his investments in seniority and acquired skills, we must remember that he may still be dissatisfied with his pay if his family or anything else on the outside makes great claims upon it: all those empty bellies to fill and empty minds to educate. But even here he may try to make injustice the reason for his dissatisfaction by getting his wife and children recognized as legitimate investments. An example is the argument that married men should be the last to be laid off in a slump.

We have assumed that, though the satisfaction quantity for any particular kind of reward varied from one person to another, it was constant for any single person, at least for brief periods of time. This assumption is reasonable enough, for the satisfaction quantity is determined by a man's investments and these change relatively slowly. But they do change: a man is always acquiring more seniority, skill, and other such investments, and as he does so, his satisfaction quantity, or what psychologists call his *level of aspiration,* rises. If his level of aspiration goes up without a corresponding increase in the rewards he is getting, the amount he still desires will increase and his satisfaction decrease.

For an example let us go back again to Nancy Morse's book. She studied the differences in satisfaction between white-collar workers under "general" and those under "close" supervision.[10] Briefly, a "close" supervisor was one who kept checking up on what the workers in his department were doing, kept "breathing down their necks." A "general" supervisor was one who, once he had told a worker what he was to accomplish, let him alone to accomplish it in his own way—allowed him, in our terms, a great deal of autonomy. The investigator knew from earlier studies that, other things equal, employees prefer general to close supervision, and so she was surprised to find in this case that the employees under general supervision were less satisfied with the pay, status, and intrinsic content of their jobs than were the employees under close supervision.

She came to attribute these results, first, to a rise in the level of aspiration of the employees under general supervision, a rise brought about by the general supervision itself, and second, to the fact that these employees got no more pay or promotion than the employees under close supervision. A person under general supervision is one who takes a great deal of responsibility: he is able to decide what ought to be done without always checking back with his boss. But a man that has learned how to do a job on his own responsibility has, by that fact, made new investments, and so should get more reward. He feels he is ready for a raise in pay and a better job, even if it is also a more demanding one. If he does not get them, he will become less satisfied than his fellow workers down whose necks the boss has been breathing all the time, even though taken by itself the latter is the worse position to be in. Things like this have persuaded some people who would prefer to believe otherwise that any effort to satisfy mankind is bound to be self-defeating. Any satisfied desire creates an unsatisfied one.

Productivity and Satisfaction

We shall end this chapter by trying to answer the second of the two questions we raised at the beginning: What is the relation between a man's satisfaction with a reward and the amount of behavior he will put out to get that reward? In American industry this is the famous

[10] N. Morse, *op. cit.,* pp. 138-40.

issue of the relation between satisfaction and productivity: Is a satisfied worker one that will work hard? Americans have been inclined to assume that he will work hard. Perhaps they believe (much to their credit) that augmenting one good thing augments all others too; or they may work on a straightforward theory of fair exchange: if management does much to satisfy the workers, the workers will do much to satisfy management. Unfortunately for their optimism careful studies of the relationship have brought ambiguous results. The workers' notion of fair exchange with management does not alway jibe with management's own. Indeed their favorite slogan, "A fair day's work for a fair day's wage," they often carry out in practice by pegging production instead of working as hard as they can. The happy worker is not always a productive one, nor is the productive one always particularly happy, and in the preceding pages we have encountered examples of both. These facts seem to provide ammunition for the hard-boiled and the cynical.

Although we have taken many of our illustrations from American industry, our interest is in social behavior as a whole. What we shall try to do now is show why there need be no single, general relation between a man's satisfaction with a reward and how hard he works to get that reward, either in industry or in any other kind of work. Our argument will be highly abstract, as it must be if it is to be general, and it will make use of one of our simplified toys. Readers who are not amused by this sort of thing and prefer not to tax their minds with even the simplest algebra had better skip the next few pages.

Let us assume that a man is emitting an activity in small, standardized units and is getting a single kind of reward, also in standardized units, either from the environment or from another man. He may, for instance, be cutting up his steak and eating it in chunks of about the same size. Let us further assume that no very valuable alternative activity is open to him, and that therefore we can disregard costs. Starting from a condition of zero reward, or full deprivation, the total quantity of reward he has received up to a given time we shall call R. The satisfaction quantity, the quantity of reward that, received over a given period of time, would satiate him either physically or according to his standards of distributive justice, we shall call Q, and we take it to be a constant for this period of time. Let us assume, finally, that within the period in question he does receive, sooner or later, enough reward to satiate him. Should he not do so, we should have to make a different analysis.

We shall now attempt to express in terms of R the two variables whose relation to one another we wish to examine: first, the man's satisfaction, S, as measured by some kind of questionnaire, with the amount of reward he has received; and second, how hard he works to get the reward, which we shall call F_A and define as how frequently, within any brief period of time, he emits the activity in question.

Let us turn first to the determinants of satisfaction. In the earlier part of the chapter, we agreed with Morse in saying that a man's satisfaction with a reward is directly proportional to the quantity of reward he has actually received, and inversely proportional to the amount by which that quantity falls short of satiating him: this latter amount is $Q-R$. We may accordingly write the equation

$$S=\frac{aR}{Q-R} \tag{1}$$

where a is a constant of proportionality. In later equations we shall take other such constants for granted. We assume that $Q-R$ cannot become negative.

The general type of curve relating S to R is shown in Figure 3. It says that as the amount of reward our man has received increases, his satisfaction increases more and more rapidly, becoming infinite when $R=Q$. We do not know that any meaning can be given to "infinite satisfaction," and in this respect our toy may be unrealistic. Otherwise we believe the curve to be realistic enough for our purposes.

We turn now to the second variable, the frequency F_A with which he emits the activity. Let us first put the matter crudely: how hard a man works depends on how valuable a reward the work gets him and on how often the work succeeds in getting him that reward. Now let us speak more carefully. According to proposition 3 in Chapter 4, the frequency with which a man emits an activity is directly proportional to the value to him of a unit of the reward. But by proposition 4 its value varies as the degree to which the man falls short of satiation with the reward; that is, its value varies as $Q-R$. And according to proposition 2 the frequency with which a man emits an activity is also a positive function of the frequency with which it is being rewarded,

Amount of Reward, Frequency of Reward, and Satisfaction

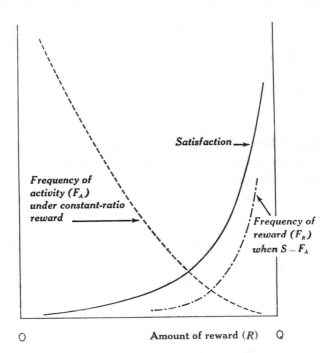

either by another man or by the environment. We shall call the frequency of reward F_R and write the equation

$$F_A = bF_R(Q-R) \qquad (2)$$

We shall recognize at once that unless we can express the variable F_R in terms of R we shall not be able to show how F_A is related to S. The frequency of reward depends not on our man's own behavior but on the behavior of some other man or the environment, and we cannot make any single, general statement about what that will be. All we can do is consider one or two of the many possibilities.

One possibility is that the other person or the environment is rewarding our man's activity at a frequency proportional to the frequency with which he emits it: every nth emission gets rewarded. This schedule of reward, reward at a constant ratio, does often occur in real life.[11] When a man cuts and eats his steak his action is rewarded nearly every time, and when a factory worker is paid by the piece he gets so many cents every time he completes a series of activities. An activity that is not emitted is an activity that cannot be rewarded; the frequency with which it is emitted depends on its value, or $Q-R$, and therefore, under the condition of reward at a constant ratio, the frequency with which it is rewarded depends on its value too. So setting $F_R = c(Q-R)$ and substituting in equation (2), we get

$$F_A = bc(Q-R)^2 \tag{3}$$

Under this condition we have at last got F_A expressed as a function of R. Look at Figure 3 to see the plot of F_A against R. We are now also able to see how satisfaction is related to the rate of doing work, at least under the condition that the reward comes at a constant ratio to the number of units of activity emitted.

What is the relationship? Equation (3) says that when our man has gotten very little reward, he will emit the activity very frequently, both because each unit of the reward is highly valuable and because the activity is being regularly rewarded: the more frequent the emission, the more frequent the reward. But as the amount of reward he has gotten in the recent past approaches the amount that would satiate him, the frequency with which he emits the activity falls off and becomes zero as $R = Q$. Our man will wolf his steak at the beginning, and then eat more slowly, giving perhaps more time to conversation, until at the end he could not eat another piece.

But this curve is very unlike the satisfaction curve. When our man has gotten least reward, he is least satisfied but working hardest. And when he is nearly sated he is most satisfied but least willing to do any further work to get the reward. For reasons of this sort we cannot say that, in general, the more satisfied a man is with a reward the harder he will work to get it. Under many circumstances, indeed, the reverse is likely to be the case: the less satisfied he is the harder he works. The point is obvious but often forgotten.

Finally, let us not jump to the conclusion that even the inverse relationship holds good under all circumstances. Let us ask under what circumstances a man's satisfaction and the frequency with which he

[11] B. F. Skinner, *Science and Human Behavior* (New York, 1953), pp. 102-04.

emits an activity might vary together, so that the more satisfied he is the harder he works. To answer this question let us set $F_A = S$ in equations (2) and (1). Then

$$bF_R(Q-R) = \frac{aR}{Q-R}$$

Solving for F_R, we get

$$F_R = \frac{aR}{b(Q-R)^2} \qquad (4)$$

Once more, the relation between satisfaction and frequency of emission depends on a third variable, the frequency of reward. For equation (4) says in effect that satisfaction and productivity will vary together only under the condition that the activity gets very infrequent reward from the environment or another person until just before the point of satiation, when it is rewarded at a rapidly accelerating rate. The curve is shown in Figure 3. This schedule of reward does sometimes occur in real life. It occurs when repeated activities that lead up to the accomplishment of some final result get rewarded very infrequently until just before the result is attained, when they begin to get rewarded in a rush. Suppose, for instance, that soldiers have been fighting a battle all day, and at dusk the enemy is just beginning to give way. Then they will put on a last big push, and their elation will mount rapidly as they get sight of victory.

If our argument has shown that satisfaction and productivity can under some conditions vary together, it has also shown that they need not do so generally. The reason is that their relation depends on the frequency of reward, and this schedule may take a number of different forms under different conditions of exchange.

Summary

This chapter has been a continuation of the last. In the last chapter we described the condition in which people are most apt to say they are satisfied with the amount of reward they are getting—if they are ever satisfied at all. This is the condition of distributive justice. In the present chapter we have been less interested in describing the condition itself than in determining how satisfied men feel with the degree to which they have reached the condition. A man is more nearly satisfied with a reward, the more he has gotten of that reward within a given period of time, and the less of the reward he still desires. What he still desires is the difference between the amount he has received and the amount that would satiate him, either physically or by his standards of distributive justice. But even this is not an adequate statement because sometimes, while a man has been approaching satiation with a particular reward, he has also been increasing his investments, which means that he thinks he deserves new rewards or more of the old ones. In psychological language, he has raised his level of aspiration, and so far as his reward has not kept pace, he is still unsatisfied.

Satisfaction is verbal and emotional behavior, and its relation to other kinds of behavior is not at all clear. We asked the old question of the relation between satisfaction and productivity, the relation between a man's satisfaction with a reward and the frequency with which he emits activity that gets him that reward. We found that there was no simple, general relation between the two. The reason is that the relation between satisfaction and productivity depends on a third variable, the frequency with which the activity is rewarded, and this schedule of reward may take many different forms under different conditions of exchange. Often, but by no means always, the more satisfied a man is, the less productive he is.

Authority

Chapter Fourteen

In the course of tucking in loose ends, we must now go back to a subject we considered at some length earlier—the subject of the influence a man exerts on others. But we go back to it from a new point of view. In earlier chapters we were concerned with the general or diffuse influence the members of a group exert on other members. We saw, for instance, that the larger was the number of members who liked other members, the larger was the number who conformed to a group norm. We were also concerned with the influence a relatively large number of members can bring to bear on a small number, or even on one alone. In the office, for instance, we saw how both Person and the Third Man brought influence to bear on Other by getting him to give them help. In the present chapter we shall turn the problem around. Instead of several men's influencing one another, one man may influence several others at a time. When he does so often and regularly, we say that he commands more leadership, power, or authority than do the others. Since our interest is in elementary social behavior, we shall be more concerned with persons who acquire authority by their own actions than with persons who have it handed to them by appointment or inheritance. We shall try to answer two questions: How does a man earn authority? and, What effects does his authority have on the behavior of people he has authority over?[1]

[1] In this chapter, I am specially indebted to C. I. Barnard, *The Functions of the Executive* (Cambridge, Mass., 1938), pp. 161-84; B. de Jouvenel, *De la souveraineté* (Paris, 1955) and *The Elements of Pure Politics* (unpublished

The Channels of Influence

At the risk of going over old ground, let us be sure that we understand what we mean by influence. Let us go back to Person and Other in the office. Person makes a suggestion that Other perform a certain action, specifically that Other help Person with his work. In making the suggestion, Person presents a twofold stimulus to Other. In the first place, the suggestion itself is a verbal stimulus describing the activity Other is to emit, and in the second place, the stimulus signals that it is Person, and not somebody else, who is asking him to emit it. In Chapter 4 we did not emphasize this second aspect of the stimulus because we were not ready to do anything with it at the time. Other's compliance with the suggestion depends on two sorts of considerations. First, is the suggested activity likely to yield Other a profit? In the present case, is it likely to get him reward in the form of social approval? Other's conscious or unconscious answer to this question will depend on his previous experience in getting rewards from activities in some way similar to the one suggested. Second, is Person the sort of man who is likely to reward the activity? Other's answer to this question will depend on his previous experience in getting rewards from people in some way like Person. In Chapter 5, for instance, we saw that men were particularly apt to comply with suggestions coming to them from others known to like them.

If Other does comply with Person's request and thus rewards Person with success, he makes it more likely that Person will come to him with a request on another occasion. Moreover, Other's compliance affects not only Person's future behavior but his own. If Person rewards him with social approval, then Person has made it more likely that Other will comply with his request on a future occasion, though we must always remember that if Person asks Other for help often, the costs of both parties may increase enough to cut off for the time being further interaction between them.

Other's compliance with Person's request is itself apt to take the form of a verbal stimulus describing a course of action to be taken.

lectures given at Yale University, 1958); and J. S. Adams and A. K. Romney, "A Functional Analysis of Authority," *Psychological Review*, Vol. 66 (1959), pp. 234-51.

Person has asked for help, and Other's compliance with the request takes the form of telling him that if he takes such and such steps, he will solve the problem that faces him at work. If Person then takes these steps and gets rewarded with success in doing his work, he will be more likely on future occasions not only to go to Other with requests but also to accept Other's suggestions, both in connection with his work and in other fields. In Person's experience Other has become the sort of man compliance with whose suggestions is apt to be rewarding, and Person will accordingly be more apt to emit activities whose chief characteristic is that they have been suggested by Other. But note again that Other has no more remained unaffected by the exchange than Person has. In Other's experience Person has become the sort of man it is rewarding to make suggestions to. Above all, Other has been rewarded for making suggestions, and so he is likely to make more suggestions, not only to Person but to others like him. To sum up: the result of the exchange has been that Other has become more apt than he was before to make suggestions to Person, and Person has become more apt to comply with suggestions coming from Other. Every time men act they change the probabilities of their future actions.

Let us now consider a group of people. Influence of the sort we have just considered is apt to be widely diffused in a group, in the sense that every member may have influenced every other member at one time or another. But we shall never understand authority if we dwell on this fact alone. The problem is not qualitative but quantitative. Even though every channel of influence is open, some channels get used more than others because members get more out of using them. The reason is obvious. In Chapter 8 on Esteem we saw that in any group the number of members possessing a rare ability to provide services valuable to others is relatively small, and by the same token the number who value these services is relatively large. When the happy few use their abilities to reward the many, the many render them high esteem and become more likely to approach them for rewards on future occasions. But if our argument in the preceding paragraphs has been correct, the few have been acquiring at the same time the ability to influence the many. They have been acquiring it by the very process of rewarding the many, by giving them instructions that the many have found it rewarding to comply with. To speak more carefully, the probability that the few will influence the many has been increased. In this way the channels of influence in the group develop a pattern. Many members bring influence to bear on a few members, and a few bring influence to bear on many members.

What we call authority does not depend just on the fact of influence but on this pattern of influence. Let us say that one man has influenced another when an activity emitted by the other conforms in some degree to a verbal or other symbolic stimulus—a suggestion, instruction, request, or order—the man has addressed to the other. Let us then define *authority* as follows: the larger the number of other members a single member is regularly able to influence, the higher is his authority in the group. The man with highest authority we shall call the leader. By this definition authority is not just influence, for each member may have influenced every other at one time or another. Authority refers instead to differences between members in the amount of influence they exert. And the first proposition we shall state about authority is this: the higher a man's esteem in a group, the higher his authority is apt to be. In earning esteem men also earn authority; they earn esteem by providing rare and valuable services to others, and therefore, the process of earning authority, rather than acquiring it by appointment or inheritance, is apt to be the hardest kind of hard work. Influence over others is purchased at the price of allowing one's self to be influenced by others. This rule is embodied in the proudest title of the head of the Roman Catholic Church: the Pope is *servus servorum Dei,* "the servant of the servants of God."

It may be ambiguous to say that authority is the ability to influence many others and to do so regularly, for the statement assumes that the number of persons influenced and the frequency with which influence is exerted vary together, and this may not always be true. Thus one man may be able to influence many others but not be able to do so very often. We all know of cases when a man held in low esteem in a group once made a suggestion that all the others happened to take up for one reason or another of their own. More common is the case in which one man influences many others but only within one rather narrow field of activity, and outside that field he has no more authority than the next man. We might say that such a man wields a specialized authority, and we shall run into an example in the next chapter. Moreover one group may differ from another in the range of activities within which its leader exercises authority. Thus a factory group may have an appointed leader, the foreman, as well as an informal leader, who has won his position through his own efforts. Under these circumstances the scope within which the formal leader exercises his authority may limit the scope available to the informal leader. Notwithstanding all these theoretical possibilities, the evidence—and it is crude—often suggests that the values of three variables wax and wane together: a man who influences many others is often also a man who influences them often and over a wide range of activities. Indeed our argument suggests that the more often he rewards them, and the wider the range within which he does so, the more regular his authority over them and the wider its range.

For a long time psychologists tried to discover some single trait of personality, or set of traits, the possession of which was apt to make a man a leader. Their results were meager and ambiguous: no single trait seemed to make a man a leader with any regularity, and recently the psychologists have contented themselves with saying that leadership does not depend on the personality of the leader but on the nature of the relation between the leader and his followers.[2] It should now be clear why the psychologists have been right in changing their views. The most important single factor in making a man a leader is the factor that also earns him esteem: the ability to provide rare and valued rewards for his followers. But, as we cannot reassert too often, followers in some groups find some of the damnedest things valuable. So long as a man by hook or by crook can provide his companions with these things, he is apt to win esteem and authority over them. Sometimes his ability to provide them may itself depend on his possession of some general trait of character like intelligence or sheer energy, but it need not do so always, and in some cases the accidents of a man's past experience and learning put him in command of abilities outlandish in themselves but such as his followers happen at the moment to demand. It is one of the more wryly amusing of human experiences to discover that we, who by definition possess intelligence and energy in abundance, do not become leaders, while others, who conspicuously lack our qualities, do make the grade.

In earlier chapters we allowed the man who provided rare and valuable services to his fellows to get esteem in return but we allowed him

---

[2] See especially C. G. Browne and T. G. Cohn, eds., *The Study of Leadership* (Danville, Ill., 1958).

hardly any other rewards. It should now be clear that his ability to influence many others, to control their behavior, puts into his hands the power to use their actions to reward himself, though they too may get rewarded at the same time. Suppose, to take the commonest of all cases, that the leader together with others in the group will be rewarded by the accomplishment of a particular result, and that the result can be accomplished only by the concerted or coordinated action of all the members. Then the leader's acquired ability to influence the behavior of a large number of the members is just what he needs to secure their coordinated action. He may, for instance, be able to get a large number of the members to do the same thing at the same time. Indeed the ability to secure coordinated action is the very heart of what we mean by leadership. If the result is accomplished the leader is rewarded along with the others, and he has at last gotten something besides esteem for all the work he has done.

But note that when the leader asks another man to take action leading to the accomplishment of a group task, he must not ask the other to do something he could not or would not do himself. Something that he would not do himself is an action that is rare and valuable indeed; he, the leader, is the monopolist of that kind of action, and on the maintenance of the monopoly his position depends. To ask someone else to take action that he would not take himself is therefore, by the rule of status congruence, to throw his own position in doubt. As he values his position he will not take the risk.

Esteem and Authority

For the moment our general argument has gone far enough. It has led to the proposition that the higher is a man's esteem, the higher is his authority, when that authority is earned rather than acquired by appointment or inheritance. Whether or not esteem and authority are associated for the reasons embodied in our argument, the fact that they are associated is often observed, and we turn now to some of the evidence.

The first piece of research we cite was carried out by French and Snyder.[3] It was quite straightforward and none the worse for that.

[3] J. R. P. French, Jr., and R. Snyder, "Leadership and Interpersonal Power," in D. Cartwright, ed., *Studies in Social Power* (Ann Arbor, 1959), pp. 118-49.

Working at an Air Force base, the investigators formed a number of groups each consisting of four men. Three of the men in each group were enlisted men and one was the noncommissioned officer who, quite apart from the research, had official responsibility for supervising the enlisted men. Accordingly, one man in each group had acquired authority by appointment, but, as we shall soon see, it was the esteem he had earned that gave him his actual authority in the experiment.

Before the experiment itself began, the investigators asked each member of every group to answer a sociometric question about each of the others. The question was blunt: "How well do you like him?" and the subject was to answer by indicating a point on a seven-point scale of liking. The investigators then presented each subject with a card on which were drawn two similar figures, labeled A and B, whose relative size was made ambiguous by lines that tended to create an optical illusion. Two of the subjects got cards in which figure A was the larger of the two, though, thanks to the optical illusion, not obviously so; and two of the subjects got cards in which figure B was the larger. The investigators adopted this procedure in order that there should be some difference of opinion about the relative size of the figures between two of the men in each group and the other two.

The investigators asked each member to record privately his judgment as to which figure was the larger, and then threw the question open for discussion among the four members, without, of course, allowing them actually to measure the figures. The investigators observed the discussion, recording the number of attempts to influence the others that each member made, and finally they asked the members once more to record their private judgments.

The investigators repeated this procedure three times, using different figures each time, and each time they paired the noncommissioned officer with a different one of the enlisted men by giving them identical cards. Thus the noncommissioned officer encountered each enlisted man once as a supporter and twice as an opponent in the discussions. In this way the noncommissioned officer had an equal chance to show how much he could influence each of the three enlisted men.

The results were just what we should have expected. The investigators referred to the noncommissioned officers as "leaders," which is what they were officially. The first finding concerned the relation between attempted influence and the results of the sociometric test. The more a leader accepted, that is, the better he liked, the other members of his group, the more often he attempted to influence them in the discussion, and, for that matter, the more often they attempted to influence him and one another. But we are naturally more interested in the degree to which the others liked the leader, that is, the esteem in which they held him. The greater was the average liking of the other members for the leader, the more often he attempted to influence them in the discussion.

We have still not reached the heart of the matter, as we are much less interested in attempted, than in successful, influence. The investigators developed a measure of a leader's effectiveness, which took into account his success in changing his opponents' opinions, as recorded after the discussion, his success in preventing his partner from switching, and his success in resisting a change in his own opinion. They found that the higher the leader's average acceptance by members of his group—or, as we should say, the higher his esteem—the more effective he was.

These findings are similar to some we have already encountered in Chapter 5 on Influence. We shall leave to the reader the job of finding his own explanation why a leader who likes his men is apt to try to influence them, and why they are apt to try to influence him and one another. We are more concerned with a leader who is also liked by his men. As we argued earlier, a man held in high esteem is likely to have made many suggestions to his followers and to have had many of them rewarded. Accordingly he is prone to making further attempts to influence them on a new occasion. But this is not all; for if he enjoys high esteem, his followers must often in the past have found compliance with his suggestions rewarding, and so they will be all the more prepared to comply with his suggestions on some new occasion: in ordinary language, they will have confidence in his judgment. In short, esteem and authority are apt to be associated, both because a man of high esteem will attempt to influence many people and because many of his attempts will be successful. Let us not forget a commonplace but important fact: no attempt has less chance of succcess than an attempt that is not made. Nothing venture, nothing have. This experiment incidentally suggests something for which there is a great deal of further evidence: an appointed leader, like the noncommissioned officers here, will be most powerful if he does not wholly rely on the authority of·

ficially assigned him but goes on to earn unofficial authority by the methods typically used by informal leaders.

In the last experiment we knew that the more influential leaders were held in high esteem, but we were told nothing about the means they used to get it. We shall now turn to a piece of research that does give us some information on this point. The characteristics of leadership are primitive: they seem to appear in groups of youngsters almost as soon as they are able to take part in social interaction at all, and the present research, by Lippitt, Polansky, Redl, and Rosen, studied the way boys won and wielded power in two summer camps.[4] The investigators observed the boys' actual behavior, particularly noting which ones influenced what others by contagion—i.e., if one started doing something the other started to do it too, without a word's being said—and which ones influenced what others by direct attempts at influence—i.e., one actually told the other to do something. The investigators also asked each boy to answer various questions about the others, such as: "Who would you like to be with? Who would you like to be? Who is best at getting others to do what he wants them to do?" Finally they asked each boy to rank the others on various criteria: goodness in sports, fighting ability, campcraft, and of course sex sophistication.

Putting the data together, the investigators found that boys were apt to let their behavior be influenced, through either contagion or direct influence attempts, by other boys they mentioned in the questionnaire as having high power. Boys mentioned as having high power made more attempts to exert influence than did other boys, and more of their attempts were successful. But this finding only tells us that boys seen as powerful were so in fact. Much more important was the finding that powerful boys were better than the others at campcraft or fighting. That is, they were in a high degree able to perform activity that was rewarding to their fellows or to withdraw activity that was punishing. For the ability to fight is the ability to hurt, and to stop beating a man up is in fact to reward him. We must never forget that a leader is often able to maintain his position by negative reinforcers, such as the threat of physical violence, as well as by positive ones—though if his followers can readily escape to some other group, the negative reinforcers by themselves will not be enough to maintain his authority. In short—it is

[4] R. Lippitt, N. Polansky, F. Redl, and S. Rosen, "The Dynamics of Power," *Human Relations*, Vol. 5 (1952), pp. 37-64.

not an original idea—a man's authority finally rests on his ability to reward and punish.

Let us now take a quick look at the relation between esteem and authority as revealed in a couple of field studies of small groups. In the Bank Wiring Observation Room at the Hawthorne Plant of the Western Electric Co., Taylor came closer than any other wireman to realizing the group's highly valued output norm.[5] When the men were suffering in their work from wire of poor quality, it was he that left the room and brought back a good supply. Socially he was always ready to take part in a game or conversation, and the men in the room had a standing invitation to play poker at his house. He was much the most popular man in the room, and the others showed their feeling toward him by helping him in minor ways at his work more than they did anyone else. The help was not of the sort whose acceptance would have undermined his position: what help they gave him anyone could have given; he was conspicuously able to do his own work well, and he often failed to return the help he got. As for his influence, he won more arguments than any other man in the room, he gave more advice that was accepted, and he took the lead in putting an end to disputes that were threatening to turn into fights.

Again, in his study of workers in a Federal law-enforcement agency, Blau showed that those agents who were not only highly competent at their work and so able to give good advice to others but also, which was not true of all the competent agents, ready and willing to give advice—those agents received much interaction and much esteem.[6] Note that the help they gave the others was of the rare kind, not the kind that any fool could give. And they also exerted most influence, particularly when many agents were on hand to be influenced and problems affecting all the agents were to be faced. The only occasions when all members of the department were assembled in one group were the department meetings, held once a week; on these occasions the agents who had earned highest esteem participated most often in the discussion, and here, as elsewhere, their suggestions were the ones most likely to win acceptance by the rest.

> The superior status of agents who received many contacts also manifested itself in the dominant role they assumed when a small group of

[5] G. C. Homans, *The Human Group* (New York, 1950), p. 78.

[6] P. M. Blau, *The Dynamics of Bureaucracy* (Chicago, 1955), pp. 97-179.

officials was engaged in a joint undertaking. They made most suggestions and their suggestions were most often followed, whether the suggestion was where to go for lunch or whether the decision referred to a project on which several agents worked together, as they occasionally did. This was particularly evident in the case of the informal leader. For example, he and two other agents were once appointed to draft a proposal for changes in one of the regulations. In their conference, he took command of the situation, making the decisions and telling the others what to do. One of them accepted a subordinate position unquestionably, and the other, an exceptionally independent person, also submitted to his directives after some protest.[7]

Obedience to Authority

The higher a man's esteem, the higher his authority. But he tests his authority afresh every time he makes a new suggestion, and the results of the test may confirm his authority or undermine it. In short, he risks his authority with every new suggestion. Suppose, then, that a man held in high esteem makes a suggestion or gives an order to his followers. Let us not worry about these words "suggestion" and "order": in both cases a verbal stimulus has specified an activity to be emitted. What are the factors that determine whether or not any single follower will comply and emit the activity? The answer was given at the beginning of this chapter, but we had better restate it here. First, there is the nature of the order itself. Does the person to whom the order is addressed find that what he has been told to do will yield him a net reward? His answer to the question will depend on how similar the suggested action is to others that in the past have rewarded him, and how different it is from others that have punished him. Second, there is the person who gives the order: he is always part of the stimulus. Does the man to whom the order is addressed find that an action ordered by this person will yield him a net reward? His answer to the question will depend on the esteem in which he holds the person who gives the order, for the latter's esteem embodies his past record of rewarding his followers. Esteem plays in informal authority the part that official authentication of an officer's position plays in formal authority: it creates the presumption that compliance with an order emanating from him will bring net reward, and failure to comply, net punishment.

The two factors interact with one another. Certain sorts of order no follower will obey no matter whom they come from: compliance would be too costly. A leader is well advised not to give such orders, for if he does so he at once raises in the minds of his followers a doubt whether compliance with other orders he may give will yield them reward. On the other hand, certain sorts of people will not be obeyed no matter what suggestions they make. Such people are in the unhappy position of never being able to show that if their suggestions had been followed, the results would have been rewarding. A suggestion not followed is a suggestion whose worth cannot be tested. But in between orders that will not be obeyed and people that will not be obeyed, there are orders that men are not sure they will be rewarded for obeying but that they will obey nevertheless if one man, rather than another, issues them. Under these circumstances the man who is obeyed is the man whose past record of giving orders, embodied in his esteem, has created the presumption that compliance with his orders will result in net reward. Even though the followers look askance at the terms of the order itself, the fact that it comes from a particular man will tip the scales toward their compliance. Such a man has acquired room for maneuver: his followers will give him the benefit of the doubt. They will give compliance a try and wait to see what the results will be.

One reason why men obey an order is that they perceive the results of obedience to be rewarding. But what results? There is more than one. Some members of a group obey an order because they find its direct results rewarding. Others may be indifferent to the direct results but obey nevertheless. If the direct results cannot be obtained unless all obey, and some members find these results valuable, the members that remain indifferent may obey for fear of losing the social approval of their fellows. For a man who disobeys, when his fellows find his obedience valuable, has withdrawn reward from them and forfeited their approval. Accordingly it has often been observed that men fight hard in battle at least as much because they will not let their comrades down as because they want to beat the enemy.

It follows that the more social approval the indifferent have to lose, the more disobedience costs them, and so the more likely they are to obey. This means further that, if a high level of good feeling has already been established in a group, if many members like other members, the larger, other things equal, will be the number of members who obey the leader's orders, so long as any of their number find obedience rewarding. The more they are bound to one another, the more they control one another, though if they happen not to accept the leader's aims, this very cohesiveness will constitute his greatest danger. Whatever else it may take, it certainly takes time to build up the good feeling: it takes time, for instance, for the members of a military unit to develop confidence in one another, and so no officer should be in a hurry to break up the unit and reassign its members if he values its fighting capacity. The argument we have been using here is no new one; we have already encountered it in Chapter 6, where we found that the more cohesive a group was, the larger was the number of its members that conformed to a group norm. But an order is very like a norm—a norm is only a standing order—and both name an activity that some members find valuable for themselves and others to emit. An order emanates from a single person more clearly than a norm does, but leaders carry more weight even in establishing norms than followers do, just as they carry more weight in issuing orders. In short, a leader's authority depends not only on his own relation with his followers but also his followers' relation with one another, and a leader will do what he can to encourage good feeling among his men for his own sake as well as theirs.

To further the spread of good feeling among his followers a leader can do nothing better than establish as best he can the conditions of distributive justice, for to establish justice is to put down resentment. If his chief external job is to be successful, his chief internal one is to be just. "He's fair," are the words in the mouths of his followers from which all other praises spring. Actually it is not a question of the leader's having a choice whether or not he will try to do justice, for the job will be thrust upon him willy-nilly. When a dispute arises between two members that cannot be settled, so to speak, by negotiation, they will be apt to refer it to someone higher than they in status. Indeed to submit a dispute to someone equal in status to oneself—unless he be so much of an outsider that his status makes next to no difference—is in fact to accord him, with higher authority, higher status. As matters affecting status may be the very ones in dispute, choosing such an arbiter may upset the social order even more; whereas if the parties go to someone whose superiority is already established, they exalt no new man. At any rate we certainly observe leaders trying to maintain distributive justice in their groups. Thus Doc, the leader of the Norton Street Gang, took the chief part in bringing Alec's bowling score into line with his other contributions to the gang.

But the establishment of distributive justice is not altogether an internal job. So far as the group accomplishes a result rewarding to its members, the question how the reward is to be distributed among them will come up. Sometimes the reward cannot be distributed. If the group has undertaken, for instance, the job of solving a problem by discussion, the rewards of success cannot be differentially distributed among the members: each must take what comfort he can out of it. But if the reward is something that can be distributed, like money, the question of its distribution will arise and fall into the leader's lap. One of a leader's chief jobs is to divide the booty fairly. He will have to hit upon some rule of proportionality between the investments of individual members, their contributions to the successful result, their costs, and their shares of the reward.

When we say that "the leader must do so and so" or that "one of the leader's jobs is to do such and such," we naturally do not mean that he always does it in fact or does it successfully. We mean only that his followers will expect him to take certain sorts of actions, the question whether or not he will take those actions will come to him, and his response will have certain consequences. We are not talking here about the leader's "functions"; we are talking about the results of his acting or failing to act.

Now let us suppose that a leader has issued an order to a number of followers, and that they have complied by emitting the specified activities. If the activities accomplish the results envisaged, and if the results reward the followers, the leader's authority is confirmed and the risk he took with it has been successful. Under these circumstances, he is even more likely than he was before to give orders on a new occasion, and they are even more likely to obey him. If he is successful often enough, they will come to follow him almost blindly: to obey his orders almost without regard for what the orders themselves may be. If, indeed, we agree that a man earns esteem and hence authority by providing services that others find both rare and valuable, the leader has provided the rarest and most valuable of all services: he has decided what the others are to do, and decided correctly, when the correct, that is, the rewarding, decision was not at all obvious. Some men would rather do anything than decide for themselves. But the leader pays a price for being right: when an ambiguous situation arises again, the followers will be all the more ready to look to him for a decision, and then he will endanger his authority just as much by not deciding at all as he will by deciding incorrectly.

But the very fact that a successful leader influences more and more other men and does so more and more often means that inferior members of the group influence fewer and fewer others, less and less often. Indeed the longer the process goes on, the more powerfully status congruence comes into play. If esteem and authority not only are associated in fact but get associated in men's perceptions, then a man held in low esteem will be behaving incongruently, and for that matter unjustly, if he makes a suggestion to a large number of other members. "Who is he," they will ask, "to tell us what to do?" and they will punish him for his presumption. The punishment will make him less ready to try to influence them on another occasion, and if he does not try he certainly cannot succeed. In these circumstances he may learn that if he does want any large number of members of the group to take some concerted action, he had better not suggest it to them himself. He had better take it to the established leader instead, and clear it with him. If the leader then takes up the suggestion and puts it out as coming from him, the others are apt to obey. Thus leaders get credit for more good ideas than their own abilities deserve. In this field nothing succeeds like success or fails like failure: "Whosoever hath, to him shall be given; but whosoever hath not, from him shall be taken away even that which he hath." The circles are vicious—or benignant, as one chooses to look on them —and they are very hard to break.

Authority and Debt

We have provided our own explanation of the association between esteem and authority. When men seek to explain it for themselves they often use a metaphor, and since the metaphor is one of indebtedness, no book that treats social behavior as a process of exchange can afford to disregard it. Indeed it may be more than a metaphor; for indebtedness brings in the notion of fair exchange, and fair exchange, or distributive justice, is part of the phenomenon of authority as it is part of most social phenomena.

A man earns high esteem by providing for others services they can-not provide nearly so easily for themselves. At least for the time being they cannot make him a return in kind, as fair exchange would require, and so they are his debtors. True, they do render him esteem, which by making him superior makes them by the same token inferior. But from this point of view esteem is a token of unpaid debt: it is a promissory note. What it promises is that at some later occasion they will redeem the pledge by doing what the creditor asks of them, by submitting, that is, to his authority. Such a promissory note has the advantage for the creditor that he can ask for its redemption at any time—it is liquid capital or call money—and that what it entitles him to ask for in the way of a return is not specified, so long as it falls within the bounds of fair exchange: it is a blank check. It gives him, then, great freedom of decision, which more than repays him for whatever costs he incurred in doing the others a service in the first place. When he does finally call his debt, asks them to do something, and they obey, they have redeemed their pledge and are once more his equals. That is, they would be were nothing else to happen. But if they find the results of what he has asked them to do as rewarding as he finds them himself, he has in effect once more done them a service and put them back in his debt. The obligations that others have to him constitute, therefore, the leader's capital. It is strictly risk capital. He risks it when he asks them to do what he wants. When they do so and find the outcome rewarding, he has replaced his capital. But he must build it up before he can risk it, and he must risk it if he is to increase it further.

If a man does in fact acquire authority over others by performing services for them that they cannot repay except by submission, it obviously follows that if he wants the authority he must perform the services. Thus politicians and other "operators" whose living depends on their getting favors done for them will almost automatically try to put anyone they meet under obligation to them. Their behavior may become embarrassing if the services they press upon a man are not ones he much wants. The assumption is not just that the receiver will at some later date return the favor but that the giver is the one to say what the return shall be and when it is due, and these features make the operator's profit on the transaction.

But an operator who shows he is one is not really in as strong a position as the true leader—a fact we recognize when we call him an operator. To ask a man to do something and refer, if only indirectly, to the favor you did him earlier is to admit that the favor was only done in order that it should be returned; and to lay bare your calculation in this way is to destroy your moral superiority. A man held in high esteem is a man who wants fewer things from others than they want from him. Accordingly you bring yourself down to their level when you show you want something badly too. It is all right for you to show you want things for the group but not for yourself. Altruistic giving is one of the rarest of activities, and one to which men's esteem is bound to pay homage. But if you give something to a man for selfish reasons, in order to get something back for yourself, he is, by the same token, quit of yielding you esteem and confessing his own inferiority in the meantime. And if he did not realize you wanted something back but later discovers you did, he will resent your enjoying all that esteem you had no right to: your original favor and his return would have satisfied the conditions of distributive justice without your getting his esteem to boot. Accordingly a leader who values his position will not use the fact that he once did the follower a good turn as an argument for compliance with an order.[8] The most calculating thing one can do may be to show no calculation in giving. And informal groups are often feudal systems, where a man gets help from another only to yield him loyalty and obedience in return.

Authority and Liking

We must now look at a problem we have left up in the air until now —the problem of the sentiments his followers express toward a man in authority. We have argued that a man holding high authority is a man held in high esteem, and we have defined his esteem as the number of other members of his group that yield him social approval. But what do we mean by social approval? If by social approval we mean liking in the ordinary American sense of the word—the sentiment we express toward someone we approach easily in the expectation that he will reward us without forcing us to incur high costs in either fear or inferiority—then it is clear that leaders are not always much liked. They may be esteemed, in the sense of being respected, but liking is another matter.

[8] W. F. Whyte, *Human Relations in the Restaurant Industry* (New York, 1948), p. 251.

The reasons why a leader may not be much liked are obvious. First, a person in authority is one who controls the activity of others—controls with their consent but still controls—and his control is almost bound to incur them costs. At the very least, compliance with his orders may force them to forgo doing what they would otherwise have found most rewarding, and to forgo reward is, of course, to incur cost. His orders may coordinate their activities toward the accomplishment of some distant goal, which means that the rewards of compliance will be long in coming while in the meantime its costs pile up. Even though the reward does come in the end, a man who incurs you costs is still a man to be avoided, still a man to be feared as much as liked. Though you will obey his orders if he can catch you, you would rather not be around when he gives them. He is the lightning, and you cannot tell where it will strike next.

Second, a man in authority is a man who, in controlling others, is apt to use punishment or the threat of punishment as well as positive rewards. The inducements to compliance are always in short supply, and if a leader does not command enough positive inducements, he will be tempted to use whatever others he can lay his hands on. When he has given orders, he may feel bound to criticize the manner in which his followers have carried them out. Though he may praise, he may also blame, and even if he does not use sticks and stones, his words will still hurt you. When he sits in judgment in matters of distributive justice, you cannot be certain that he will give you fair treatment according to your lights: to have many chances to make decisions is to have many chances to make mistakes. And he will make them, never fear: no one can be a leader who cannot live with this ineluctable fact. A leader, then, is a man who can punish as well as reward, and punishment, as we know, arouses a very different kind of behavior from that aroused by reward: punishment is a reason for avoiding and fearing the punisher. Finally, by his very position as a man held in high esteem, a leader may be standing in your light—you who but for him might be top dog yourself: he is depriving you of reward. We have perhaps not had enough to say about envy in this book.

In short, a leader may be dangerous, and such men are to be approached with circumspection. He is apt to hurt his followers as well as reward them—indeed to hurt them in the very process of rewarding them—and so they will have good reason for avoiding and fearing him as well as for approaching and liking him. The sentiments they express toward him will accordingly be mixed or, to use the modern word, ambivalent, and perhaps the best he can do is maintain a surplus of positive sentiments over negative ones. If a person held in low esteem has no such opportunity for arousing positive sentiments, neither does he run any such danger of arousing negative ones. In any event, liking is hardly the right word for describing the attitudes of followers toward a leader—respect, esteem, or deference perhaps, but not liking.

Whether or not the reasons we have given are the correct ones, the ambivalent nature of followers' sentiments toward a leader is often observed. It is most often observed in the case of leaders whose presumptive authority—the presumption that they will give orders and that the orders are to be obeyed—has been established by appointment or inheritance. Compliance with the orders of such men is enforced in case of necessity by sanctions coming from outside the group in question: the foreman's orders to his workmen will, for instance, be backed up by higher officers in the firm. Accordingly such men are freer to control their followers by punishment or the threat of punishment, and so more liable to arouse hostile sentiments, than are informal leaders, who usually have to earn at least their initial esteem, the initial presumption that their orders will be obeyed, by providing positive rewards for their followers.

A good example is provided by fathers in some primitive societies. In patrilineal societies, for instance, a father inherits from *his* father the right to exercise authority over his family and sometimes over his brothers' families too. In words of the social anthropologists, he possesses jural authority: he acquires and wields his authority according to the recognized norms of the society in question. In these societies, a son's sentiment toward his father is apt to be very far from what we call liking. He may respect or even admire the old man, but liking in the form of easy friendliness is not the sentiment he displays, and he is even apt to keep clear of his father except when they have a job to do together. The attitude of respect gets more firmly established the more regularly he works with his father and under his father's orders, for instance, in tilling the family land, and the more fully the father's means of controlling him are limited to punishment or threat. Poor fellow, we must not blame the father too much for using negative sanctions: they may be almost the only ones at his disposal. In this respect, a father is usually at a disadvantage compared with a mother, who especially in a child's early years has many and valuable rewards of a positive sort that she can give him; and accordingly a boy's sentiment toward his mother is apt to be warmer and less ambivalent than his sentiment toward his father.

In certain matrilineal societies, on the other hand, where jural authority over a boy is vested in his mother's brother and not in his father, the boy tends to take the characteristic attitude of respect toward this authority figure, and then he is free to be much more of a friend and companion to his father than he could have been in a patrilineal society. In societies where many families live in the same circumstances, these attitudes toward jural authority get generalized or copied from family to family throughout the society, and get enshrined in their turn in its norms. They may also have wide repercussions on behavior toward other kinsmen.[9]

As students of elementary behavior, we should not be much interested in reactions to jural authority if the same tendencies were not observed in informal groups. Let us look at an example. We are already familiar with the general procedures R. F. Bales and his associates use in their research in small groups. They put a number of undergraduate volunteers into a room, set them a problem to be solved by discussion, and make a variety of detailed observations of their interaction. Note that they always give the members of the group a joint task, and we have no reason to believe that just the same findings will be reached in such a group as will be reached in one like the cash posters in the Eastern Utilities Co., whose job did not require collaboration.

In the particular research we are now concerned with, Bales and his associates formed four different five-man groups and made their usual observations on a total of twelve sessions of these groups.[10] In addition, they asked every member at the end of each session to put the members of his group, including himself, in rank-order on four different criteria: Who contributed the best ideas for solving the problem? Who did most to guide the discussion and keep it moving effectively? Whom do you like most? And whom do you dislike? Had the answers to these ques-

[9] See G. C. Homans, *op. cit.*, pp. 190-280; G. C. Homans and D. M. Schneider, *Marriage, Authority, and Final Causes* (Glencoe, Ill., 1955).

[10] R. F. Bales, "The Equilibrium Problem in Small Groups," in T. Parsons, R. F. Bales, and E. A. Shils, *Working Papers in the Theory of Action* (Glencoe, Ill., 1953), pp. 111-61.

tions been scored in a straightforward way, the sum of all scores on any one question would have equaled the sum of all scores on any other. But the investigators in their report of the research say that they did not in fact treat the data in quite the straightforward way we have described, and as a result the total scores on the different criteria are not in fact equal. Disliking scores, for instance, are much lower than the others, which seems to mean that the general level of disliking was low.

We shall remember that in Chapter 10 on Interaction we studied a Bales matrix made from observations on six-man groups. The present groups had only five members, but we have no reason to believe that their matrix would have shown a different pattern. We shall remember also that the investigators set up the matrix by putting the members in rank-order of the number of unit-acts each one initiated, both to other members and to the group as a whole, which turned out also to be their rank-order in interaction received. At that time we complained that the investigators told us nothing about the relation between the rank of members in interaction and their rank in esteem. In the present research they made the deficiency good. As before, they put the members in their initiating-rank at each session, but then tabulated the scores each member got on the four sociometric questions against his initiating-rank, and summed up the results of all twelve sessions in the following chart. It suggests some central tendencies in the relation between interaction and sentiment in discussion groups.

From this chart we see first that the curves for "best ideas" and "guidance" are much alike, suggesting that these two criteria are really a single one, which might be called "contribution to the group task." We also see that the more often a member initiated interaction the higher the score he got on this criterion: the more he did in fact contribute to the discussion, in quantity of talk if not in quality, the more highly he got named as contributing; but the relatively low score of the No. 2 initiator prevents the relationship from being a completely linear one. As for the No. 1 initiator, the investigators at the end of the whole series of sessions asked the members of each group who had acted as their leader, and they were specially likely to name him.

Much more interesting are the curves for "likes" and "dislikes." The general tendency or slope of the liking curve suggests a positive relation between interaction and friendship, such as we found among the cash posters. But the relation was obviously not linear. The second initiator

Choice in Relation to Initiation-Rank

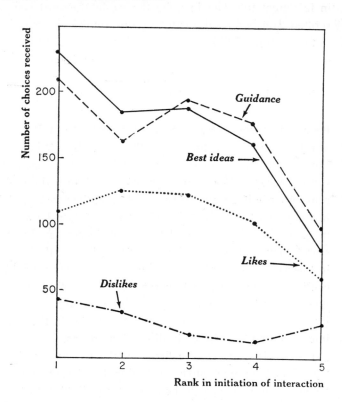

was the best-liked man, followed closely by the third, and the top initiator only got a fair amount of liking. Moreover he was the most *dis*liked member, which suggests an ambivalent attitude toward him on the part of the rest, although disliking seems in general to have been less intense than other forms of choice. In short, choice for liking was rather differently distributed from choice on guidance and best ideas, and the top position in guidance, initiation, and leadership tended to get in the way of a man's being liked.

Further analysis of the data confirmed these results. Examining the whole set of intercorrelations between the measures they had made, the investigators found that the correlations between liking and the other variables, while positive, were the lowest in the set, and that the correlations tended to decrease with time. For instance, the top initiator was more apt to be also the best-liked member at the first session of a group than at the last. In a sociometric study of a series of group meetings Lippitt found something of the same sort: choices on the two criteria of working with another member and spending leisure time with him tended to be much more highly correlated at the beginning of the series than they were later. At the beginning, a member named by many others as someone they would like to work with was also named by many as someone they would like to spend leisure time with. As time went on the members' social standing became better established, we may suspect that choice on leisure shifted toward the Hudson pattern: members began to choose for leisure other members who were their equals in esteem on the working criterion.[11]

The question now is why the top initiator in the Bales groups, the man seen as contributing most to the discussion, should not have been better liked. First and always we must remember that the investigators gave each group a definite task to accomplish: it was to reach by discussion some solution to a set problem. The top initiator tended to be the leader of the group in the sense that he was most occupied with directing it to its goal and supplying it with ideas for a solution. In Bales' terms he was the task, or instrumental, leader. And as leader he necessarily had to evaluate and criticize the contributions of others and even, deliberately or in effect, to choke them off in the middle of speeches that were not pertinent to a solution. In so doing he inevitably and to some extent punished the others, depriving them of rewards in freedom and approval they might otherwise have enjoyed. But to make a man forgo reward, no matter how small, is to arouse his hostility, no matter how little. As Bales puts it: "The more 'directive' and 'constricting' the quality of activity, the more likely it is to arouse negative reactions."

No doubt the leader's activity rewarded the other members by helping them reach a solution to their problem. The reward may not have been great—they may not have been much interested in solving the problem—but it was probably better than nothing. In return they gave him their respect, as shown by their choices for "best ideas" and "guidance." But in rewarding them the leader also made them incur costs,

[11] R. Lippitt, "A Program of Experimentation on Group Functioning and Group Productivity," in W. Dennis, R. Lippitt, *et al.*, *Current Trends in Social Psychology* (Pittsburgh, 1948), pp. 14-49.

and so they turned their liking choices away from him and toward others with whom they could interact at lower cost—with whom they were more at ease and less constrained—particularly to the men who were second and third in interaction and guidance.

This argument is supported by further evidence of Bales'. In a new series of five-man groups he paid particular attention not only to interaction initiated but to the relation between interaction initiated and interaction received: the receipt/initiation ratio.[12] He found that members were much more apt to dislike leaders who talked more than they were talked to than leaders who behaved the other way around and received more interaction than they gave. Indeed leaders whose ratio of receipts to initiations was high were apt to be chosen highly for both guidance and liking, and in their groups the relation between interaction and liking became linear: the more a man led the better he was liked. Now we may guess that a leader who talked more than he was talked to was one who spent a particularly large part of his time bossing the group around, telling the members how they ought to think and act, doing, that is, the sort of thing most apt to be immediately punishing to the members, however effective it might have been in accomplishing the group task. Accordingly such a leader would be particularly likely to arouse some hostility in his followers. But a leader who was talked to much more than he talked was apt to be more encouraging to his followers' ideas, more willing to allow them free expression, and so more rewarding to them. Accordingly such a leader was more apt to be liked than was the other kind.

As he wins his leadership, perhaps the best a man can hope for is that the things he is liked for should increase a little faster than those he is disliked for. In a sociometric study of students in the ninth and tenth grades of several different high schools, Riley and Cohn arranged the subjects in classes by order of status, status being measured as it was in another study by Riley and her associates, described in Chapter 9 on The Matrix of Sentiment.[13] The investigators then counted the number of traits that other students praised each subject for possessing and the number of traits they condemned him for possessing. The

[12] R. F. Bales, "Task Status and Likeability as a Function of Talking and Listening in Decision-Making Groups," in L. D. White, ed., *The State of the Social Sciences* (Chicago, 1956), pp. 148-61.

[13] M. W. Riley and R. Cohn, "Control Networks in Informal Groups," *Sociometry*, Vol. 21 (1958), pp. 30-49.

higher the status of a student, the larger, they found, was the number of traits for which he was favorably mentioned, and the larger also the number for which he was mentioned unfavorably. But the ratio between the two, the proportion of favorable mentions to unfavorable ones, increased steadily with increasing status. Speaking roughly, we may say that a person of low status, which usually means low authority, makes neither many friends nor many enemies: he makes little difference; while a person of high status makes many of both: he makes a big difference for good or ill. But so long as he can stand some dislike —and there are people that cannot stand any—a person of high authority may on balance stand to gain by it.

The Degree of Ambivalence Toward Authority

It is one thing to show that a leader is apt to inspire some hostility in his followers, another to show what determines how much hostility he gets. Our argument suggests that there should be two sorts of determinants. The activity on the part of the leader that is most likely to arouse hostility is his giving orders to a large number of his followers in the endeavor to coordinate and control their behavior toward the attainment of a relatively distant goal; for compliance with such orders is apt, as we have seen, to make some of the followers incur costs, including the special kind of cost called punishment. We should therefore expect that the more often a leader gave such orders, relative to the number of times his activities rewarded his followers as individuals, the greater should be his followers' hostility and ambivalence toward him. But we must also consider the goal to the attainment of which the leader's efforts at coordination are directed. If the goal is attained and is very rewarding to the followers, it will more than make up for the costs the followers incurred in attaining it. We should therefore expect that the less successful a leader is in attaining the goal, or the less rewarding the followers find the goal when attained, the greater should be the followers' hostility and ambivalence.

On the first determinant Bales' results have already given us some information. Although on the average the leaders in his groups were respected but not much liked, those leaders who spent a particularly large amount of their time directing the group, relative to the time they spent accepting communications from individual followers, were disliked even more than the average leader; whereas those leaders who be-haved the other way, and spent a particularly large amount of their time accepting communciations from individual followers, relative to the time they spent directing the group—those leaders were liked much more than the average leader: indeed they got much respect and much liking too.

Sometimes the frequency with which a leader tries to direct his fol-lowers depends on the circumstances in which the group is placed. In-formal leaders, for instance, in groups that already have formal ones are unlikely to exercise authority over a full range of fields of activity; the formal leaders pre-empt some of the fields, and incidentally attract much of the potential hostility to themselves: they are the conspicuous targets. Thus in industrial groups, where the formal supervision of manufacturing is in the hands of foremen, informal leaders are less apt to take full control of their followers than they are in more independent groups like gangs. Taylor in the Bank Wiring Observation Room, while giving much help and advice to individuals, did rather little to coordi-nate the activities of the members toward the accomplishment of a joint task, and this was probably one of the reasons why he was so well liked: his popularity was more prominent than his leadership. For the kind of authority on the part of the leader that will incur his followers the high-est costs—costs in criticism received, rewards postponed, and imme-diate pleasures forgone—is authority exercised in coordinating their activities. When people are prevented, as they must be by coordination, from doing what they want when they want to, they will find the experi-ence to some degree costly. And cost, being deprivation, is apt to arouse some dissatisfaction and hostility. Accordingly we may put the matter bluntly and say that the less a man of high esteem is also a leader, the more apt he is to be liked.

And now for the second determinant. Even though a leader often co-ordinates the activities of his followers in accomplishing a group task, he may still be well liked if the task produces results sufficiently re-warding to the members. Then the immediate costs he has made the fol-lowers incur will be swallowed up in the ultimate rewards his efforts have brought them. This, or something much like it, has been demon-strated in research by Theodorson.[14] The investigator studied two pairs

[14] G. A. Theodorson, "Leadership and Popularity Roles in Small Groups," *American Sociological Review,* Vol. 22 (1957), pp. 58-67.

of discussion groups, making four groups in all. The two groups in the first pair were artificially formed and met in a social-science laboratory; their members discussed problems of family adjustment. The groups in the second pair were naturally formed, in the sense that people attended or failed to attend who happened to feel like doing so, and their members discussed current problems of world politics.

The first variable the investigator examined he called *cohesiveness,* which Festinger and his associates define, as we have seen, as the degree to which members are attracted to take part in a group.[15] In the present instance, the investigator based his measures of cohesiveness on the answers each member made to questions on how much he enjoyed a meeting, how much he liked every other member, and how much he was "concerned about and willing to sacrifice for the group." Members that expressed high concern in answer to the last question were, we suppose, members that found the group goal more valuable than any incidental rewards; and members who answered the other questions favorably, particularly the first, must have been members who felt the group goal had in fact been attained to a high degree. In each pair of groups, one group was significantly more cohesive than the other on these counts. The investigator did something to make one of the laboratory groups more cohesive than the other by giving it a desirable meeting place and assigning it an observer of high status; he did nothing to make one of the natural groups more cohesive than the other, but one did in fact become more cohesive in the course of time.

As we have seen, the investigator used the liking-choices members gave to other members as the basis of one of his measures of cohesiveness: a group was more cohesive the higher the average level of liking within it. But he also used the choices to put the members of each group in rank-order of popularity. And after every meeting he asked each member to rank the others on the amount of leadership each had exercised and on the number of good ideas each had contributed to the discussion. The investigator used the answers to put the members in rank-order of recognized leadership and contribution.

He then examined the correlations between group cohesiveness and the rank-order of individual members in popularity, leadership, and

[15] L. Festinger, G. Schachter, and K. W. Back, *Social Pressures in Informal Groups* (New York, 1950), p. 164.

contribution. He found that in each pair the more cohesive group showed higher positive correlations between popularity and leadership, on the one hand, and between popularity and contribution on the other, than did the less cohesive group. On our interpretation, the more rewarding the members found the group task and the more successful they were in accomplishing it, the more the leaders and others who had contributed much to its accomplishment were apt to be popular too. Under these conditions leadership and popularity overlapped. Even though you coordinate the activities of others and so make them incur heavy costs, you may nevertheless recover the esteem you have put in jeopardy, provided that by exercise of your authority you can accomplish a result highly valuable to them. You may then manage to be a leader and be popular too, but you should not count on having this happy condition last. A good example is provided by military leadership. Many officers are not particularly popular with their men, indeed an officer who is merely popular is a little suspect on that account; but an officer who has brought his men successfully through a situation of great danger, and so has accomplished a result highly valuable to them, is apt to win something as close to adoration as we are likely to see this side of Paradise.

According to this argument the leaders in the Bales groups may have found it particularly difficult to reconcile effectiveness with popularity; for they were apt to fall between two stools. On the one hand, there was a group task to be accomplished, and they did a great deal to direct the members toward its accomplishment; on the other, the task may not have been one that brought the members very valuable rewards. After all, the members did not volunteer for the groups because they were interested in the problems under discussion, which were set by the investigator and not chosen by themselves. Thus the leaders exercised much authority in accomplishing a not very valuable result, and on both counts they were likely to endanger their popularity.

Familiarity Breeds Contempt

In describing the followers' reaction to the leader, we are in danger of forgetting his reaction to them. If they incur costs in accepting authority, he incurs costs in exercising it. That the costs are real and severe will come as an unpleasant surprise to a man once merely popular who has been elected or appointed to leadership. Thus a popular workingman who has just been elected shop steward is apt to complain that "no one is your friend any more." Indeed the chief problem in creating successful groups may be that of finding men who can stand the costs of command. A leader must accept the worry of making decisions and bear as best he can the guilt of making wrong ones; nor will he find it easy to be natural and unself-conscious in the face of his followers' ambivalent attitudes toward him. A leader, we have said, is dangerous: his followers will have some reason to avoid him, especially when they may do so legitimately. On the more "social" occasions, unless the occasion is also supposed, like an office party, to symbolize the unity of the group, his followers are apt to keep out of his way. Accordingly a leader, in his own group, is likely to be a lonely man. Not that the loneliness altogether lacks compensation: a leader earns esteem, and hence the presumption of authority, by performing services for others; their demands on him may become importunate, and he may yearn for an excuse to escape. A leader is a man whose time is not his own.

From loneliness, from the burden of decision, from the ambivalence and importunity of his followers, the leader will seek occasional escape in the society of men with whom he can relax and be at ease. In the nature of the case, the only such society open to him is the society of his equals: people who have nothing to ask of him—for to ask for something is to confess inferiority—and people whom he in turn has no leave to command—for to command is to assert superiority. Because leaders in any single group are few in number, a leader is apt to find his social equals in the leaders of other groups; and it is a matter of observation that persons of high status in any one group are apt to have more "outside" contacts and friends than persons of low.[16] But if outsiders are hard to get at, the leader will be denied even this resource: a good example is the captain of a ship at sea.

The leader, then, is apt to stand in some degree of enforced aloofness from his followers. It may be a burden to him, and yet there is an ancient maxim saying that aloofness, too, has its compensations, that a man cannot slough it off and still remain a successful leader. This maxim is "familiarity breeds contempt."

Few maxims have more aroused the scorn of democratic Americans.

[16] G. C. Homans, *op. cit.,* pp. 185-86.

Democracy has been uncomfortable with institutions as authoritarian as armies. Americans look on military life as an imposition, and on officers as incompetent until proved otherwise—until they have actually saved their outfit and the Republic. But military officers have been especially fond of citing the maxim, sometimes even to justify "social" distinctions that do not correspond to the realities of American life. Indeed we do right to scorn it if it justifies a man's avoiding other men and so implying his superiority to them on grounds, such as mere birth or money, that our society does not recognize as legitimate. Yet properly translated and circumscribed in its application, "familiarity breeds contempt" only states the facts of social life.

It simply means that authority over a man and social equality with him are, in our terms, incongruent. If I am "familiar" with a man I treat him and he treats me as a social equal: we interact often and we are without reserve toward one another, in which case he has a right to treat with contempt any pretentions I may put forward to authority over him. If, on the other hand, he has in fact accorded me authority over him, it will make us both uncomfortable to be familiar: my greater power is at odds with the equality in influencing and being influenced that is the heart of familiar friendship. Indeed if I persist in treating him familiarly I may by the rule of status congruence cast doubt on my superior authority. To be sure, if I am a man of tact I may be able to remain more familiar with him and still keep more authority over him than another man in my place could have done. All the maxim says is that it will take tact: there is a limit to what I can get away with, and sooner or later I cannot have things both ways. The general point has been well made by Barnard: "Much experience demonstrates that those who are unequal cannot work well for long as equals. But experience also demonstrates that where differences of status are recognized formally, men of very unequal abilities and importance can and do work together well for long periods."[17]

If the success of a group in accomplishing a task depends to some extent on the leader's exercise of authority, and if the maintenance of his authority depends on his staying to some extent aloof from his followers, then we might expect the leader's aloofness to be associated with the group's success. And there is a piece of research by Fiedler

[17] C. I. Barnard, *Organization and Management* (Cambridge, Mass., 1948), p. 223.

that may be interpreted as bearing out this conclusion.[18] It is true that studying the effectiveness of formally organized groups takes us beyond the boundaries of elementary social behavior, but the opportunity to illustrate the results of the leader's aloofness is too tempting to be forgone.

Fiedler studied a number of different types of groups, running from basketball teams through bomber crews to open-hearth steel shops, always choosing groups whose effectiveness he could measure. Within each type he compared the effectiveness of a number of groups identical in organization. Thus he compared basketball teams by the number of games they won, bombers by their scores in target bombing, open-hearth crews by the time it took them to make a given amount of steel.

The investigator also made various measures of the sentiments of the members of the different groups, both the followers and the official leaders, like the captains of the basketball teams. Besides a simple sociometric test, he used questions designed to get at the leader's "assumed similarity" with his followers. We shall not go into the methodology of the "assumed-similarity" score, but only take the investigator's word that it measured "an attitude toward others which may best be described as emotional or psychological distance." We believe that it measured what we have called aloofness.

The investigator then correlated the effectiveness scores of the groups of each type with their members' sociometric and "assumed-similarity" scores. For groups of every single type he found that effectiveness was higher, the more nearly two conditions were realized: first, the followers gave the leader a high degree of sociometric choice, that is, they approved of him highly—though we may suspect that the approval was of the sort we have come to call "respect" rather than the more intimate "liking"; and second, the leader himself had a low score on "assumed similarity," that is, he felt himself somewhat aloof from the others. In a few of the groups a third condition seemed also to play a part in effectiveness, namely, that the leader himself should give high choice to his "keyman," the member of the team who, next to himself, did most to make it effective. If leader and keyman were personal allies the group was particularly likely to succeed in its endeavors.

[18] F. E. Fiedler, *Leader Attitudes and Group Effectiveness* (Urbana, Ill., 1958).

But the relationship between the leader's emotional distance and the effectiveness of his group is the finding we most want to emphasize here. The investigator was all the more surprised to find it holding good so regularly because it ran counter to his original hypothesis, which was that effectiveness would be associated with the leader's psychological *closeness* to his followers. His original assumption is just the one many American social scientists would have made. Indeed they have had so much to say against "authoritarianism" (which may have little to do with authority) and so much to say in favor of "democracy" (which may have little to do with political democracy) that their students have learned to shudder with guilt if they ever catch themselves giving a man a direct order or standing in the least apart from him socially.

Summary

A man influences another when he asks the other to do something and the other does it. Each member of a group may have influenced, in this sense, every other member. We say that a man who regularly influences more members than another does holds higher authority than the other; and the man who holds highest authority we call the leader of the group. A man earns authority by acquiring esteem, and he acquires esteem by rewarding others. What he does for them often takes the form of giving them advice that, when taken, they find rewarding. Accordingly they come to recognize him as a man compliance with whose instructions is apt to be rewarding, and they get to be all the more prepared to comply with his instructions on some new occasion. This allows him the opportunity of giving them instructions when they have not asked for them, particularly instructions that, if obeyed, coordinate their activites toward the attainment of some group goal. Their obedience depends on the nature of the activities he orders and on the fact that it is he that has ordered them. If the followers do obey, and find the results rewarding, the leader has confirmed their confidence in him and re-established the esteem he risked in giving the order. He will be still more ready to give them orders on the next occasion, and they will be still more ready to obey.

Because a man acquires esteem by providing rare and valuable services for others, men held in high esteem, and therefore men holding high authority, are relatively few in number. Requests tend to flow toward them from many other members, and orders tend to emanate from them to many others. Interaction in the group tends to focus on them, which means that other channels of interaction get relatively less use. Indeed as differences in esteem get established in a group, members will find it incongruent to accept orders coming from a man of low esteem. If such a man wants to influence a large number of others, he will learn to take his proposal to the leader and get it issued as an order in the leader's name, and this process focuses interaction on the leader still further.

But in issuing orders that are obeyed, particularly orders coordinating the followers' activity toward the attainment of some distant goal, the leader will almost inevitably make them incur costs, including punishment. And these costs will lead them to hold mixed feelings toward him, feelings both negative and positive: he may be respected but not much liked. He can best reconcile leadership and popularity if, first, he spends a good deal of time rewarding them as individuals relative to the amount of time he spends coordinating their joint actions, and second, he succeeds in attaining a goal highly rewarding to them, for then the reward will offset the costs he has made them incur in the process.

Not only a follower but also the leader himself incurs costs through his exercise of authority, and these costs will tend to make him stand somewhat aloof from his followers. Though his aloofness helps him avoid some of the costs of authority, it also carries with it positive advantages. For as the leader's authority gets recognized and established, it becomes more and more incongruent with that social equality with his followers which we call familiarity. If, indeed, he persists in acting familiarly he will cast doubt on his superiority in power. Since the success of the group in attaining its goals depends, among other things, on his authority, and since the maintenance of his authority depends in part on his aloofness, this aloofness, provided he can keep up his esteem at the same time, contributes to the effectiveness of his group.

Equality

In my earlier book *The Human Group* I stated the proposition that, other things equal, "persons who interact with one another frequently are more like one another in their activities than they are like other persons with whom they interact less frequently,"[1] and I cited evidence that this was true of at least a few groups. In the present book we have encountered further evidence on the relation between personal similarities, on the one hand, and liking and interaction, on the other. In Chapter 9 on The Matrix of Sentiment the Swedish university students showed some tendency to choose others with scores near or equal to their own as well as others with better scores; and in Chapter 11 on The Nature of the Givens we saw how persons with similar backgrounds and hence similar values were particularly apt to reward and like one another.

We have also encountered evidence that the similarity in question is often a similarity in esteem or recognized status: that is, the persons concerned are social equals. By equality we do not mean the equality of all members of a group but equality within layers or strata—the rough equality with one another of members who are at the same time superior or inferior to others. Thus the Swedish students showed some tendency to choose students from their own school within the university—students, that is, whose status was equal to their own in the recognized ranking of schools. And in Chapter 10, in the study

[1] G. C. Homans (New York, 1950), p. 135; see also p. 243.

of interaction among American high school students, the students tended to receive most interaction from others who fell within their own or neighboring status-classes.

Finally, we saw in the last chapter that when one man exercises authority over another, both parties, besides reaping rewards from the interaction, also incur costs, and that these costs lead them sooner or later to escape to the society of their equals—that is, to the society of people to whom they are neither superior nor inferior in authority. With equals, they are particularly apt to be relaxed and at their ease, and they are particularly apt to seek out their equals on "social" occasions in the special sense of "social," meaning occasions when there is no compelling job to be done.

In the present chapter we shall try to understand that these phenomena are not independent but, on the contrary, are often related to one another so as to form a complex of behavior. We shall try to understand why persons who are similar to one another in some respect are apt also to be social equals; why equals are apt to interact with one another and find one another rewarding when the cost of interacting with superiors or inferiors is high; why these occasions are often "social" occasions; and why equals tend to feel particularly at their ease with one another.

Equality and Inequality in Primitive Exchange

Rather than plunging into equality directly, we shall creep up to it roundabout. Social behavior is an exchange of rewards (and costs) between persons. Sometimes a man has good reason for exchanging with another who is in some sense his superior, and sometimes he has good reason for exchanging with another who is his equal. Both tendencies are always present, and we are now interested in the relation between the two. We also believe that the propositions we put forward hold good of all men everywhere. The kinds of things men find rewarding differ from society to society and from group to group within a society, but propositions about the nature of elementary exchange itself, apart from the kinds of things exchanged, hold good of all men. That in this respect at least human nature is the same the world over is a matter of faith with us. We certainly have not tried to prove that it is so, and the research we have cited comes almost wholly from a single society, that of the United States of America. But because it provides some evidence to justify our faith and also serves as a useful introduction to the nature and consequences of the two tendencies—to exchange with a superior and to exchange with an equal—we shall take a little time to study exchange in so-called primitive societies.

In particular, we shall study the exchange of material goods. Over many centuries modern man has developed institutions, beginning with the market, that have tended to take the exchange of material goods out of the domain of elementary social behavior. He has tried to make this sort of exchange impersonal and has pretty well succeeded. When I go into a drugstore and pay money for toothpaste, the exchange implies almost nothing about, does almost nothing to create, a personal tie between the clerk and myself. The segregation of economic exchange from other social relations is always breaking down, and on some occasions, like the exchange of Christmas presents, a little of the older attitude persists. But on the whole in modern societies the exchange of goods is far more impersonal than it is in primitive ones. There it is Christmas all year long: the exchange of goods always has implications for the personal ties between people, and so we speak of it as gift exchange instead of buying and selling.

The assumptions primitive people make about exchange are well summarized in Marcel Mauss' famous little book, *Essai sur le don.*[2] If Primitive Person gives something to Primitive Other, Other is generally bound to return something of equal value according to the terms of exchange current in the tribe in question. If, indeed, Person covets something that Other owns, he will try, like an "operator" in our own society, to force a gift on Other so that he can establish a claim on him—a phenomenon that the pioneers of North America, who were already accustomed to more impersonal rules of exchange, called "Indian giving." Person is in a good position to force Other to accept the gift, for to refuse it would be a refusal to enter into exchange and thus equivalent to a declaration of hostilities: the man who refuses has deprived the other of what he wants.

Should he accept the gift, Other may try to return an object of slightly greater value—which gives rise in primitive societies to some-

[2] M. Mauss, *The Gift,* I. Cunnison, trans. (Glencoe, Ill., 1954); see also D. L. Oliver, *A Solomon Island Society* (Cambridge, Mass., 1955), pp. 335-448.

thing a little like interest, especially if some time goes by before Other makes the return. But the important point is this: just as failure to accept a gift implies hostility, so taking the gift and making a fair return implies friendship. And more than friendship: it also implies that the exchanges will continue indefinitely, that the two have become trading partners, and that, if either party breaks off the exchange later, he has declared hostilities just as much as if he had refused a gift in the first place. With the primitives as with us, an exchange of rewards between two men leads to their friendship and further inter-action. But the primitives have gone further than we have in turning what happens into a set of rules about what ought to happen. Where we have institutionalized the market, they have institutionalized the gift.

Should Other spurn the gift, he admits himself an enemy. Should he take it and make a fair return, he becomes a friend. But what if he takes it and fails to make a return? Since the man that makes a fair return is by that fact the giver's social equal—he has demonstrated his ability to provide equally rare and valuable rewards—the man that fails to do so confesses himself neither the giver's enemy nor his friend but his inferior. He loses status relative to the giver. What is more, he may, in becoming an inferior, become also a subordinate: the only way he can pay his debt may be to accept the orders of the giver. In the last chapter we saw that something of the same sort occurs in our own society.

The point is that to take a gift and fail to make a return is to incur cost in the form of social inferiority. The gift may be so valuable, Other may need it so badly, that he may take it, accept the cost, and still feel he has done well. But again he may not, and much will depend on his past history. If up until this time he has been Person's social inferior, he will not feel the cost much. By the rule of status congruence, his inferiority in exchange is in line with his inferiority in other respects, and so he loses no further status. But if he has so far been Person's equal, he will feel the cost much more: he will have come down in the world.

The secondary mechanisms of human behavior ride on the backs of the primary ones. Men learn new kinds of behavior whose rewards depend upon the fact that the old are already recognized. That taking a gift one cannot return from a man hitherto one's equal is to confess one's inferiority to him is not only a generalization about actual behavior; it is also a rule a man can turn to his own advantage. He can now with deliberate intent give others gifts they cannot repay in order to humiliate them and make them his inferiors. The final twist of primitive gift giving is the *potlatch* of the Indians of the Northwest Coast: two men of high status try to snow each other under with gifts; the one whose presents fail to match the other's in value loses face, fiercely resents the victor's triumph, and vows social revenge. But the Northwest Coast only carries to a bizarre extreme what is implicit in all primitive gift giving—and some not so primitive. One has from time to time detected the same overtones in the giving of Christmas gifts in modern North America. After all, the differences between the primitives and ourselves are only matters of degree.

These rules apply not only to gifts of material objects but also to to the rendering of services. Anyone who accepts from another a service he cannot repay in kind incurs inferiority as a cost of receiving the service. The esteem he gives the other he forgoes himself. The service may be valuable enough to outweigh the cost and return him a profit, but the cost is there. We already have reason to believe that it may not be the only cost he incurs in interacting with his social superiors. Even an American, at any rate, will often hesitate before he asks a favor or help, of a kind he cannot return, from someone who has hitherto been his equal. In these circumstances a man must be a true Christian who fails to feel or, worse, to show his inferiority if he asks for help or his superiority if he gives it.

Equality and Similarity

With this introduction we are ready to enter upon our main line of argument, using for supporting evidence the research at the New York State Training School for Girls at Hudson, New York, only part of which we considered in Chapter 8. We shall remember that the investigator asked the girls to make sociometric choices of the others on three main criteria: living with another girl, working with her, and spending leisure time with her. Choices on living and working were much alike in the sense that if a girl chose another for living, she was apt to choose her for working too, and so the investigator lumped the two sets of choices together. The chief finding on choice for living-working was that the more choices a girl received, the more apt she was to emit activities valuable to the other girls under circumstances in which a number of them lived and worked together, as they did in the cottages and workshops at Hudson.

In earlier chapters we postponed study of the choices for leisure time because we knew they fitted in better here. What are the facts? First, choice for leisure overlapped with choice for living and working less than the two latter did with each other. Whereas a girl was apt to name the same other girls for both living and working, she named different ones for leisure: of all girls chosen for leisure 64 per cent were chosen for leisure only. Second, a girl chose, on the average, fewer other girls for leisure than she did for living and working, but, third, a higher proportion of these choices were mutual choices. Fourth and last, though there was little overlap in choice between living-working and leisure, the two were nevertheless related in an interesting way.

As the investigator says, a girl in making her choice for leisure tended to direct it elsewhere than to the girls highly chosen for living and working. But where is "elsewhere"?

> The "elsewhere" is not very far afield from her own position: it is predominantly to those members of the community's population who have approximately the same choice-status as the chooser herself shows. . . . In other words, although she directs a predominant amount of choices towards a relatively few well-chosen individuals for living working, when she is choosing for spending leisure time with others she seldom selects those very individuals, shifting instead to those who are more nearly within her "sociometric class" in the official life of the community."[3]

In short, a girl was more apt to choose another for leisure, the more nearly the other's esteem was equal to her own.

This last finding goes far toward accounting for some of the others. If a girl confined her choices for leisure to her equals in esteem, she had fewer others to choose from than she would have had if the whole population had been open to her choice. And in fact fewer choices were made for leisure than for living and working. Since the chosen other was limiting her choice in the same way the girl did herself, and since for both the number of others open for choice was small, we

[3] H. H. Jennings, *Leadership and Isolation*, 2nd ed. (New York, 1950), pp. 257-58.

might indeed expect purely as a matter of chance that mutual choice for leisure would be frequent. And although there was in general little overlap between choices for living-working and choices for leisure, we should expect—which was the fact—that what little overlap did take place was most apt to take place among girls of high esteem: they were specially likely to choose one another for both living-working and leisure. Yet we may doubt whether the small number and high mutuality of choices for leisure were wholly due to the play of chance.

The esteem a girl earned depended on the degree to which others found her activities rewarding, and therefore two girls held in roughly equal esteem must have emitted activities that were in some respect similar. But, as we have seen, persons that emit similar activities are apt to hold similar values, and so they are apt to reward and like one another even more than they do others. To use the current phrase, they have much in common. Similarity, to be sure, is not the only basis for mutual reward, but it is surely one of the bases. Thus one of the criteria for a pleasant ringer-bundler team in the supermarkets was that the two workers should have similar backgrounds and so find it easy to make conversation. The more similar, moreover, are the values of two persons, the more likely they are to reward each other in ways that go beyond whatever earns them esteem in the larger group. Thus at Hudson a taste for, say, bird watching might not be relevant grounds for choosing a girl as a good one to live with in company with a large number of others. What would count there would be behavior that helped the whole joint enterprise go more pleasantly. But we must never forget that we are talking now about choices for leisure. The point about leisure is that it leaves one free to indulge one's idiosyncrasies, and a shared taste for bird watching might make all the difference in a leisure-time companion. When we come to think about it, then, the fact that girls held in equal esteem were particularly apt to choose one another for leisure seems perfectly natural, for girls of equal esteem were apt to be similar in other ways as well, and similars are apt to reward one another.

Whatever the reasons for it, the fact itself was clear. The investigator at Hudson talked informally and unsystematically to the girls about the reasons why they chose others, and she found that they were, indeed, particularly apt to choose for leisure other girls whose values resembled their own. One girl went so far as to say: "You'll think this is a crazy reason but it's the truth. She likes noise like I like noise. I'm always holding myself in in the house, don't yell around or nothing. Susan and I race all over the place in our spare time . . . ."[4] We cannot tell whether the similarity in values was itself determined by a similarity in the girls' backgrounds, a subject the investigator did not go into. Note that the more idiosyncratic were a girl's values, the fewer people, naturally, she could find to share them—which was undoubtedly one of the reasons why the girls at Hudson made fewer choices for leisure than they did for living and working.[5]

Equality and "Social" Interaction

But it was not just their similarity in values, their liking and doing the same things, that led girls to choose for leisure other girls whose esteem in the larger group was equal to their own. If the commonest explanation was that "she likes the same things I do," the next was that "I can be myself with her." But this very explanation implied that a girl could not be herself with everybody, that with some people she felt under constraint. In interacting with some people she incurred, in our language, costs.

What were these costs and where were they incurred? In the last chapter we saw that persons held in high esteem are also apt to hold high authority, and that persons who submit to authority are apt to incur some costs in doing so. We must now consider in more general terms the costs of inferiority. A person held in high esteem is one that has been accorded social approval by many others; and so if two or more different spheres of activity are open to members of a group, the sphere in which esteem is won—and lost—is the more public one, the one in which the larger number of members is brought together. At Hudson this was the sphere of living and working, in cottages and shops. Here a few girls won high esteem by providing

[4] *Ibid.*, p. 260.

[5] See S. M. Lipset, M. Trow, and J. Coleman, *Union Democracy* (Glencoe, Ill., 1956), pp. 154-75. The investigators find that workers in a big shop are more apt to have really close friends who also work there than do workers in a small shop, because the larger number of workers in the former makes it more likely that any one worker will find others in the shop whose values resemble his own. The whole discussion is interesting.

services much in demand by many others, but here too, by the same token, the girls that did not win much esteem found their inadequacies shown up. The process that put some up put others down: one man's superiority implies another's inferiority. No doubt the girls were glad to get the services of their superiors, but the price they paid was a tacit confession of their own inferiority.

The girls of high esteem, moreover, in whom others could find little to criticize, felt free in the course of exercising their authority to criticize others. And even if a girl of lesser rank managed to escape criticism and live up to some of the public norms of the group, she was likely to find the effort painful. Whatever offsetting advantages she got from living and working with the rest, her conspicuous inadequacy, the criticism she received, and the strain of measuring up to group standards were costs to her, costs that tended to increase as the working day went on, until she was ready to escape. In the nature of the case she could best escape by leaving the public sphere for the private sphere of leisure and by associating at leisure with her social equals. For the girls below *her* had just as much reason for wanting to escape from her as she had for wanting to escape from those above. The only girls left were her equals, but equals are people who emit equally valuable activities. Accordingly they can exchange rewards on even terms and thus escape the costs of inferiority. Her equals could not make a girl feel inferior—nor could she make them feel so. Only with them, therefore, could she relax and "be herself," free of judging or being judged, and only them could she really "like" in the American sense of liking; for "liking" implies an absence of constraint, and constraint is rarely absent from our relations with superiors.

The investigator at Hudson made clear the costs of criticism and, in general, the costs of trying to live up to the standards of the larger group, the group that lived or worked together. For instance, she quoted one girl, who had not yet found a companion for her leisure time, as saying: "Lena's wonderful in our house but for me she's useless as a personal friend—one minute she says she understands you and the next she's telling you you're just awful."[6] And the investigator spoke of "the responsibilities, cares, and awarenesses which come with participation in work relationships or common

[6] H. H. Jennings, *op. cit.,* p. 270.

living relationships wherein the . . . individual may be urged to 'improve,' 'raise the standards,' and, in general, may feel threatened with guilt, the cause of which he may be at a loss to discern."[7]

Mind you, a girl that chose another for leisure seldom spoke of her as being "wonderful," as she often did of the girls she chose for living and working. She was seldom deceived as to her companion's absolute worth: "a poor thing but mine own" was apt to be her apologetic attitude. This was only natural. She could hardly help knowing how much—or little—the other girl had to offer the general society and how much esteem she earned there. What made the other a suitable companion for leisure was not that her behavior was highly rewarding in itself. Since it was behavior that became valuable only after the prior demands of living and working had been satisfied, it was likely to consist of the small coin of sociability—though sociability may then, of course, become very valuable indeed. Whatever its value, the crucial feature of the other's behavior was that it resembled the chooser's own, and so could not make her feel small. No matter how little the other had to offer, it was at least purchased at a low cost in social inferiority. For even if one's reward is low, one still has a profit if its cost is even lower.

Finally the secondary elaboration of social behavior must have come in to strengthen the tendency for social equals to interact during their leisure time. Once a girl had been established as another's equal in the public sphere of living and working, she might well hesitate to approach her in that sphere under circumstances that could put their equality in doubt. For instance, to ask the other for help at work might, by the rule of status congruence, raise a question whether she was really the other's equal. Thus in the machine shop described in Chapter 12 on Justice, we saw that workers who held the title of "machinist" hesitated to ask other machinists for advice, though the lowly "operators" had no such qualms. But if a girl hesitated to approach her equal at work, she had all the more reason to approach her at leisure, where the kinds of activity that created differences in esteem were much less likely to be in demand. To associate with her equals in that sphere could only help establish her position.

We have explained the tendency for people to interact with their

[7] *Ibid.*, p. 272. I am indebted to Seymour Perlin for a description of somewhat similar tendencies in a mental hospital: "Group Behavior: The Perception and Tolerance of Psychopathology on a Hospital Ward" (unpublished ms.).

equals by showing why an inferior has some reason *not* to interact with a superior, especially when at leisure. But as we saw in the last chapter, a superior also has reason to avoid an inferior under the same circumstances: the avoidance may be mutual. And again status congruence comes in to strengthen the tendency. For once the equation between social equality and interaction during leisure gets established as a recognized social fact, then a man who associates with his inferior under these conditions tends to suggest to his companions that he is not really the other's superior but only his equal after all. By the rule of status congruence he tends to cast doubt on his own superior status, and thus, as we know so well, our pretended superiors often try to avoid being seen with us on "social" occasions. Alas! that the laws of elementary social behavior should be the laws of snobbery—but they are.

On the other hand, a man whose superior status is so firmly established that he need not worry about it, a man who has reached the condition we call social certitude, may allow his inferiors "social" access to him. His status is congruent on so many counts that he can afford to let it be incongruent on this one. Association with him can bring up the apparent status of others and thus reward them, and accordingly he has gained a new way of earning their esteem to add to those he commands already. But note that we have now argued ourselves into assuming two contradictory tendencies: both a tendency for inferiors to avoid interaction with superiors and for them to seek it. Which tendency gets the better of the other seems to depend on the degree to which the relative status of the two parties is established and unshakable. We shall return to this problem a little later.

We must not assume that the phenomena we have been considering were limited to Hudson. On the contrary, the association between social equality and interaction on what Americans call "social" occasions—spending leisure time, going to parties, or eating in company—is a conspicuous feature of status, class, and caste systems in all times and places. The explanation of the phenomena is not simply that people similar in status are apt also to be similar in other respects, and so apt to reward one another. This plays its part, but it does not altogether account for the prominence of the fact that the interaction is "social." Status is won or inherited in the more public sphere of activity, the sphere in which rather large numbers of people are related to one another, the sphere, like making a living, in which very valuable rewards are to be gained. Because the rewards are high, people will pay highly for them. They will be ready to accept them from others at the cost, for instance, of confessed inferiority to the others. But the more such rewards they get, the less their value becomes and the higher their cost. The time when the profit men get from transactions of this kind sinks toward zero is apt, in the nature of the case, to be the time when "work," however it be defined, is coming to an end and "social" life beginning. In the nature of the case too, men can escape the costs of associating with their superiors only by seeking out the society of their equals; for their own inferiors have the same reasons for avoiding *them* as they have for avoiding their superiors. What their equals have to offer them in the "social" sphere may not be inherently very valuable, though it becomes relatively valuable to the degree that the higher priorities have already been met, but whatever its value it is at least purchased at low cost. For these reasons social equals are apt to spend some of their time interacting with one another on "social" occasions.

A Resultant of Superiority and Equality

In earlier chapters and now in this one we have encountered two tendencies: a tendency for men to express approval of, and to interact often with, others who are in some sense "better" than they, and a tendency for men to like and interact with their equals. It is at least conceivable that under some circumstances, especially when no sharp distinction can be made between "work" and "leisure," the two tendencies might combine to produce a resultant tendency for men to interact with, and express liking for, others who are a little "better" than they are themselves but not much better—to choose "up" but only a little "up." To examine this possibility, let us go back to the research by Bales and his associates that we considered in the last chapter.[8]

We shall remember that in studying several discussion sessions of five-man groups, the investigator found that, on the average, the member who interacted most often received most choices from the

[8] R. F. Bales, "The Equilibrium Problem in Small Groups," in T. Parsons, R. F. Bales, and E. A. Shils, *Working Papers in the Theory of Action* (Glencoe, Ill., 1953), pp. 111-61.

other members on the criteria of "best ideas," "guidance," and "leadership." In fact the relationship between frequency of interaction and a combined measure that might be called "contribution to the group task" was approximately linear: the more often a member interacted, the higher the choice the others gave him as a man who had done much to help the group reach its goal.

The investigator also asked the members to choose others on the simple criterion of "liking," and he found that in this case the relationship with interaction was not linear but curvilinear. The best-liked members were only second and third in frequency of interaction, and the top interactor was only third in liking received, followed by the two least frequent interactors. In short, the curve bulged upward in the middle and drooped at both ends, though more toward the low end in interaction than toward the high. (Look once more at Figure 4 on p. 304.) In the last chapter we concentrated on the top leader, and used Bales' data to illustrate the ambivalent sentiments men express toward persons in authority, sentiments better called respect than liking: members who contribute little are little liked, and members, such as the top leader, who contribute much but in doing so make the others incur high costs, are both liked and disliked. In the present chapter we must stop concentrating on the top leader and consider the whole shape of the curve.

In explaining his results, the investigator has much to say about the best-liked man, who was also No. 2 in frequency of interaction. Just because the No. 1 man concentrated on getting the job done, the investigator argues that the No. 2 man was forced to specialize in another kind of activity, particularly apt to win him the liking of others: he specialized in what the investigator calls the "socio-emotional" field— patting people on the back, approving without criticizing, and easing tense situations with jokes. Indeed the fact, which is apparent in Figure 4, that the No. 2 man was not named quite as often for "best ideas" and "guidance" as he would have been if the relation between interaction and choice on this criterion had been perfectly linear does suggest that he may have been performing other services than those contributing directly to the solution of the group problem. Bales also feels that a particularly stable solution to the struggle for status that often rends the upper levels of a group may be an alliance of personal friendship between the No. 1 interactor who is, in Bales' terms, the "instrumental-adaptive" leader and the No. 2 man who is a specialist in the "socio-emotional" field. Bales' argument is borne out, in part at least, by Fiedler's finding, which we considered in the last chapter, that the leader of a successful group was apt to be on particularly good terms with his key man or second in comand.

But the behavior of the No. 2 man cannot fully explain the pattern of liking in Bales' groups. After all, the No. 3 initiator got almost as much liking as did No. 2, and yet there seems to be little evidence that he too was a "socio-emotional" specialist. Some more general force must have been at work. What we should like to know is not just the total score in liking that each member received, but the way each member distributed his liking among the others. That is, we should appreciate having a liking matrix. Since Bales does not provide us with one, let us choose some hypothesis, construct a toy matrix embodying it, and then see how close it comes to generating Bales' results. Our hypothesis is that liking in Bales' groups tended to resemble leisure-time choice at Hudson, and tended to go from a man to his fellow members to the degree that they were his sociometric equals on other criteria, but that when two men were equally near the chooser's own rank, he chose the higher man ahead of the lower one. In short, he chose "up" but only a little "up." A further justification for the last feature of the hypothesis is provided by the Swedish students whose behavior we examined in Chapter 9 on The Matrix of Sentiment: a student choosing others on grounds of equality was apt to give higher choice to the higher scorer of two members whose scores were equally close to his own.

The detailed rules for constructing the toy matrix are the following:

1. O, P, Q, R, and S are the five members of the group, and this is their order from high to low in frequency of interaction.
2. Each member gives a score of 4 to the man he likes best, 3 to the man he likes next best, and so on.
3. Each member likes best the man whose rank on interaction is nearest his own, second best the man whose rank is next nearest, and so on.
4. When a member has two others equally near him in rank, as Q has P and R equally near him, he gives more liking to the man who is higher in rank.

The matrix that results from these rules is shown in Table 19.

In this matrix the important thing to look at is the bottom line of figures, which shows the total liking received by each member and so corresponds to the curve showing the relationship between interaction and liking in the Bales data. We submit that the two curves are of the same general character. The best-liked men, and nearly equal to one

TABLE NINETEEN

Sentiment Matrix: Equality and Superiority

		Liking-choice to					Total given
		O	P	Q	R	S	
	O		4	3	2	1	10
	P	4		3	2	1	10
Liking-choice from	Q	2	4		3	1	10
	R	1	2	4		3	10
	S	1	2	3	4		10
Total received		8	12	13	11	6	

another in liking received, are the Nos. 2 and 3 interactors. From this high tableland the amount of choice drops off at both ends of the curves but more toward the lower end in frequency of interaction than toward the upper. Our matrix, to be sure, makes liking for the top interactor and task leader even lower than the Bales results indicate: he was better liked in reality than we allowed for in the rules for constructing the matrix. Nevertheless we may guess that the hypothesis embodied in the matrix corresponds to a real tendency in the Bales group.[9] In these groups liking-choice was the same sort of thing as leisure-time choice at Hudson. Just as the girls were apt to choose for leisure other girls who were nearly their sociometric equals on the living-working criterion, so the members of the Bales groups were apt

[9] O. J. Bartos has shown that the rules for constructing our matrix will predict actual popularity rankings in ten-man Bales groups to a rank-order coefficient of 0.76 (unpublished memorandum).

to choose others who were nearly their equals in contribution to the group task. The only difference is this: we have no evidence for Hudson that when members were faced with two others equally close to them in rank, they tended to give higher choice to the member of higher rank.

We must believe that the similar tendencies had similar causes: the increasing costs incurred by men in interaction with their superiors in esteem make it worth their while to exchange rewards of a different kind with, and to express a less respectful approval for, their equals. Although the design of Bales' experiment gave the members no opportunity for interaction during their leisure time, the kind of behavior he calls "socio-emotional" is in fact the kind that people are most apt to exchange on "social" occasions.

Alternate Status

We have seen that equals tend to like and interact with one another particularly on "social" occasions. But how about people who fall short of complete equality, particularly people who, just because they are nearly equal, find that their status relative to one another is in doubt? Earlier we gave brief consideration to the effects of social certitude and incertitude on the interaction between men, and now we must return to the problem. In this field we possess very few good studies, which gives us all the more reason to consider one whose results were clear-cut even though it is less concerned with elementary social behavior and more concerned with status as formally recognized in society at large than we should like it to be.

The research in question was carried out by Zander, Cohen, and Stotland.[10] In six large American cities the investigators and their associates interviewed three different kinds of professional people concerned with mental health: psychiatrists, psychologists, and social workers. In all, they interviewed about 150 members of each profession. They first asked each subject to assess the authority and influence of members of the other two professions in comparison with his own authority and influence. As we should expect from our general knowl-

---

[10] A. Zander, A. R. Cohen, and E. Stotland, "Power and the Relations among Professions," in D. Cartwright, ed., *Studies in Social Power* (Ann Arbor, 1959), pp. 15-34.

edge of American society, all three professions agreed that the psychiatrists, who of course held medical degrees, had more authority and influence than the other two groups—though the psychologists and social workers were not quite as sure about it as the psychiatrists were themselves. As for the relation between psychologists and social workers, these two professions saw themselves as about equal in power.

The investigators then asked each subject to say how much he wanted to be respected and liked by members of the other two professions and to have professional and social contacts with them. In accordance with the higher status of the psychiatrists, the other groups were more likely to express such wishes about psychiatrists than the psychiatrists were to express them about the other groups. And in accordance with their higher recognized authority, the psychiatrists were more ready to complain about the behavior of the other two professions than the other two were to complain about the psychiatrists.

Much more interesting and much closer to elementary social behavior were the differences within each profession. Those psychologists and social workers who saw themselves as having relatively high power expressed less desire for professional or social contact with psychiatrists than did psychologists and social workers who saw themselves as having little power. Among the psychiatrists, on the other hand, the relationship reversed itself, and those psychiatrists who saw themselves as having relatively high power expressed more desire for contact with members of the other professions than did psychiatrists who saw themselves as having little power. We may guess that most of the people who believed they had relatively high or low power must in fact have held high or low status, respectively, within their professions. And then we may say that the people who wanted least contact with the other group were the low-status members of the high-status group (the psychiatrists) and the high-status members of the low-status group (the psychologists and social workers). That is, the persons closest in status wanted least contact. This finding may seem to run counter to our proposition that equals will seek out interaction with one another, but we must remember that we are not concerned with equals here: by the standards of American society psychiatrists in general are accorded higher status than the other two professions.

We are concerned instead with people who, though divided by status, were still relatively close to one another.

As we saw earlier, a man established as another's equal hesitates before doing anything that might suggest his inferiority to the other; but a man already established as the other's inferior shows no such hesitation. In the present case, there is no question of absolute equality, yet something of the same sort occurred. In the presence of two broad status-classes, the members of the lower class who stood highest within their class were most anxious to avoid contact with members of the upper class, presumably because such contacts would have given the upper class a chance to remind them of an inferiority they were far from feeling within their own group. If frequent social contacts could have ended, as they do in some cases of social climbing, by winning for a psychologist full acceptance as a member of the upper class, no doubt he would have been more eager to make them. But only a medical degree could make him a psychiatrist, and in these circumstances he had little to gain and much to lose by mere interaction. In the same way, the members of the upper class who stood lowest within their class were most anxious to avoid contacts with members of the lower class, presumably because they might have had a hard time maintaining, over against these others, a superiority they were far from feeling within their own group. But the members of the upper class who were firmly established as high in status and the members of the lower class who were firmly established as low had nothing to lose by the contacts and welcomed them at least as a possibility. These people were more congruent in status than the others, who were either low men in a high group or high men in a low group. We are forcibly reminded of the classic peasant who, because after all "he knows his place," can speak up to the lord of the manor, and of the lord who can be perfectly at his ease with "the lower orders" because after all they cannot conceivably unnerve his effortless superiority. It is the *bourgeois,* the man in the middle, who is nervous about his relations with other classes.

Phenomena like this bear a family resemblance to what anthropologists have come to call alternate generations.[11] In some primitive kinship systems, the members of the two generations that are closest to one another, like fathers and sons, are apt to express respect rather than close affection for one another and to avoid one another except

[11] G. C. Homans, *op. cit.,* pp. 215-16, 251.

Equality   333

when required to work together. But members of alternate generations —that is, generations separated by an intervening one, like grandfathers and grandsons—cannot be rivals and are apt in consequence to express close affection for one another and to interact frequently and easily. In the one case the differences in status are determined by generation and in the other by differences in occupation, but in both cases the persons nearest in status, short of complete equality, are the persons whose relations are most strained.

Summary

Unless all the members of a group are equal, social equality between any two of them implies that the members have previously become differentiated in esteem and then in recognized status. Men win high esteem by providing for many others services that the others cannot return except in the form of esteem and obedience. Though these services are rewarding, they are also costly, one of the costs being the status a man loses by the very fact of giving it to another. But as men get their fill of the rewards provided by persons of high esteem, other rewards, the rewards of sociability, increase in relative value. Men can best get these rewards outside the public sphere of activity, in which esteem is won and lost, and therefore inside the sphere of "social" life; and they can best get them from people neither superior nor inferior to themselves by the standards of the public sphere. Social equals are people who provide equally valuable services, therefore they can exchange on equal terms; and though the services may not be very valuable in themselves, they at least cost nothing in confessed inferiority. Accordingly a man's social behavior displays two tendencies: a tendency to interact with, and respect, persons in some sense "better" than himself and a tendency to interact with, and like, persons in some sense similar to himself. The two are not independent tendencies but closely dependent on each other. Finally, though equals tend to interact with one another, people who are nearly equal but still different in status—and because nearly equal most in doubt about their relative status—these people may not be ready to test their social standing and so may tend to avoid one another. This means further that the tendency for a man to interact with his "betters" may be especially strong when he is not just a little inferior to them but definitely a good deal inferior.

Since we have often been concerned in this chapter with snobbish behavior, and since snobbery arouses strong moral feelings, we had better put in a disclaimer, once and for all. We do not mean to imply, either here or elsewhere in this book, that men *have* to behave in the ways we have described. For instance, we can readily conceive how a man might go through a course of social training from childhood onward that would leave him free from worrying about his status under any circumstances, and undoubtedly some men have been lucky enough to get this kind of training. In this sense men never *have* to behave as we say they do. But they often do in fact behave that way, and when they do, the causes of their behavior arc thc oncs wc have given.

Status, Conformity, and Innovation

Chapter Sixteen

Our study of the substantive findings of research began in this book with Chapter 5 on Influence. In that chapter and the ones immediately following we were concerned with the processes by which a group develops a structure—that is, the processes by which it reaches the condition we call practical equilibrium—when the kinds of behavior any one member gives to any other tend to repeat themselves time and time again. We looked, for instance, at the way members try to change the behavior of a deviate, and if they fail to do so, give him little interaction or social approval. We looked also at the way members get differentiated in esteem. But as we have gone on, we have become less and less concerned with the way structure develops and more and more concerned with the nature of the structure itself.

In parallel with this changing interest, we have become steadily less concerned with esteem and more concerned with status. This does not mean that esteem has become any less important in the social behavior we have studied: it only means that our intellectual interests have been changing. Esteem is the actual social approval many members emit to one of their number. One of the most important, but still only one, of the determinants of his status is their recognition—and his own recognition—that he is getting the esteem. What we recognize are stimuli; any item of behavior is not only a reward (or punishment) but also a stimulus to the person to whom it is directed, and a stimulus not only to him but to interested spectators. A man's status in a group is a matter of the stimuli his behavior toward others and others' behavior toward him—including the esteem they give him—present both to the others and to himself, stimuli that may come to make a difference in determining the future behavior of all concerned.

As time has gone by, we have also had to consider more and more complex forms of social behavior. Once status gets recognized, it sets the stage for new developments in behavior, developments we call secondary because their appearance depends on the prior establishment of the more primitive forms. We ran into this secondary development early in the book, but the study of status congruence first forced us to take serious account of it. Men not only behave in the ways described by our propositions but often come to recognize that they are doing so. Though they would never state the propositions in quite our language, they do become aware of general relationships between different forms of behavior. Which stimuli shall become crucial in determining a man's status depends on which relationships his companions have become aware of, and the stimuli in turn create new rewards and costs for new kinds of behavior. To return to the example we have used so often: once two men get recognized as equals in status, and once it is recognized that equals are commonly people who emit equally valuable activities—once the relationship between equality in status and equality in value gets recognized as a congruent one—then a man who goes to another and asks for a service for which he cannot make an equivalent return has cast some doubt on his equality with the other in the eyes of his companions. He has presented them with a stimulus suggesting that some different kind of behavior from what they have hitherto adopted toward him may bring them reward. To cast doubt on his status may, therefore, be a cost to a man, a cost he could not have incurred until the other members had become aware of the congruent relationship, and accordingly he may refrain from asking for the service in question unless he stands in dire need of it. The service itself may be valuable, but the stimulus he presents to his companions in asking for it is something else again. In short, one of the potentially rewarding activities of men is the presentation of stimuli, and they try to manipulate, to their advantage, the stimuli they present to others.[1]

[1] The great, and fascinating, expert in this field is E. Goffman, *The Presentation of the Self in Everyday Life* (New York, 1959).

The secondary mechanisms may help the primary ones maintain stability in a group. If, for instance, our man refrains from asking another for a service he is unable to return, he has by that fact maintained his equality with the other and thus contributed to the general stability of social relations. But we are far from arguing that the recognition of status and the secondary mechanisms it brings into play always contribute to social stability. They may, on the contrary, introduce important possibilities for further change and innovation. It is appropriate that these should be the subject of the present chapter, for it is the last chapter in which we shall encounter altogether new material. To put the matter a little too neatly: we began by showing how change creates group structure and we shall end by showing how group structure creates change.

In particular we shall be interested in showing how, when differences in status between members have once become recognized and established, these differences tend from then on to stimulate further differences in their behavior. From this point of view, we shall consider that members may occupy three different types of social position: upper, middle, or lower status. We do not claim that every group possesses just three levels of status, no more and no less, or that a member can always be assigned unambiguously to one of the levels. We do claim that a threefold division is not arbitrary but inherent in the strategy of the situation, and indeed it appears in many class structures in society at large. Upper-status people have many others below them but few or none above; lower-status people have many above them but few or none below; but middle-status people have others both above and below them. These differences are obvious but not trivial; for as we shall soon see, they create differences in the risks people take when they emit new behavior. In the present chapter we shall consider the threefold division in its relation to innovation, on the one hand, and conformity, on the other. We shall also have to bring in a variable we have already encountered in earlier chapters: the degree to which a man's status is established and unambiguous or fluid and ambiguous, that is, the degree to which social certitude prevails.

Status and Conformity: Field Research

Without more ado, let us look at some of the evidence, first the evidence from field research and then, at greater length, the evidence from experiments. In natural groups, as we cannot repeat too often, a man of high status gets his position by providing for other members services that they find valuable and rare. So far as members set a high value on conformity to certain norms, for instance, an output norm in an industrial group, the man who conforms is doing them a valuable service, though not a particularly rare one—unless like Taylor in the Bank Wiring Observation Room he conforms more closely than anyone else.[2] Therefore, a man of high status will conform to the most valued norms of his group as the minimum condition of maintaining his status.

In *The Human Group* I said that a man of high status would conform to a high degree to all the norms of his group, but this was certainly an overstatement; indeed the book itself supplied evidence against it.[3] To keep his high status a man must provide rare and valuable services to others, but so long as he does that, the other members may allow him some leeway in lesser things. He may even take the leeway. Mere slavish conformity to any old norm may put him back among the masses instead of keeping him set apart from them, where he belongs. He is apt to be a leader, in a position of authority. If there is any correcting to be done, he is the one to do it: it is his business to correct others, not others' to correct him. If, then, he violates group norms in minor ways, it will take some presumption on the part of other members to tell him he is wrong.

The margin of freedom from group control enjoyed by a man of high and established status has been well described by Everett Hughes:

> Here is an apparent paradox: Admittance to the group may be secured only by adherence to the established definitions of the group, while unquestioned membership carries the privilege of some deviant behavior. This is, of course, not a paradox at all; for it is characteristic of social groups to demand of the newcomer a strict conformity which will show that he accepts the authority of the group; then, as the in-

[2] G. C. Homans, *The Human Group* (New York, 1950), p. 78.
[3] *Ibid.*, p. 141.

dividual approaches the center of the group and becomes an established member, they allow him a little more leeway.[4]

At the moment we are not particularly interested in the newcomer to a group, but since Hughes has brought him up, let us say a word about him in passing. At this end of the book we are dealing with complex forms of behavior, and of their complexity justice is always a part. A newcomer is a man who has acquired little investment in a group; if his returns from membership are to be, in accordance with the rules of distributive justice, proportional to his investment, his rewards must be kept low and his costs high. So far as it constrains behavior and restricts freedom, conformity to norms is costly. Hence other members often try to make newcomers conform strictly to the norms of the group. Whether they will conform is another matter. Probably they will if esteem is not too long denied them. What happens when they cease to be newcomers without having won much esteem we shall soon consider. On the other hand, a man who has fully earned his footing may be exempted from rigid compliance.

We have looked briefly at the man of high status as he appears in field studies; let us now look at the man of low status. In his study of sixteen agents in a Federal law-enforcement agency, which we have already cited and which we shall describe at length in the next chapter, Blau pays special attention to the behavior of one unpopular agent, unpopular because he violated important norms of the group. He reported to his superior a bribe offered him by the management of one of the firms he investigated and took a threatening attitude toward management in general. The other agents interpreted his reporting the bribe as an effort to lick his superiors' boots, and they disapproved of it for other reasons too. The firms, they felt, were under such great temptation to offer bribes that it was unfair to tell on them when they succumbed; the offer of a bribe also gave an agent an unofficial hold over a firm and so helped him in his investigatory work, but the hold would be lost if bribes were ever reported. This agent also talked too much, completed more work than the others thought right, and refused to help them out with their technical problems.

For these reasons he received little esteem; indeed he was ostracized: so far as possible the others cut off interaction with him. But note that

[4] E. C. Hughes, "The Knitting of Racial Groups in Industry," *American Sociological Review*, Vol. 11 (1946), p. 517.

to ostracize a man is to remove him from social control: if he holds out against that pressure there is nothing more the group can do to bring him back into line, short of physical violence. The group has lost its leverage on his behavior. The next time he has a choice whether or not he will do something they want, he is the less apt to do it the less they have left to take away from him in the way of esteem and interaction. He has nothing to lose by nonconformity and perhaps even something to gain by vexing them.

The investigator says of this agent:

> To be sure, his deviant behavior contributed to his continued isolation, but this position also encouraged lack of conformity. . . . His overproductivity had made him an isolate and, once in this position, he became the only member of the agency who ignored a very important unofficial norm. The individual who had adapted himself to an isolated position could more readily violate the norms of the group.[5]

His preceding actions had won him low esteem from others, and his low esteem in turn made it likely that his next actions, too, would be unacceptable to the group, confirming him in his low esteem. Social behavior is full of such vicious spirals, as it is of favorable ones. Note also that once he had built up a record of bad behavior, no single action in conformity to group norms would have done much to raise his esteem. It would take time to live down his past, which meant that on any particular occasion he had little to gain by conformity as well as little to lose by its opposite. This sense of being trapped by their pasts makes some people anxious to start fresh in new groups. "They know me," they say, "too well in there."

If this agent had had anything to hope for from the group, if he had still been vying for acceptance by it, no doubt he would have been less prepared to violate group norms. But this was not the case: not only was his status low but it was firmly established as low. Accordingly we may say that members of established low status in a group are particularly apt not to conform to its norms. Since they get little reward from the group, they are also particularly apt to leave the group altogether—if there is anywhere they can go.

[5] P. M. Blau, *The Dynamics of Bureaucracy* (Chicago, 1955), p. 155.

Status and Conformity: Experimental Research

In the scanty evidence of field research we have found some reason to believe that men of both upper and lower status, in their different ways and for different reasons, show some tendency toward nonconformity. As yet we have had nothing to say about men of middle status. In contrast to the other two, are they particularly apt to be conformists? To answer this question let us turn to the experimental evidence, and first to research carried out by Kelley and Shapiro.[6]

The investigators brought the subjects, who were college freshmen, into the experimental room in groups of five or six at a time. There the members introduced themselves to one another; each told the others something about himself, and then the investigators had each one answer a simple sociometric test in which he was to say, on the basis of this brief acquaintanceship, how acceptable as a co-worker he found each of the other members. After this, the investigators put each member into an alcove by himself and asked him not to communicate with the others. While he was there, they handed him a slip of paper apparently showing how he had scored on the sociometric test: whether his fellow members had chosen him as an acceptable co-worker or not. As soon as he had read the slip, the investigators hastily withdrew it as if they had handed it out inadvertently, never meant to do so at all, and only now realized their mistake. Naturally this little act had the effect of stamping their scores all the more indelibly upon the subjects' minds. Some of the subjects were thus persuaded that they were highly acceptable to the others, and some that they were not in the least acceptable. A further questionnaire asked each member to say whether he wanted to keep on as a member of the same group. Not surprisingly, members in the high-acceptance condition were much more apt than the others to want to continue.

The investigators then told each member that he was to carry out a task, that his score on it would be pooled with those of the other members of his group, and that the group with the highest average score would get a fifteen-dollar prize. The task was this: he was shown a

[6] H. H. Kelley and M. M. Shapiro, "An Experiment on Conformity to Group Norms where Conformity is Detrimental to Group Achievement," *American Sociological Review*, Vol. 19 (1954), pp. 667-77; see also J. M. Jackson and H. D. Saltzstein, *Group Membership and Conformity Processes* (Ann Arbor, 1956).

series of ten pairs of white cardboard squares, the two squares in each pair being labeled A and B. He was to say which square contained the more dots; the investigator told him that the same square was the correct answer every time, but did not tell him which one it was, A or B. Unknown to the subject, the squares in the first pair contained an equal number of dots, but thereafter with each presentation square A lost a few dots and B gained a few so that it became more and more clear to an unprejudiced observer that B had more. After every presentation, each member gave his choice of square and indicated his confidence in it. At that time he was allowed to write notes to his fellow members. These were collected but not delivered. Instead, by a procedure that became familiar to us in the chapter on Influence, the investigators delivered to each subject a set of notes, actually the same for each member, but purporting to come from other members. All the notes suggested that the right answer in every case was square A and not square B. That is, each member received visual evidence that one answer was correct, while being informed by his fellow members that another one was. He also knew that a correct answer would help his group get a prize. Would he conform to the apparent influence of other members even though conformity might be detrimental to group achievement?

From each member's choice of square in each presentation, and from the degree of confidence he expressed in that choice, the investigators calculated his conformity score, a measure of the degree to which he had given in to group influence; and they then correlated these scores with members' acceptance or nonacceptance by the others and their willingness or unwillingness to continue in the group.

The most interesting findings were the following. Members who set a low value on membership in the group, most of whom also believed they were not acceptable to their fellow members, tended to show little conformity. This appears to be an experimental reproduction of the phenomena Blau described: a group that has withheld esteem from a member has by that fact lost control over him. Faced with a choice between doing what the group wanted and doing what would at least satisfy his own self-respect—in this case naming the square that really had the more dots—the man of low status was apt to choose the latter. Since the group could not hurt him any further, he had nothing to lose by not conforming.

The second finding was even more interesting. Members that set a high value on membership in the group were, on the average, somewhat more likely to be conformers than the others. But individually they varied in their conformity far more than did the nonconformers in their nonconformity: some conformed very much and some very little, as if they had fallen heavily on one side of a dilemma or the other.

It seems to have been from a desire to explore further the bearing of this last, ambiguous finding that Kelley, this time in company with Dittes, embarked on a second study.[7] Since the procedure of the new experiment was in many ways the same as that of the last, we shall only report the ways in which it differed. Several groups met separately to discuss the question which of two gangs of juvenile delinquents should be judged more worthy of help. The discussion was based on two sets of fictitious court records, so doctored that the members of a group were almost certain to reach the decision that one of the gangs was more worthy than the other, but only after they had talked the matter over for some time. In their instructions, the investigators emphasized that a group's decision should be unanimous, like a jury's, and when the group did reach unanimity each member was to register the fact by rating the gangs, both in public and in private, on a number of different scales.

The investigators interrupted the discussion three times and asked each member to rate the others on the desirability of their remaining in the group. At the end of the discussion they announced the average score the group as a whole had received on these tests, and then let each member look in private at what purported to be his own score in relation to the average. In fact, of course, the scores were fictitious, and they were designed to produce a finer discrimination among degrees of acceptability than had been achieved in the earlier experiment. Of the six members of each group, one found his score to be above the average (the "high" condition), two found theirs to be about average ("average"), two found theirs to be slightly below the average ("low"), and one found his to be far below ("very low"). The investigators also discussed his score with each member and allowed the highs and the averages to believe that their ratings were pretty

[7] J. E. Dittes and H. H. Kelley, "Effects of Different Conditions of Acceptance on Conformity to Group Norms," *Journal of Abnormal and Social Psychology,* Vol. 53 (1956), pp. 100-07.

stable and unlikely to change in the future, while they persuaded the lows and very lows that their ratings were liable to change and get even worse. The higher a man's status the more stable his status, the investigators suggested. Besides status itself, they tried to manipulate the degree to which status was perceived as established.

After each man understood his apparent standing in the group, the members renewed their discussion of the gangs; but this time the investigators introduced new evidence designed to suggest that the group's original and unanimous decision was wrong, and that the other gang was probably the worthier of the two. The experimental question then became the following: Under what conditions of perceived acceptance by the others were members more or less likely, in the face of the new evidence, to cleave to the group's original decision? The investigators used three different measures of conformity: the degree to which a member expressed agreement with the group's decision in a private rating of the gangs, the degree to which he did so in his public rating, and the degree to which in discussion he tended to discount or explain away the new information. The investigators also noted how long it took each member to make his new ratings, their assumption being that a man who took little time was probably sticking automatically to the original decision. They also measured how big a part each member took in the discussion following the release of the new information.

The investigators then asked each group to work on another problem, the members this time judging, in a succession of pairs of squares, which square contained the more dots. Since this procedure was much like that of the previous experiment we shall not describe it further. When work on both problems had come to an end, each member answered a final questionnaire, reporting how highly he valued his membership in the group, how free he felt to express opinions contrary to the group's judgment, and how secure he felt in his social standing— especially how strongly he believed that the group would in the future reject him even more than it had already.

And now for the results. As we might have foretold, the order of the four classes in acceptance was their order in evaluation of their membership in the group: the more highly a member felt he was accepted by the others, the more highly he valued his membership; but the differences in this respect between the very lows and the lows, and between the lows and the averages were much more significant statistically than the difference between the averages and the highs. In other respects the averages and the highs behaved quite differently. The previous experiment had, in effect, lumped the two together in the high-acceptance condition, and got from them much conformity as well as much of its opposite. The present experiment separated them, and in so doing it managed also to separate conformists from nonconformists. For by almost every measure the present highs conformed less to, and expressed more freedom to differ from, the group judgment than did any other class, whereas the averages, in sharp contrast, were the greatest conformers of all. The averages also turned in their new ratings sooner than did any other class and participated most in the discussion of the new information, though largely by discounting it and explaining it away. The investigators suggest that the averages found it rewarding to belong to the group and felt considerable acceptance by the others, but that they thought they had still more acceptance yet to win. They suggest that the conforming behavior of the averages reflected their aspirations to still higher social standing.

Turning now to the lows, we find that, like the earlier experiment, they were somewhat nonconformist, but that, unlike the earlier one, they were not as much so as the highs. With the very lows, the same general tendency presented a slightly different twist. We shall remember that there was only one of them in each group: he was both low and alone in his status. More apt than any other status to feel they were about to be rejected altogether, setting at the same time a low value on membership, and expressing little conformity in their private judgments, the very lows nevertheless expressed in public more conformity than did any other status, took less part in discussion, and felt less freedom to disagree. As the investigators say: "In the extreme case . . . where acceptance is so low that actual rejection is presumably an imminent possibility, anxiety about rejection is especially high, and the result seems to be a pattern of guarded public behavior."

Upper Status and Originality

We now have experimental evidence that it is not just members of low status, but members of high status as well, who are prone at times to nonconformity. But before we ask whether both lows and highs are nonconformists for the same reasons, let us look at one more piece of research, this time carried out by Bartos and carried out on natural groups rather than on artificially formed, experimental ones.[8]

The subjects of the research were 231 active members of six teen-age Y.M.C.A. clubs in a small Midwestern town. At the first meeting of the year each club elected eight officers, four of whom were to serve for the first term of the school year and four for the second; and after his election the president of the club appointed several other officers to help him with the work.

The clubs may appear somewhat over-officered, but that only helped the investigator to divide the membership into four classes differing in status. From high status to low they were: (1) the presidents, or leaders, (2) the remaining elective officers, whom the investigator called elected lieutenants, (3) the appointed officers, or appointed lieutenants, and (4) the members not holding office, or followers, this last class being obviously the largest. Whereas the preceding studies were forced to create differences in status by experimental manipulation, here the investigator had them handed to him naturally by the election and appointment system. But note that, if any comparison at all is valid, the "lows" and "very lows" in the last study corresponded to only a small section of the followers in this one, and that most of the followers were equivalent to the "averages."

The investigator had each subject look at a series of twelve pairs of cards and asked him "to match one of the three lines appearing on each of the right hand cards with the one line appearing on each of the left hand cards." Since the line on the left was always just the same length as one of the lines on the right, the job of matching should have been simple. But naturally the investigator did not mean to let his subjects off as easily as all that. While a subject was making his choice of lines, he heard off-stage the voices of six persons, which he was led to believe were the voices of members of his club, urging that one of the lines in the right hand card was the proper match for the line on the left; and in seven instances out of the series of twelve the voices unanimously urged the choice of the wrong line. The investigator in fact played the voices from a tape recorded in advance of the experiment.

After putting each subject through this experimental condition, the

[8] O. J. Bartos, "Leadership, Conformity, and Originality," unpublished paper presented at the 1958 meeting of the American Sociological Society.

investigator had him do the same matching job all over again with what seemed to be a new set of cards but was actually the same one, and this time without the chorus of voices. As a good experimenter, he wanted to make sure that the subjects would not make the same mistakes when not under the apparent influence of their fellow members as they had when they were under it. Not surprisingly they made many more mistakes in the first condition than in the second, and they made them by doing what the voices told them. Accordingly the investigator concluded that the number of mistakes a subject made by giving in to the influence brought to bear on him was a valid measure of his conformity.

The investigator had the subjects take two further tests. The first, called the independence-of-judgment scale, consisted of a series of fifteen statements with each of which the subject was to say whether he agreed or disagreed. For instance, one such statement was: "It is easy for me to take orders and do as I am told." Not unnaturally, agreement with statements like this was held to be evidence of a propensity to conformity. The experiment itself was modeled on an earlier one by Asch, and answers to such statements had in fact discriminated between those of Asch's subjects that conformed and those that did not.[9] Finally in the second test the subject looked through a series of drawings, both freehand drawings of strange asymmetrical figures and ruled drawings of symmetrical and geometrical shapes, and decided which ones he found most pleasing aesthetically. These drawings the investigator had borrowed from another piece of earlier research, which had seemed to show that the number of "complex" cards a man chose was a valid measure of his "originality."

The problem now was to relate the statuses of the members to their differences in the various measures of conformity and originality. On the line test the leaders of the clubs were far less conformist than other members. Most conformist were the elected lieutenants in the next highest status, but there was no great difference in conformity between them and the people holding the two lowest statuses: the appointed lieutenants and the followers. Much the same thing was true of the independence-of-judgment test: the leaders were far less conformist than the others; this time the followers were most conformist but not much more so than the elected and appointed lieutenants. In the readiness of the members of highest status to resist influence from the rest of the

[9] S. E. Asch, *Social Psychology* (New York, 1953), pp. 450-501.

group, these results are in accord with the Kelley experiments. But there is little hint, such as appeared in the final Dittes-Kelley study, that the members lowest in status, the followers, were also prone to nonconformity. We must remember that the followers in the present study made up more than half of the whole membership and so included many people equivalent to the "averages" of Dittes and Kelley. The "averages" were, of course, strong conformists.

As for the results of the originality test, the leaders were the most original, followed by the elected lieutenants, with the other two classes —the appointed lieutenants and followers—at the bottom of the list and about equally unoriginal. But we lay much less weight on these findings than we do on the results of the line-matching test, where people were actually under the influence of the apparently unanimous and incorrect judgments of other members of their groups. This test, it seems to us, comes closest to simulating actual social behavior.

Though the last three studies we have examined—Kelley-Shapiro, Dittes-Kelley, and Bartos—do not reach absolutely identical results, they do tend in the same general direction. The members of middle status in a group, whether they are so actually or only believe themselves to be so, seem most disposed to give in to influence coming apparently from a large number of other members or to cleave to an opinion that other members have once accepted. Less prone to conformity are members of either upper or lower status. We suspect that this latter finding would have emerged from the research even more clearly if, in the Kelley-Shapiro study, the membership had been divided into three statuses instead of two and if, in the Bartos study, the lower status had not embraced more than half the whole membership. Be that as it may, let us accept as established the main tendencies of the research and ask how we shall account for them. Above all, let us ask whether the same general kind of explanation will account for the behavior of men in all three statuses.

Status and the Risks of Action

We should not treat the last three experiments as simply studies in conformity to group norms. In each experiment, what faces the subject is not just an established group norm but rather information to the effect that the other members are agreed in believing a certain state of affairs to exist, when the direct evidence suggests that it may not exist at all. Were not the subject faced with information conflicting with the apparent group judgment, there would be no question of his not conforming. But the fact is that he does have alternative courses of action open to him—and this is true of most cases of conformity. Under the circumstances, what determines his choice of alternative?

In reaching his decision, a member is presented with two sorts of stimuli: those making up the situation itself, and those making up his own status. In the past, the appearance of similar stimuli have been occasions when his acting in different ways has brought him different degrees of reward. Some of the stimuli in the situation are similar to those present in the past when he uttered a judgment and was rewarded by having it turn out to be correct. Some of the stimuli making up his status are similar to those present in the past when he conformed to a group norm and was rewarded with social approval. The question is: How similar are they? Which combination of stimuli will govern his behavior and make it more probable that he will emit one of the alternatives rather than the other?

To put the matter in less cumbersome, though possibly also less fundamental terms: the member perceives, on the basis of his past experience, that he takes risks in adopting either of the two alternatives. He may either agree with the apparent group judgment or disagree and assert his independent judgment. Both courses of action promise rewards and costs in both self-respect and status, and neither the rewards nor the costs are certain. The risks, moreover, are of two kinds. First, if he agrees or disagrees, will he turn out to be correct? And second, if he is correct or incorrect, what will he gain or lose? If he is correct, he certainly will enhance his self-respect, but what will he do to his status? He must bear both kinds of risk in mind, which need not mean that he must do so consciously. For it is conceivable that even if he agrees with the group and turns out to be correct in doing so, he will not do his status much good. Under these circumstances, it may be a better bet for him to disagree with the group, even though he judges that his chances of being correct are doubtful, so long as he will do his status a lot of good should he turn out to be correct after all. When the ratio between the values of two rewards is greater than the ratio between the probabilities of attaining them, it is wiser to go for the greater value than the greater probability.

In the light of this analysis, what are the risks faced by men of different status in agreeing or disagreeing with an apparent group judgment? If an upper-status man conforms and the group's judgment turns out to be correct, he is just where he was before: no damage is done to his status but he has not improved it either. Much the same is true if he conforms and the group's judgment turns out to be incorrect. He may not lose much: although the event will have proved him wrong, everyone else will have been wrong too—for he must presume that there will be no treachery and that all the others will in fact have reached the same conclusion they asked him to reach. Still, it will do him little good to be wrong with the rest when upper-status people get their position by being different from the rest and better.

If, on the other hand, he does not conform, and the group's judgment turns out to be correct, he will at least have been "different"; and though he will have sacrificed a certain amount of esteem, it is conceivable that as a man of high status he is relatively satiated with esteem, and that the pleasures of indulging his independent judgment have risen in value. Even, moreover, if he does lose esteem, he will still have a lot left to play with. We are talking about people whose status is high and established, and the point about such people is that they have a long way to go before hitting the bottom. The further one can fall before all is lost, the more opportunity one has for retrieving one's position, and so the more room for maneuver.

But what, finally, if the upper-status man refuses to conform and the group's judgment turns out to be incorrect, if, that is, he turns out to be right and the rest wrong? Not only will he, by backing his own independent judgment, have forgone no self-respect; but he will also have increased, as he could have done in no other way, the esteem in which the others hold him as a possessor of rare abilities. He will especially have increased it if his correct judgment brings rewards to the other members, as it did in the first of the experiments we examined. He will not have been simply indulging for his own pleasure in the license the group sometimes allows to upper-status people, but will once more have made a unique contribution to the welfare of the group, which it is the business of upper-status people to do. His behavior will have been in keeping with his position; he will have acted out his role, for what we mean when we say a man has a role is that a certain kind of behavior has become established as congruent with his status in other respects.

Under these circumstances, the balance of risk makes it likely that an upper-status man will choose nonconformity. Naturally we do not mean that he need make the calculations consciously, or that all upper-status people reach, consciously or unconsciously, the same conclusions. We only assume that their very status makes nonconformity a good bet for them, and that enough of them take the bet to make a difference in the statistics.

In these experiments, we may think of the men who refuse to conform as being potential innovators. Under new circumstances they follow their own judgment instead of taking the old course of sticking with the group. And in Chapter 14 on Authority we saw that leaders are actual innovators in the sense that they take the initiative in changing the behavior of a large number of others. Whether or not they do so because they have more energy or intelligence than others, our present point is that they are further encouraged by their strategic position as upper-status people. For leaders must take risks, and only the success of the changes they bring about can replace the capital they have put up. But if the risks of innovation are there to be taken, upper-status people are better able to take them than others, for they have less than the others to gain by doing the same old thing and less to lose by trying something different.

Now let us face a person of middle status with the same predicament and ask what he stands to gain and lose by conformity and nonconformity. Remember that in the nature of the case his position is less secure than that of either of the other two: the lower-status man, already at the bottom, has no more status to lose; and the upper-status man, just because he has a lot of status to lose, can afford to risk some of it; but the middle-status man can less easily stand the loss of his little all. In this sense the division of a status system into three levels is not arbitrary but corresponds to three different strategic positions. At any rate, if the man of middle status conforms to the group's judgment and the group turns out to be right, his position as an accepted member is confirmed, and it needs confirming more than does that of an upper-status member. If he conforms and the group is wrong, he does not lose anything: he has only been a boob with the rest, who are in no condition to turn on him. If, on the other hand, he refuses to conform, and the group's judgment turns out to be right, he may really hurt himself in status; he is not so far from the bottom that a single misstep will not bring him appreciably closer to it. And if, finally, he refuses to conform, the group's judgment turns out to be wrong, and he, accordingly, is right, he will indeed gain status; but it will take more than one such achievement to get him to the top. Nor does he rise in a vacuum: his gain in status is at the same time a challenge to someone above him. He cannot afford to be right unless he is ready to accept the risks of future rivalry. A middle-status person who has behind him, in his past, only a moderate amount of activity rewarding to the other members needs more to bring him up and less to bring him down than does a man of higher status, who has already done the work of establishing himself. Under these circumstances, where nonconformity offers gains but also serious risk of loss, a man is apt to bet on conformity instead: it cannot hurt his position, it may even help it a little, and it is in either case less risky than the alternative.

No doubt the middle-status man who is determined to get to the top can only put some of his money on nonconformity regardless of its risks. Though he will have to repeat his successes and face the rivalry of men who have already arrived, nothing else will get him where he wants to be. But such men must naturally be few compared with those that set their sights less high or even worry about staying where they are. As Peter Blau says of his agents in the Federal law-enforcement agency: "Officials whose standing in the group was intermediate, particularly relatively new members, who were still trying to improve their position, semed to conform more strictly with group norms than those of higher status."[10]

Let us finally turn to the people at the bottom of the social heap. If a lower-status man conforms to the group's judgment and the group is correct, he does not get very far. Our assumption in this chapter is that a man's past behavior largely determines the present behavior of others toward him. If in the past a long run of his behavior has been "bad" by the others' standards—and that is what we mean when we say his position as a man of lower status is established—then one example of "good" behavior will not do much for him: it will take more than that to bring him up. If, moreover, there must be someone at the bottom of every group, any improvement in his behavior that does not

[10] P. M. Blau, *op. cit.*, p. 242.

clearly put him ahead of somebody else will leave him relatively where he was before. The same is true if he conforms and the group's judgment turns out not to be correct.

If, on the other hand, he rejects the group's judgment and the group is correct, he has nothing in the way of status to lose because he is at the bottom anyhow. And if he rejects the group's judgment, the group turns out to be wrong, and he therefore turns out to be right, he has something to gain. He has saved his self-respect and has been justified in doing so. If he resents the position the group has assigned him, if he feels that they are depriving him of something rightfully his, then showing them up when they are wrong is a delightful way of getting back at them. There are compensations for even the worst of positions, and God tempers the wind to the shorn lamb.

However delightful being right when the rest are wrong may be for its own sake, it is, against all justice, a poor method for a lower-status man to use who wants to get accepted by the group. Status congruence gets in its way. Though the event has proved him correct in his judgment, yet as a man who has been assigned lower status he has no business being correct: it is out of character; whereas for an upper-status man to do the same thing is perfectly in character and not resented, for it constitutes just one more proof of what the group knows already. One of the difficulties a man encounters with rising in the world once his companions have safely consigned him to a low status is that no matter how good, how valuable, his activities later become, they will deny him the credit of them. "It wasn't really he that did it," they say, "and anyhow who is he to put himself forward?" Try as he will, he cannot do anything right.

The upper-status man has little to gain by conformity, the lower-status one little to lose by its opposite, and so for different reasons the behavior of both is biased in the same way. The latter is apt to bet on nonconformity for the rewards other than status that it can bring him. But note that if he does so, it only confirms him as an outsider in the eyes of the group, and makes it still less likely that on the next occasion any single item of "good" behavior will raise his standing. If the nonconformity of the upper-status man only plays into his own hands, only gives him a chance to raise his status further, the nonconformity of the lower-status one works increasingly against him. In elementary social behavior, as we have pointed out more than once, "whosoever hath, to him shall be given; but whosoever hath not, from him shall be taken away even that which he hath." And as we saw at the beginning of the chapter, a group that has assigned a man low status is apt by that fact to have sacrificed control of him, for it has left itself nothing to deprive him of should he behave badly, by its standards, the next time. It has already done its worst.

Low-status members of a group are, therefore, apt to go still lower. They are apt, indeed, to leave the group altogether unless they can find some reward to take the place of the esteem that has been denied them. Such reward may be provided by other people in the same boat, other people rejected by the group, who cling together all the more fiercely for that reason, giving to one another the approval denied them elsewhere. The phenomenon of companionship in misery—a few people each of whom chooses each of the others for many different activities, both at work and at leisure—seems to appear especially often at the very lowest levels of groups.

The three experiments we have considered presented the subjects with a choice between doing and not doing what the group apparently wanted them to do, when the other information they were given left them with a clear alternative to conformity. Although the experiments seemed thoroughly artificial, the kind of problem they set for a member does come up again and again in real groups. Accordingly we may guess that the research does tell us something of general importance about the relationship between status and behavior.

Vying for Acceptance

So far we assumed that the status of the persons concerned was pretty well established. If it is not established, the relationship between status and behavior may be of a wholly different sort. We have seen, for instance, that a man of established lower status is apt to be a nonconformist. In Blau's words, "The individual who had adapted himself to an isolated position could more readily violate the norms of the group." But if a man has not given up, if he still sees a chance to be accepted, if he is still vying for membership, his behavior is more apt to be conformist, indeed overconformist, than the reverse. We shall remember the experiment by the Sherifs, in which they separated the boys in a summer camp into two rival groups. As hostility between the two groups increased, the lower-status members of each group became more vociferous than the rest in venting their opposition to the other, as if they hoped thereby to demonstrate that they were full-fledged members.[11]

People are the more ready to go on vying for membership, the more fully they accept their original assignment to lower status as being in accord with the rules of distributive justice; and this depends on their investments. A man whose investments justify a higher status than the other members have been ready to accord him will add resentment against them to the other reasons for failing to conform to their norms, and so will speed up the vicious spiral that separates him from the group. But a man whose investments are low to begin with, because he is a newcomer or for some other reason, has no occasion for resentment, and since his investments can only improve with time, may hope that if he is patient and does nothing to upset things, he will sooner or later be taken in.

In the study of the machining and assembly department of the Industrial Controls Corporation, which we have spoken of several times, the investigators found two small subgroups, which were of equally low status but reacted differently.[12] One subgroup consisted of workers, low in pay and skill, whose backgrounds were apt to have one or more of the following characteristics: they were Protestant, middle-class, or white-collar. As such they were different from, and in their own eyes better than, the urban, lower-class Irish Catholics who made up half the membership in the department and dominated it. By working as hard as they could they violated the output norm praised and perpetuated by the dominant cliques, and so confirmed their low status. No doubt the moral value set on hard work, which has been called the Protestant Ethic and which they had inherited along with their background, helped them to behave as they did, but so did their pleasure in showing up the workers of higher status, whose judgment they resented. They were typical nonconformists who were not vying for membership and whom their group had accordingly lost control of.

The other subgroup consisted of workers whose backgrounds resembled those of the dominant cliques, except that they were not Irish

[11] M. Sherif and C. W. Sherif, *Groups in Harmony and Tension* (New York, 1953), p. 284.

[12] A. Zaleznik, C. R. Christensen, and F. J. Roethlisberger, *The Motivation, Productivity, and Satisfaction of Workers* (Boston, 1958), pp. 375-80.

but Italians or members of other nationalities lower than the Irish in ethnic status. The dominant members tended to joke at their expense, the jokes emphasizing the ethnic element: for instance, they might call them "Guineas." But the joking was not enough to stop their vying for full-fledged membership in the group. They took the jokes in good part; they hung around on the outskirts of the games the "regulars" played; they were ready to accept menial jobs as coffee-carriers; and they started various low-valued activities, like temporary betting-pools, which high-status people were ready to take part in but not to organize. They were, moreover, ultraconformists: they abided by the output norm and "articulated all the subtleties of the sentiments involved in restriction of output." It was as if they felt that their investments entitled them to no higher status than they started with, and that if only they stuck to the rules time was bound to be on their side. They were lower-status conformists whom, because they were still vying for membership, their group still kept control of. We may well ask how long a group can keep people vying for a rise in status without doing something to satisfy them.

Status and Conformity in Society at Large

Instead of summarizing, let us end this chapter by looking briefly at some large-scale phenomena that bear a little resemblance to the ones we have just been examining on a small scale. We should never assume that the informal group is a microcosm of society at large, that what holds good of the one holds good also of the other. It would be hard, for instance, to make out that upper-class people in society at large, like upper-status ones in small groups, are especially apt to be innovators. And yet, though the resemblances may be superficial, some characteristics of some social-class systems at some times seem to resemble what we have noticed about status in small groups—particularly the tendency for members high and low in status to resemble one another in their nonconformity and to differ from members of middle status. In the recent past of the South of this country,[13] and in England in the seventeenth century, there are hints that both upper and lower classes were less restrained in the fields of gambling, drink, and forni-

[13] J. Dollard, *Caste and Class in a Southern Town* (New Haven, 1937), pp. 75-97.

cation, more ready to indulge in the simple sensuous pleasures of life than were the climbers, the strainers, the insecure of the middle classes.

The landed aristocrat, already at the top, has little to gain from a rigid compliance with the minor moral standards of society. Since his social position is secure, whatever his economic position may be, he finds other rewards—including an indulgence in his eccentricities and in the pleasures of the flesh—relatively more rewarding than further striving for status. And the poor farm laborer, who has little to gain by respectability and nothing to lose by its opposite, is similarly attracted by the simple sensuous pleasures—riot and debauchery—which have the further charm of not costing much money. Respectable people treat him like an animal, and his natural response is indeed animalian, which comfortably confirms the respectable in the moral judgment they have passed on him. Yet they have their moments of envying him his license, above all, his freedom from striving. He can afford to relax and be a natural man. In a wry way, he is making the best of a bad society. But the people in the middle, particularly if they see some chance of rising in the world, must seek, by close adherence to a rigid morality, to differentiate themselves from what they call the rabble and establish their claims to social recognition. Middle-class people are more apt to be puritanical than either upper- or lower-class ones. Yet in saying this we are immediately reminded how dangerous it is to generalize from the small group to society at large. For in the England of the seventeenth century, middle-class people, though they certainly were conformists in morality, were far from being conformists in other respects. Puritanical in the general sense in manners, they were also Puritans in the special sense in religion: they were religious reformers. And at the crisis of the seventeenth century, when King and Commons faced one another in arms in the Civil War, middle-class people were specially likely to support Parliament, while the other two classes—not all but many of them—tended to identify themselves with one another and with the king.[14]

[14] J. M. Lloyd Thomas, ed., *The Autobiography of Richard Baxter* (London, 1931), p. 34.

A Summary Group

Chapter Seventeen

In my last book, *The Human Group*, I examined field studies of five different groups and tried to show that some of the same propositions held good in all of them. My primary emphasis was on the groups, my secondary, on the propositions. In the present book we have come close to reversing the process. We have now taken up a wide range of propositions about elementary social behavior and found evidence from both field and experimental research to support them. The emphasis has necessarily fallen on the isolated proposition: we have not done much, though we have done more in later chapters than we did in earlier ones, to show how a number of the phenomena manifest themselves together in a single situation. In this chapter, by way of a summary of what has gone before, we shall try to do just this: we shall take one excellent field study of a single group, a study that had not appeared at the time *The Human Group* was published, and show how a number of the phenomena we have described earlier made their joint appearance in the behavior of its members. The group in question is one of the two described by Peter Blau in his book, *The Dynamics of Bureaucracy*.[1] We have spoken about it several times already; in fact it suggested the situation we used as our model for the interaction of those two hard-worked characters, Person and Other. In using it as a summary group we shall have to repeat some of the things we said about it in other

[1] (Chicago, 1955) pp. 99-248.

connections; for whatever may be the needs that a summary meets, it certainly meets them at the cost of repetition.

We must not mistake our sample group for a typical group: there is no such thing. In Chapter 11 on The Nature of the Givens, we tried to show that a single set of propositions about social behavior would not lead us to expect, under different givens, any one form of group organization but a wide variety of forms. Far from being typical, the present group was rather simply organized, as groups go. We should not look on it as "the" eternal group but as a highly individual instance, which by very reason of its simplicity sets off to advantage the phenomena we want to summarize.

A Federal Agency: Consultation Among Colleagues

The group consisted of a supervisor, sixteen agents, and one clerk, who formed in 1949 a department in a local branch of a Federal agency that had its headquarters in Washington, D.C. In order to protect the anonymity of the group, the investigator does not tell us what the precise job of the agency was. Broadly it was concerned with the enforcement of a certain set of Federal laws. Since we are not interested in formal organization, and since he was hardly a member of the group, we shall not have much to say about the supervisor; nor was the clerk a member. Our business is with the sixteen agents.

The members of the department were fairly experienced in their work: only one had been with the agency for less than five years. Two held the civil-service grade 9, which was the highest represented among the agents; two were in grade 7; and the rest, the great majority, were in the middle with grade 8. But regardless of their different grades, all did much the same kind of work. Only three were women, and only one was a Negro. On the average an agent spent about 40 per cent of his time in the home office, where he had a desk of his own along with the other agents. But because their duties took them often into the field, not all the agents were together in the office at any one time.

An agent's main duty was investigation. On assignment by the supervisor, he went to the office of a business firm, obtained from it a wide variety of information, then came back to the agency where, from the information he had collected, he wrote a report stating whether or not and in what way the firm had violated Federal law. In order to determine whether a violation had occurred, an agent had to know how a large and complex body of legal rulings applied to the circumstances of a particular case. And since his report might become the basis of legal action against the firm, an agent had to be sure of his facts, his argument, and the clarity of his presentation.

The quality of the reports an agent turned in to the supervisor determined more than anything else the kind of efficiency rating the latter gave him, and this in turn affected his chances for promotion to a higher grade in the civil service. Thus an agent had to do a job difficult in itself, and his success in doing it made a difference to his future. Moreover, unlike the members of many industrial groups, the agents believed strongly in the value of the work the agency was doing, and so were doubly motivated to do it right.

Yet in spite of his long experience, an agent was often in doubt which legal rules might be applicable to the case under consideration and what decision he ought to reach about it. An agent was left free to make his own decision, the only formal rule being that if he had any doubt or question, he was to bring it to the supervisor without consulting any of his colleagues. But like many formal rules, this one was disregarded. Not unnaturally the agents believed that to take a question to the supervisor was to confess one's incompetence and so to prejudice one's efficiency rating; accordingly they did go to their colleagues for help and advice, and the supervisor seems to have winked at the practice.

Although the agents all had much experience, they still recognized that some of their number were better than others at solving the problems that came up over writing reports. Blau's first job was to ask every agent to put all the others in order of their competence as he saw it. The individual rankings were highly in agreement with one another, and they agreed also with the supervisor's ranking of the competence of the different agents.

The investigator next tried to relate the perceived competence of the different agents to the number of times other agents went to them for help and advice. In the course of his observations of behavior in the department, the investigator kept a record of every contact between agents, however brief it might have been, such as a word spoken in passing. He discovered that an agent, while he was in the office, had an average of five contacts per hour with colleagues. Some of these were casual and social conversations, but many were discussions of technical problems. The investigator decided that the latter were probably the longer, and so in studying the distribution of technical consultations he included only contacts that lasted more than three minutes. The investigator also asked every agent to name the other agents whom he consulted when he ran into difficulties with his work.

The results showed a rather marked pattern. As we should expect, the more competent an agent, the more contacts he was apt to receive, and the higher was the esteem in which he was held.[2] But the correlation was not perfect. Two of the agents who their colleagues believed were competent seem to have discouraged people that came to them for help and so to have choked off further advances. As Blau says, "The two experts who were considered uncooperative by their colleagues were generally disliked and received only few contacts. To become accepted, an expert had to share the advantages of his superior skill with his co-workers."[3]

But most agents were ready to help. A few of them, and these among the most competent of all, were consulted by a large number of others, but did not themselves go regularly for advice to any one agent. Thus four agents had no regular partners, but all four were highly competent. Three of them were also very popular as consultants. "These three were by no means isolated from the exchange of advice. On the contrary, they participated so widely in it that they did not spend much time with any single co-worker."[4] The fourth agent had only recently been assigned to the department and had not yet been brought into much use as a consultant. The rest of the agents, on the other hand, were apt to take regular partners. Each one of them, though occasionally consulting the few highly competent men, was apt to be especially closely linked with one or two others whose competence was more nearly equal to his own. On any occasion when he needed help, he felt free to consult his partner, as long as he was ready to allow the latter the same kind of privilege in return.

[2] In a later study of a social-work agency, Blau found no relation between esteem and contacts received. The reason was that in the social-work agency, unlike the Federal agency, the workers set a negative value on expert knowledge of procedures. Accordingly, an expert was less apt to be approached for technical advice, and less apt to get esteem in return, than he was in the Federal agency. See P. M. Blau, "Social Integration, Social Rank, and Processes of Interaction," *Human Organization*, Vol. 18 (1959-60), pp. 152-57.

[3] P. M. Blau, *The Dynamics of Bureaucracy, op. cit.,* p. 119.

[4] *Ibid.,* p. 108.

Rewards and Costs of Consultation

Now let us see what the investigator has to say about the social economics of consultation:

> A consultation can be considered an exchange of values; both participants gain something, and both have to pay a price. The questioning agent is enabled to perform better than he could otherwise have done, without exposing his difficulties to the supervisor. By asking for advice, he implicitly pays his respect to the superior proficiency of his colleague. This acknowledgment of inferiority is the cost of receiving assistance. The consultant gains prestige, in return for which he is willing to devote some time to the consultation and permit it to disrupt his own work. The following remark of an agent illustrates this: "I like giving advice. It's flattering, I suppose, if you feel that the others come to you for advice."[5]

The expert who was willing to give advice got various advantages incidental to his rise in esteem. From the consultation he drew renewed confidence in his own capacity to solve technical problems. He might, indeed, pick up ideas useful to him in doing his own work without paying the price of an admission of inferiority. Each of the three most popular consultants, whom many others asked for help, could, moreover, when he needed help in return, scatter his requests among these many and did not need to concentrate them on any single agent, which would have made more conspicuous the fact that it was help he was asking for. As the investigator puts it: "Besides, to refrain from asking any particular individual too many questions helped to maintain his reputation as an expert. Consequently, three of the most popular consultants had no regular partners."[6]

The cost that an expert incurred in getting his prestige is obvious: he had to take time from his own work. "All agents liked being consulted, but the value of any one of very many consultations became deflated for experts, and the price they paid in frequent interruptions became inflated. . . . Being approached for help was too valuable an experience to be refused, but popular consultants were not inclined to encourage further questions."[7]

[5] *Ibid.,* p. 108.
[6] *Ibid.,* p. 108.
[7] *Ibid.,* p. 108.

The investigator is quite explicit that asking a colleague for help incurred an agent costs: "Asking a colleague for guidance was less threatening than asking the supervisor, but the repeated admission of his inability to solve his own problems also undermined the self-confidence of an agent and his standing in the group. The cost of advice became prohibitive, if the consultant, after the questioner had subordinated himself by asking for help, was in the least discouraging—by postponing a discussion or by revealing his impatience during one."[8]

The cost in inferiority of asking a colleague for help was rendered greater in this group than it would have been in some others by the fact that, formally, the agents were not greatly unequal: all held the same job-title, all did the same kind of work, and most of them held the same civil-service grade. A man who is already another's inferior has much less to lose in asking a service of him than one who began as his equal.

That asking for help did indeed incur a man costs is shown by the practice some agents adopted of asking for help while elaborately pretending that they were doing nothing of the sort. Such an agent would bring his problem to a colleague as if it were a case presenting special points of interest well worthy of dispassionate analysis between two discriminating judges. As one of the agents said, "Casey asks me sometimes, too, but he does it with a lot of finesse. He will just seem to ask what my opinion is, not as if he were worried about the question."[9] And the investigator makes the comment: "Such manipulative attempts to obtain advice without reciprocating by acknowledging the need for the other's help were resented. . . . If his advice was needed, the agent demanded that the respect due him be paid by *asking* for his assistance. An official whose deliberate disguise of a consultation was discovered created resentment without averting loss of esteem."[10] In short, this maneuver broke the rules of fair exchange: it attempted to get help without conceding superiority in return. We have encountered behavior of the same sort in the machine shop described in Chapter 12.

As we have seen, three of the most competent agents did not enter into partnerships, did not regularly exchange help and advice with particular other agents. Two highly competent agents did take regular

[8] *Ibid.,* pp. 108-09.
[9] *Ibid.,* p. 112.
[10] *Ibid.,* p. 113.

partners, but upon the whole partnerships were confined to people of middle and low competence. The investigator implies that it was precisely the costs a man incurred in asking the most competent agents for advice that led the rest to seek out partners among people more nearly of their own rank, with whom they could exchange help without losing status; for the essence of partnership was that if one man asked his partner for help on one occasion, the partner might ask the same favor back on the next. Speaking of the fact that an agent who tried to consult one of his more competent colleagues might meet with a refusal, Blau says:

> To avoid such rejections, agents usually consulted a colleague with whom they were friendly, even if he was not an expert. . . . The establishment of partnerships of mutual consultation virtually eliminated the danger of rejections as well as the status threat implicit in asking for help, since the roles of questioner and consultant were intermittently reversed. These partnerships also enabled agents to reserve their consultations with an expert whom they did not know too well for their most complicated problems.[11]

That is, the advice a man got from his partner might not be of the highest value, but it was purchased at low cost since a partner was apt to be his social equal. And thus he was enabled to save his really difficult problems for the most competent agents, whose advice, since it did come high in confessed inferiority, he did not want to ask often.

It should be clear how these findings illustrate the arguments we put forward in the earlier part of this book. Social behavior is an exchange of more or less valuable rewards. The expert agents provided for the others a service that these others found valuable and rare. In return, the experts received much interaction and were able to command from the rest a high degree of esteem, thus establishing a social ranking in the group. But in getting these rewards both parties to the exchange incurred costs—the experts in time taken away from their own work, the others in implicit admissions of inferiority. The costs, moreover, increased and the rewards declined with the number of exchanges, thus tending to cut off further exchange. The experts began to rebuff new requests, and the rest began to hesitate before approaching the experts. Indeed the rest began to look for sources of help they could exploit at lower cost. In the nature of the case, these sources could only be agents

[11] *Ibid.*, p. 109.

more nearly of their own rank than the experts. With such people they could both give and take advice without net loss in esteem.

Finally, most agents met the conditions of distributive justice. For instance, the experts who were ready to give help got much esteem but incurred heavy costs in time taken away from their own work: their costs were proportional to their rewards. Therefore the other agents not only respected but liked them. To win esteem it was not enough to *be* expert: a man had to devote his expert knowledge to the service of others. Thus a couple of agents, known to be competent, who repelled others approaching them with requests for help, were much disliked and left much alone. In failing to enter into exchange at all they had deprived the others of services that the others had come to expect of people with so much to give.

"Social" Interaction

The investigator next turned to the relations between the agents' competence and their more purely "social" behavior. Of the latter he made two different kinds of observations. In his period of watching the group he had kept a record of all the contacts (interactions) an agent received from others, but in mapping out the pattern of consultations he had included only the relatively long contacts—three minutes or more—on the ground that long contacts were more likely than short ones to have to do with the official business of the agency. Now, in mapping out "social" behavior—passing the time of day, gossiping, telling jokes—he included all the contacts an agent received, long or short, and called this a measure of *contacts received*. The investigator also asked each agent to keep a record every day of the colleagues he lunched with. "If a luncheon engagement is defined as eating with one colleague once, the total number of engagements reported (which often included several colleagues on the same day, and the same colleague on repeated days), divided by the number of days on which the respondent went out to lunch from the office, defines the value of this index,"[12]—which the investigator called a measure of an agent's *informal relations*.

He then proceeded to study the interrelations of these three variables: competence, contacts received, and informal relations. For this

[12] *Ibid.*, p. 237.

purpose, he divided the rank-order of the agents on each variable into two parts, but the division did not necessarily come at the mid-point of the distribution. Thus seven agents were rated as high in competence and eight low, but six were rated as high in contacts received and nine low. (One agent transferred out of the department in the course of the study, reducing the total number of the agents considered for the present purpose to fifteen.)

Agents high in competence were statistically likely to be high also in contacts received. Not all were: the two highly competent agents who were unwilling to give the others the benefit of their competence and who were accordingly disliked received few social contacts; but the tendency was in this direction. By the same token, the less competent agents tended statistically to get few contacts.

Perhaps this finding tells us little more than we know already. An expert who was willing to share his knowledge with others was much sought after by the others for consultation, and we know that many of the contacts an expert received were of this sort. But not all were: some were more purely "social." Once a man has won esteem by providing others with rare and valuable services, another reason for their seeking him out comes into play: he is now able to offer a new kind of service. In Chapter 15 on Equality we explained why a man tends to seek out his equals for interaction on "social" occasions. But once this is recognized to be the case, then for Person to interact with Other socially and be seen doing so is to provide the outward and visible sign that he is Other's equal, and this, paradoxically, creates a new reason for his interacting with his social superiors. For if Other is a man of high status, then Person by being seen in his company has offered prima-facie evidence that he is of high status too. Accordingly some members of a group, those not unduly troubled about their self-respect, seek out social interaction with a member of high status for reasons other than getting the service that first won him the status. But how will a member of high status receive their advances? If he is in any doubt about his status, social contacts with his inferiors will tend to bring him down to their level, and he is apt to rebuff them; but if his status is so firmly established that he need not worry about it, his willingness to allow them social access to him provides them with a new and valuable service and enhances the esteem in which they hold him.

"Contacts received" was measured by the number of interactions a man received in the office, and this might include "business" contacts as well as "social" ones. The best index of purely "social" contacts was "informal relations," which was measured by luncheons. The investigator found that, statistically speaking, agents of high competence were apt to have few informal relations and agents of low competence to have many. Some of the competent agents did not use their competence to help others; therefore they did not enjoy high status, and the others were not much interested in getting their company for lunch. Some enjoyed a status both high and secure, and could afford to wait until others approached them. And some may not have been quite sure of their high status, which may have led them to rebuff the advances of their inferiors. All of these effects tended to reduce the informal relations of the more competent people. But the less competent people, who on the average were less secure in their status than the more competent ones, tended actively to seek others out for luncheon dates. They sought out the agents of high status if they could get them, but if they could not, they found lunching with somebody better than lunching alone. No doubt man is a gregarious animal and enjoys lunching with his fellows regardless of what it does to his status. Our only point is that differences in status provide additional reasons for (or against) social contacts. By lunching with any one of his fellows an agent of low status could at least make good the fact that he was the other's equal, that he was at least an accepted member of the group. At any rate, the less competent agents "lunched in larger groups than experts and made greater efforts to arrange their work so that they would have to eat alone as rarely as possible."[13] By eating in large groups they necessarily rolled up a high score in informal relations, since each person present at the table added to the score.

Though the competent agents tended to have fewer informal relations than the less competent, lunching more often alone or with fewer companions, the relationship was statistical and did not hold good of all of them. One agent of whom it did not hold good was the one who, in the office, was most encouraging to people who came and asked him for help. He was better liked than any other agent, and became, as we shall soon see, the informal leader of the group. In short, his status was both high and secure. "His great willingness to assist others," the inves-

[13] *Ibid.,* p. 120.

tigator comments, "was his price for maintaining this position."[14] But this was not the only service he did for them: he was also willing to provide them with the secondary reward of lunching with him. "He was particularly hospitable to colleagues who consulted him, and he deliberately fostered informal relations with them. 'If anyone asks me for lunch,' he told the observer, 'I never say, "I have a date with another fellow; I can't." I always say, "Of course, come along." ' In contrast to most experts, this agent had very extensive informal relations."[15]

The investigator finally turned to the third of the possible relations between the three variables, the relation between informal relations and contacts received, and he found that agents who had many informal relations (luncheons) were statistically likely to receive many contacts. Now this may seem curious. For if x varies as y, and x also varies as z, we might expect y to vary as z; but in this study it did not. Contacts received (x) varied as competence (y), and contacts received (x) varied as informal relations (z); but we saw earlier that informal relations (z) did not vary directly as competence (y) but rather inversely: the greater the competence, the fewer the informal relations.

This apparent departure from common sense was made possible by the statistical method used and by the fact that the correlations, while often significant, were never perfect. Enough of the competent had few informal relations, and enough of the incompetent had many, to establish the inverse relation between competence and informal relations, but not all men in either class behaved as the greater part did. And the same was true of the direct relation between competence and contacts received. Accordingly it was possible for the few competent agents who both enjoyed extensive informal relations and received many contacts to combine statistically with the few less competent ones who also did both things and so create a direct relationship between informal relations and contacts received.

But to show that the reported results are possible results does not add very much. It is much more interesting to reconstruct from the investigator's data what the actual pattern of social engagements among the agents must have been. We shall not give here the tedious reason-

[14] *Ibid.*, p. 236.
[15] *Ibid.*, pp. 122-23.

ing that leads to the reconstruction but only its conclusions. The less competent agents must have lunched with one another a great deal, and in large groups, without the more competent agents' being present —indeed the investigator implies as much. The competent agents must also have lunched with one another a good deal without the less competent agents' being present—but in small groups. This suggests that they may have rebuffed some of the social advances made to them by the less competent agents. And finally some of the less competent managed to get some of the more competent to lunch with them fairly often, in large groups. In fact the investigator tells us that the informal leader was one of the competent men who thus allowed himself to be lunched with by his social inferiors. Equals, then, tended in general to lunch with equals, but some inferiors made successful advances to their superiors in status.

We have here further evidence of the complex interplay of two tendencies we have encountered again and again in this book: a tendency for a man to interact with his superiors in status, and a tendency for him to interact with his equals. A man establishes superior status by providing superior services for others. By the same token, accepting the superior services becomes a cost to a man, since he thereby recognizes his inferiority. Sooner or later he will turn to others who can provide him with services that no doubt reward him less but that also cost him less in inferiority. In the nature of the case, these others can only be his equals. As the partnerships in the Federal agency show, he will turn to his equals for services at work that he can return in kind; but he is particularly apt to turn to them in the "social" field of activity, just because it is *not* the field in which his superiors win their high esteem—and he his low. A secondary development then builds on this primary one. The rest of mankind can "see" the equations of elementary social behavior just as clearly in their way as we social scientists can, and once the relation between social interaction and equality of status is established, it provides new rewards for interaction. By interacting with his fellows a man can then provide evidence for himself and for them that he is at least their equal. Still better, if he can get his superior to interact with him he may do something to raise his apparent status.

Esteem and Authority

As we have just seen, and as earlier chapters have taught us, people of high status tend to receive much interaction. Indeed to maneuver a man into coming to you is to establish the presumption that you are his superior. But people of high status also give much interaction, especially in the sense of originating activity. They tell a relatively large number of others what they ought to do, and the others often do it. The higher the esteem, the higher the authority, is a proposition for which the Federal agency provided much evidence.

Let us consider particularly the agent who the investigator believes was the top informal leader in the department. (The supervisor was of course the formal leader.) He was highly competent at his job, and recognized as being so both by the supervisor and by the other agents. Of the more competent agents, he was also the one most receptive and least discouraging to requests for help from others. That is, he was the most willing to incur the cost of taking time off from his own work. And he was highly popular. Note here his status congruence, his willingness to follow the rules of distributive justice, his acceptance of *noblesse oblige*. He received high rewards in esteem from the group, but in so doing he incurred, as they saw it, high costs too.

He rewarded the others not only in the business side of their life but in the social one too. He was always ready to accept an invitation to lunch with his social inferiors, and in this he was unlike most of the other competent agents. But the very liberality with which he distributed his favors prevented his becoming identified with any one of the cliques whose members met regularly for lunch. He was in touch with everybody and not exclusively in touch with any single person or subgroup. We have seen this combination of aloofness and closeness in the leaders of other groups we have looked at, and we have encountered evidence, in Fiedler's research reported in Chapter 14 on Authority, that such behavior may make leadership more effective in attaining group goals.

As we saw in Chapter 14, the more competent agents tended to take the lead in any undertaking in which several members of the group were engaged. They made most suggestions, and their suggestions were most often followed, whether the question was where to go for lunch or what to do about a project on which a number of agents were working together. And of all the competent agents, the one held in highest esteem was the one who also held highest authority. When a committee was appointed to draft a change in one of the regulations, he dominated the discussion, and his opinion was the one finally adopted. Above all, like some of the popular girls at the New York State Training School, he stood up for the other agents against the supervisor. In this connection the investigator says of him:

> This agent became the informal leader of the group, whose suggestions the others often followed and who acted as their spokesman. For example, in a departmental meeting the supervisor criticized certain deficiences in the performance of most agents, clearly exempting experts from his criticism. Nevertheless, this official spoke up on behalf of the group and explained that agents could not be blamed for these deficiences, since a legal regulation that restricted their operations was responsible for them. Generally, the high regard in which this agent was held made his advice and opinion influential among colleagues, and even among superiors.[16]

A man to whom many others come singly for valuable services, in this case advice on how to do their work, and who in rendering the services incurs costs visibly proportional to the esteem they have given him, earns the right to tell them jointly what to do in new conditions that may affect the welfare of many of them, himself among the rest. By serving he becomes a leader. We must always remember that the services he provides need not be ones that you or I should find rewarding or even approve of. Leaders get to be where they are by doing some of the strangest things, and the rest of us are always asking ourselves, "What's he got that I haven't got?" The answer is that what he has got does actually reward some other men, whether or not it ought to do so, and what he has got is rare in the actual circumstances, whether or not it would be rare in others.

Nor should we lay too much stress on the difference between the followers' coming to him singly and his telling them jointly what to do. In both cases, whether he gives them advice they take or orders they obey, the important point is that he controls their behavior; and the fact that a new occasion may call for his advising them jointly is a nonessential detail. His past behavior has won him the capability of doing so, should the occasion present itself, but it may not. The advice

[16] *Ibid.*, p. 123.

he has given them singly they have in the past rewarded with approval, and so he is more likely to give advice again on a new occasion. He has, as we say, acquired confidence in his ability to give them advice. Nor is it just that he has more confidence but that the others have less: persons whose status is less than his own are persons whose advice has less often won approval in the past, and who are therefore less apt to have the gall to speak up now: what wise ideas they may have do them no good if they lack the confidence to come out with them.

The relation between past behavior and present that holds good for the leader holds good also for the followers. Having taken his advice singly and found it rewarding, they are more ready to take it jointly— to obey him when he tells them what to do for their welfare and his own. In doing so, he puts his social capital at hazard, since if they obey and fail to find the outcome rewarding, he has done injury to his esteem and their future willingness to obey. But he has much capital to risk, and if they do find the outcome to their satisfaction, he has replaced his capital and more. Finally, though the leader may lay himself open to the social advances of his followers, he cannot allow himself to get too close to any one of them or any single clique; for frequent social interaction implies equality, and equality between people tends to be incongruent with the fact that one of their number gives orders to the rest. But the best guarantee that he shall not be too close to anyone lies in the very profusion with which he scatters his favors abroad.

Nonconformity and Isolation

A member of a group acquires high esteem by providing rare and valuable services for the other members. But these are obviously not the only services a member can perform: he can also perform services that, without being rare, nevertheless have their value. Prominent among them is conformity to the norms of the group —a norm being a statement of what behavior ought to be, to which at least some members of the group find it valuable that their own actual behavior and that of other members should conform. Since a norm envisages that a relatively large number of members will behave similarly in some respect, conformity to a norm cannot be a rare service: any fool can conform if he will only take the trouble; and therefore if all a man did was conform, he would never get much esteem, though he would always get some. But it does not follow that if conformity will not win a man much esteem, nonconformity will not lose him much—if he has any to lose. For his failure to conform, when the other members see no just reason why he should not, deprives them unfairly of a valuable service, and so earns him their positive hostility.

Among themselves the agents had, over time, worked out several unofficial norms. They felt that no agent, as a maximum, should complete more than the eight cases a month that the supervisor expected of every agent as a minimum. And they felt that no agent should take a report home from the office in order to work on it in the evening. Agents who showed any sign of doing these things were kidded until they stopped. Violation of these norms was an injury to the members of the group, and conformity a value to them, because an agent who finished more than eight cases a month or worked on cases at home might have gotten an advantage over the others in the race for promotion; and if everyone had started to violate the norms, they would all have found themselves, through competition, working harder than they ever had before—not that the supervisor was at all discouraged with the quantity and quality of their present work: the agents were devoted civil servants. In practice, these output norms conspired to perpetuate existing differences in competence, since they prevented slower agents from catching up with their superiors by working harder.

The agents laid an even more severe taboo against reporting to the supervisor that firms had offered them bribes, though by the official rules of the agency they were bound to report such offers. It was not that the agents accepted bribes and wanted to prevent a colleague who was puritanical about such matters from spoiling their game. Far from it: when they suspected that an officer of a firm was working up to offering a bribe, they did their best to cut him off before he could commit himself openly. In the agents' view, it was inevitable that businessmen, given the pressures they worked under, should think of bribery; therefore it ought not to be held against them, and an agent reporting them and so making them subject to legal action was a "squealer." The agents also had a more practical interest in the norm against reporting bribes. If possible an agent was expected to induce the firm he was investigating to obey the law voluntarily and not under the complusion of legal action expensive to both parties. An offer of a bribe, however tactfully it was made, put into an agent's hand a lever by which he might without legal action get the firm to comply with the law. But it was a lever that became worse than useless once the proffered bribe was officially reported. Indeed the report might make the company all the more ready to fight it out with the government in the courts. Accordingly agents discouraged all tendencies in their colleagues to "get tough with" and "crack down on" companies, except as a last resort. Should the agency get the reputation of behaving this way, their work would become much more difficult: all companies would meet every agent with automatic hostility, and the chances of persuading them instead of compelling them to compliance would be gone forever. For these reasons most agents felt they had a direct personal interest in seeing that all their colleagues conformed to this norm.

With these norms in mind, let us look at one of the isolates in the department. When we call him an isolate, we mean that he received few social contacts and often lunched alone. Although he appears to have been considered fairly competent, he not only was not ready to use his competence for the benefit of others but spent his time instead turning out more work than the others considered right. Already held in low esteem for behavior of this sort, he proceeded to take a "get tough" attitude toward the firms he investigated; indeed this was generally more apt to be true of the less popular agents than of the more popular ones. And he was the only agent who violated the strongest taboo of all and reported to the supervisor that a bribe had been offered him. The investigator tells us little or nothing about the social background of any of the agents, including this one, and so we cannot tell what features of his past history may have predisposed him to behave as he did. He himself admitted he had made a mistake: though he had violated the norm, he was ready to say it was a good one.

For his action the group had for a time deliberately ostracized him. Cutting off interaction with a member and thus depriving him of any social reward whatever is the most severe punishment a group can inflict on him; in fact he ceases to be a member. But once a man has stood that, he can, so to speak, stand anything; and the group has lost control of him, for it has left him with nothing more to lose. Certainly the department had pretty well lost control of this agent. Though he reported no more bribes, he did much as he pleased in other ways. For instance, the agents felt that he wasted their time by talking a great deal too much in department meetings, where the agents of higher esteem usually took the largest part in discussion. But in spite of the laughter his remarks provoked, he kept at it and would not be cowed. In a better cause he might have been a hero. The investigator believes that this agent provided only the most conspicuous example of a general tendency: that agents of established low status conformed least closely to the norms of the group, while those of middle status—particularly those, like newcomers, whose esteem was least well established —were the greatest conformers of all.

Social behavior, in a group as elsewhere, is a continuous process of members influencing other members, and the success of influence in the past changes the probability of its success in the future. One result of the process of influence is that the members of a group become differentiated in a more or less stable way—stable so long as external circumstances do not change much. As some members, for instance, succeed in providing, under the influence of requests from others, more valuable services for these others than they can provide for themselves, the members become differentiated in esteem. This fairly stable differentiation in some pattern other than a random one is what we mean by the structure or organization of the group. But the structure is never so stable that it does not itself sow the seeds of further change, and we have been studying a particular example of this. The process of influence that has landed a man at the bottom of the ladder of esteem may render any future influence, so far as it comes from other members, still less likely to succeed with him. Suppose he would ordinarily lose esteem by doing something other than what they want, but he happens as a result of his past behavior to be left without any esteem to lose. If there is any other way in which he finds the action rewarding—and it may be rewarding just because it vexes *them*— the fact that its costs have been reduced to zero raises the odds in favor of his taking it.

A group controls its members by creating rewards for them which it can then threaten to withdraw. If the group has to make good the threat too often, it may wind up with nothing left to withdraw. Its control is always precarious as long as the members have any alternative to accepting the control, such as the alternative offered by another group they can make their escape to. We have been speaking of the low-status member who is going lower. But very high status may have something of the same effect as very low. A man who has so much status to lose that he will not mind if he loses a little of it can afford to try something new and take the risk that it may not turn out to be acceptable to the membership. He too, in his way, is exempt from the control of the group. There are deviates and deviates; some from the point of view of the group are bad deviates, some are good ones. But both are innovators; and if one looked only at the innovations they propose, it would often be hard to tell which is which.

In this book we try to describe what happens in human behavior without taking any moral stand about it—unless laughter is a moral stand. Or rather we take only one stand out of the many open to us. We have nothing to say in favor of conformity or against it. All we have done is point out that a man who does not conform takes certain risks. But a man is born to take risks. Morally we cannot object to him unless he wants his nonconformity made easy, unless he wants to kick the group in the teeth and have it like him too. For then he is being unfair to the rest of us by asking that an exception to the human condition be made in his favor.

The Institutional
and the Subinstitutional

Chapter Eighteen

According to my lights, a last chapter should resemble a primitive orgy after harvest. The work may have come to an end, but the worker cannot let go all at once. He is still full of energy that will fester if it cannot find an outlet. Accordingly he is allowed a time of license, when he may say all sorts of things he would think twice before saying in more sober moments, when he is no longer bound by logic and evidence but free to speculate about what he has done.

I propose to take my orgy out in putting a frame around this book. In this last chapter I shall return to a question I raised in the first, when I tried to set up some sort of definition of elementary social behavior. It is an exchange of rewards (or punishments) between at least two persons; the exchange is direct rather than indirect; and it is actual behavior and not just a norm specifying what behavior ought to be. Granted that they grade into one another by degrees, and that nothing more than an arbitrary line can be drawn between the two, what are the relations between the elementary and the more complex forms of social behavior, between the informal and the formal, between the sub-institutional and the institutional?

The Group as a Microcosm

In their private speculations, some sociologists were once inclined to think of the small, informal group as a microcosm of society at large: they felt that the same phenomena appeared in the former as in the latter but on a vastly reduced scale—a scale that, incidentally, made detailed investigation possible. And no doubt there are striking resemblances between the two. We have seen how members roughly equal in status within a small group are apt to associate with one another on "social" occasions more often than with either their superiors or inferiors in status; and their behavior has obvious points of resemblance with the more salient features of class and stratification systems —where members of families equal in status as recognized in the larger society are especially apt to visit, go to parties with, and even marry one another. No doubt the resemblances are not fortuitous: some of the same processes are at work in both cases. But to say that the two phenomena have points in common is not to say that one is a microcosm of the other, that the one is simply the other writ small. The two are not alike, if only because in an informal group a man wins status through his direct exchanges with the other members, while he gets status in the larger society by inheritance, wealth, occupation, office, legal authority—in every case by his position in some institutional scheme, often one with a long history behind it.

When, to take another example, a number of followers get help from an informal leader, to whom they yield some power to control their behavior, the situation does look a lot like that of an appointed supervisor whose designated subordinates report to him and to whom in return he gives orders. Perhaps in the distant past, when formal organizations were first deliberately designed, the span of control—the number of men put under the command of a single officer—may have been modeled on what is apt to spring up spontaneously in a small group. But of course the situations are not really the same. The fact that higher authority has appointed the formal leader, that he is responsible to it, and that the punishments he inflicts are made possible by its support, makes all the difference, as anyone who has been both an informal and a formal leader knows. In the formal situation, moreover, both leader and followers get some of their rewards, not from exchange with one another, but from the exchange of work for pay with the organization of which they are a part. Both parties are more independent of one another than they are in the small, informal group. It is true that a formal leader may be more successful in his own job if he has something of the informal leader about him too—but this only adds to the evidence that the two are not the same.

The Complexity of Rewards

If the informal group, like elementary social behavior in general, is not a true microcosm of society at large, the reason is not that the fundamental processes of behavior—the way the emission of an activity is governed by its pay-offs and its stimuli—are different in the two cases: far from being different, they are identical. The reason lies rather in the fact that, in the institutions of society at large, the relations between the fundamental processes are more complex. The increased complexity seems to take two main forms, which are themselves related to one another. First, a particular activity gets to be maintained not just by what I shall call its natural or primary reward but also by other, contrived rewards, particularly by generalized reinforcers like money and social approval. For instance, a man cuts wood, not because he needs it for his fire, but because a firm will pay him for cutting it. Second, the process of exchange by which an activity gets rewarded comes to be roundabout rather than direct. For instance, the man gets his pay at the end of the week, not from his own supervisor or somebody else he cut the wood for, but from a clerk who is himself rewarded by still another member of the firm. What the two processes have in common, compared with elementary social behavior, is an increased reliance on explicitly stated norms and orders: the man is told that he is to cut wood, and he is told how he will get his pay at the end of the week. These and other differences between institutional and subinstitutional behavior are differences in degree only. If we like, we may consider the differences in degree to be so great as to amount to differences in kind, so long as we do not observe—but it is always open to us to observe—how the one kind of behavior is forever growing out of the other. Then the continuity of the two is borne in on us.

Consider the first process as it must go on at the lowest level; consider, for instance, the expression of grief. In every society some people, not all, must find it rewarding to make some kind of outcry when a beloved companion dies. If this were not so, if this were not a common human trait, but simply something accepted as a convention by the members of particular societies, we should hardly find mourning at death as widely distributed among mankind as in fact it is. Cultures cannot pick up any old sorts of behavior and hope without more ado to carry them on generation after generation. What they pick up must be compatible with some fundamental repertory of human nature, though the compatibility may, of course, be complex.

Once a number of people have cried a number of times at a number of deaths, they begin to make a norm of it—to say that it is the thing one does or ought to do—and the verbal statement of a rule is the first step in the making of an institution. Then other members of their group, whose eyes would otherwise have been dry, may find themselves crying too, because other rewards and punishments have come to sanction the behavior. If they do not cry, they fail in showing respect for the dead, and so lose the esteem of people who are sincere in weeping. Since they do not feel much themselves, they will be ready to adopt as a convention any idiom of mourning the others offer them. And the first thing you know, the formal expression of grief at a bereavement has become an institution, taught to younger members of the society as part of their manners.

No doubt the origin of many institutions is of this sort. The behavior once reinforced for some people in one way, which I call primary, is maintained in a larger number of people by other sorts of reinforcement, in particular by such general reinforcers as social approval. Since the behavior does not come naturally to these others, they must be told how they are to behave—hence the verbal description of behavior, the norm.

Indeed we can see the process taking place before our eyes, and we have touched on it in the earlier part of the book—though only just touched because our main business was not with institutions. Restriction of output in an industrial group undoubtedly arose in the beginning because some members found its results rewarding. But restriction gets its results only if a rather large number of members conform to the output norm, and therefore nonconformists deprive the rest of a reward. Accordingly the members who would have been indifferent to the primary reward are nevertheless apt to conform, for fear of losing the esteem of their fellows; and then restriction of output is well on its way to becoming an institution, taught to new members and even to new generations as one of the laws of life in the factory. Such combinatory processes can snowball into immense institutional piles. Indeed the secondary sanctions of an institution can become so many and so marked that the people following the norms may cease to be conscious of the primary reward, which continues to do its work, but out of sight.

In moments of unguarded talk, some anthropologists have sounded to me as if they thought that the members of a society or some section of it maintained an institutional rule simply because it is a rule, taught them in their youth as something they must obey, and sanctioned by social approval. Were this really the case, I think we should observe far less change in human society than we observe in fact. For social approval does not operate alone: its power as a sanction depends on the continuing vigor of the primary reward. Social approval can come in to reinforce obedience to a rule only so long as some members of the group continue to find obedience rewarding for reasons other than the approval it gets them. As soon as they cease to find it rewarding, a member who disobeys is not depriving them of anything, and so does not forfeit their esteem. No doubt a norm may govern behavior for a while after its primary reward has lost its power, if only because each conformist is a victim of a conspiracy of silence. No one, for instance, dares admit he feels no grief, for fear of offending others who, for reasons like his own, give him no hint they are insincere.

But an institution that has reached this stage is vulnerable and apt to collapse if alternative behavior with a new primary reward presents itself as a possibility. Then someone of very high status or very low, who has little to gain by conformity or little to lose by its opposite, breaks away, and then the hollowness of the belief that disobedience will bring overwhelming social disapproval is soon exposed. The alternative, to be sure, may for a long period of time fail to present itself, because for one reason or another the society has remained shielded from change in the physical or social environment. The first point I should like to make about the relations between institutions and elementary social behavior is that institutions, as explicit rules governing the behavior of many people, are obeyed because rewards other than the primary ones come to be gotten by obeying them, but that these other rewards cannot do the work alone. Sooner or later the primary rewards must be provided. Institutions do not keep on going forever of their own momentum.

When asked to explain why the institutions of a society are what they are, some anthropologists seem reluctant to point to the primary rewards of behaving in accordance with institutional rules. Instead they are apt, as I have suggested, to point to the fact that the rules are taught to new members of society as they come along. When asked why these rules are taught rather than others, the anthropologists then point to the relations between one rule and another. If in a matrilineal society —to take one thoroughly hypothetical case—the rule is that a man's goods are inherited by his sister's son, then a rule of marriage specifying that a sister's son should marry his mother's brother's daughter might mean, if obeyed, that the man's daughter would get some benefit from her father's goods. The first rule, the rule of inheritance, provides a reward for obedience to the second rule, the rule of marriage. But this argument, sound as far as it goes, leaves something tacitly unexplained. Why does the father find it rewarding that his daughter should get some of his goods, or even the daughter find it rewarding that she should get the benefit of her father's goods? This kind of question the anthropologists have a harder time answering. They may argue, as before, that the society—actually specific members of it—has taught a man that he must love and care for his daughter, but this is no explanation and only another description of what happens. Again we have a right to ask why the society has taught the man that rather than something else.

The fact is that some anthropologists have become so obsessed by the cultural uniqueness of particular societies that they have lost sight of what men have in common. If the anthropologists' reasoning is not to become circular, I think they must admit that they cannot fully explain their own findings unless they make certain assumptions about what men find rewarding, not just as members of a particular society but as members of a species. For instance, I do not think anyone can explain why so many societies in which legal authority over the family is vested in the father are also societies in which a boy develops a close relation with his mother's brother, unless he assumes that men, as men, react to authority in some such way as we have described in this book.[1] Of course the societies in question teach their youngsters how they ought to behave toward mother's brothers, but why do they teach them "closeness" rather than something else? Because "closeness" is rewarding under the circumstances, and rewarding for many men even apart from the norm and the sanctions attached to it. Otherwise, how did the norm itself come into existence?

It does not follow from my argument that social scientists should be particularly interested in "cultural universals," if this means actual institutions that appear in all societies, as marriage and the incest taboo are said to appear, though in fact they vary greatly in form from one society to another. But it does follow that they should be much interested in the underlying mechanisms of human behavior, like those we described in Chapter 4, for the underlying mechanisms can work themselves out in a wide variety of actual institutions. Human nature is the only true "cultural universal."

We social scientists talk as if "society" were the big thing. But an institution is functional for society only because it is functional for men. There is no functional prerequisite for the survival of a society except that the society provide sufficient rewards for its individual members to keep them contributing activities to its maintenance, and that it reward them not just as members of that society but as men.[2] Even when we talk as if "society" provided the rewards, we always, ultimately, mean that men provide them. No doubt they are men whose ancestors have learned, and who have learned themselves, to find specific kinds of behavior rewarding in specific historical circumstances, some of them long past; and they may have continued to find some of the behavior rewarding right up to the present. Since their historical experience may have been different from that of the members of another society, their present institutions may well be different from those of the other. But whatever they learned, they learned because they were men as well as members; and therefore the institutional differences, or similarities, are to be explained by the conjuncture

[1] See G. C. Homans and D. M. Schneider, *Marriage, Authority, and Final Causes* (Glencoe, Ill., 1955).

[2] For an opposing view see D. F. Aberle, A. K. Cohen, A. K. Davis, M. F. Levy, Jr., and F. X. Sutton, "The Functional Prerequisites of a Society," *Ethics*, Vol. 60 (1950), pp. 100-11.

between the nature of man and the nature of the circumstances. This is easy to say but not, of course, easy to do.

If you look long enough for the secret of society you will find it in plain sight: the secret of society is that it was made by men, and there is nothing in society but what men put there.

The Complexity of Exchanges

Let me now look at the second of the two processes by which institutions develop out of elementary social behavior—the increasing roundaboutness of the exchange of rewards, which is sometimes called the increasing division of labor. Some primitive societies seem to have developed a complexity of organization that hardly goes beyond what appears, for instance, in a street gang in our own society. The same simple types of transactions stand clearly revealed in both. The society is so hard up, physically or socially, that it has not been able to afford any very elaborate institutional development. One of the reasons why students of elementary social behavior are charmed with the very primitive societies is that they reveal mankind stripped down socially to its fundamentals. In the words of the anthropologist Lévi-Strauss, returning from the Nambikwara of central Brazil: "I had been looking for a society reduced to its simplest expression. That of the Nambikwara was so far reduced that all I found there was men."[3]

At the origin of even the most modern industrial society lies a social unit of much the same sort. Look back, for instance, at the earliest description of the society that, in my view, should count more than any other—more than Greece, Rome, and Israel—as the principal ancestor of our own: look back at Tacitus' description of the tiny Germanic tribal kingdoms of the first century A.D.[4] Of course the society is already highly institutionalized, governed to a high degree by rules inherited from the past, perhaps from a remote past. But the rules outline an organization that is closer to what naturally and spontaneously appears in any small group than anything we have known in more modern times. Consider the kingship itself. It is already in theory something a man inherits and does not acquire by

[3] C. Lévi-Strauss, *Tristes Tropiques* (Paris, 1955), p. 339.
[4] P. Cornelius Tacitus, *Germania*.

his own actions—though if he is incompetent his high birth is unlikely to save him. But the relation between the king and his "companions" (*gesiths, comites*), who drink in his hall in peace and follow him in war, and whom he rewards with food, with jewelry, and finally with land, much more resembles the relation between the informal leader of a group and his followers than do most political systems that we have known in our society since that time. At the back, historically, of any of the great modern societies we shall find some such society as this—institutionalized indeed, but institutionalized in a pattern that betrays its kinship with the primeval small group.

Now suppose such a society has created a capital of some sort. By capital I mean anything that allows it to postpone actions leading to some immediate reward in order to undertake others whose rewards, though potentially greater, are both uncertain and deferred. The capital may take the form of unusually well-disciplined soldiers; it may take the form of a surplus of food or money; most important of all it may take the form of a moral code, especially a code supporting trust and confidence between men: a true belief that they will not always let you down in favor of short-term gains.

Without some capital no institutional elaboration can get off the ground. But given the capital, the society—really some man or group of men within the society, perhaps always ultimately a single man— is apt to invest it by trying out some set of activities that departs from the original or primeval institutional pattern. The new pattern envisages an intermeshing of the behavior of a larger number of persons in a more complicated or roundabout manner than has hitherto been the custom. Having, for instance, conquered new territory with the help of his companions, the king may try to maintain permanent control over it, and to do so he will have to rely, since he now has more people under his rule, not just on his own ties with his companions but on his companions' ties with companions under them. That is, he may have to encourage the development of some sort of feudal system, and in doing so he will have to spell out, to make a matter of explicit norms, the behavior toward one another of the people now made interdependent. He will have to do so for the same reason that makes a modern factory, when it has grown beyond a certain size, begin to spell out its organizational chart. But the question always remains whether the new arrangement will pay off before the capital runs out. Probably most such attempts by most human societies have failed.

Instead of handling his own finances and dispensing his own justice, the king may appoint a full-time treasurer and full-time judges. These institutions may ultimately increase the efficiency of his administration, attract to his rule, by the prospects of speedy justice, men who might otherwise have been drawn elsewhere, and maintain the peace on which his ability to levy increasing taxes finally depends. They may even set him free of his exclusive, and therefore dangerous, dependence on the loyalty of his companions. But these rewards take time to come in; and while he waits for them, he must invest capital to pay the treasurer and the judges enough to make up, and more than make up, for the time they take from other affairs. He must arrange that the rewards they get from doing their duty are greater than those they would get from appropriating the king's funds to their own uses or selling the king's justice for money in their own pockets. But to do all these things the king must have the capital; he must, for instance, be able to spare enough land from other uses so that his officers can be paid out of the rent, and this means that he must have effective control over the land. In all these undertakings the king is a risk-taker just as surely as is any venture-capitalist today: the institution of royal judges, for instance, may not pay off. Indeed the risks the king takes are greater, for they include his life.

Once the king has succeeded in maintaining his peace so that common men feel that mere anarchy is no danger to their enterprises, other kinds of things may happen at a lower level of society. A man who once made woolen cloth by performing every operation from the original carding and spinning to the final retail sale may decide to specialize on one operation, let us say the weaving itself. In so doing he may gain advantages in applying a more specialized skill to a larger volume of work, but he can get these advantages only if he is sure of his suppliers, the spinners, and of his outlets, the finishers, who must now become specialists too. Unless the whole chain of transactions can be maintained, so that the consumer gets his cloth in the end, every single specialization collapses. The volume of business may finally become great enough to provide a pay-off for a man whose specialization is the coordination of specialists—in the medieval cloth trade they called him a draper or clothier—and then we are at the threshold of modern society. We are also at the point where increased taxes on cloth may help pay off the king for his maintenance of the peace.

Of course I cannot go into all the details, nor are they the point. All of these innovations, whether political or economic, whether at the top of society or at the bottom, have the following characteristics. They require some form of capital to be attempted at all, for their pay-offs are not immediate but deferred. And the capital must increasingly take the form of generalized reinforcers like money and social approval. But note that even the ability of a society to provide rewards of this sort depends on the previous accumulation of some little capital. Money is no use unless people are confident that it can be converted into goods, and a man who is worrying about where his next meal is coming from is unlikely to find social approval particularly rewarding.

The innovations are apt to require a longer chain of transactions before the ultimate reward is achieved—before, for instance, the customer gets his cloth—than did the systems that immediately preceded them. And the chain is more roundabout: if a man is to walk from one place to another he just starts straight out, but if he is to ride on a subway, someone has to build a steel mill first. The length and roundaboutness of the chain of transactions mean that the innovations link a larger number of people together than were linked hitherto: a customer once depended on a single weaver for his cloth; now he depends on a whole team of cloth-workers. But the innovations imply increased specialization, and as the number of people tied together increases, the richness of any particular tie is apt to decrease. After the Industrial Revolution people were apt to complain that the relationship between master and man had been impoverished, reduced to a mere cash nexus. The larger, finally, the number of persons concerned and the more complicated their interdependence, the less it is possible to leave their mutual adjustments to the rough and tumble of face-to-face contact. They must go by the rule, work by the book, which also means that institutional behavior tends to become impersonal. Although all recurrent behavior tends, sooner or later, to get described and consecrated in explicit norms, now the process is hastened. Indeed one of the institutional innovations without which the others cannot get very far must be an organization that specializes in the sanctioning of norms, that is, a legal system.

Except for a few recent economic historians who specialize in the study of economic development, scholars seldom, it seems to me, examine in detail the processes of institutional growth. Above all, they do not explain them. They tell us, for instance, that Henry II was the first king of England to send royal judges regularly on circuit throughout the country. They never ask what capital, social or economic, enabled him to undertake the innovation, what risks it ran, or what returns replaced the capital and allowed the institution to persist. But only answers to these questions would explain the most important developments in human history. After all, there are other entrepreneurs than economic ones, nor are the economic ones always the most important. Given the capital, every society tries institutional innovations. If they turn out to pay off—and a great deal of capital may be spent before they do—they persist. They may even replace the capital, and allow the society to go on to another innovation. But there must be a pay-off; it is never automatic and always problematical; and it may not continue. External circumstances may change; other parts of the social organization may fail and bring the institution down in their ruin; and the institution itself may exhaust the sources of its own reward—as when an advanced agriculture works out the soil available to it.

All history is there to remind us how precarious is the process of civilization. The decline of the Roman Empire is there to remind us of it, for the first large-scale experiment in Western civilization. But even the recovery of the West from the Roman collapse has been far from uninterrupted. Feudalism in northwestern Europe was in trouble from the beginning; indeed it could never have corresponded in the least to what doctrine said it ought to be, had it not been supported by sources outside itself: by national loyalties transcending the feudal tie and by a kingship that only just managed to remain something more than the top rung on the feudal ladder. The expansion of the twelfth and thirteenth centuries was followed by the stagnation of the fourteenth, as if the very success of medieval institutions in eliciting some kinds of reward had used up the supply available. And in the sixteenth century English industry made tentative approaches to factory organization, which could not be maintained in the face of a market collapse and which were not revived until the eighteenth, when the application of steam power gave factory organization a pay-off that no other form of industrial production could match. The same refrain repeats itself over and over: institutions do not keep going just because they are enshrined in norms, and it seems extraordinary that anyone should ever talk as if they did. They keep going because they have pay-offs, ultimately pay-offs for individuals. Nor is society a perpetual-motion machine, supplying its own fuel. It cannot keep itself going by planting in the young a desire for those goods and only those goods that it happens to be in shape to provide. It must provide goods that men find rewarding not simply because they are sharers in a particular culture but because they are men.

The Persistence of Elementary Social Behavior

As the institutions of civilization depart further and further from elementary social behavior, the latter does not disappear in proportion. Far from it, it persists obviously and everywhere, ready to take its revenge. It may persist in its most elaborate form in areas where institutional arrangements have broken down and left gaps. I have argued that street gangs show an elaboration of informal pattern not unworthy to rank with that of a primitive hunting band. If street gangs included girls and allowed marriage the resemblance would be even closer. And the characteristics of elementary social behavior reassert themselves the more fully the further the institutional breakdown goes, in disaster, revolution, or defeat in war.

But I am not much interested in the elementary social behavior that lies outside the institutional system, as the street gang does. Much more important is the behavior that lies within the system. It sprouts in the "grapevine"; it is as well developed in the personal loyalties of some executives and political leaders as it is in the group of workers who will not let the exuberant production of one of their number show up the deficiencies of the rest. It appears in the invention of, and concern for, outward and visible signs of rank and status never warranted by the formal organization itself. Sometimes the activities exchanged in elementary social behavior get their value from the rules of the institution. Thus the help people exchanged for esteem in the Federal agency I have described so often would have had no value if the men concerned had not been employed at a certain kind of organized work. But though the institution gave value to the help, the process of exchange itself remained just as elementary, just as subinstitutional, as anything seen in a street gang. Elementary social behavior does not grow just in the gaps between institutions; it clings to institutions as to a trellis. It grows everywhere—if only because the norms established as institutions and the orders given in instituted organizations can never prescribe human behavior to the last detail, even if they were obeyed to the letter, which they are not. Indeed the elementary behavior helps explain how and why they are disobeyed.

We should not look on the subinstitutional as necessarily a kind of friction holding the institutional back, to be gotten rid of only to the advantage of the latter. On the contrary, the motives characteristic of elementary social behavior often mobilize solid support behind institutional aims. An obvious example is the way in which the soldiers' determination not to let their comrades down contributes more than anything else to the fighting power of an infantry outfit. Of course this is an instance of the phenomenon I started this chapter with—how institutions are maintained by other rewards than the one each is primarily set to achieve. Infantry combat is meant to defeat the enemy; this is undoubtedly a reward, though often one long in coming, but effective combat may also be rewarded, and more immediately, by the approval of your fellow soldiers whom you have covered as they have you. And sometimes elementary social behavior manages to support an institution in the institution's spite. The help exchanged in the Federal agency may well have made the work of the agency more effective than it would have been otherwise—but it was exchanged only by disregarding an official rule against helping.

The Conflict of the Institutional and the Subinstitutional

Elementary social behavior, then, is not driven out by institutionalization but survives alongside it, acquiring new reasons for existence from it. Sometimes it contributes to the support of the institution. But sometimes, as we also know, the two work against each other. Since the relatively bad situations are the ones we are most interested in, because we might want to do something about them, I shall spend the rest of my time on the conditions in which the two are at odds.

Consider then a working group in an American office or factory—a group like those we have studied so often in this book. Exchange—it has been our main theme—is the basis, acknowledged or unacknowledged, of much human behavior, and each member of the group has obviously entered into exchange with the company. But the exchange as institutionalized, as subject to explicit rules, is a limited exchange: each member has agreed, in return for a money wage, to contribute his labor as directed by the company. To be sure he may get many rewards from his labor besides money: a pleasant place to work, a job that ranks high in the community, and sometimes interesting work to do. But the most fully institutionalized aspect of the exchange is that of labor for money: the company is not legally bound, as part of its bargain, to provide the other things. Industrialization has specialized exchanges. As it has advanced, it has ceased to recognize many of the sorts of things that entered into the exchange between superior and subordinate at a time when society had moved less far away from elementary social behavior. No transaction engages as much of the man as it used to.

What happens, we may then ask, to the behavior that has been simplified and rationalized away, that goes unrecognized institutionally? Has it really disappeared, or has it only been swept under the rug? As the worker gets down to his job in his department, he encounters many activities in his fellow workers that reward or punish him, and he learns activities that reward or punish his fellow workers. Though their nature may depend on arrangements made by the firm, they are treated as institutionally irrelevant to the exchange of labor for money. Thus the ledger clerks in the Eastern Utilities Co. found that their job was more skilled and more responsible than that of the cash posters, but it got the same pay and was allowed less autonomy. By the standards of elementary social behavior, justice had not been done them, and their status was threatened in consequence. But none of this was institutionally relevant to the bargain between them and the company.

I do not mean in the least to imply that the management of the Eastern Utilities Co. was unconcerned with justice. Just as much as the union did, it believed in "a fair day's work for a fair day's wage," though the two might have disagreed about the exact value either term of the equation should take. But the notion of fair exchange, so far as it was institutionalized, took little into account besides work and money, and treated as outside its scope many of the aspects of justice that elementary social behavior in fact brings up. This may easily be seen in the replies the supervisors made when the ledger clerks complained. In effect they pointed out that the clerks had made a bargain to do what they were told in the way of work, in return for a fair wage. So long as management stuck to its part of the bargain, what call did the clerks have to ask for more than theirs? Institutionalization makes more complex the chains of transactions between men, but achieves it at the price of simplifying any one link. Elementary social behavior may compensate for the simplification, as it does at times in military units, but it may also find the simplification intolerable, as it did here. The ledger clerks expected the company to maintain justice in general and not justice in particular. Incorrigibly, and against the whole tendency of human history, they expected the management to behave like men, and not like actors playing an institutionalized role. Thank God they did; but at points like this elementary social behavior begins to break in on institutionalization and, instead of supporting it, does it damage. This is only one example of the way the two can fall at odds.

Let us recognize that the ledger clerks and others like them might not have found their status so threatened or trying to do something to improve it so rewarding had they not already enjoyed other sorts of reward in relative abundance. There is a hierarchy of values, and not till the lower ones have been met do the higher ones attract: it is a rich man who can afford to worry about his status. Only in a few places like America are wages so high that workers can begin to interest themselves in the finer points of distributive justice; and this has consequences for both management and organized labor. Business has been so successful in providing money that other values have risen in relative importance; its old assumption, child of past penury, that money would be enough to enlist the full energy of labor no longer works quite as well as it did, and business cannot make it work at all without creating a demand for new products to be bought with money. As for organized labor, the more successful it is in getting the general level of wages raised, the more likely it is to undermine its own unity; for then workers can begin to interest themselves not just in the absolute amount of wages but in wage differentials, and wage differentials are obviously apt to set one group of workers against another. A working class is perhaps most unified when its members have gotten enough above mere subsistence so that the bosses cannot buy them off one by one—they can wait out a strike together—but not so far above that wage differentials rise in value relative to the general level of wages. The nineteenth century reformers, by the way, must have founded their demand for universal suffrage on the assumption, which was true then, that the poorest class was also the largest: if all these people got the vote, they would be able to get their other deserts. But now that the curve of income distribution has changed in shape, and so many families have moved up that the middle-income levels have become the largest, we Americans may be able to oppress the poor by perfectly democratic methods: the poor have got the vote but they no longer have the votes. What I am suggesting here is that the very success of the specialized exchange of money for wages is one of the conditions that allows subinstitutional behavior to break in on the institutional. We are at last rich enough to indulge our full humanity.

But let me get back to the office. The ledger clerks complained to their supervisor of the injustice of their position over against the cash posters, expecting him to take the matter up with the officer above him in the managerial pyramid. When he did little or nothing, they added his behavior to their complaints: "He doesn't stand up for us." They were expecting from him the sort of action that would have indeed been natural in an informal leader: in return for the loyalty they would have given him, an informal leader would certainly have represented their interests against any outside party. Once more the assumptions of subinstitutional were coming up against those of institutional behavior: as the ledger clerks had demanded a less specialized justice from their company, so now they asked for a less specialized leadership. They were asking again for a man and not a supervisor. But how could their supervisor stand up for them? He too was trapped by the institutional rules. He might report to higher authority the disaffection of the ledger clerks, but he had no further power to do anything about it. Institutionally speaking, he too was paid to do as he was told. To do anything effective he might have had to use with higher authority his own informal ties rather than his formal ones.

At this point the story of the ledger clerks ends. Although they were thinking of going to the union and asking it to take the matter up, they had not in fact done so. Nor is their case particularly striking in itself: I use it only to illustrate what I believe to be a large class of cases. Suppose that the office were not unionized and that many groups were nursing grievances—not only grievances about the actual amount of wages, that is, about a matter the institutional bargain did take cognizance of, but also grievances, like the ledger clerks', about matters it did not. Certainly these groups would approach their supervisors first; when they found that many of the supervisors could not effectively stand up for them, they would cast about for something else to do. Many of the groups would have developed informal leadership, and if the complaint were at all deeply felt, the leaders, as a condition of keeping their positions, would have to try to bring the complaints home to the management. The first thing you know they would have gotten together and organized a strike; and if their followers had enough of what I have called social capital, material and nonmaterial, to keep the strike up, they would have forced the company to accept a union—collective bargaining, grievance procedure, and all. Some such event is often the origin of unionization in a plant.

Note what has happened: subinstitutional has come into conflict with institutional behavior. The result is not a collapse of the old institution and a return to the elementary, but the founding of a new institution, the union, of a peculiar sort—an institution designed to maintain subinstitutional values: to make the company take a less specialized view of justice—for the grievance procedure in some degree does this—and to recapture for the workers some control over their environment by giving them more effective representation than either their supervisors or their informal leaders could have done. Of course the new institution, once formed, may in time run into the same trouble with elementary social behavior as the old one did earlier.

I suspect that many of our institutions have the same kind of origin. Indeed in an earlier book I claimed this of the complex of institutions we call democracy.[5] In informal groups it is hard for government *not* to be carried on with the consent of the governed. Democracy aims at re-establishing this elementary value in a much more complicated institutional setting. It is an institution designed to make good the human deficiencies of other institutions.

The invention of new institutions is not the only way of coping with the conflict between subinstitutional and institutional behavior. The conflict may be resolved, and resolved for long periods of time, by "good administration"—the sort of thing the ledger clerks would have

[5] G. C. Homans, *The Human Group* (New York, 1950), pp. 46 :-66.

enjoyed if their supervisor had managed to bring their complaints home to his own boss, and he in turn had begun to consider what adjustments he might make. Good administration is intelligent behavior within a more or less unchanging institutional framework, and it can compensate for many defects in the latter. If it were not so, we should not see so many autocracies and tyrannies so successful for so long—and successful even apart from their use of terror in governing their subjects.

But the problem need not be solved at all, temporarily or permanently. The society may tear itself apart in conflict without ever creating a new institution that will stick. Still more often the problem may simply persist without issuing in overt conflict but without resolution either. New forms of behavior that might have proved rewarding enough to establish themselves are not invented; or no one is able to risk the social capital to try them out. The result is a society of people to some extent apathetic, of institutions to some extent "frozen" in an unnatural equilibrium—unnatural in the sense that out of the elements lying around here and there something better might conceivably have been made.

Something of this sort seems to some of us to have happened to American industry even with the unions.[6] The original institutional compact, of money for obedience to orders, has not encouraged management to turn the worker into a slave of a machine—as the humanists would have it—but to turn him into the machine itself, into something, that is, which has the admirable property that if you will only feed it the right materials and power it will do just what you want it to, no more no less. If you will only feed the worker money, you should get out of him just exactly what you want. When you do not get it, and since elementary social behavior is always breaking in you never do, you never conclude that your theory is inadequate but only that you have not applied it rigorously enough. You redesign the controls on the machine so that now—you hope—it simply cannot get off the track. For this purpose the assembly line, where manpower is machine-paced, is the best thing yet devised. But it is so unnatural that you must feed your human machines still more money to get them to work on it at all. And the more money they get the more

[6] See A. Zaleznik, C. R. Christensen, and F. J. Roethlisberger, *The Motivation, Productivity, and Satisfaction of Workers* (Boston, 1958), pp. 394-411.

valuable to them relatively becomes the elementary social behavior you have done your best to eliminate. The worker is left so apathetic, so many activities in his repertory have gone unrewarded, that management seems justified in its thinking that he is incapable of independent responsibility and that he can only be treated as a machine fueled up with money and made to run on a track. And so the wheel comes full circle.

What industry often lacks is what we have seen to be characteristic of strong and lively institutions: not one motive alone but a wide variety of motives held by the men whose activities the institution coordinates is enlisted in support of its aims and not left to work against them or at best at cross-purposes. Industry might consider joining the forces it has so far shown itself unable to lick. As usual, this is easier said than done.

Of course you are at liberty to take a moral stand and approve the present situation, though for reasons opposite to the ones an industrialist might bring up. You can argue that workers ought not support the purposes of management, which cannot help being utterly at odds with their own. They ought to stick to the original narrow bargain and make it work for their interests. They ought to get as much money, for doing as little work, as they can. They will not behave quite the way you think they ought to, but the price a man pays for having high moral standards is seldom seeing them realized. And at least your moral stand will allow you to disregard the immediate problem: for all practical purposes you will be just as conservative as the most hard-boiled businessman. But the general problem you will have a harder time disregarding. Sooner or later, in this society or another, you will find an institution whose purposes you approve of, and then you will have to consider how the many motives of many men can be brought to support it.

The trouble with civilized men is that they cannot live with the institutions they have themselves invented. In rewarding some kinds of social behavior better than savage society could ever have done, the new institutions drive other behavior underground. But it does not stay there forever. Sometimes the very success of the institutions gives an opening to behavior that men could little afford to indulge in while they were still on the make. If a poor society must be human because it has nothing else, and a rich society can be human because it has everything else, we moderns are *nouveaux riches* trying to acquire aristocratic tastes. Sometimes the great rebellions and revolutions, cracking the institutional crust, bring out elementary social behavior hot and straight from the fissures. They always appeal, for instance, to the simplest principles of distributive justice: When Adam delved and Eve span, who was then the gentleman? To call them simple is not, of course, to call them bad: the question of value comes later. For the institutions the rebels invent in the endeavor to realize justice on earth are just as apt to sacrifice something human as the institutions that preceded them: they come corrupted by the very anger that gave them birth. And then men wonder whether the struggle was worth its cost that left them still facing their old problem: how to reconcile their social institutions with their social nature. Yet men have invented one peculiar institution that may just conceivably help them get out of their rat race. To call it science is almost as embarrassing as calling your wife Mrs. Smith: the name is too formal for the bedroom. If men are to feel at home in the world of their making, they will come to understand better what it is their institutions are to be reconciled with —and "better" means in just those ways science has committed itself to. This is the only reason for studying the familiar chaos that is elementary social behavior—except, of course, the sheer pleasure of the thing.

Index

Exchange, activity changes in kind, 64-68
complexity, 385-90
cost, 57-61
descriptive terms, 32-35
distributive justice, 72-78
economics, 68-70
example, 31-32
primitive, 317-20
profit, 61-64
propositions defined, 51-52
quantity variable, 36-39
rationality, 79-82
stimuli proposition, 52-54
total reward, 70-72
value and quantity propositions, 54-56
value variable, 39-49
variables in descriptive terms, 35-49
Explanation, definition, 10
External system, 231

Festinger, L., 85, 88, 97, 100, 103, 120, 122, 167, 208, 309
Festinger group, 85
Fiedler, F. E., 313
French, J. R. P., Jr., 288
Frequency, value proposition, 55
see also Quantity
Friends, interaction, 183

Geographical location, influence, 208-14
Gerard, H. B., 85, 93, 103
Gewirtz, J. L., 35
Goffman, E., 337
Gullahorn, J. T., 208

Hartley, E. L., 161
Homans, G. C., 8, 9, 13, 32, 33, 35, 37, 149, 162, 163, 186, 188, 201, 213, 220, 230, 234, 235, 237, 292, 302, 311, 316, 333, 339, 384, 395
Howe, M. DeWolfe, 9
Hudson study, 158-60, 167-70, 213, 320-23, 323-26
Hughes, E. C., 340
Human exchange, see Exchange

Hurwitz, J. I., 224
Hymovitch, B., 103, 224

Indifference, mutual, 168-69
Induction, definition, 10
Industrial Controls Corp. project, 217-19, 221, 222-24
Inequality, and equality in primitive exchange, 317-20
Influence, approval and interaction, 90-93
approval and productivity, 85-90
cost and profit, 93-99
deviation from production level, 87
failure, 106-09
group induction, 88
research on, 83-85
reward, alternative sources, 100-102
similarity as source, 103-06
Institutionalization, 391-98
Interaction, aggregate matrix of six-man groups, 194
corrected matrix, 193
defined, 35
equality, 323-27
with equals, 197-200
liking, 181-90
matrix of, 190-97
model matrix, 191
measures of the frequency of, 38-39
origination, 201-03
"social," summary group, 366-70
status and disposition to communicate, 198
Investments, distributive justice, 74-75
profits proportionality, 242-47
reward and cost proportionality, 237-42
reward proportionality, 235-37
Isolation, summary group, 373-77
Israel, J., 170

Jackson, J. M., 342
Jennings, H. H., 156, 166, 168-70, 213, 321, 324, 325

F
G
H
I 9
J 0
K 1